David Simon Lee

ART&IDEAS

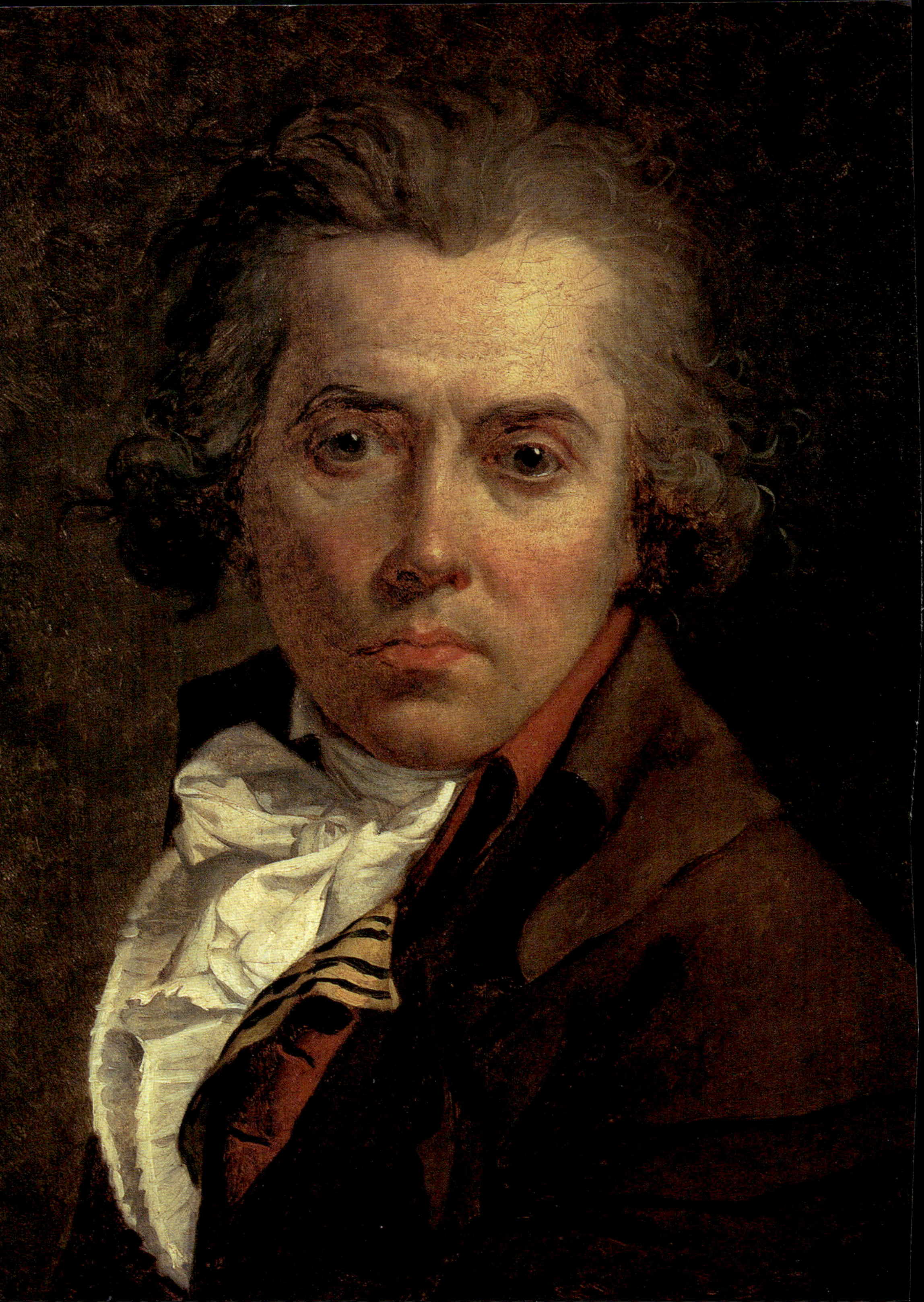

David

Opposite
Self-Portrait
(detail of 93),
1791.
Oil on canvas;
64 × 53 cm,
$25^{1}/_{4} \times 20^{7}/_{8}$ in.
Galleria
degli Uffizi,
Florence

Jacques-Louis David (1748–1825) was the single most important European painter between 1785 and 1815. His working life spanned a period of extraordinary change and upheaval: the intellectual ferment of the Enlightenment, the French Revolution, the abolition of the monarchy, the Napoleonic era and the return of the Bourbon kings to France. During the 1780s he perfected a style of dramatic and noble painting that matched exactly the contemporary desire for morally elevating images. David's superior social connections meant that he was exposed to liberal intellectual ideas, and as a result he became highly politicized. This initially took the form of agitating against the stifling influence of the Royal Academy of Painting and Sculpture, and of personal assertions of artistic independence. As a liberal he welcomed the promise of social change that the Revolution offered, and he became actively involved in politics in 1792, when he was elected a deputy of the National Convention.

Though as a politician he was no prime mover, he took an increasingly radical stance on most issues. More significantly, he devoted his brush to the cause of the Revolution, and produced propagandist paintings that glorified republican martyrs. In his position as 'Pageant Master of the Republic', he organized great revolutionary festivals that involved almost the whole population of Paris. These worked as powerful instruments of propaganda: to unify the new Republic in celebrations of brotherhood and liberty. When revolutionary extremism was replaced by more moderate attitudes, his involvement almost cost him his life, and when, after a period of imprisonment, he returned to work, he vowed never to engage in politics again. The lure and attraction of Napoleon Bonaparte, however, was enough to galvanize him to become the emperor's chief painter, capturing the pomp and magnificence of the imperial court and the cult of military heroism in huge commemorative pictures. With the defeat and exile of Napoleon, David was forced to leave France, and went to live in Brussels, where he continued to paint until his death in 1825.

It is appealing to try to see David as a kind of artistic barometer of his age, and to view his paintings as illustrations to the history of France. This is to fall into the trap of considering him as a figure who stood outside history, a 'genius' gifted with an extraordinary degree of prophecy and detachment. He is also, of course, much more than just a witness of his times. David's works, based on both ancient history and contemporary events, present a view that is shaped by a desire to communicate certain social, cultural and political values, and are thus necessarily partial views, though bound up with his particular experiences and preoccupations. Another commonplace in studies on David is to term him the greatest exponent of Neoclassicism. Again, this is to limit his achievement by imposing on him an artificial uniformity of concerns. Some discussions of him simply characterize such key works as *The Oath of the Horatii* (see 62) as 'masterpieces', and thus place them outside critical debate. It is also worth remembering that the term Neoclassicism was not used until the 1880s, and that David would have considered that he was producing works in the 'Grand Manner' or 'Great Style': paintings concerned with exemplary deeds and actions from ancient history or the Bible that were expressed in a clear and edifying way. It is also true that David's work does change a great deal throughout his career, and that the values embodied in his history paintings of the 1780s are very different from the Napoleonic works, such as *The Coronation of the Emperor and Empress* (see 152), and from the paintings produced in exile at the end of his life. David's concerns, far from being consistently Neoclassical, often depart considerably from its ideals of understatement, harmony and restraint.

In addition to the public notions of patriotism, education and propaganda, we also have to consider David's personal motivations: a desire for fame, material success and power within the artistic world. David thus emerges as a complex and often not very sympathetic character. He was unpopular with fellow artists because of his undisguised sense of competition and rivalry, and the way that he took advantage of his financial security to challenge the establishment and assert his individuality. Such elements must then be balanced with his revolutionary political stance: his call for democracy and the subjugation of narrow self-interest on behalf of the nation. On numerous occasions David has been called an opportunist, thanks to his ability to survive and prosper through changes of regime. However, each of his conversions seems to have been genuine, if rather tardy. Perhaps the characteristic of David that emerges most clearly is his combination of powerful commitment and extreme pragmatism.

David had very strong views on the profession of the painter, and was determined to free himself from the traditional view that painting was merely a craft. To him it was an intellectual undertaking; he was exceptionally well read and cultivated in comparison to other painters of the day. He believed that: 'To achieve their goal, masterpieces must charm but also penetrate the soul and make a deep impression on the mind that is similar to reality ... Therefore the artist must have studied all the motives of mankind and he must know nature thoroughly. In short he must be a philosopher.' This stress on the nobility of the calling of the painter was nevertheless underpinned by a shrewd financial brain. David's activities as an entrepreneur meant that he attracted commissions from both French and foreign patrons, and only the sculptor Antonio Canova (1757–1822) achieved a larger international clientele. Through his approach to teaching (1) and through his legions of students – he had over 400 throughout his career – David exerted an enormous influence on both French and European art. When he wrote in 1824 that: 'I founded a brilliant school; I painted

1
Jean-Henri Cless,
David's Teaching Studio in the Louvre,
1804.
Pen, ink and wash;
46·2 × 58·5 cm,
18⅛ × 23 in.
Musée Carnavalet, Paris

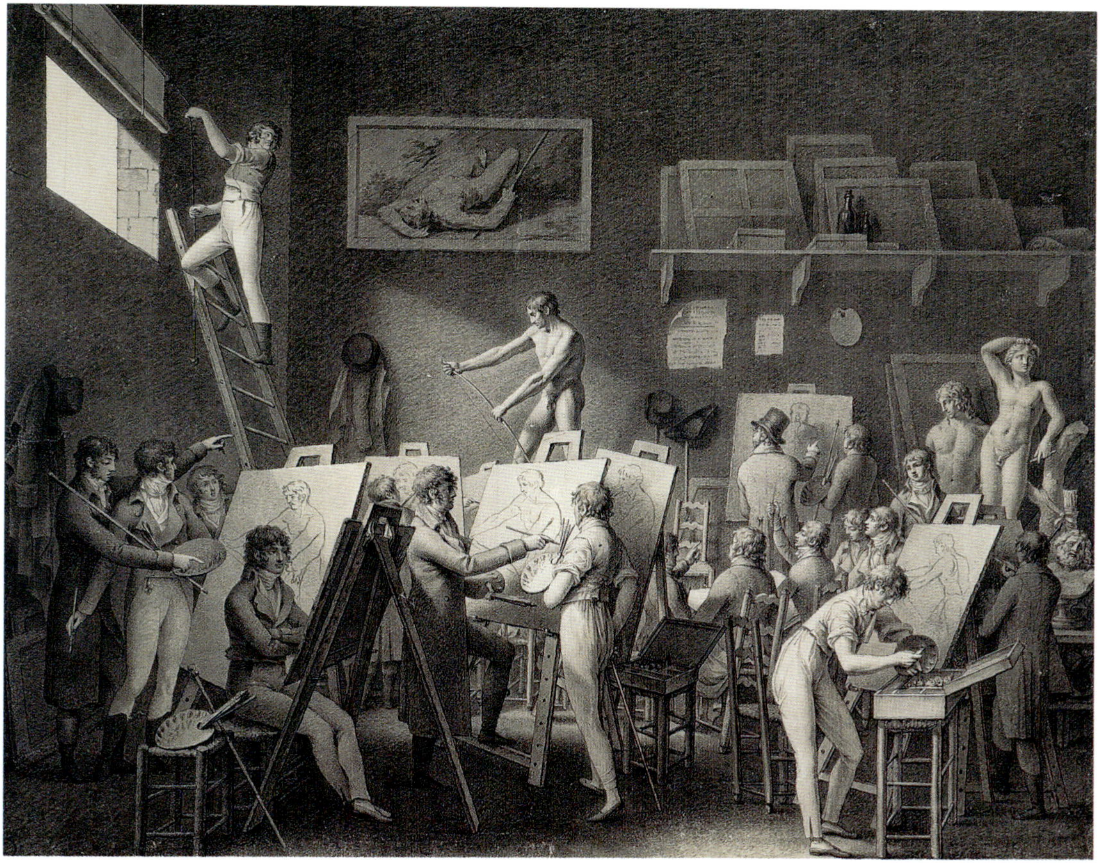

classic pictures that the whole of Europe came to study', he was not overstating the case. David's success was achieved by an ability to create works that both challenged and encapsulated the differing ideological aspirations of successive regimes. His works were simultaneously controversial and appealed to 'the public'. The later eighteenth century saw 'the public' emerge as an active rather than a passive force, its approval or disapproval profoundly affecting the fortunes of works of art. David rapidly seized on the possibilities of the power of public opinion, and pitched his works at a level of narrative, rhetoric and contemporary relevance that was likely to gain at least attention, if not actual support. As part of this strategy he also carved out a highly individual artistic identity for himself. Under the Bourbon monarchy this placed him as a virtuous and independent outsider, but during the Revolution and Napoleon's empire he wanted to be seen as a patriotic servant and the proponent of a new order.

This study of David has been written to set the artist in the context of Bourbon, Revolutionary, Napoleonic and Restoration France, and as an introduction to debates which have preoccupied modern scholars concerning his stylistic innovations, political engagement, his search for new audiences and his changing attitudes to the depiction of morality, virtue and patriotism.

Finding a Voice   Parisian and Roman Beginnings

1

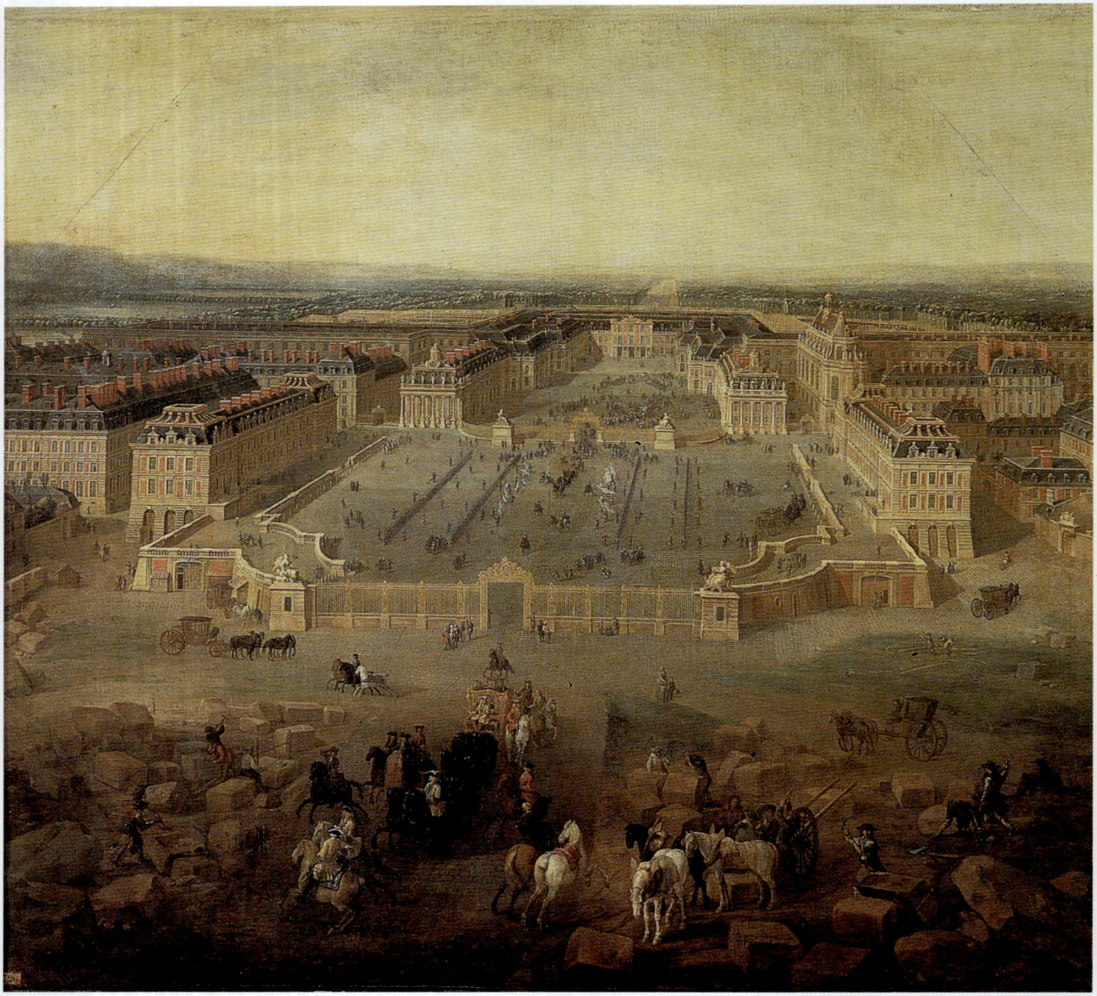

A visitor to France in the second half of the eighteenth century would have seen a land of immense contrasts, and found a society of deep divisions. Prosperous towns were approached through derelict and ill-kept countryside, and the gap between rich and poor seemed ever increasing. Birth, privilege and the ownership of land determined a person's rank and position; only the very enterprising, the favoured or the lucky could hope to improve their lot. As in almost all other European countries, the lower classes were kept in order by repressive laws and harsh punishments, and the French administration and dispensation of justice only served to emphasize society's divisions. Depending on who you were, if you were found guilty of a crime, you might be exiled or imprisoned in not too wretched surroundings, or you might alternatively be thrown into a filthy, fetid hole and forgotten, or you might be executed. Social status also determined the manner of execution: while nobles were quickly and honourably dispatched by beheading with the sword, commoners suffered torture and the agony of being burnt alive, hanged or broken on the wheel. Even in death there was no equality.

2
Pierre-Denis Martin, *Versailles*, 1722.
Oil on canvas; 139 × 150 cm, $54\frac{3}{4} \times 59\frac{1}{8}$ in. Musée National du Château de Versailles

This nation of twenty-three million people was ruled by the Bourbon king Louis XV (r.1715–74) from the élite isolation of the Palace of Versailles (2), 20 km (12 miles) from the centre of Paris. A weak and indecisive ruler, Louis came to the throne in 1715 at the age of five, with his cousin Philippe, Duke of Orléans, governing in his stead until he came of age. His inept personal reign, which began in 1723, was characterized by a series of military defeats, humiliating peace treaties and financial deficits that resulted in tax increases which placed an intolerable burden on the poor. Below the king in the hierarchical structure came the old-established aristocracy and nobles who depended on inherited wealth, income from estates and royal preference to keep them in their positions. For many observers, Louis and his ministers had mismanaged or neglected their duties, and had brought the country into decline. Once the most powerful nation in Europe, France had now conceded that position to England, and in any military or economic comparison between the two nations, France inevitably came off the worse – a severe blow to national pride and confidence. English superiority was jingoistically celebrated by William Hogarth (1697–1764) in his *O the Roast Beef of Old England (The Gate of Calais)* of 1748 (3), a satirical comment on the state of France as a place of poverty, religious bigotry and vainglory. As a succulent joint of English sirloin arrives, it is greeted by a fat friar and a group of half-starved soldiers, and it makes a substantial contrast to the cauldron of thin soup being carried away. At the sides, hideous fishwives resemble their wares, and an exiled Jacobite rebel skulks miserably with a meagre meal of a raw onion and a piece of bread.

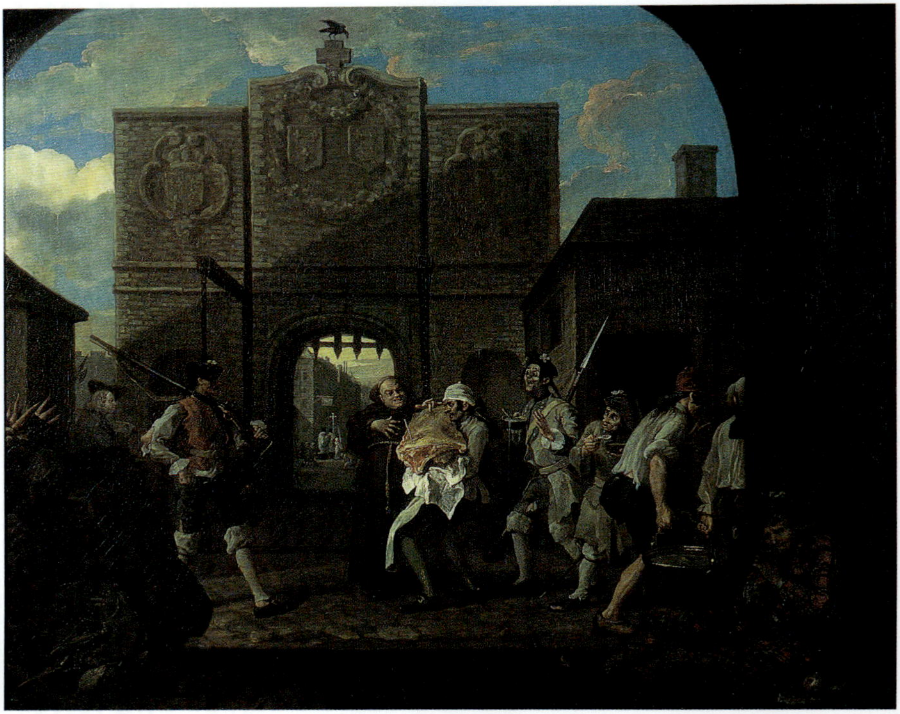

Nevertheless, France was undergoing slow but sure change, and the growing bourgeois class – bankers, financiers, lawyers, merchants and businessmen – began to seek power and status to go with their newly acquired wealth. For some this meant joining the landowning aristocracy by buying a title and an estate, but for others it lay in challenging the Crown's authority by seeking political office. This was also a time of great intellectual excitement and inquiry: philosophers and writers such as Jean-Jacques Rousseau, Voltaire and Denis Diderot were beginning to question orthodox and traditional beliefs about kingship and religion, to advance scientific and rational investigation and to call into question the inequalities that could be seen all around. This phenomenon was dubbed the Enlightenment, and in France its main proponents were called *philosophes* (philosophers). Radical new ideas about individual liberty and self-determination were put forward, with education and learning being seen as the key to progress. The whole of human knowledge (as well as a hefty dose of

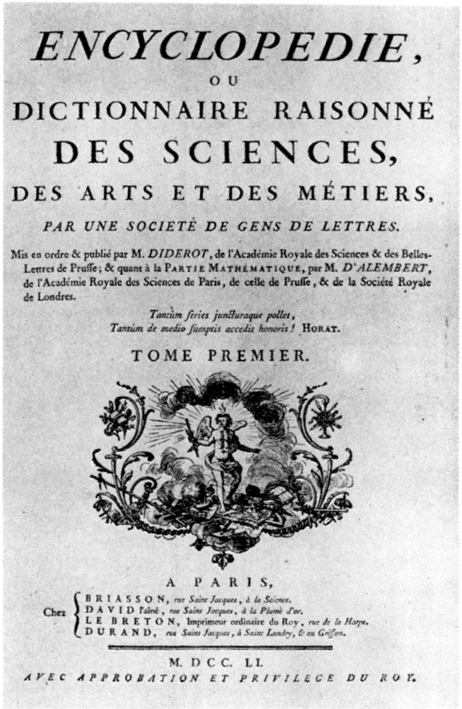
ENCYCLOPEDIE,
OU
DICTIONNAIRE RAISONNÉ
DES SCIENCES,
DES ARTS ET DES MÉTIERS,
PAR UNE SOCIETÉ DE GENS DE LETTRES.

Mis en ordre & publié par M. *DIDEROT*, de l'Académie Royale des Sciences & des Belles-Lettres de Prusse; & quant à la PARTIE MATHÉMATIQUE, par M. *D'ALEMBERT*, de l'Académie Royale des Sciences de Paris, de celle de Prusse, & de la Société Royale de Londres.

Tantùm series juncturaque pollet,
Tantùm de medio sumptis accedit honoris! HORAT.

TOME PREMIER.

A PARIS,
Chez BRIASSON, *rue Saint Jacques, à la Science.*
DAVID l'aîné, *rue Saint Jacques, à la Plume d'or.*
LE BRETON, Imprimeur ordinaire du Roy, *rue de la Harpe.*
DURAND, *rue Saint Jacques, à Saint Landry, & au Griffon.*

M. DCC. LI.
AVEC APPROBATION ET PRIVILEGE DU ROY.

3
William Hogarth,
O the Roast Beef of Old England (The Gate of Calais),
1748.
Oil on canvas;
78·8 × 94·5cm,
31 × 37¼ in.
Tate Gallery,
London

4
Title page of the *Encyclopédie,*
1751

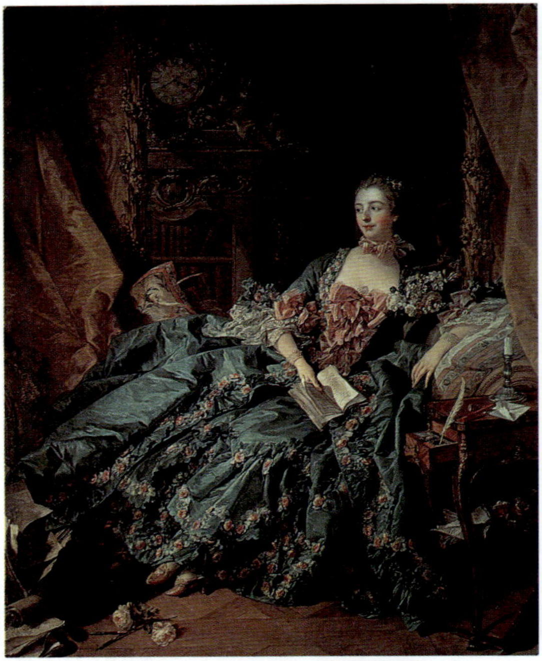

5
François Boucher, *Portrait of Madame de Pompadour,* 1756.
Oil on canvas; 201 × 157cm, $79^{1}/_{8}$ × $61^{3}/_{4}$ in.
Alte Pinakothek, Munich

6
The interior of the Salon de la Princesse in the Hôtel de Soubise, Paris. Paintings by Charles-Joseph Natoire, 1736–9

radical thinking) was published by Diderot and Jean le Rond d'Alembert in the monumental thirty-five volume *Encyclopédie* (*Encyclopedia or Rational Dictionary of the Sciences, Arts and Crafts*) of 1751–80 (4), which was a blueprint for the social and technological modernization of the nation.

In the fine and decorative arts the power and influence of the court was dominant, and Madame de Pompadour (5), Louis XV's beautiful mistress and close companion, was instrumental in shaping artistic taste and fashion. The prevailing style was for elegant and delicate forms derived from interior decoration. It was characterized by elaborate gilded plasterwork and carving in the form of curves and scrolls, and made extensive use of mirrors and glass (6). Pleasure, fantasy, delight and escapism were the principles behind this style that later became known as the Rococo. Typical subjects for painting were mythological stories of the amorous pursuits of gods and goddesses, and pastoral scenes of nymphs and shepherds. Figures often appeared like precious porcelain dolls, and stood

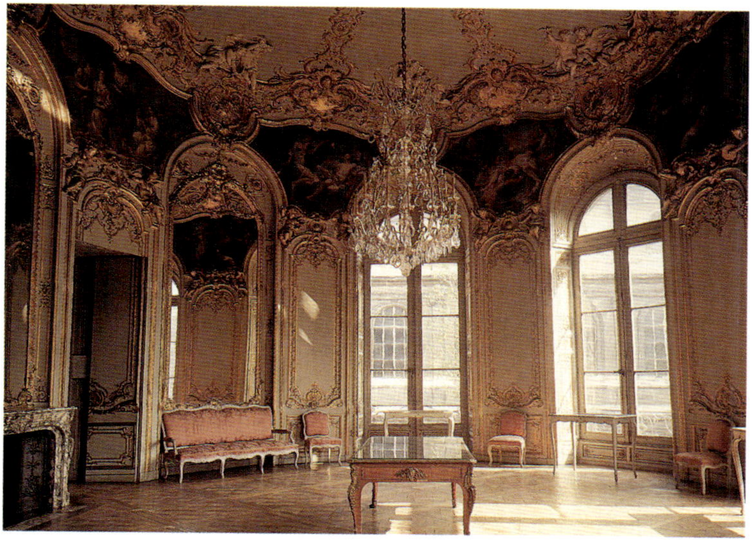

in unlikely poses, floating rather than occupying space. Pastel pinks, yellows, blues and greens were used to enhance the decorative appeal. Yet gradually, from the middle of the century, a moral backlash began. Rococo paintings might be a feast for the eyes, but they were a famine for the soul and spirit. Enlightenment critics and writers claimed that art should not simply be decorative and sensual. They urged artists to create an art of substance, that would touch the emotions of the spectator while at the same time educating, improving and providing models of behaviour. Diderot proclaimed: 'First move me, astonish me, tear me to pieces; make me shudder, weep and tremble, make me angry; then soothe my eyes, if you can.' The loves of the gods and flirtatious shepherds and shepherdesses were to be replaced by the heroism, nobility and self-sacrifice of ancient heroes and philosophers, and by the virtuous devotion of wives and children to family ideals. Yet these exhortations by moral commentators often fell on deaf ears. The newly rich did not want to be surrounded by dull lessons of virtue in their opulent town houses, and artists invariably chose to paint what was popular and saleable, rather than what the non-picture buying intellectuals told them to.

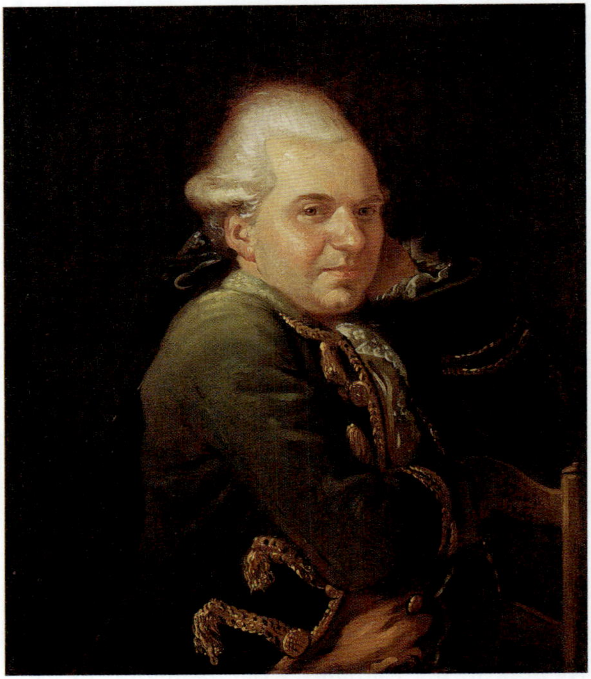

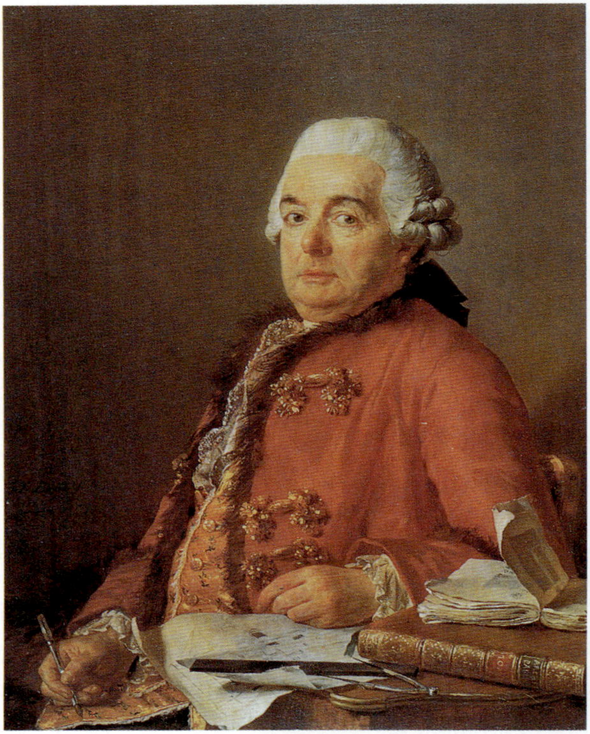

The social and artistic backdrop against which Jacques-Louis David grew up was therefore full of tensions and a desire for change. He was born on 30 August 1748 in Paris, in a house on the Quai de la Mégisserie, close to the Seine, and was baptized on the same day in the artists' church of St Germain-l'Auxerrois. David's father, Louis-Maurice, a wholesale iron merchant whose business affairs were rather shaky, nevertheless had pretensions to better himself. On 26 May 1746 he had married Marie-Geneviève Buron, who came from a family of Freemasons and architects, and who was a distant cousin of the celebrated Rococo painter François Boucher (1703–70; 5). Determined to raise his status in society, Louis-Maurice bought himself a minor administrative post (a common practice in the eighteenth century); he then indulged in the gentlemanly pursuit of duelling, and died following a pistol duel in December 1757, aged thirty-five. Thereafter, David's mother played only a minor role in her son's upbringing; he was placed successively in the care of two uncles, François Buron (1731–1818; 7) and Jacques-François Desmaisons (*c*.1720–89; 8), who were both architects and building contractors. Although he received a good education in the classics – at a boarding school and at the Collège des Quatres Nations – David was no great scholar. Despite this, his family hoped that he would take up a profession such as architecture, medicine or law, and were dismayed when he announced that he wanted to become an artist – a career then regarded as little more than a trade, lacking the status of a profession and thus unsuitable for a young bourgeois. Conscious of this, David made it his life's ambition to demonstrate that art was an intellectual and noble pursuit, and not merely a manual craft.

7
Portrait of François Buron,
1769.
Oil on canvas;
65 × 54 cm,
25⅝ × 21¼ in.
Private collection

8
Portrait of Jacques-François Desmaisons,
1782.
Oil on canvas;
91·5 × 72 cm,
36 × 28⅜ in.
Albright-Knox Art Gallery, Buffalo

Becoming an artist was not entirely unheard of within David's family circle. An old tradition maintained that an unnamed forbear had been an assistant to Charles Le Brun (1619–90), Louis XIV's First Painter, and Boucher had achieved great financial success and been appointed First Painter to Louis XVI in 1765. Boucher was initially approached to teach the budding young artist but he declined, pleading old age and probably disinclination. Instead he recommended Joseph-Marie Vien (1716–1809), a fifty-year-old professor at the Academy who had a reputation for progressive teaching, and who had made some attempts to move away from the prevailing Rococo prettiness towards subjects inspired by classical antiquity. Boucher said that Vien was a good painter but 'a bit cold', and told David to, 'come and see me from time to time and when you bring me your work I will correct Vien's coldness and teach you my warmth'. Around 1765 David joined about fifty to sixty other

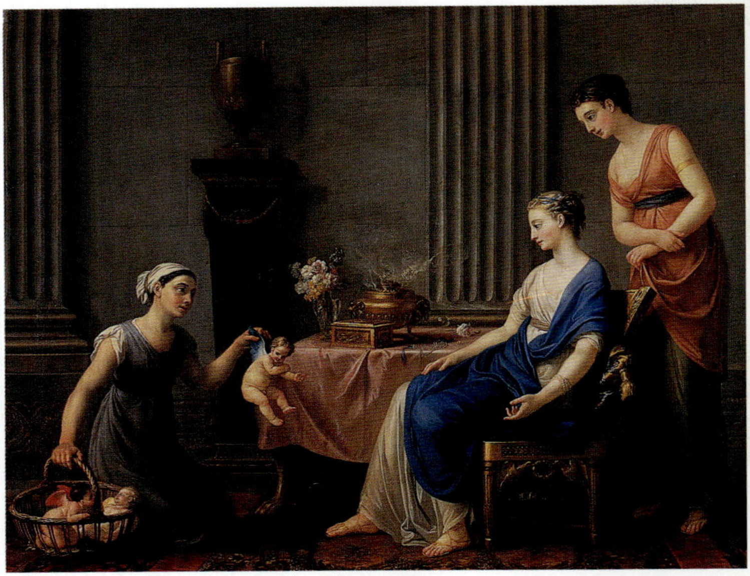

9
Joseph-Marie Vien,
The Cupid Seller,
1763.
Oil on canvas;
95 × 119 cm,
37⅜ × 46⅞ in.
Musée National du Château de Fontainebleau

10
Portrait of Marie-Françoise Buron,
c.1769.
Oil on canvas;
66 × 54 cm,
26 × 21¼ in.
Musée National des Beaux-Arts, Algiers

students in Vien's studio in the rue Montmartre, where he made steady, if unspectacular, progress. Vien became a kind of surrogate father to his new pupil, one of a number of paternal substitutes that David was to have throughout his young life. Although Vien encouraged his students to paint directly from the life model and to study Renaissance artists, his work suggests that he did not always follow his own advice. A painting such as *The Cupid Seller* (9), though inspired by an engraving of a recently discovered ancient wall-painting from Gragnano, near Herculaneum, treats the subject as a

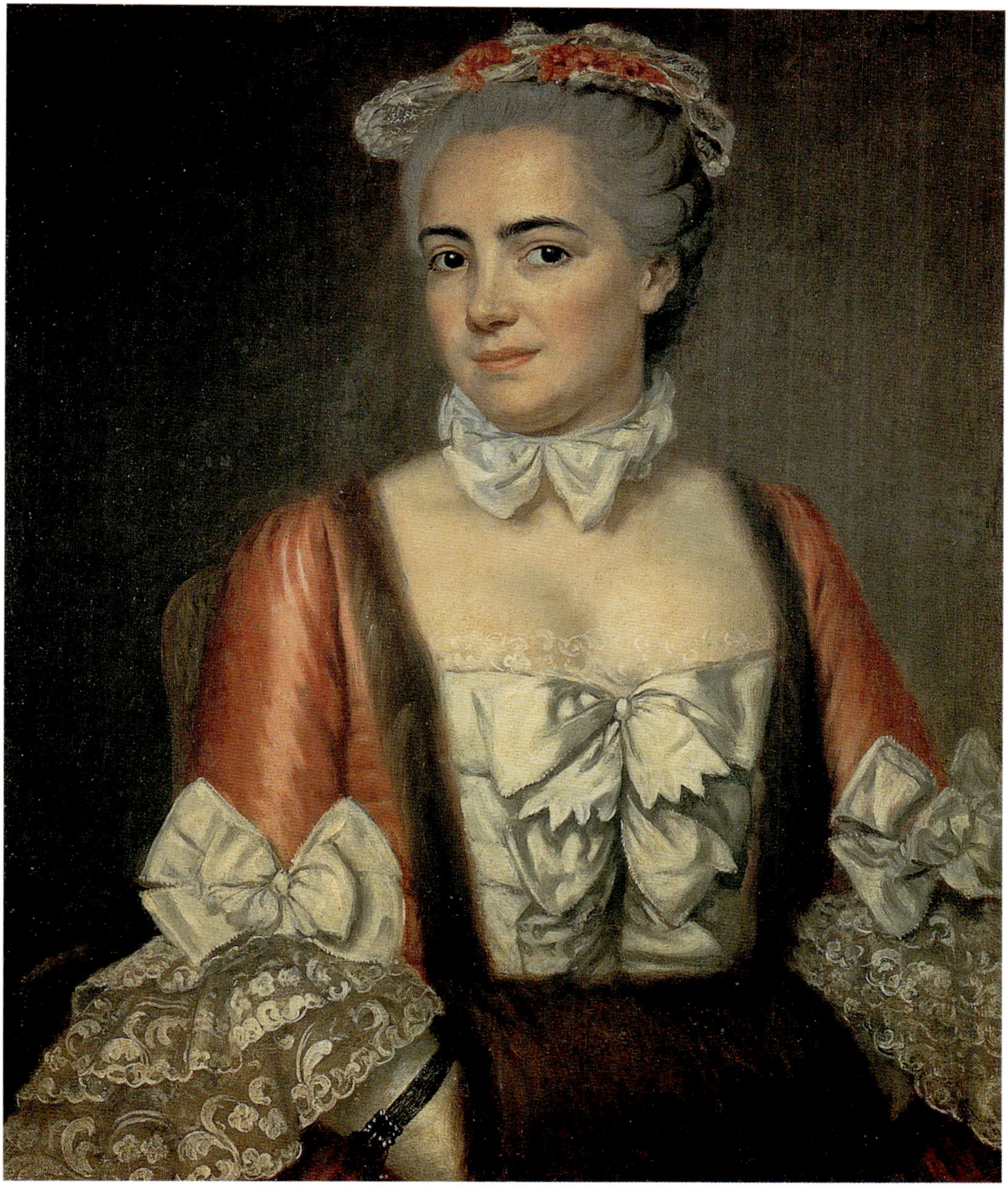

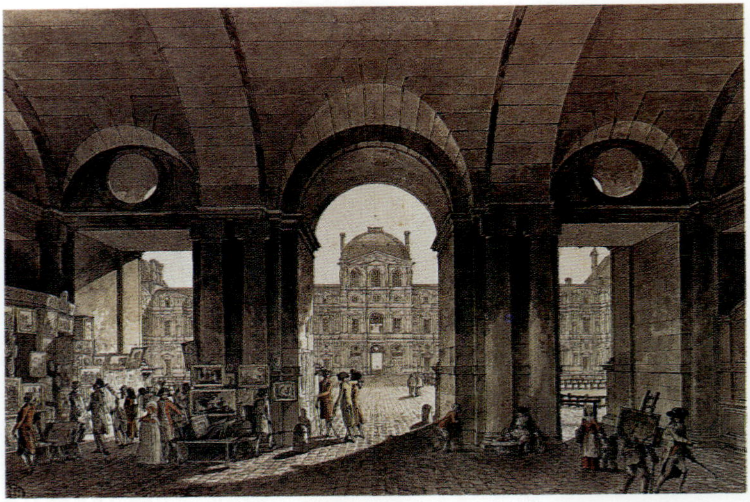

11
Drawing
by Meunier,
engraved
by Née,
The Louvre at the End of the Eighteenth Century

piece of veiled erotica: the image of the cupid held by his wings promising sexual fulfilment. Despite its classical inspiration, it is effectively a Rococo subject in antique clothing.

As with many other young artists, both before and since, David used his close relatives as models for his first portraits. As well as his uncle Buron (see 7), he also painted his aunt, Marie-Josephe, and her daughter, Marie-Françoise (10), who had supported his wish to become a painter. Although no demonstrations of youthful genius, both paintings show a directness of approach and a sympathetic contact between artist and sitter that anticipate David's later successes in portraiture.

David enrolled at the school of the Royal Academy of Painting and Sculpture in September 1766, his family connections ensuring that his student years would not be marked by poverty and hunger. The Academy, founded in 1648, was housed in rooms in the former royal palace of the Louvre (11), which served as the location for other learned bodies, and also formed a warren of artists' studios and lodgings. The students were only taught drawing, because it was considered to be the fundamental basis of both painting and sculpture. For tuition in painting, a pupil would enter the studio of an established master, who was usually an Academician. Pupils began by

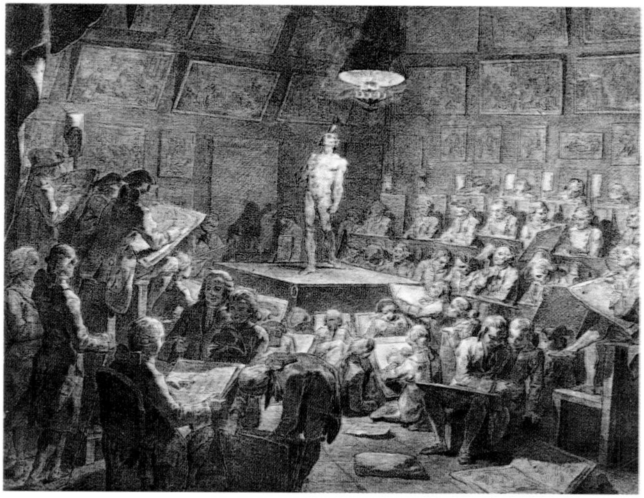

12 Charles-Nicolas Cochin, *The Life Class of the Academy,* c.1760. Chalk on paper. Private collection

copying from drawings and engravings, then progressed to study from plaster casts of famous ancient sculptures; only when they had gained a deal of skill and experience were they let loose in the life class, the pinnacle of the whole teaching system. Only male models were used (12) because it was thought that young male students might be corrupted by drawing naked females for hours on end. The reason that so much emphasis was placed on mastering the human form was that the Academy sought to train history painters – artists who depicted and interpreted scenes from the Bible, ancient history and mythology. Because history painting was based on the authority of the written word, and suggested models of virtue and morality by depicting the selfless actions of heroes and patriots, it was held to be the most elevated category of painting (ranked above portraiture, landscape and genre), and the one to which all true artists should aspire. Naturally, David aimed to become a history painter.

The goal of practically every Academy student was to win the premier student prize: the Grand Prix, or Prix de Rome. The victors in this annual history painting competition, where a student was given ten weeks to produce a picture on a set subject in a tiny studio cell, spent between three and five years at the French Academy in Rome. Study in the Eternal City was thought essential to complete a young artist's education, and the attraction of doing so at the government's expense meant that the Prix de Rome was the subject of intense competition. But David was neither a brilliant nor a precocious student, and it took him five attempts to win the coveted prize. At each failure he became increasingly frustrated with the Academy for denying him the prize, and this dissatisfaction sowed the seeds of a long-standing grudge against the institution.

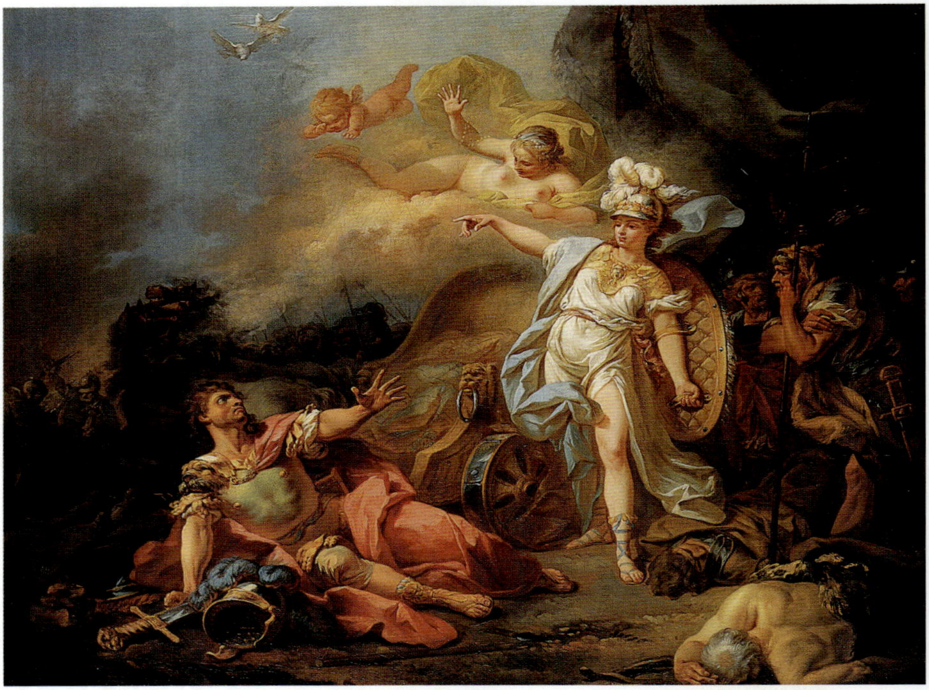

The works he produced for the Prix de Rome were in the decorative and rather playful style of the day, and gave few hints of the direction that his art would eventually take. In 1770 he was eliminated in the preliminary competition, and in 1771 he came second with *The Combat of Mars and Minerva* (13), a subject taken from Homer's *Iliad*. At the time of the Trojan War, Minerva, goddess of wisdom and supporter of the Greeks, defeated Mars, god of war and an ally of the Trojans, in a battle. After Mars was felled, his lover Venus came to his rescue. The work by the first-prize winner Joseph-Benoît Suvée (1743–1807; 14) was clearly more balanced and elegant than David's rambling and unconvincing effort, which showed serious shortcomings in both the gestures and the anatomy of the figures. Despite his rival's superior work, David was a poor

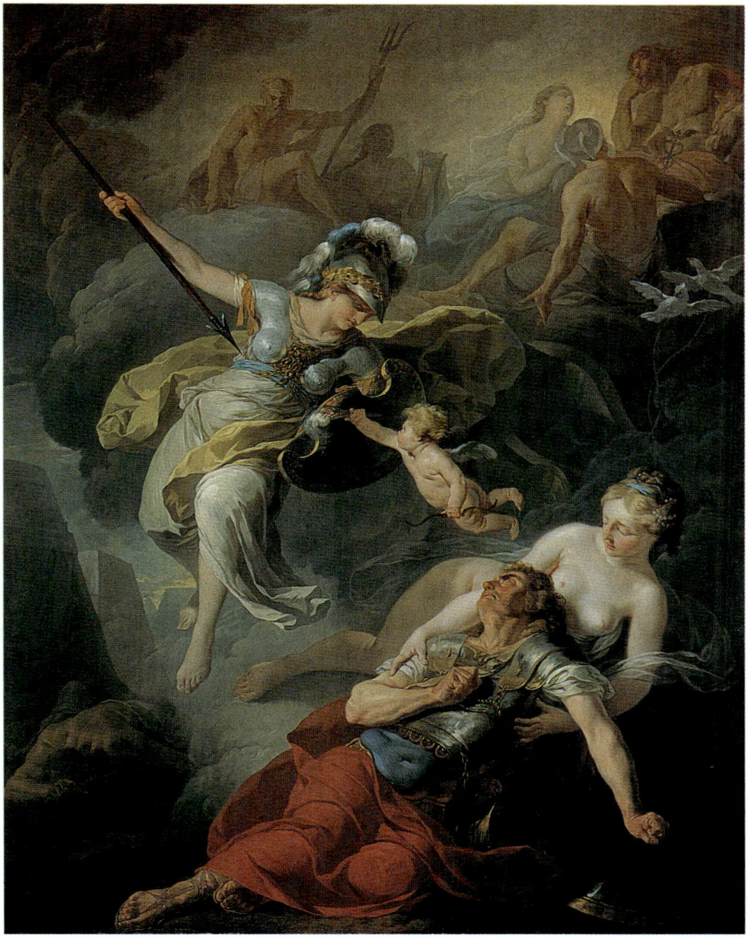

13
The Combat of Mars and Minerva, 1771. Oil on canvas; 146 × 181 cm, 57½ × 71⅜ in. Musée du Louvre, Paris

14
Joseph-Benoît Suvée, *The Combat of Mars and Minerva*, 1771. Oil on canvas; 143 × 103·5 cm, 56⅜ × 40¾ in. Musée des Beaux-Arts, Lille

loser and retained a lifelong dislike of Suvée, later calling him 'ignorant and horrible', and also saying that this failure, 'was harmful to my development; for without it I'd have left four years sooner the bad style of the French school which I later had so much difficulty in shaking off in Rome'. David had entered for the prize without informing his master, Vien, and had been warned that such a serious competition was not to be taken lightly. He was also angry because he strongly suspected that some judges, and perhaps even Vien, had used their influence to sway the result. This was the first instance of the fear of conspiracies, bordering on paranoia, that surrounded David throughout his working life. The next year he lost again, and this time his suspicions were well founded: he had initially been allocated one of the two first prizes, but then a plot was hatched, the votes were changed, and he saw the excellent Pierre-Charles Jombert (b.1748/9) and the mediocre and undeserving Anicet Charles Gabriel Lemonnier (1743–1824) carry

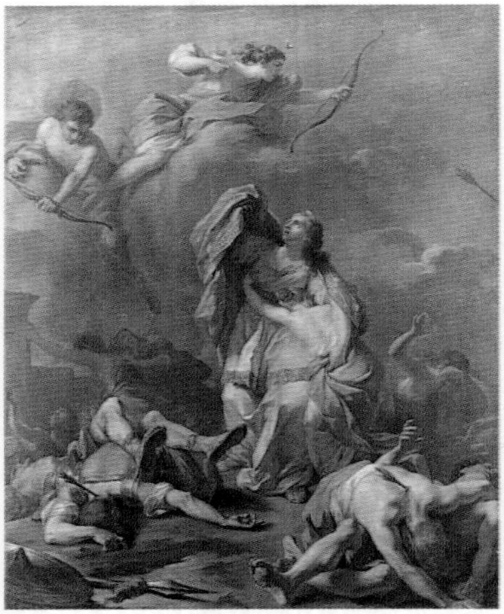

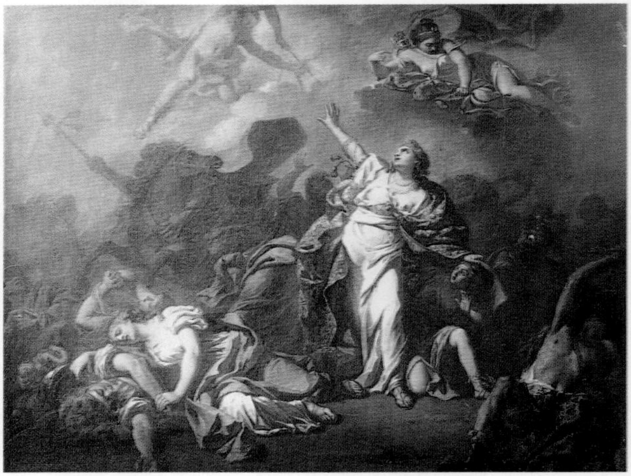

off the prizes (15, 17). The subject was *Apollo and Diana Attacking Niobe and her Children,* an episode from Ovid's *Metamorphoses,* in which Apollo and Diana destroy the children of the arrogant and presumptuous Niobe with a rain of arrows, because she had declared herself superior to Leto, their own mother. David's cause in the competition had not been helped by his impulsive temperament: he had repainted over his first attempt before the lower paint layer was dry, with the result that the new surface blackened and lost vibrancy (16). Bitterly disappointed, he made a half-hearted attempt at suicide by starvation, but was soon coaxed back to

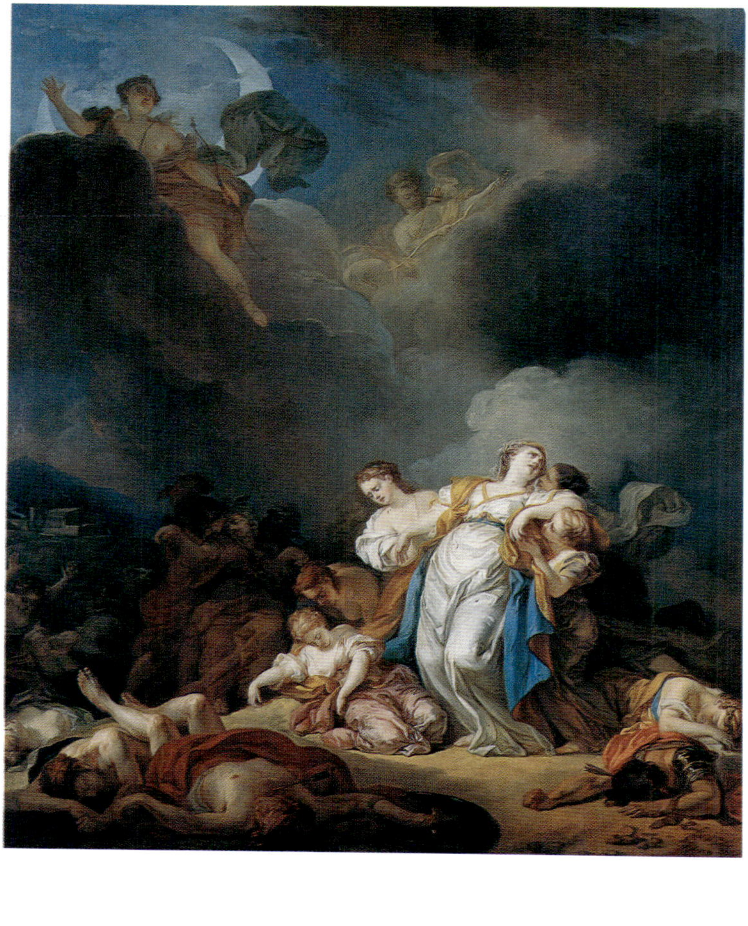

15
Pierre-Charles Jombert,
Apollo and Diana Attacking Niobe and her Children,
1772.
Oil on canvas;
140 × 110 cm,
$55\frac{1}{8} \times 43\frac{3}{8}$ in.
École Nationale Supérieure des Beaux-Arts, Paris

16
Apollo and Diana Attacking Niobe and her Children,
1772.
Oil on canvas;
120 × 152 cm,
$47\frac{1}{4} \times 59\frac{7}{8}$ in.
Private collection

17
Anicet Charles Gabriel Lemonnier,
Apollo and Diana Attacking Niobe and her Children,
1772.
Oil on canvas;
141 × 112 cm,
$55\frac{1}{2} \times 44$ in.
Musée des Beaux-Arts, Rouen

nourishment, thanks mostly to the intervention of a friendly and sympathetic Academician, Gabriel-François Doyen (1726–1806). In 1773 David was again beaten, this time by a very accomplished rival, Pierre Peyron (1744–1814). Peyron's painting of *The Death of Seneca*, now lost and known only from an engraving (18), was simple, noble and severe – the very qualities that Enlightenment thinkers had demanded to take French art away from the frivolous and hedonistic Rococo towards a serious and moral style that taught a virtuous lesson.

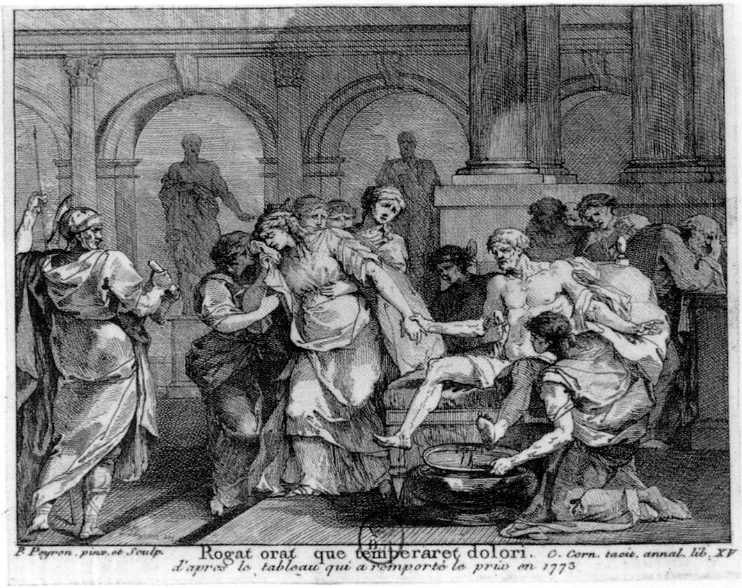

18
Pierre Peyron,
The Death of Seneca,
1773.
Engraving;
12·5 × 14·5 cm,
$4\frac{7}{8} \times 5\frac{3}{4}$ in

19
The Death of Seneca,
1773.
Oil on canvas;
123 × 160 cm,
$48\frac{1}{2} \times 63$ in.
Musée du Petit Palais, Paris

By contrast, David's work (19) was turbulent, theatrical and lacking in gravity, giving no hint of Seneca's dignified and restrained suicide, forced on him by order of the tyrannical Emperor Nero. Instead, the painting seems more concerned with the emotional farewell between Seneca and his wife Paulina.

Although defeated in the Prix de Rome in 1773, David had the satisfaction of winning the prize for the best drawing of an expressive head, with his image of *Sorrow* (20). Drawing and painting such heads was to become a speciality of his, and their careful study was given great importance, as they could add meaning and subtlety to history paintings. At this time he was also commissioned to produce paintings to decorate the newly built grand town house of the famous ballet dancer Marie-Madeleine Guimard. This welcome employment came about because of an argument between Mlle Guimard and her first choice, Jean-Honoré Fragonard (1732–1806). It was said that Fragonard wreaked his revenge on her by slipping into

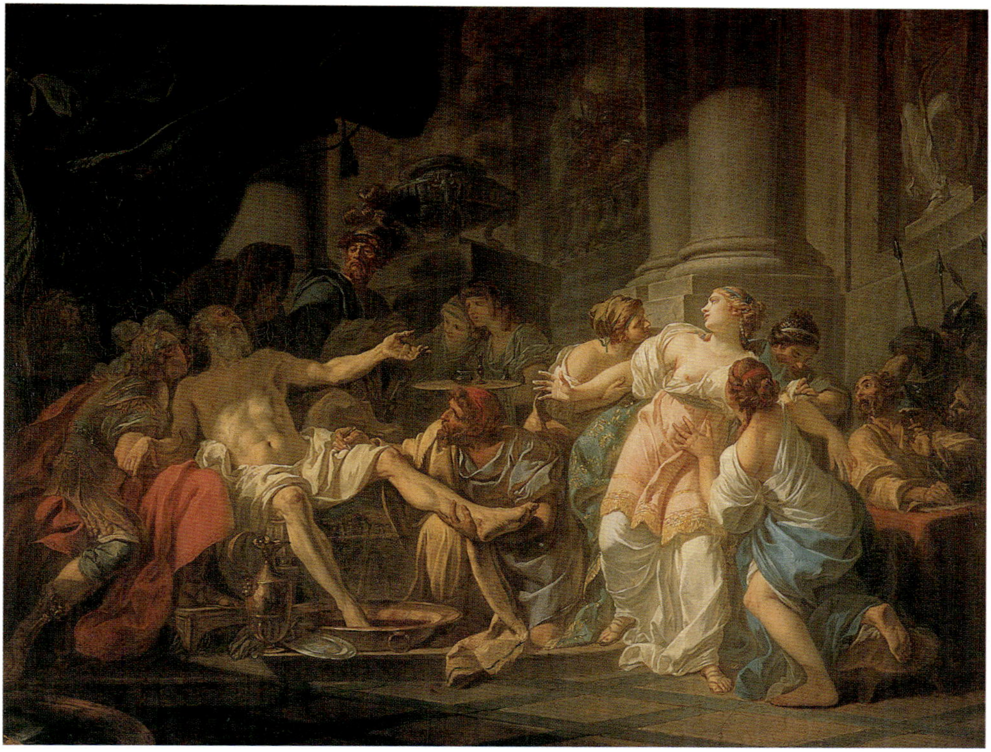

the house unnoticed when the work was complete and defacing a picture of her as Terpsichore, the Muse of the Dance. With just a few brushstrokes he changed the figure's expression from a smile to a grimace, but fortunately David was able to return the painting to its original state. Fragonard was one of the most prominent and sought-after artists of the day, and for David to have been asked to take over from him indicates that the young artist was considered a promising (as well as

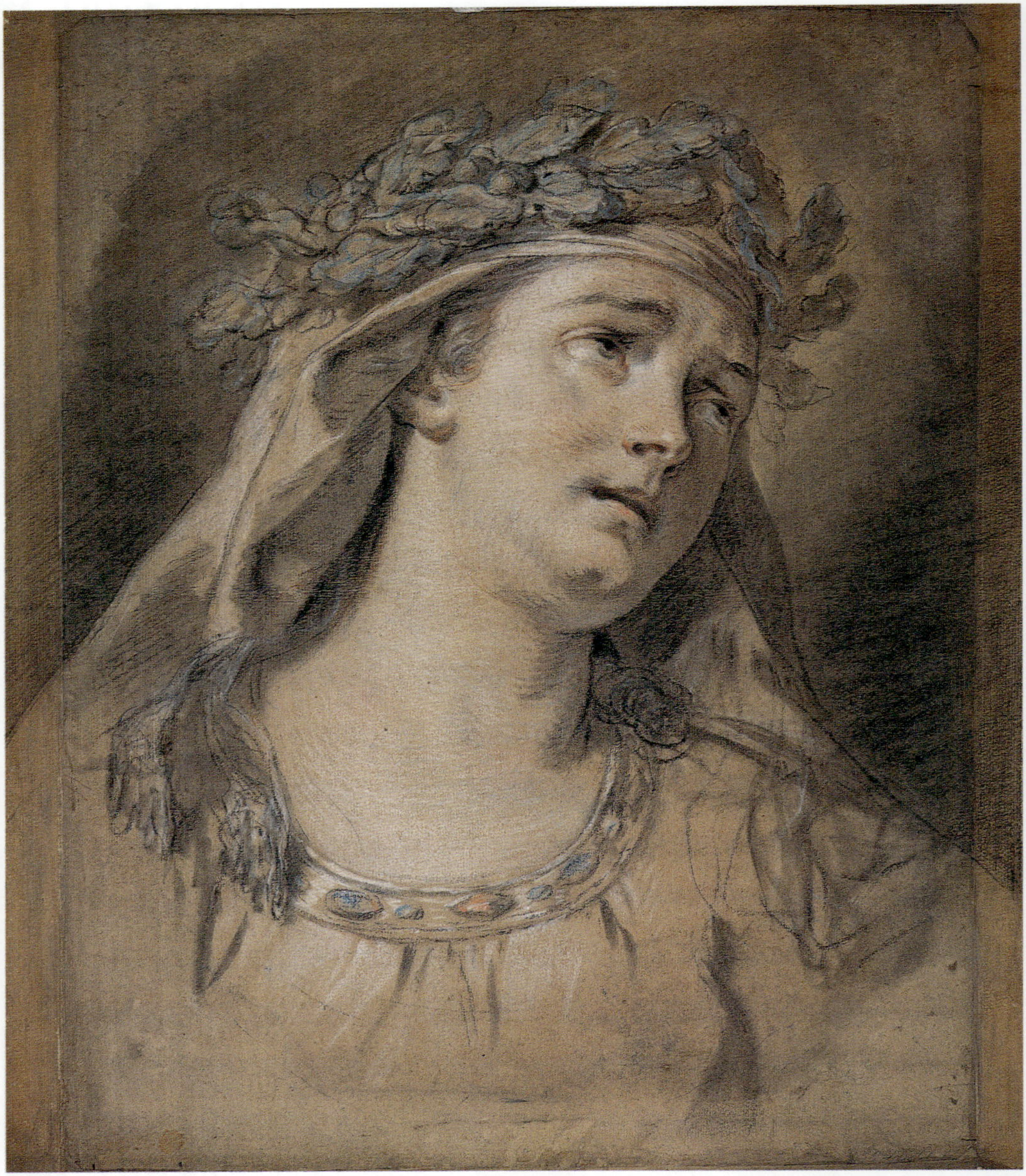

20
Sorrow,
1773.
Coloured chalks
on paper;
53·5 × 41cm,
21 × 16⅛ in.
École Nationale
Supérieure des
Beaux-Arts,
Paris

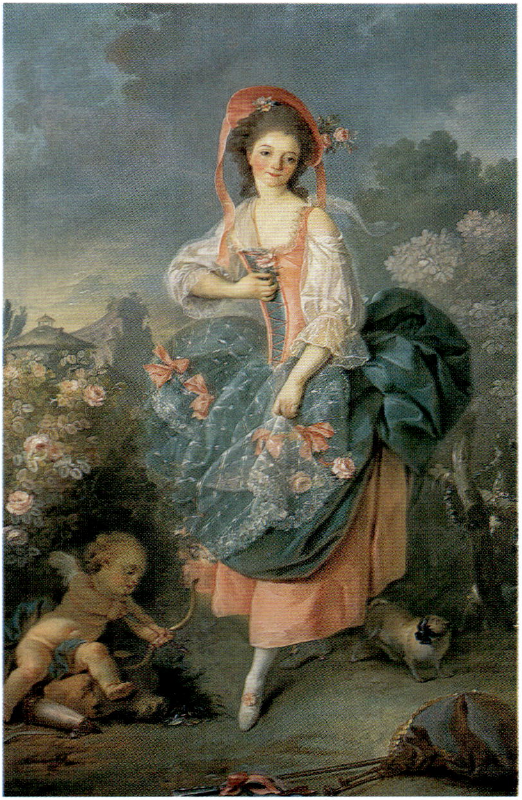

21
Portrait of Mademoiselle Guimard as Terpsichore, 1773/4.
Oil on canvas; 195·5 × 120·5 cm, 77 × 47½ in.
Private collection

cheaper) practitioner of the Rococo. But even though Fragonard and Mlle Guimard were on bad terms, there was no animosity between him and David; on the contrary, David visited the older artist to ask permission to complete the work that he had started, and Fragonard very graciously agreed, probably relieved to be rid of an awkward patron and an unrewarding job. Unfortunately, David's interior decorations have disappeared. The profligate Mlle Guimard went bankrupt in 1786, and the house was later demolished and its decorative paintings auctioned off. The only reminder of this episode is a charming portrait that David painted of his patron which demonstrates how capable and proficient he was of working in a light and frivolous manner (21). Although once again cast as Terpsichore, Mlle Guimard appears more like an elegant shepherdess than an antique muse.

David's painful Prix de Rome odyssey finally came to an end the following year, when he won with a much calmer and dramatically focused picture – *Antiochus and Stratonice* (22). On hearing the news of his victory David is supposed to have said: 'This is the first time in four years that I have been able to draw breath.' The subject dealt with the young Syrian Prince Antiochus, who had taken to his bed with a mortal sickness. The wise physician Erasistratus observed that whenever

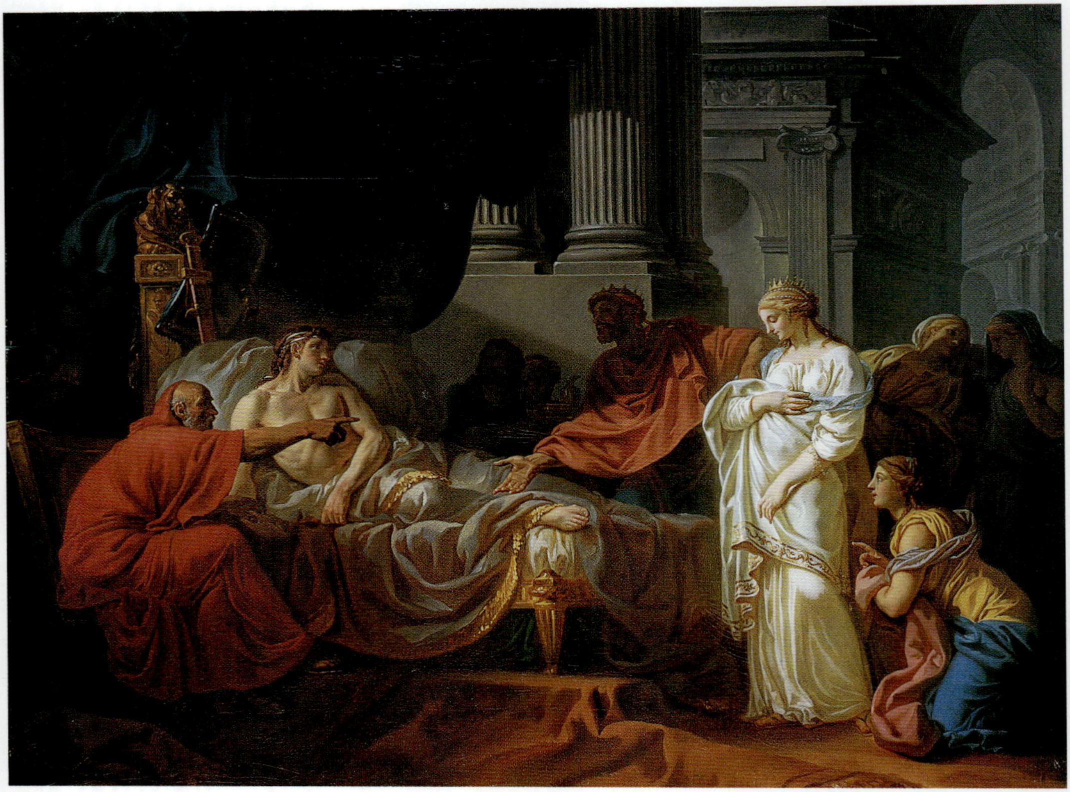

Antiochus' new stepmother Stratonice entered the room, his patient's spirits rallied dramatically. The prince was lovesick, and the only cure was for his father, Seleucus, to give up his new bride, which he reluctantly did to save his son's life. David skilfully condenses the moment of diagnosis and the moment of donation into a single scene, and he probably also subdued his natural exuberance in order to please the judges. It also seems likely that he had learnt from Peyron's example of the previous year; at Peyron's funeral in 1814, David is reported to have said: 'He opened my eyes.'

At this time David was lodging with his godfather, the playwright and opera librettist Michel-Jean Sedaine (23), who was also the secretary to the Academy of Architecture, and lived in comfortable rooms in the Louvre. He became yet another father figure to David; so close was their relationship that it was even rumoured that Sedaine was David's natural father. Through Sedaine, David was introduced to intellectual society, and he evidently had the necessary social graces to feel at home in such circles. But although his relatively privileged

22
Antiochus and Stratonice, 1774. Oil on canvas; 120 × 155cm, 47¼ × 61in. École Nationale Supérieure des Beaux-Arts, Paris

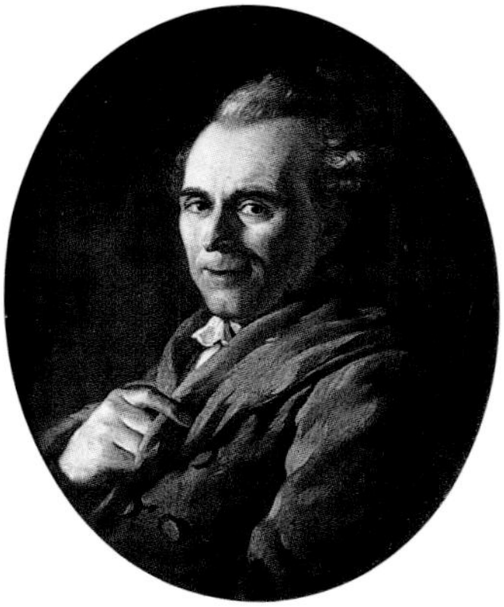

23
Portrait of Michel-Jean Sedaine, c.1772. Oil on canvas; 55 × 45cm, 21⅝ × 17¾in. Private collection

upbringing had given him many advantages over his fellow students, there was one problem over which money and social connections had no influence. As a schoolboy David had a speech impediment, later made worse by an injury on the inside of his left cheek which was sustained during a fencing match with a fellow student in Vien's studio. This gradually formed into a fleshy non-malignant tumour which made his speech difficult to understand. It can be no coincidence that David chose to express himself through visual means, and it might even be said that as his ability to make himself understood in words deteriorated, his determination to ensure that his paintings were clear and emphatic increased.

In the same year as David's Prix de Rome triumph, France had a new king. In May 1774 Louis XV died of smallpox at the age of sixty-four, and was succeeded by his twenty-year-old grandson, Louis Augustus, who became Louis XVI (24). Although the new king's passion was for hunting rather than the arts, his advisers persuaded him of their importance. By the careful selection of appropriate subjects, history painting could help

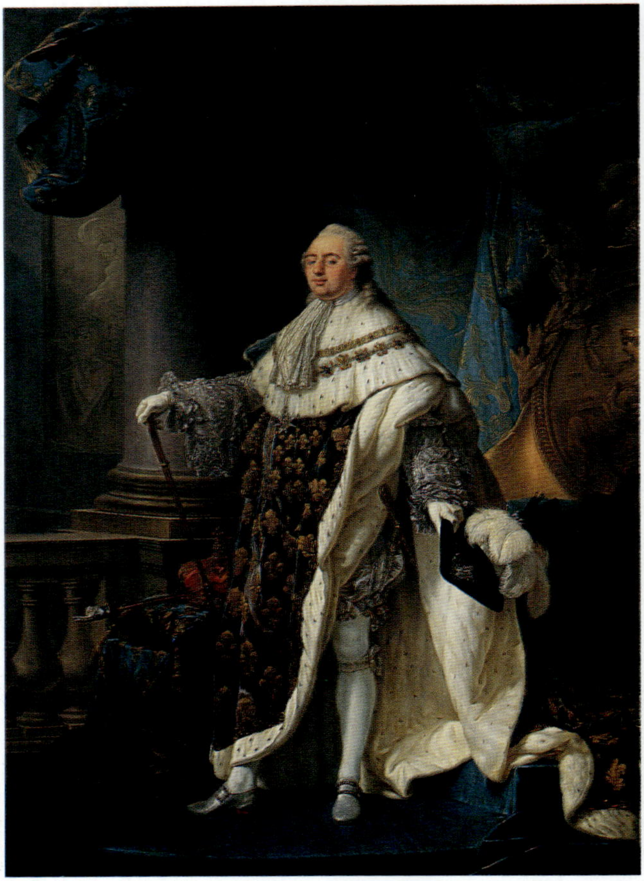

24
Antoine-François Callet,
Portrait of Louis XVI,
1788.
Oil on canvas;
278 × 196 cm,
$109\frac{1}{2} \times 77\frac{1}{8}$ in.
Musée National du Château de Versailles

25
Joseph Siffred Duplessis,
Portrait of the Comte d'Angiviller,
1779.
Oil on canvas;
144 × 106 cm,
$56\frac{5}{8} \times 41\frac{3}{4}$ in.
Musée National du Château de Versailles

to cement national identity, encourage morality and patriotism, and also promote the image of an enlightened absolute monarch sponsoring the fine arts. To this end, in 1775, a former soldier and personal friend of the king, Charles-Claude de Flahaut de la Billaderie, the Comte d'Angiviller (25), was made the Directeur des Bâtiments du Roi (Director of the King's Buildings) – a kind

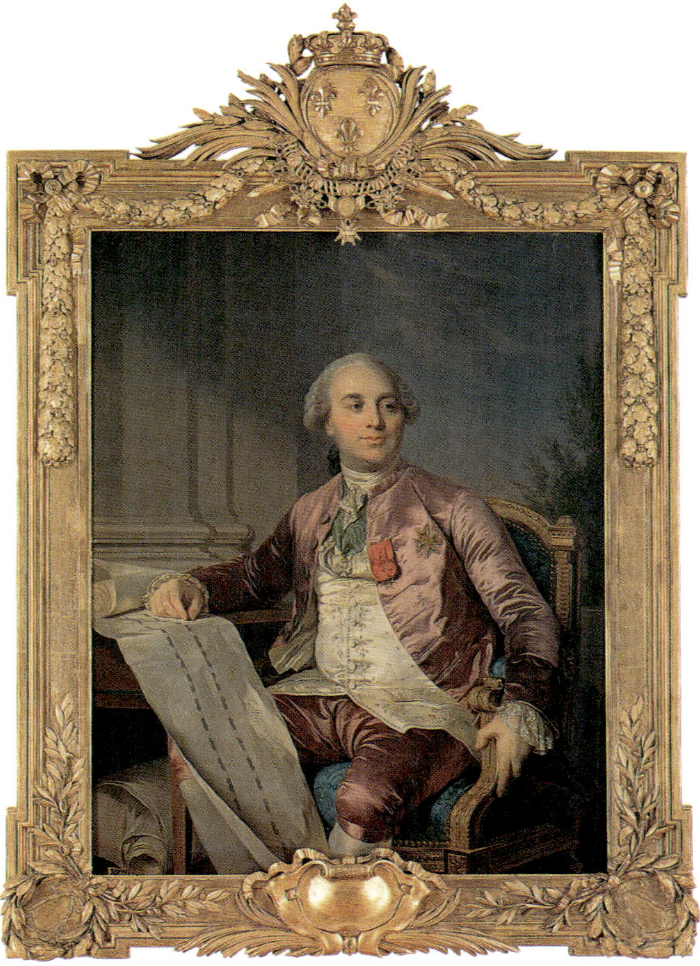

of minister of fine arts. Through him more money was made available to commission paintings that were patriotic and didactic. Serious painting, for so long starved of sufficient funds, was at last given adequate resources; it was a fortunate time for an aspiring painter to be embarking on a career.

After spending a year in Paris following his success, David set off for Rome in October 1775. The journey, which was slow, uncomfortable and not without some danger, took just over a month, and included stops in Bologna and Florence to study

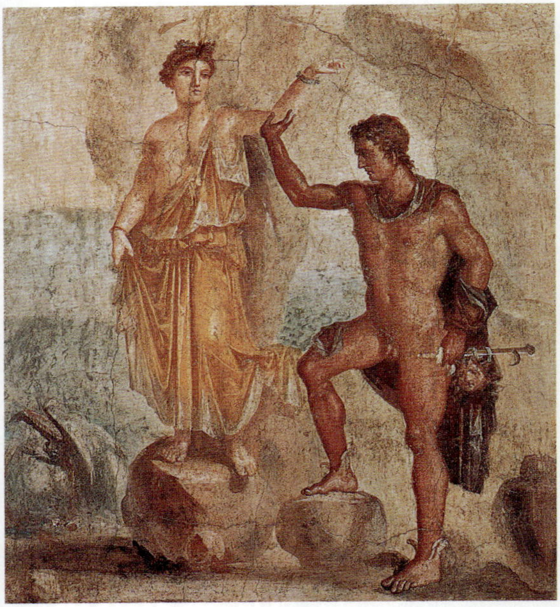

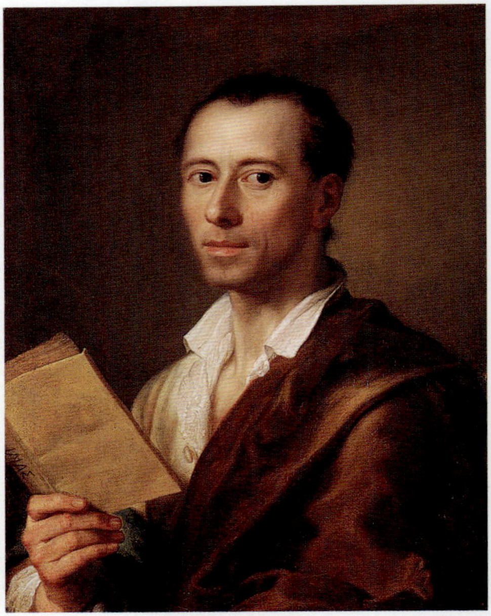

major works of art. David travelled as a member of Vien's party, as his master had been recently appointed director of the French Academy in Rome. From the mid-eighteenth century, Rome had been re-established as the centre of the European art world, partly due to the rekindling of interest in antiquity sparked off by the archaeological discoveries of Herculaneum in 1738, and Pompeii in 1748 (26), and partly through the influential writings on ancient art by the German Johann Joachim Winckelmann (27), the principal theorist of Neoclassicism. In his *Reflections on the Imitation of Greek*

Works in Painting and Sculpture (1755), Winckelmann had written that: 'The sole way for us to become great, and if possible inimitable, is by the imitation of the ancients.' By this he did not mean merely copying ancient works, but a process of total immersion in the world of the ancients, followed by the creation of works of art imbued with the spirit of antiquity. Winckelmann thought that art had reached its supreme expression in ancient Athens at the time of the sculptor

26
Perseus Freeing Andromeda, mid-1st century BC. Wall-painting transferred onto panel from the House of the Dioscurides, Pompeii; 122 × 100 cm, 48 × 39⅜ in. Museo Nazionale, Naples

27
Anton Raphael Mengs, *Portrait of Johann Joachim Winckelmann*, c.1761/2. Oil on canvas; 63·5 × 49·3 cm, 25 × 19½ in. Metropolitan Museum of Art, New York

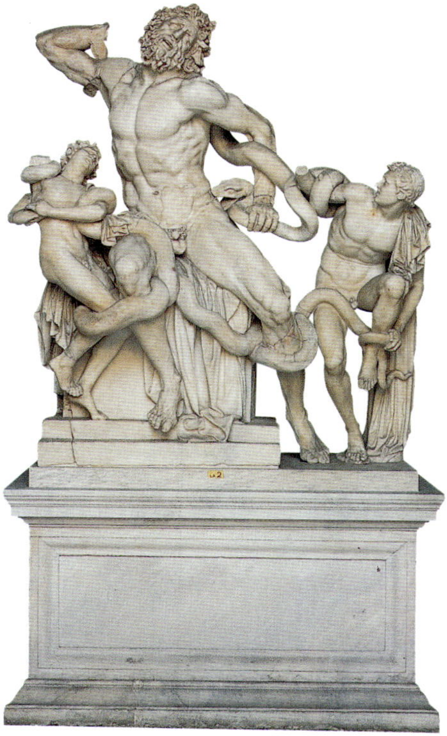

28
Laocoön, Roman copy of a Greek bronze original c.150 BC. Marble; h.242 cm, 95¼ in. Vatican Museums, Rome

Pheidias in the fifth century BC – the period known as the 'golden age' for its achievements in art, literature and politics. He also stated that 'the most eminent characteristic of Greek works is a noble simplicity and sedate grandeur in gesture and expression', and that he had found exactly these qualities in the sculptural group of the *Laocoön* (28), which had been rediscovered in Rome in 1506, and was considered one of the greatest works to survive from antiquity.

Rome at this time was a city with a huge international colony of artists, dealers in art and antiquities (some of them fakes), and a great number of foreign visitors and connoisseurs. Prominent among these were young British aristocrats making the 'Grand Tour' of the continent to complete their classical education. These 'Grand Tourists' often returned with portraits of themselves in Roman settings (29), and with some piece of ancient sculpture for their stately home. Although exposure to the civilizing influence of antique culture was the primary aim of the Grand Tour, it was also an opportunity to escape close parental supervision, and many young travellers took full advantage of their freedom to indulge in debauchery.

But what did David expect of Rome? Evidently not a great deal. For all its artistic glories, the city was hot and unhealthy and a prime example of underdevelopment, with run-down roads, fields lying fallow and noxious marshes that bred mosquitoes in their millions. The trip was sometimes considered more of a duty than a privilege, and David initially seems to have been rather lukewarm about going and reluctant to change his approach to art. Before departing from Paris he had been advised not to let the Roman experience affect his work, to which he replied: 'The antique will not seduce me; it lacks liveliness and does not move.' Yet in the five years he spent in Rome (1775–80), his art underwent a total transformation. But this was no sudden conversion whereby the scales dramatically fell from his eyes, even though David later claimed that this had indeed happened following a visit to Naples in July and August of 1779. In reality the change was slow and gradual, but nonetheless ultimately complete and decisive.

29
Pompeo Batoni,
Portrait of Thomas Dundas,
1764.
Oil on canvas;
298 × 196·8 cm,
$114\frac{3}{8} \times 77\frac{1}{2}$ in.
Private collection

Under Vien, the regime of the French Academy in Rome – housed in the Palazzo Mancini on the Corso, Rome's main thoroughfare (30) – became much more strict. The new director was determined that the slack conditions of the past, whereby students had a sort of extended holiday, should be replaced by discipline, diligence and application. Students were to rise at

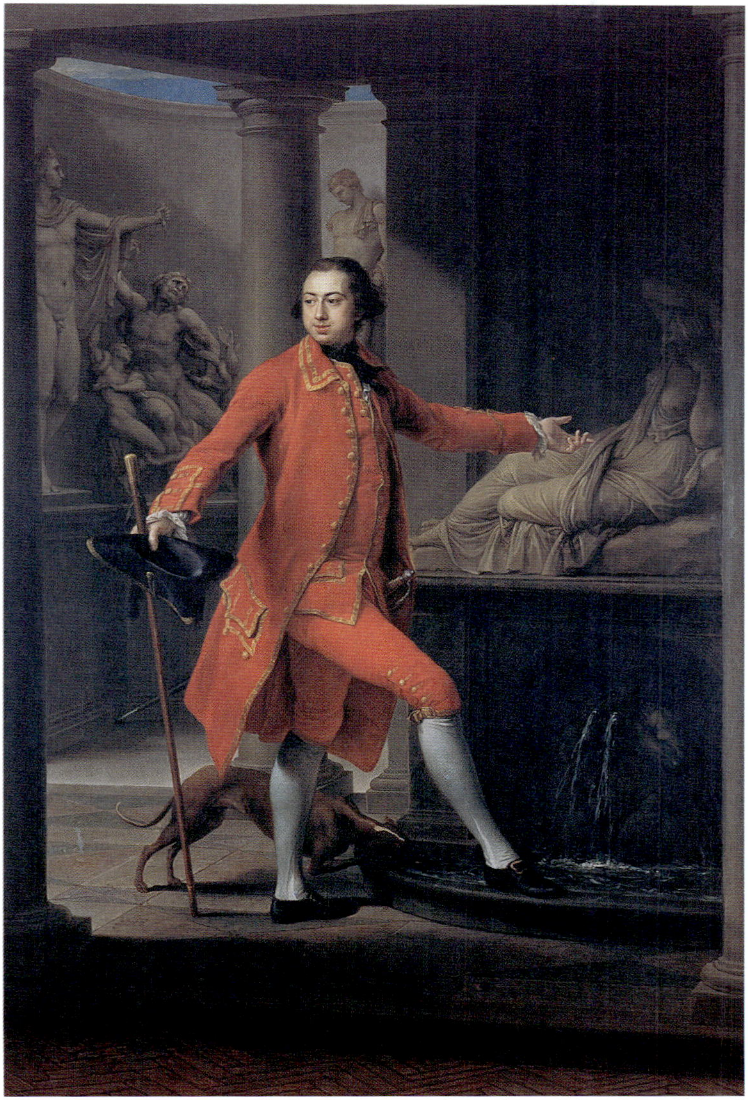

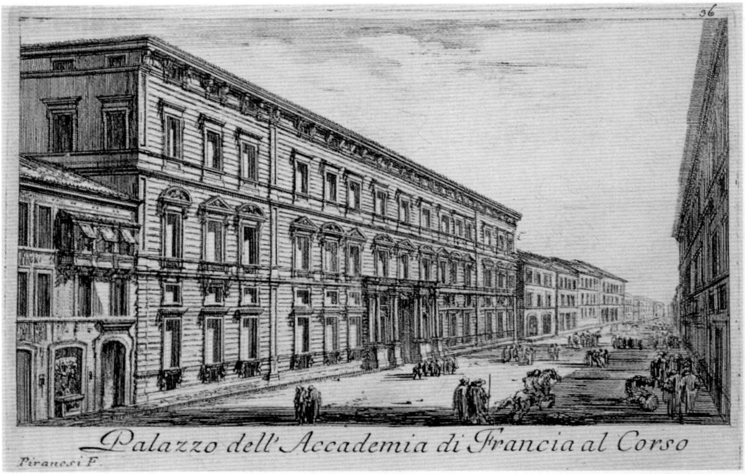

five in the summer and draw the life model from six until eight, when the light was at its best, and in winter to work in the evening under artificial light. A rigorous programme of drawing and making copies in the Vatican museums, in churches and in palaces also existed, and paintings of the students' own composition had to be sent back to Paris for assessment. A student's social life was also regulated: they had to be back inside the Academy by 10 pm in the winter and by 11 pm in the summer. Vien even proposed that they be made to wear a uniform, but this was not adopted for fear of antagonizing the people of Rome. Some students found this regime too restrictive and lacking in inspiration, and in 1779 a friend of David's, the sculptor Antoine Léonard Dupasquier (1748–1831/2), was sent back to Paris in disgrace for insolence and insubordination towards Vien.

David's first studies from this time were drawings of Roman antiquities and landmarks – the usual stuff of student sketchbooks (31, 32). He filled two albums with drawings from ancient sculpture. The intention was that these would provide visual material when he returned to Paris; artists drew extensively and intensively from the antique because most of them would only make one trip to Rome in their lifetime. The first painting that David produced in Rome, a large oil sketch of

30
Giovanni Battista Piranesi, *The Palazzo Mancini on the Corso, Rome.* Etching and engraving; 38 × 61·5cm, 15 × 24¼ in

31
Minerva, 1776/7. Pen, ink and wash; 21·2 × 15cm, 8⅜ × 5⅞ in. Musée du Louvre, Paris

32
View of the Tiber and Castel St Angelo, 1776/7. Grey wash over black chalk; 16·6 × 22cm, 6½ × 8⅝ in. Musée du Louvre, Paris

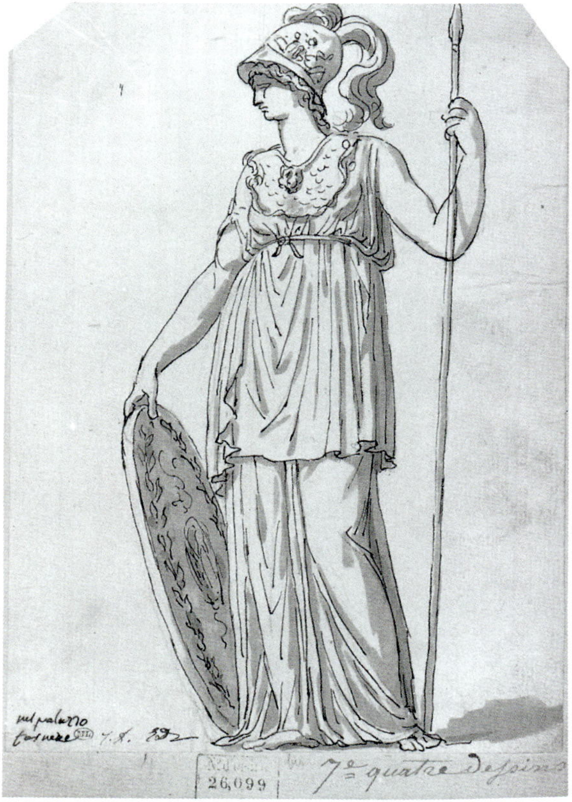
26,099

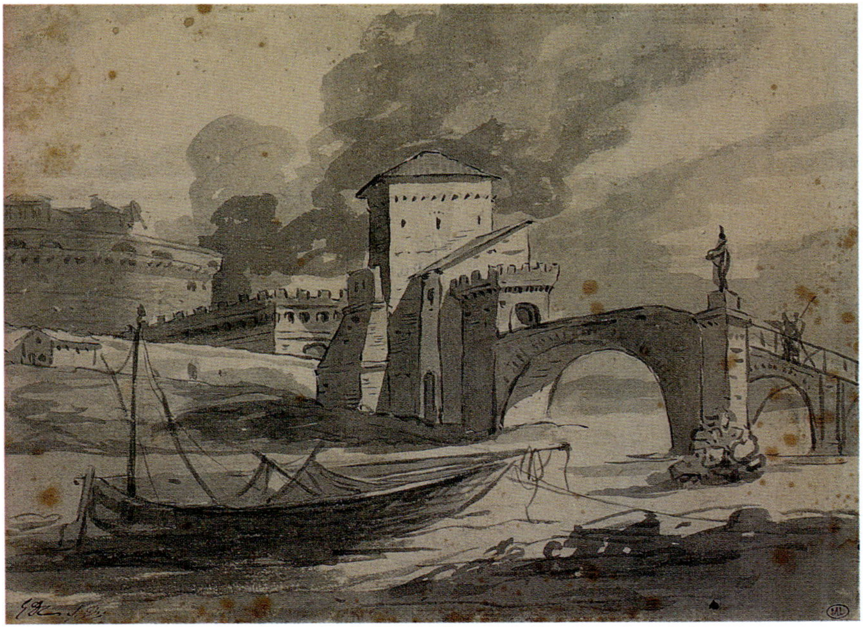

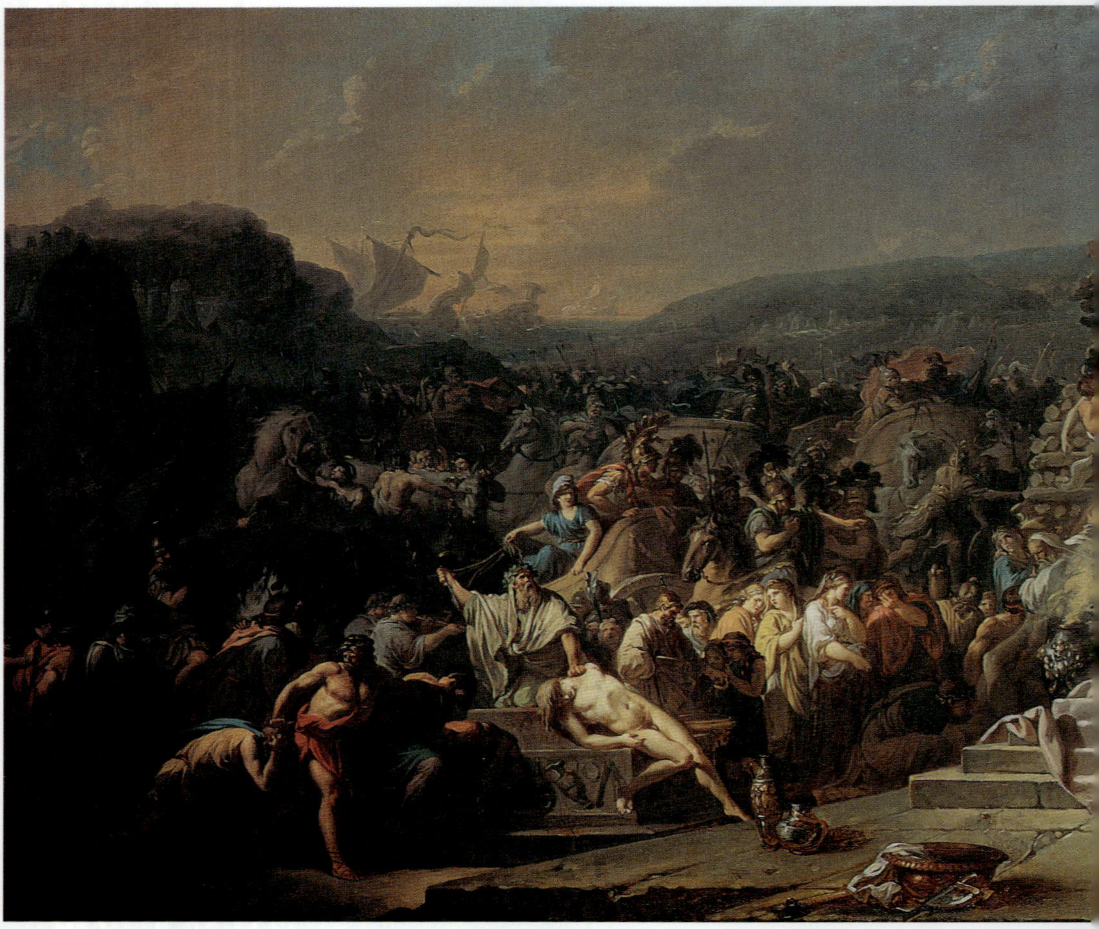

33
The Funeral of Patroclus, 1778.
Oil on canvas;
94 × 218 cm,
37 × 85⅞ in.
National Gallery of Ireland, Dublin

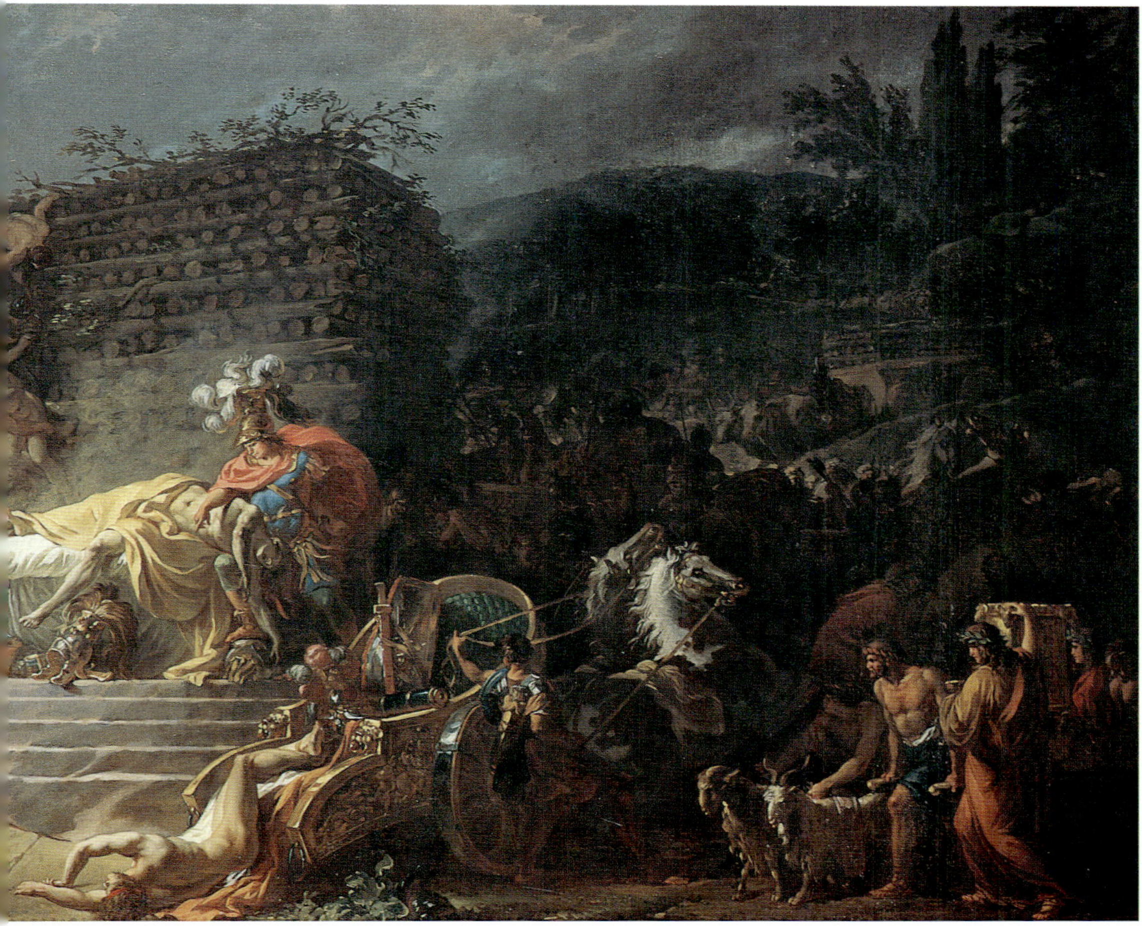

The Funeral of Patroclus (33), bore no signs of the direct influence of the city. A large and rambling scene of small-scale figures, with a subject taken from Homer's *Iliad*, it continued where David had left off in Paris. The central portion shows the Greek warrior Achilles embracing the body of his friend Patroclus who has been killed by Hector, the son of the king of Troy. Below, tied to the back of a chariot, is the body of Hector, who was killed in revenge by Achilles and is about to be dragged back to the Greek camp. At the left a group of Trojan princes are being sacrificed and their bodies added to the pyre. Yet such a dark and bloodthirsty theme is rendered with flickering touches of highlight and shadow, and so no great sense of either sadness or horror is created. Perhaps David would have made the whole thing more dramatic if he had decided to develop the sketch into a finished picture, but he never did. The work was sent back to Paris for consideration by the Academicians in April 1779: their report stated that, while they detected some promise, they noted that the flickering highlights interfered with the clarity of the composition, and that David needed to refine his treatment of light and shade. They also saw spatial ambiguities in the work, and suggested that he undertake a deeper study of perspective – in fact David was to struggle with perspective throughout his career. It was recommended that, 'It might be useful for him to practise with some themes whose action would occur on a single plane; then he would have to take into consideration the placement of all the groups.' The report ended by saying that, 'Our detailed criticism must not discourage him but should incite him to live up to the great promise he shows.'

Although David's talent was recognized, at this stage in his career he was not considered to be the most gifted artist of his generation, and greater hopes were held out for others, in particular Peyron. But shortly after painting *The Funeral of Patroclus*, David's art began to change decisively due to his discovery of seventeenth-century art, especially the dramatically lit and forceful canvases of Caravaggio (1571–1610; 34) and his followers, and the measured and rational compositions of Nicolas Poussin (1594–1665). David's art gained in strength, and the *académies* (full-length male nude and semi-nude studies) such as the *Hector* of 1778 (35), the *Patroclus* of 1780 (36) and the *St Jerome* (also of 1780), show how he had begun to use light and shadow to give weight and density to his figures. He also became a much more scrupulous observer of the life model. A command of drawing was fundamental to the development of David's style; a mastery of the purity of line allowed for a purging of the decorative and the inessential. Contour was used as both an outline and to suggest volume; this new style was formed thanks to the influence of student sculptors resident at the French Academy in Rome, such as Jean-Baptiste Giraud (1752–1830), Jacques Lamarie (1750–82) and the previously mentioned Dupasquier. Dupasquier favoured frieze-like compositions, Giraud recommended the antique as a valuable corrective to the mannerisms of academic drawing, and Lamarie advocated a concentration on outline. Watching Lamarie draw, David asked: 'Aren't you going to put shadows inside your figure?' Lamarie replied by saying: 'Do you believe that drawing lies in some more or less well-executed hatching? No, it lies wholly in contour. Put inside what you like.'

David's new style of draughtsmanship was demonstrated in a very long and spectacular drawing resembling an antique frieze, *The Funeral of a Hero* of 1778/80. Wishing to emulate the bas-reliefs on Roman sarcophagi, this was an experiment in narrative, and represents a compendium of many of the antique details that he had seen in Rome. Within this work David placed great emphasis on the body language and gestures of the figures, and his whole attitude to pathos and the expression of the emotions became strengthened and clarified. Curiously, the drawing is now in two sections. The shorter section, in Grenoble (37), shows a warrior slain by his adversary between the watching Athena and Hercules on the left and the Three Fates on the right. Atropos turns away from the warrior and snips the last thread of his life from the spindle that is held by Clotho. The reclining Lachesis idly observes the thread's measure. The longer section, in Sacramento (38), shows the warrior's body borne in a funeral procession complete with mourners, priests and sacrificial animals. Although in two parts, there is no doubt that they originally formed a single entity because of the style of draughtsmanship, the media and the width of the paper.

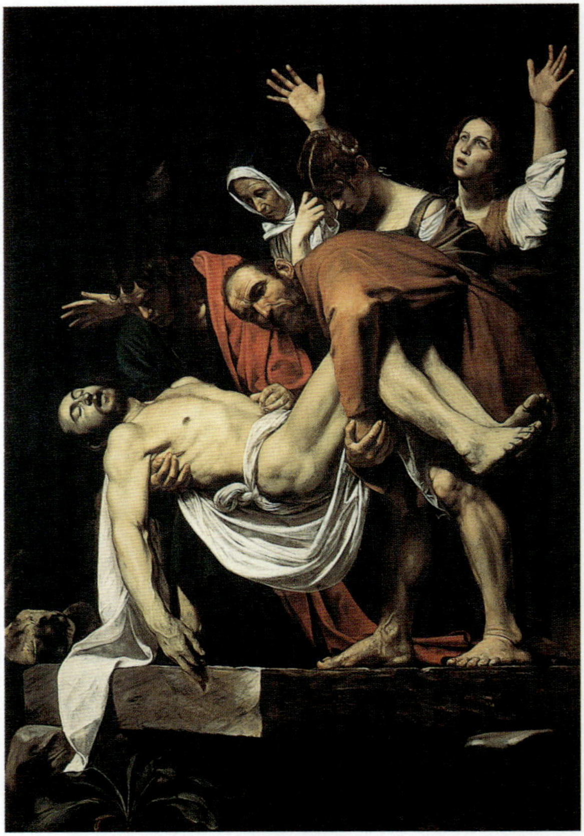

34
Caravaggio,
The Entombment,
1602–4.
Oil on canvas;
300 × 203 cm,
118$\frac{1}{8}$ × 79$\frac{7}{8}$ in.
Vatican Museums, Rome

35
Hector,
1778.
Oil on canvas;
123 × 172 cm,
48$\frac{1}{2}$ × 67$\frac{3}{4}$ in.
Musée Fabre, Montpellier

36
Patroclus,
1780.
Oil on canvas;
122 × 170 cm,
48 × 66$\frac{7}{8}$ in.
Musée Thomas Henry, Cherbourg

David also made much of the impact that Raphael (1483–1520) had had on him in Rome – 'Divine Raphael! It was you who led me, step by step, to antiquity. It was you sublime painter who managed to come closest to these inimitable models ... Their beauties were revealed to me by your graceful and erudite paintings. In return for my admiration, will you do me the favour to recognize me – even with three hundred years

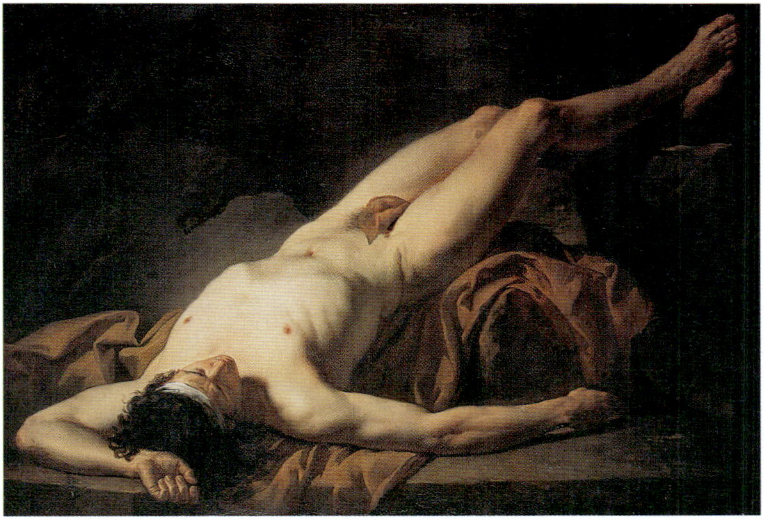

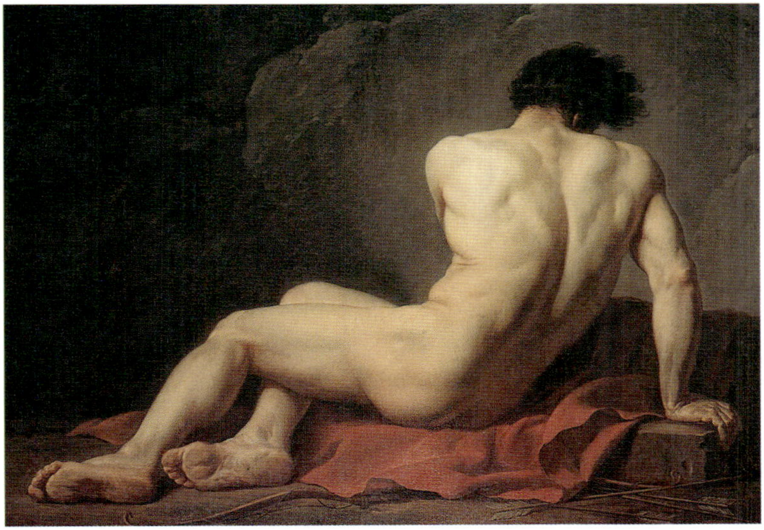

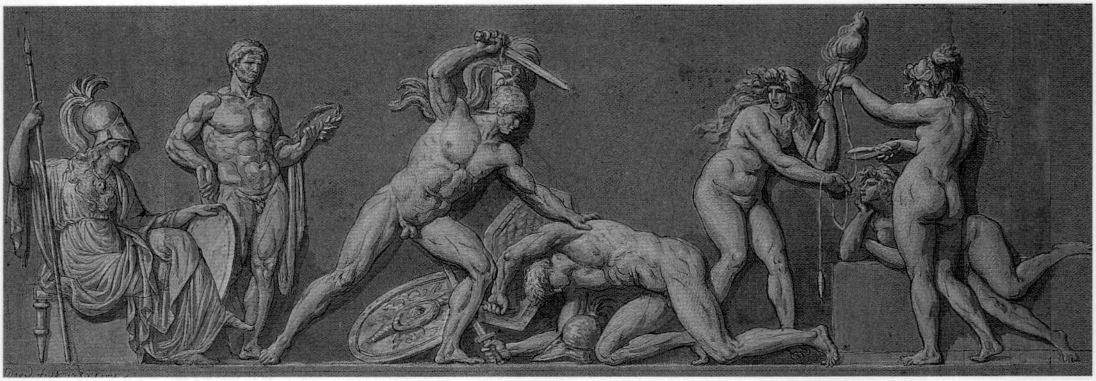

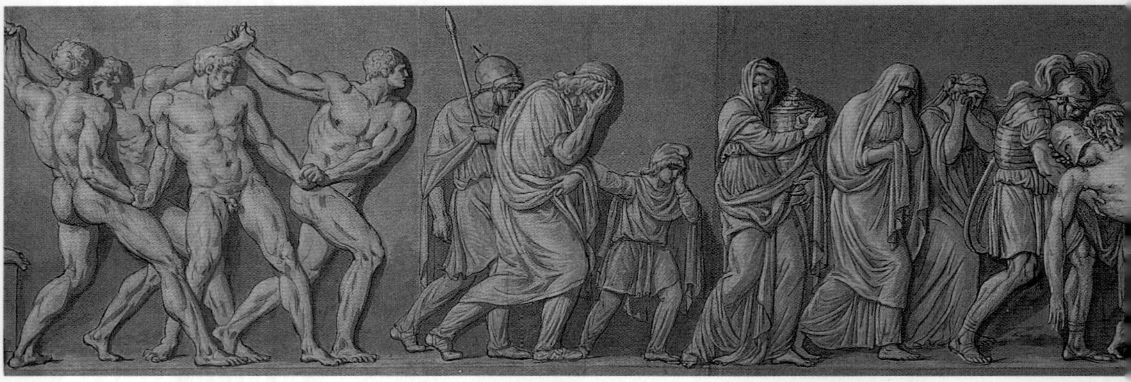

37–38
The Funeral of a Hero, 1778/80.
Pen, ink, wash and white highlights
Top
26 × 74·6 cm, 10¼ × 29⅜ in.
Musée de Peinture et de Sculpture, Grenoble
Bottom
26 × 153 cm, 10¼ × 60¼ in.
E B Crocker Art Gallery, Sacramento

between us – as one of your pupils?' In fact there is little in David's work at this time to suggest such a profound debt to Raphael, and this passage, written around 1808, is surely more about David subsequently reinventing and placing himself within the tradition of Western painting than a documentary account of his Roman experience. In another later source he also greatly dramatized and embellished his supposed discovery of the significance and true meaning of antiquity. David made a visit to Naples in late July to early August 1779 with a fellow student, the sculptor François-Marie Suzanne

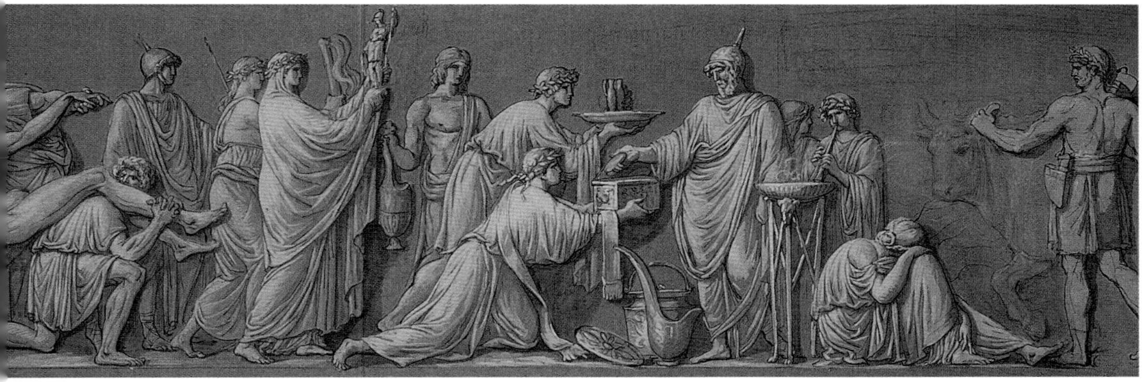

(b.*c*.1750), and possibly the young archaeologist and future writer on art, Antoine Quatremère de Quincy. Such was the revelatory power of the ancient works he saw there that David declared: 'I felt as if I had been operated on for a cataract.' It seems a little odd for any artist to have considered Naples as being richer in antiquity than Rome, and indeed one of David's first letters from Naples to Vien contradicted this reminiscence by stating that after seeing Naples he better appreciated Rome. Although the sight of the wall-paintings of Herculaneum and Pompeii, which he almost certainly visited, probably contributed to his increasing awareness of the importance of contour, David's feeling that he now comprehended antiquity was not attributable to the sight of any single work. Such a conversion is perhaps best understood by considering David's discovery as the realization that antiquity held a degree of relevance and actuality that was far removed from his initial dismissal of its remoteness and distance from the present. This episode also informs us that neither David nor his biographers, when writing retrospectively, are very reliable witnesses concerning his art.

The process of change and development occurring in David's art proved difficult for the highly strung young man. Even before going to Naples his work was not progressing well. On his return his health suffered, and he became sullen, morose and depressed by his inability to give visual form to his new discoveries. In August 1779 Vien became worried and wrote to d'Angiviller in Paris: 'I try to encourage him and calm him as best I may, but if this melancholy settles down, I shall be the first to advise him to return to France.' Jean-Baptiste Pierre (1714–89), the king's First Painter, observed a month later that, 'We are dealing with a man who is open, honest, but at the same time excitable enough to need careful handling.' Though the major factor, work alone was not necessarily the only cause of David's problems – it was also variously rumoured that David was pining for Suzanne Sedaine, the daughter of Michel-Jean Sedaine (see 23), and even that he had an affair with Madame Vien's chambermaid, and that the liaison had produced a child. But this crisis in David's life was very brief and, by late September, he was restored to health and accepted the renewal of his scholarship in Rome for a further year.

39
St Roch Interceding with the Virgin for the Plague-Stricken,
1780.
Oil on canvas;
260 × 195 cm,
$102\frac{3}{8} \times 76\frac{3}{4}$ in.
Musée des Beaux-Arts, Marseille

Soon afterwards David received his first independent commission, thanks to the recommendation of Vien. It was for an altarpiece for the chapel of the Lazaret (or quarantine centre) in Marseille, France's major Mediterranean port, and a place that lived in continual fear of contagion brought by travellers from the East. The picture was to commemorate *St Roch Interceding with the Virgin for the Plague-Stricken* (39), a miraculous episode from the 1720 outbreak of the disease in the city when the fourteenth-century saint, who had suffered from the plague himself, reappeared and came to the aid of the

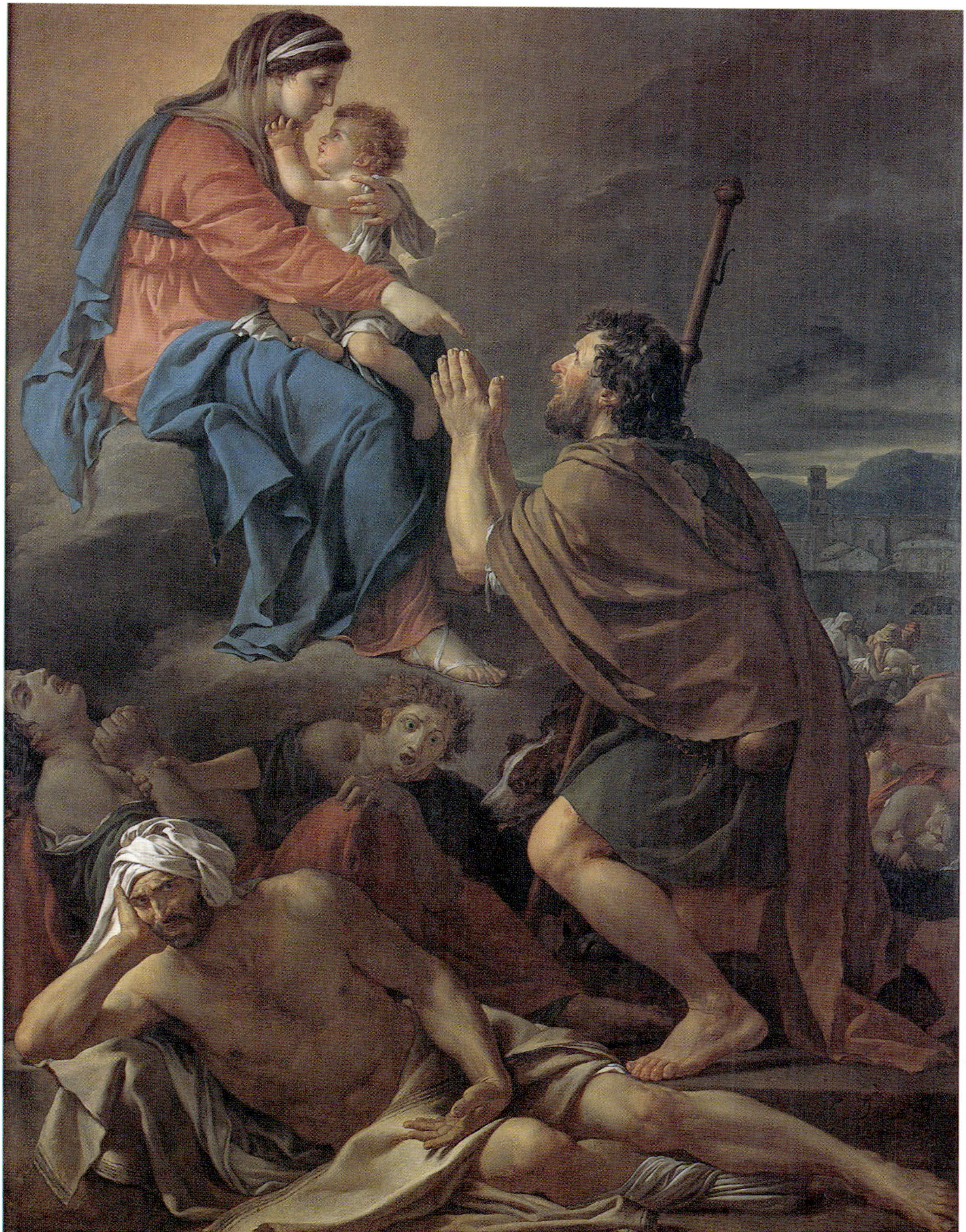

sick. As the painting would only be seen by people held in quarantine in the Lazaret, only a modest fee of 550 livres was offered. David immediately shut himself away in his studio and refused to let anyone in until the work was finished. He adopted a well-tried religious format, with the plague victims at the bottom, the Virgin and Child at the top, and St Roch acting as the intermediary between heaven and earth. He took compositional inspiration from the works of such artists as

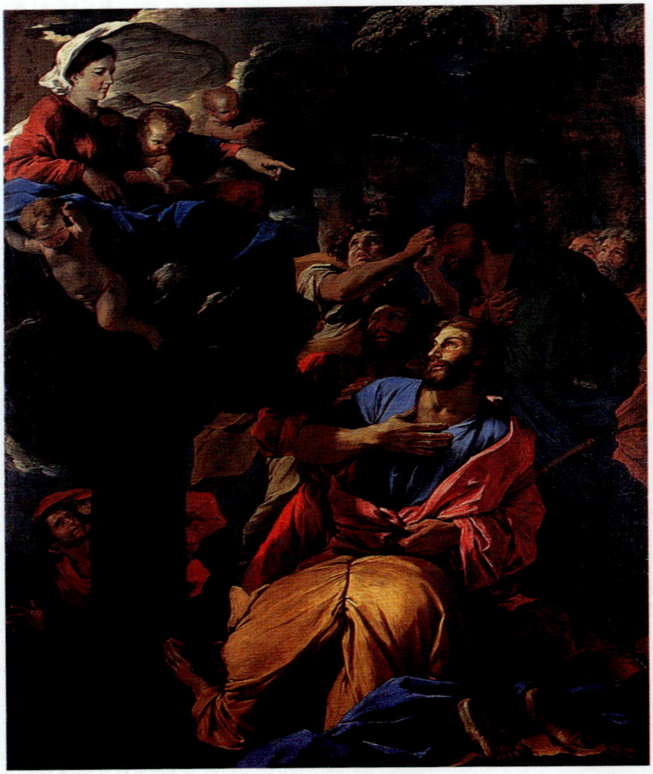

40
Nicolas Poussin,
The Virgin Appearing to St James the Great,
1629/30.
Oil on canvas;
301 × 242 cm,
$118\frac{1}{2} \times 95\frac{1}{4}$ in.
Musée du Louvre, Paris

Guercino (1591–1666), Caravaggio and, in particular, Poussin (40). The agitated youth below the Virgin is modelled on the sculpted bust of the *Anima Damnata* (*Damned Soul*) of *c*.1619 by Gianlorenzo Bernini (1598–1680), which was itself derived from Caravaggio's *Boy Bitten by a Lizard* of 1592–3. While painting this picture, and indeed many later ones, David was troubled by doubts and uncertainties. At one point he asked

Vien to come and see the completed head of the plague victim on the left. He found it admirable and, later the same day, was surprised by David's request to come and look at the picture again. 'What?', Vien said, 'I saw it this morning.' 'No,' replied David, 'I've re-done it.' Exasperated at his pupil's impetuosity, Vien responded: 'You wretch, you might have spoilt and destroyed it altogether with your urge to do better.' But David's judgement was sound, and the *St Roch* was very well received: Rome's most senior Italian artist, Pompeo Batoni (1708–87), said to David that, 'I have lived in this city for over fifty years, and have seen painters from all nations. I know all of the works they have produced and I do not recall a single one that is the equal of yours.' He encouraged David to pursue his career in that city – 'Young man, do not return to France, you are worthy to succeed me here.' Vien was delighted with his pupil, and according to one contemporary report, the success went to David's head to the extent that he began to treat his fellow students at the Academy as inferiors. David clearly thought that he had surpassed what the clients could justifiably expect for such a small fee, and pressed for increased payment. He was always to have a highly developed (some said overdeveloped) sense of the monetary worth of his paintings, and did not shrink from telling patrons or buyers what payment he thought appropriate. He kept the picture for two years before sending it to Marseille, and d'Angiviller regretted that the work had not entered the royal collection in Paris. On its arrival it was so highly prized that it was not hung in the publicly inaccessible Lazaret chapel, but was given pride of place in the city's Bureau of Health. Following its installation David was given an extra 350 livres.

The publicity surrounding the *St Roch* also led to David being given a lucrative commission for a grand portrait of a Polish nobleman, Count Stanislas Potocki (41). Although begun in Rome, the painting was actually completed a little later in Paris. Potocki came from one of the most celebrated Polish families, and had recently become very wealthy thanks to his wife's dowry. This gave him the money to start collecting works of art, to travel to Italy, and to pay for a monumental portrait. He was also a scholar, and translated and commentated on the work of Winckelmann, which led to him being dubbed 'The Polish Winckelmann'. Obviously his portrait had to be impressive and suggestive of his status. Therefore David depicted him on horseback, subduing a skittish horse with consummate ease – not only the mark of a gentleman, but also reminiscent of the classical story of Alexander the Great taming the wild stallion Bucephalus. The equestrian portrait had long been a favourite device to suggest power and authority in rulers, by the analogy between their control of the animal – that knows nothing of titles and only responds to firm and confident handling – and their fitness to rule their subjects. David turned to the example of the great Baroque portraitist

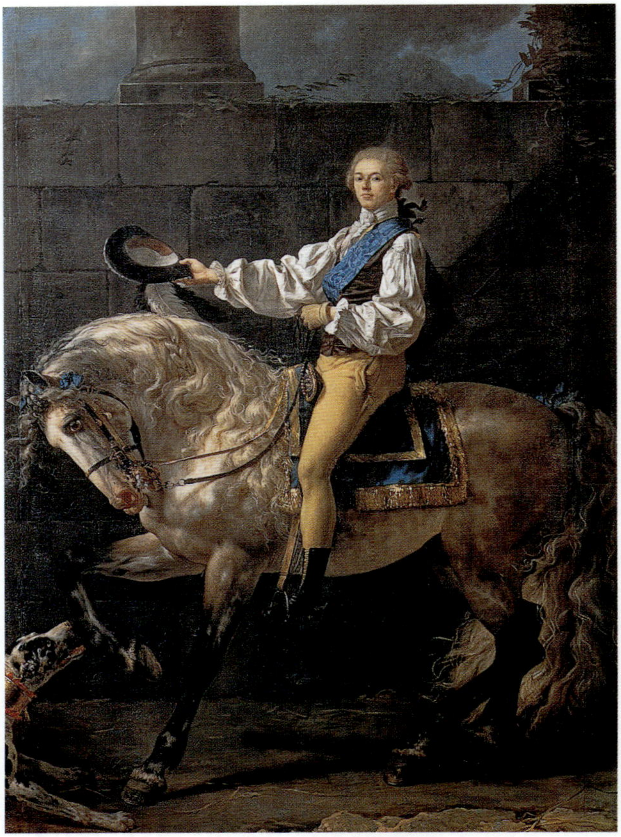

41
Portrait of Count Stanislas Potocki, 1780.
Oil on canvas; 304 × 218 cm, $119\frac{5}{8} \times 85\frac{7}{8}$ in.
Muzeum Narodowe, Warsaw

42
Anthony van Dyck, *Prince Thomas of Savoy on Horseback*, 1634.
Oil on canvas; 315 × 236 cm, $124 \times 92\frac{7}{8}$ in.
Galleria Sabauda, Turin

Anthony van Dyck (1599–1641; 42) to create a work that was similar in scale and impact. With its vibrant colours and lively treatment of paint, the portrait differed from David's other works at this time, and he thus revealed another facet of his developing skills. The end result is strictly controlled and the lighting is evenly distributed and does not have the randomly scattered highlights of his earlier portraits. The shaft of diagonal light at the right does not sharply illuminate Potocki's left side, and its most dramatic effect is to cast long shadows of the horse's legs on the riding school floor. Potocki is given rather bland features, and his aunt Kossakowska later ordered the face to be repainted with a better likeness. Fortunately the overpainting was later removed, and what we see now is original. David also placed his signature and the date on the collar of the Dalmatian at the lower left. Was this simply a little joke

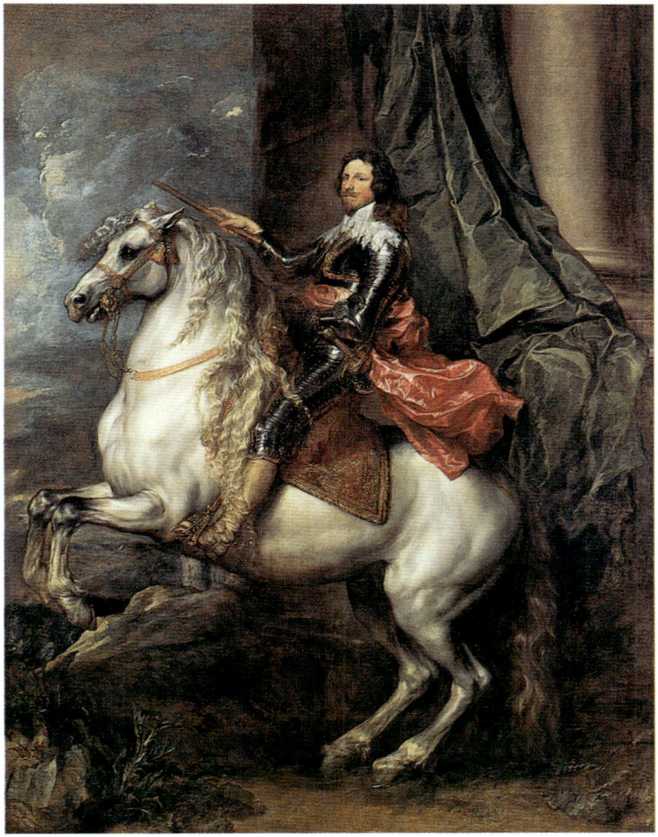

at his own expense, or was it a deeper comment on the servile nature of the portrait painter who was dependent upon the patronage and good will of wealthy clients? Whatever the answer, David was very handsomely paid for the work, receiving between 3,500 and 5,000 livres from Potocki.

In Rome, David came of age as an artist. The pretty and decorative superficiality of the Rococo was replaced by an approach that was both more dramatic and more realistic. It is a mark of David's single-mindedness and determination that his development of a personal style was based on exemplars other than those usually expected to affect the artistic visitor to Rome. Instead of the calm and harmonious aesthetics of antiquity and the Renaissance, David seized upon the rhetoric of seventeenth-century art, mediated by a vision of the ancient world as a place of vitality and strength.

The success of the *St Roch* and the Potocki commissions banished David's self-doubts, and convinced the ambitious young artist that the time was now right to return home, and he refused the extension of his scholarship for a sixth year. In doing so he boldly deviated from the career path that was being mapped out for him by Vien and d'Angiviller. David had his eyes on higher goals – membership of the Academy and prestigious and lucrative royal commissions. In his own mind, at least, fame and fortune awaited him in Paris.

Painted Virtue and Patriotism   Success in Enlightenment Paris

2

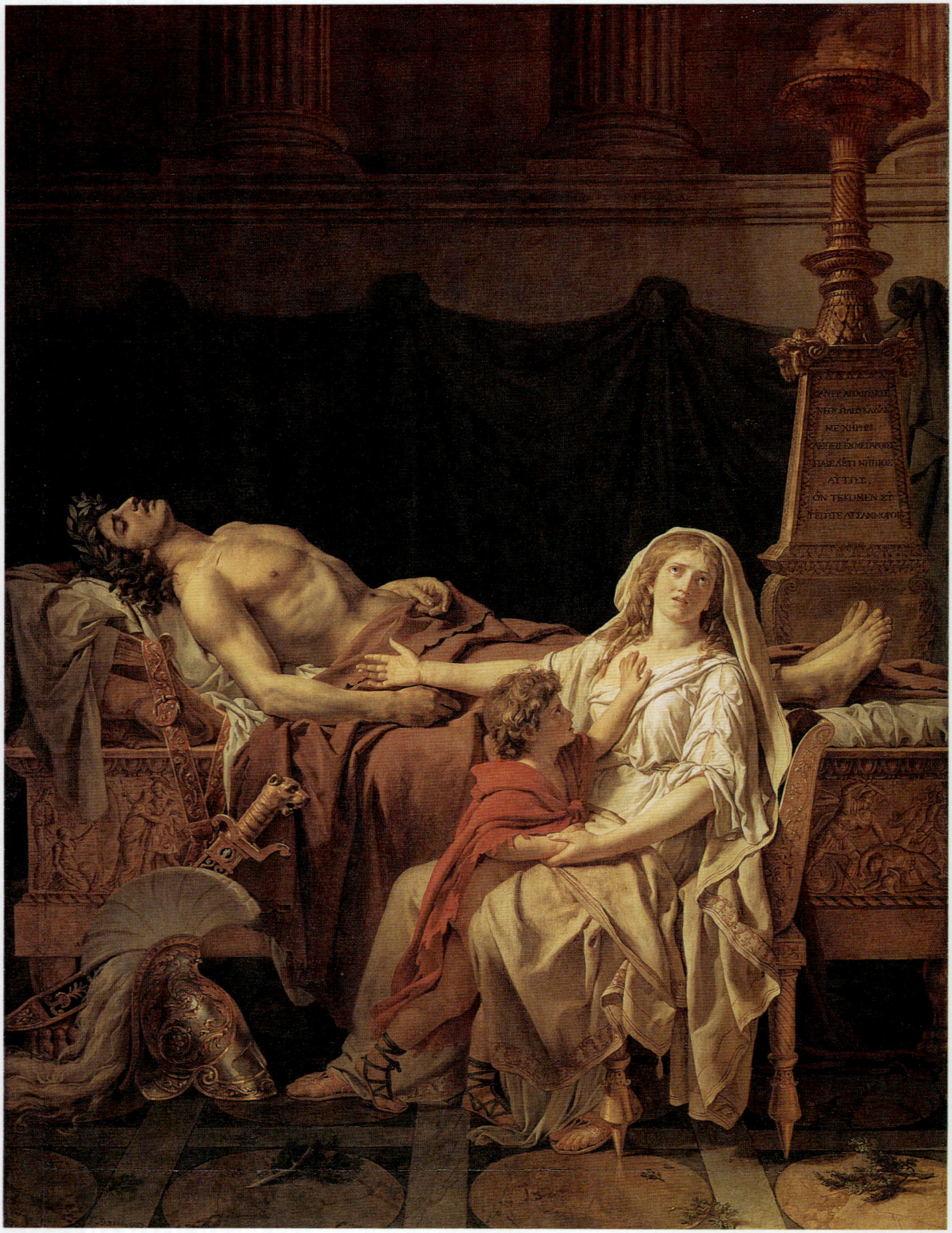
ΑΥΤΩΣ,

David left Rome on 17 July 1780, and arrived in Paris towards the end of September. In Paris his first priority was to become a member of the Academy, since Academicians were given the most prestigious projects when royal commissions were distributed. They also had the monopoly on exhibiting at the only large-scale public art show, the Salon, which took place every two years in the Louvre. To become an Academician, an artist had to present his or, very rarely, her works to the assembled members, and if they were thought to be good enough, the candidate would be accepted as an Associate (*agrée*). A reception piece on a subject chosen by the Academy then had to be painted in order for them to become a full Academician (*reçu*). David wanted to show the Academy the *St Roch* and some of his other Roman work in order to gain admittance, but this was not acceptable to the king's First Painter, Jean-Baptiste Pierre (44). On 1 December Pierre wrote: 'The picture [*St Roch*] by the sieur David can be accepted for his *agrément*, as can his nudes; but he cannot present his candidature until he has done a work in Paris. This is a custom that has assumed the force of law.' This insistence on precedent obviously rankled with David, and when, in August 1793, he spoke out against the Academy and its privileges, outdated customs and inertia, he must have had this incident in mind:

43
Andromache Mourning Hector, 1783. Oil on canvas; 275 × 203 cm, 108¼ × 79⅞ in. École Nationale Supérieure des Beaux-Arts, Paris, on loan to Musée du Louvre, Paris

A young man who, on his return from Italy was preceded by a disquieting reputation, wanted to apply to the Academy; a member of this Academy [probably Doyen because Vien was in Rome] who had not been won over by the prevailing spirit of the institution, examined the artist's work and enthusiastically praised the work of the young candidate. An old Academician [Pierre] who had been through all of the honours offered by the Academy and whose lethargic perseverance had occupied all of its positions … said

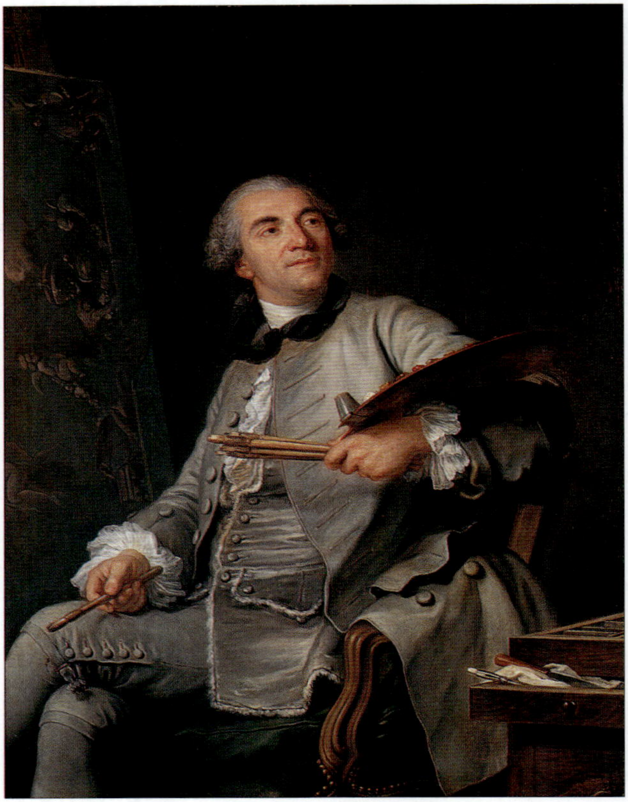

44
Guillaume Voiriot,
Portrait of Jean-Baptiste Pierre,
1759.
Oil on canvas;
130·5 × 97·5 cm,
$51\frac{3}{8} \times 38\frac{3}{8}$ in.
Musée National du Château de Versailles

gravely, 'Gentlemen, if as it is said, this young man has so much talent, I myself see no need to admit him into our midst. Gentlemen, remember the equilibrium of talents, the equilibrium.' Seized by a holy respect for such a clearly reasonable argument … they inclined their heads and crossed their hands over their chests, commending their colleague's good idea. They all cry out together 'The equilibrium of talents! The equilibrium!' and all this simply to hold back for two years a young man's rise to fame, for at that time the Salon was only held every two years. They even claimed that he should not be admitted until after the public exhibition, that all the places were filled, that too many candidates had applied at the same time …

As the king's First Painter and director of the Academy, Pierre worked closely with d'Angiviller in pushing through the reforms in history painting and reinforcing the authority of the Academy. A rich snob who had virtually given up painting to concentrate on administrative matters, Pierre enjoyed wielding power and humiliating artists, whom he habitually addressed in the 'tu' form, normally used for children and servants. He was highly unpopular among his colleagues and, although sometimes supportive of David, the two were soon to form an intense dislike for one another.

To create his new work, David chose a subject from ancient history which also had contemporary appeal – Belisarius (45). The story of Belisarius, as related by Procopius of Caesarea (Belisarius' secretary) and the twelfth-century Byzantine writer Johannes Tzetzes, was that of a loyal and successful general in the service of the Byzantine emperor Justinian. He had won major victories against the Vandals, Goths and Bulgarians, but he then became implicated in political intrigues, was accused of treason and disgraced. He became an outcast and was even reduced to begging; one version of the story also said that his eyes were put out. Belisarius had also been the subject of a novel by Jean François Marmontel in 1767, which recast the ancient general as a greatly wronged philosopher, and criticized weak and corrupt kingship and the lack of civic virtue. Marmontel's Belisarius remained loyal to the emperor when falsely accused and sentenced, and was eventually vindicated when Justinian and his heir Justin II secretly sought out the aged general for advice. Parallels were soon drawn between Justinian's treatment of Belisarius and the unheroic reign of the then king, Louis XV, which the *philosophes* saw as characterized by corruption, vain luxury and laxity of morals. Belisarius' call for religious tolerance of pagans, which could be related to the contemporary persecution of Protestants, also meant that Marmontel's book was condemned by the Faculty of Theology at the Sorbonne in Paris. Modern life had also thrown up a kind of present day Belisarius when the Comte Thomas Arthur de Lally, Baron de Tollendal, formerly a military hero, became the scapegoat when the French were forced to surrender to the English at Pondicherry in 1761, a loss which meant the end of their

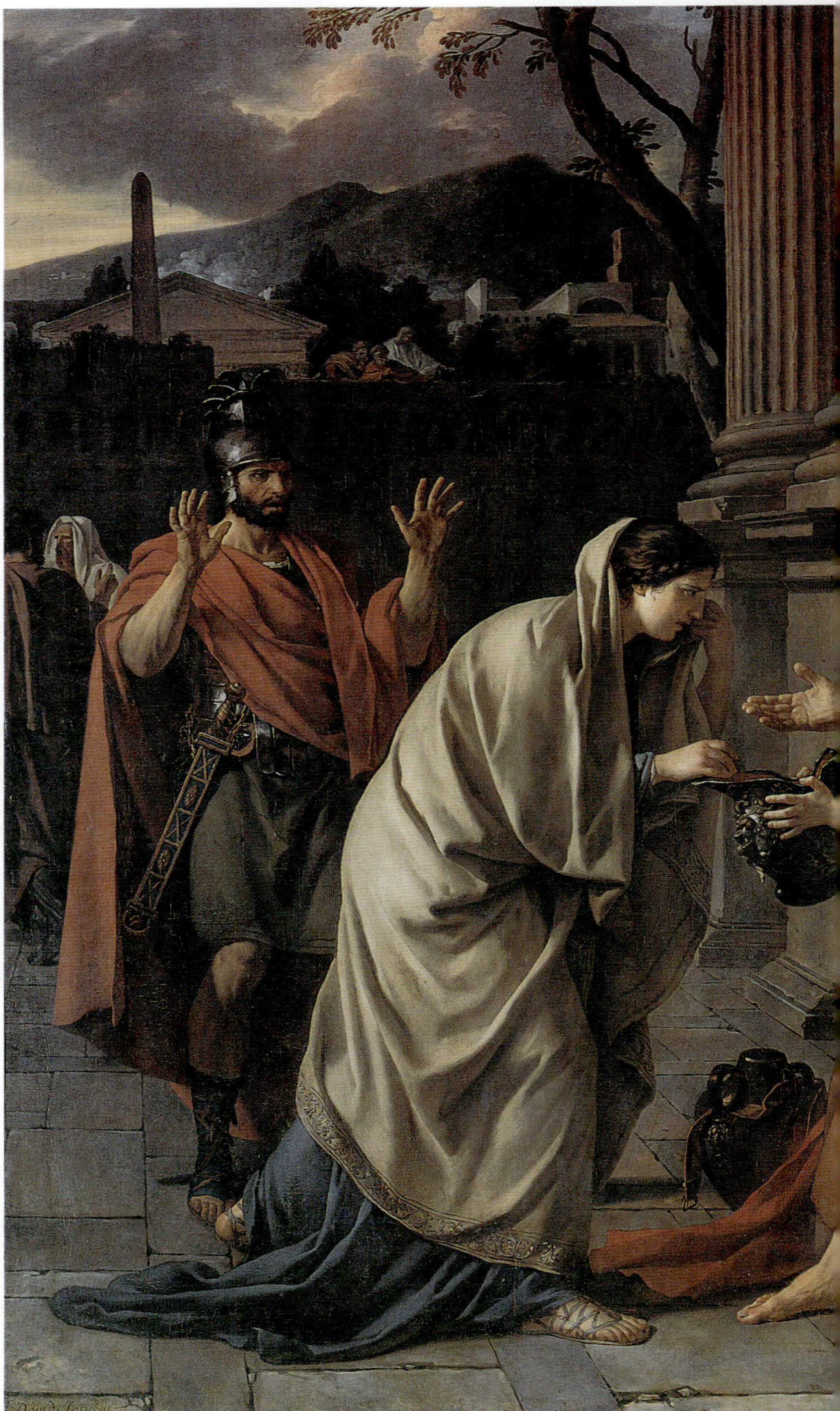

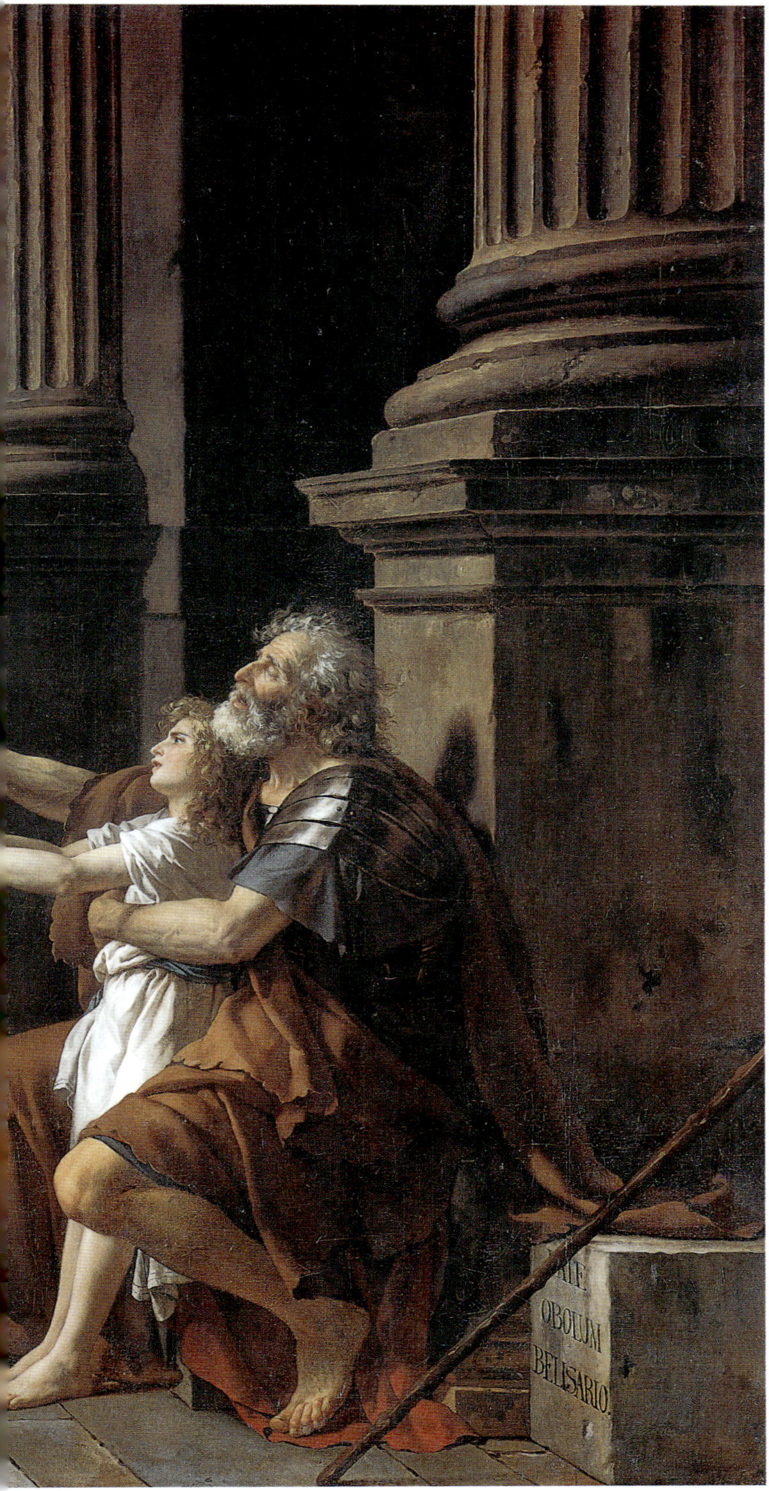

45
Belisarius Receiving Alms,
1781.
Oil on canvas;
288 × 312 cm,
113$\frac{3}{8}$ × 122$\frac{7}{8}$ in.
Musée des Beaux-Arts, Lille

colonial aspirations in India. Accused of treason and cowardice, he was imprisoned for two years before being tried and condemned to death in 1766. This outrageous and unjust treatment prompted a sustained campaign, led by his son and Voltaire, which succeeded in clearing his name in 1778. In selecting the story of Belisarius, David demonstrated a shrewd grasp of current trends at court and in liberal intellectual circles. Under the administration of the former soldier d'Angiviller, history paintings with military subjects were being encouraged, and so David very astutely chose to paint

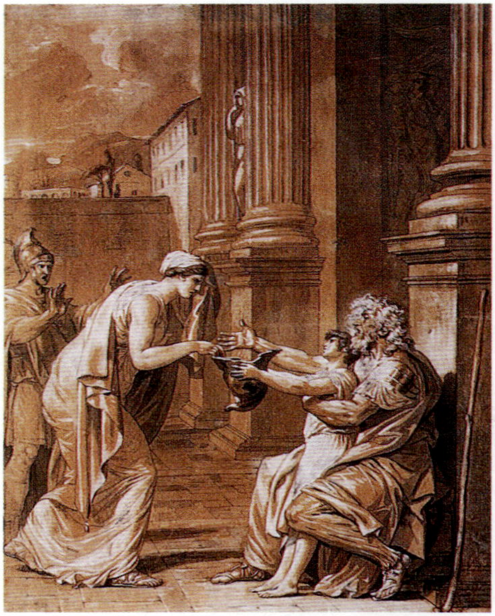

46
Belisarius Recognized by a Soldier, 1779.
Pen, ink, wash and white highlights; 45 × 36 cm, 17¾ × 14⅛ in.
École Polytechnique, Palaiseau

47
Belisarius Receiving Alms, c.1620s.
Engraving by Bosse after Luciano Borzone

a picture that had both a classical appeal and a contemporary resonance. In doing so he courted both the attention of officialdom and the recognition of a public sensitized to the pathos and topicality of the subject.

David had actually first worked on the theme of Belisarius when he was in Rome in 1779, after Peyron had lent him his copy of Marmontel's novel. He then produced a detailed drawing of the subject (46). The general disposition of the scene was probably inspired by an engraving of a painting then thought to be by Van Dyck, now attributed to the seventeenth-century Genoese artist Luciano Borzone (1590–1645; 47). This shows the blind Belisarius begging with an outstretched hand while surrounded by a group of women, a child and one of his former soldiers. All are dressed in seventeenth-century costume, and there is no attempt to recreate sixth-century Byzantium. David also looked to Hubert Gravelot's illustrations to Marmontel's book for the details of the architectural setting. He probably began the painting around November 1780 in a studio that he had acquired on the top floor of one of the

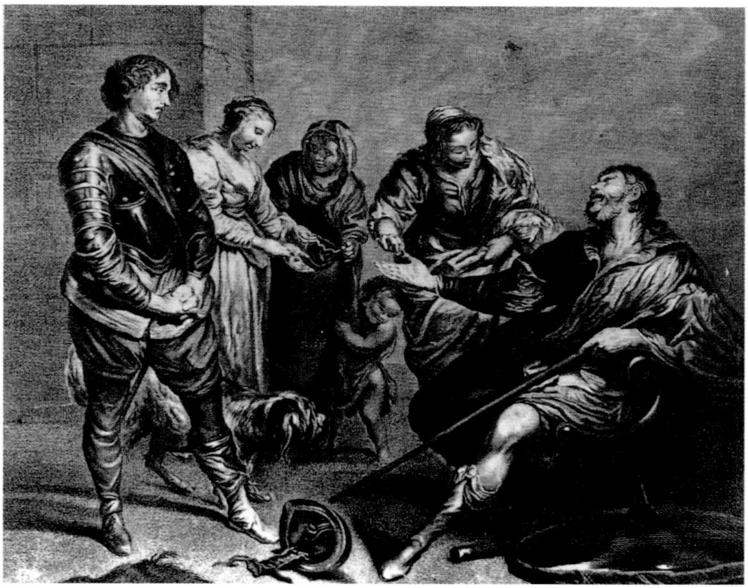

pavilions of the Paris town hall. With a typical economy of effort he adapted the vertical format of the drawing into a horizontal presentation. Both the drawing and the painting showed the same scene – *Belisarius is recognized by one of the soldiers who served under him just as he receives alms from a woman* – which was David's own invention, not having occurred in any of the written sources. For the painting David took note of the work of the expressive characterizations of his contemporary Jean-Baptiste Greuze (1725–1805), who created simple and direct scenes of rustic morality such as *The Village Betrothal*

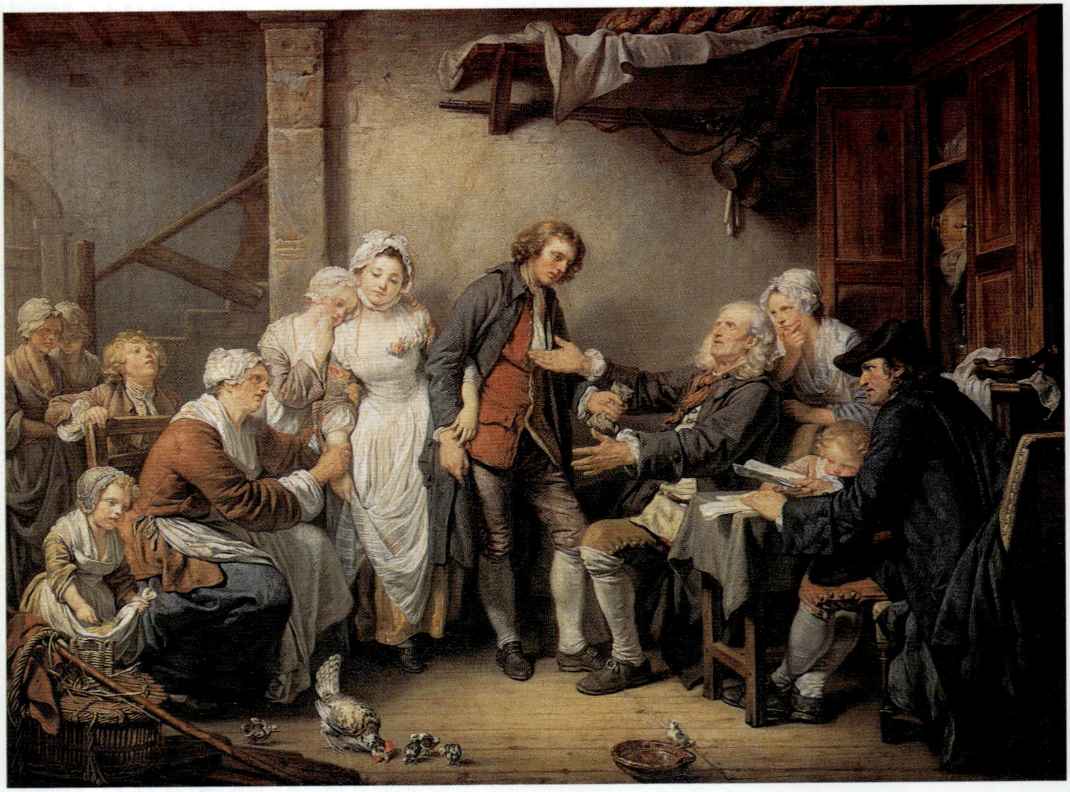

of 1761 (48). There is also much evidence of figures being drawn from life; one of David's first pupils, Philippe-Auguste Hennequin (1762–1833), posed for the figure of the boy helper.

The theme of Belisarius was much in vogue from the 1770s, and rival artists of David's own generation, such as Peyron and François-André Vincent (1746–1816), had painted their own versions of the subject. In Peyron's work (49), Belisarius is recognized by a peasant who had served under him, and praised as their protector and saviour by the rural family that now give him hospitality. Vincent's Belisarius (50) is reduced to begging, and receives the charity from a soldier in Justinian's army. Here there is no sense of recognition, the blind former general is oblivious to the identity of his benefactor. Vincent also took the unorthodox step of creating a group of half-length figures, an unusual device in France at this time. David, sensing competition, was determined to outdo both Peyron and Vincent, and the choice of such a dramatic moment combined with a powerfully direct presentation was calculated to provide a striking and appealing reading of the story. He also painted his *Belisarius* on a scale he had never yet tackled: it measures 2·9 × 3·1 m (9 ft 5 in × 10 ft 3 in), more than seven times larger than the works by Peyron and Vincent.

48
Jean-Baptiste Greuze,
The Village Betrothal,
1761.
Oil on canvas;
92 × 117 cm,
36¼ × 46 in.
Musée du Louvre, Paris

The *Belisarius* was the first fully resolved example of the new heroic and austere style that is now known as Neoclassicism. It is a picture with a serious subject that is painted in a sober and rational style. Few characters, set as if on a stage, exchange meaningful and easily understood gestures. *Belisarius* is a painting about charity, sympathy, dutiful patriotism and the reversal of fortune. At the very moment that the woman drops a coin into the upturned helmet held by Belisarius' boy helper, something perhaps borrowed from Vincent's work, one of the general's former soldiers recognizes him and raises his hands in shock and surprise. Announcing the old man's desperate situation, and appealing to the spectator's charitable sensibilities, the Latin inscription *Date Obolum Belisario* (Give an obolus – an ancient Greek silver coin – to Belisarius) is displayed on the marker stone in the bottom right-hand corner. This was a scene from Christian antiquity that clearly had lessons for the present. Belisarius' wanderings, exile and blindness also gave him something of the character of a Homer figure, and the facial features employed by David reflect these similarities. As if to underline his change in circumstances, the old general sits begging by a structure that is either a triumphal arch or a city gate. Whichever is the case, a sense of victimization and isolation brought on by the vagaries of fortune is suggested. The irony of the inclusion of a triumphal arch – erected to honour a successful commander following a military victory – is immediate. If banished to beg outside the city walls, Belisarius is patently an outcast from society.

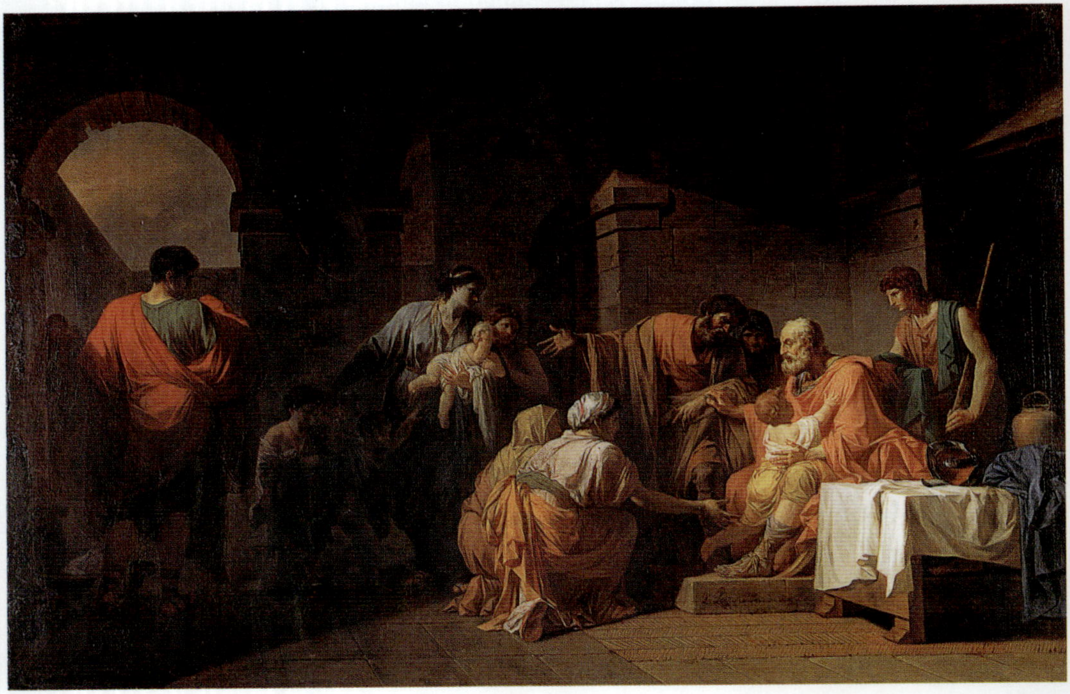

The overall organization of the picture, and the major role assigned to the architectural setting of the fluted half columns, the distant obelisk and pedimented building, owe much to the influence of Poussin. His work was continually cited by critics such as Diderot as the prime example of the noble, severe and intellectual qualities of painting, and was seen as a model for the regeneration of French art. Peyron was the first of the new generation of history painters to consciously follow Poussin, but David soon began to adopt compositions and the disposition of figures from him. This is first seen in the *St Roch* (see 39) and the *Belisarius*, but in the *Belisarius* David attributed greater characterization and emotional response to his figures than the mask-like and understated figures employed by Poussin. However, lessons drawn from past artists did not help David with his perennial problems of recession and perspective. On the left, the spatial relationship between the woman's back foot and the feet of the soldier is faulty, and the orthogonal lines of the pavement recede incorrectly. This was, as

49
Pierre Peyron,
Belisarius Receiving Hospitality from a Peasant who had Served under him,
1779.
Oil on canvas;
93 × 132 cm,
36⅝ × 52 in.
Musée des Augustins, Toulouse

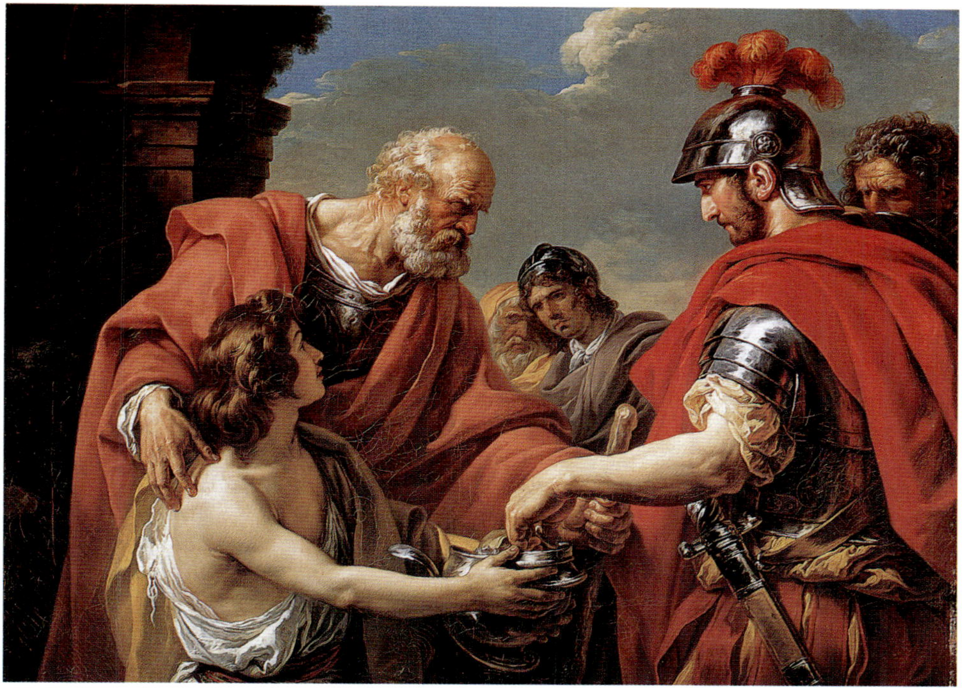

50
François-André Vincent,
Belisarius,
1776.
Oil on canvas;
98 × 129cm,
38½ × 50¾in.
Musée Fabre,
Montpellier

Thomas Crow has observed, probably the result of David's enlargement of Gravelot's small book illustrations, combined with the unfamiliarity and inexperience of working on such a large scale. At the bottom left of the canvas, David signed the work with the Latin inscription L DAVID FACIEBAT ANNO 1781 LUTETIAE ('L David was making this in the year 1781 in Lutetia' – the ancient name for Paris). Such a Latin signature not only underlined David's classical learning, but was perhaps a sideswipe at the Academic ruling requiring an artist to paint a picture in the capital to qualify as an *agrée*. By using the imperfect form *faciebat* (making) instead of the perfect form *fecit* (made), he drew attention to the fact that he was living in Paris while he was painting it.

David presented this work, along with some others, to the Academy on 24 August 1781, contrary to a decision of the Academy of 4 August which expressly forbade candidature for the Academy at the time of the Salon. This was introduced because in that year a number of potential *agrées* were late in submitting their entries, and a halt to submissions was called to save the Academician charged with the hanging of the Salon (called the *Tapissier* or decorator) the troublesome task of re-hanging the exhibition to accommodate the works of any newly admitted artists. David claimed to be unaware of this rule and said that he was only seeking 'advice and instruction' by submitting his work. This is hard to believe, since David knew that, as a new member, he would have the right to show these works at the Salon, which opened the next day. Whatever the case, he was unanimously elected an Associate Academician and his works were hung on the walls of the Salon after the official opening, their sudden appearance naturally creating great interest. Other artists had used this stratagem before, although not everybody approved of such a practice; David was to adopt this attention-grabbing device for almost all of his subsequent public exhibits. The Salon, which was open for a month from 25 August (the feast day of St Louis), was the capital's main entertainment during that time, and attracted large crowds drawn from all classes of society. In fact it was one of the few places where a labourer might rub shoulders with a nobleman, and a fishwife with a lady of quality. Such social integration was a shock to the middle and upper classes who could neither bear the sight nor the smell of the lower orders.

The Salon received much attention from both the official and the unofficial press, and dozens of pamphlets, ranging from considered and balanced opinions to scathing and mocking attacks, were written and sold. David's *Belisarius* was very favourably received, and the elderly Diderot, writing his last account of a Salon, said of it: 'I see it every day, and each time I think I am seeing it for the first time (in a paraphrase of Racine's *Bérénice*, Act 2, Scene 2). This young man works in the grand manner, he has a soul, his faces are expressive without being contrived, the attitudes are noble and natural, he can draw, he can dispose a drapery and make handsome folds; his colouring is fine without being garish.' The proud artist wrote excitedly to his mother in Normandy: 'I did not receive one blackball from the Academy, which is most unusual. Monsieur the Comte d'Angiviller was at the meeting of the Academy and he gave me the greatest encouragements ... If you come to Paris to see my pictures you will know them at once by the crowds around them. The important people, the Cordon Bleus [members of the Order of the Holy Spirit, the highest order of knighthood] want to see the author, and at last I am rewarded for my troubles ... At present I am only rich in glory, certainly less so in hard cash, but I trust that this too will not be long in coming.' David's modest circumstances at this time meant that he was forced to lodge in the upper storey of a house belonging to an iron merchant, Hecquet, who was probably a friend or business acquaintance of his late father, and so he received visitors in the more comfortable surroundings of his uncle Sedaine's rooms in the Louvre instead.

Although his main Salon piece was a grand work on an elevated subject, David was also anxious to demonstrate the variety of his productions to the Parisian audience. In addition to the *Belisarius* he exhibited the *St Roch* (see 39), *The Funeral of Patroclus* (see 33), three Roman *académies* – *St Jerome*, *Hector* (see 35) and *Patroclus* (see 36), a *Head of an Old Man* (possibly the *Philosopher* now in the Musée Baron Gérard in Bayeux), a lost *Woman Nursing her Child* and a number of other studies. He had also taken the precaution of exhibiting the portrait of Potocki (see 41) in his studio before and during the early part of the Salon. Whatever happened, the public would be aware of his work. History painting, portraiture, expressive heads and sentimental genre were chosen to herald his arrival and announce his versatility.

But even though the *Belisarius* was well received, it was not the most successful painting at the Salon. That accolade was awarded to *The Death of Leonardo da Vinci in the Arms of Francis I* (51) by François-Guillaume Ménageot (1744–1816), a former colleague of David's in Vien's studio. This was a completely different sort of picture from the *Belisarius*, and it owed its success more to the subject matter – a French king's compassion and reverence for a famous artist – than to any startling stylistic development. Nevertheless, by calculation and audacity, David had engineered a brilliant Parisian debut. He had attracted the attention of the people that mattered, and he could soon expect to receive important and prestigious commissions. One critic writing about David's *Belisarius* obviously suspected a favourable disposition towards the young artist from the Directeur des Bâtiments du Roi, and wrote, with a mixture of jealousy and spite: 'Happy is he with talent when one has d'Angiviller.' As David's letter to his mother says, he was as yet only rich in glory, and hoped that the Crown would purchase the *Belisarius* – he had, after all, lavished a lot of time and trouble on it. But Pierre went back on a promise to buy the work – more proof of the strained relations between the two. Fortunately, Pierre's superior, d'Angiviller, liked the *Belisarius* so much that he ordered a reduced scale replica for himself from David. In this work, painted in 1784 with the assistance of his pupil François-Xavier Fabre (1766–1837), David rectified the spatial problems of the original. But although this was a variant replica of an existing work, David treated his task conscientiously; it was, after all, for an important client, and he therefore gave it a reasonably high (though not total) degree of personal attention.

51
François-Guillaume Ménageot, *The Death of Leonardo da Vinci in the Arms of Francis I*, 1781.
Oil on canvas; 278 × 357cm, 109½ × 140½ in.
Musée de l'Hotel de Ville, Amboise

As soon as he moved into his studio in the town hall in 1780, David began to take on pupils. They were of twofold importance to him: firstly, their tuition fees provided a regular source of income, and secondly, they could be used as assistants on his major commissions. The best of them could even be entrusted with working independently on reduced replicas. As well as the *Belisarius* replica, there is also one of *The Oath of the Horatii* (see 62), painted in collaboration with Anne-Louis Girodet (1767–1824) in 1786, and an unfinished full-size copy of *The Death of Socrates* (see 66), probably also painted with Girodet's assistance. Although the idea of a replica of an

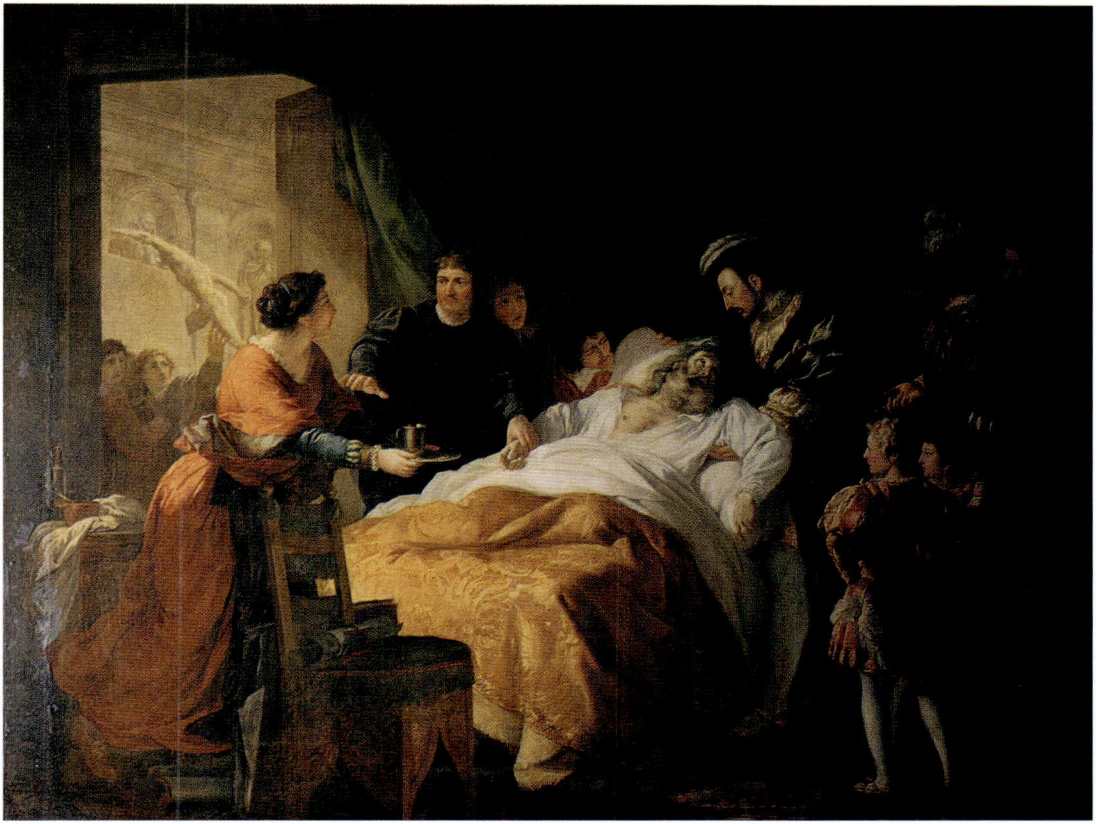

original work runs counter to twentieth-century sensibilities about the uniqueness of the art object as the expression of the individual creativity of the artist, such matters of discrimination did not feature so greatly in the eighteenth century. Critics and writers had yet to fix the notion of the artist as the creative genius whose works were predominantly an extension of the self. To the eighteenth-century collector, buying a replica of a successful work was a practical way of owning a key example of an artist's output, and the fact that there was one or more of them did not drastically diminish its status. In David's case he exercised an extremely high degree of quality control over what left his studio, and there are only isolated examples of patrons being unhappy with the result. In painting another version of a successful Salon piece, David was also following established practice. There are numerous other contemporary examples of artists repeating royal or public commissions on a smaller scale for private collectors. In its size and organization, David's studio was both a place of instruction and a setting where suitable pupils were gradually introduced into the process of production. A marked division of labour was established to enable several projects to be executed at once, and although a small scale operation in the 1780s, under Napoleon's patronage the system enabled vast canvases to be undertaken with little loss of quality.

If any fault had been found in the *Belisarius*, it was that its colours were too dull, and so in the autumn and winter of 1781–2, David spent three or four months travelling around northern France and Belgium making a detailed study of Flemish artists, particularly Peter Paul Rubens (1577–1640), who were renowned for their vibrant treatment of colour. On his return to Paris he had to resolve a disciplinary matter with one of his pupils. He had left the studio key with a trusted student, Philippe-Auguste Hennequin, but it then emerged that Hennequin had used some expensive blue ultramarine pigment that David had been reserving for himself; he was also suspected of having stolen an engraving from the master's portfolio. Hennequin's accuser in this matter was a jealous fellow student, Jean-Baptiste Wicar (1762–1834), and although Hennequin pleaded ignorance to the first charge and innocence to the second, David was inflexible and dismissed him from the studio. Disputes and rivalries were never very far from the surface in the hothouse atmosphere of David's studio, and his pupils were not necessarily friendly comrades with mutual goals.

The success of the 1781 Salon led to David being allocated a studio and lodgings in the Louvre, a substantial perk and proof of official favour. Places in the Louvre were eagerly sought after by artists, and David's family connections probably helped him once again. He was given the former rooms of the painter Pierre-Antoine Baudouin (1723–69), whose widow was the daughter of David's cousin, Boucher. She, in turn, had remarried Charles-Etienne-Gabriel Cuvillier, d'Angiviller's Premier Commis at the Direction des Bâtiments du Roi. The new location meant that David could now take on more pupils, and also expand his operations. The most talented young artists joined him and began to paint under his influence: these included Jean-Germain Drouais (1763–88), an enormously gifted artist who died tragically young, Anne-Louis Girodet (a male artist – Anne is the French equivalent of the Hebrew name Annas) and François-Xavier Fabre.

When he moved into the Louvre in 1782, David asked one of the building contractors, Charles-Pierre Pécoul, whose son he had known in Rome, to build him a small bed alcove. 'Why then a small one?', Pécoul replied, 'I'll make it big, suitable to receive your wife.' He then promptly suggested his daughter Marguerite-Charlotte as a bride, although at only seventeen she was half the age of David. As a further enticement, Pécoul added: 'You wish to live for art, well then work for glory, I will work for your fortune.' David consulted with his godfather Sedaine, who had hoped that the up-and-coming artist might marry his own daughter Suzanne, but it was agreed that the match would be advantageous, especially as Mademoiselle Pécoul brought with her a substantial dowry. The couple married on 16 May 1782 in the church of St Germain-l'Auxerrois, close to the Louvre. The witnesses to the wedding contract of 2 May included Pierre (the unpleasantness over the *Belisarius* forgotten, or put to one side), Vien and the king's chief architect Etienne-Louis Boullée (1728–99). According to the marriage contract, David's financial resources were modest, but his new wife brought with her a fortune that gave him the financial independence that he had not previously had. Nine months later the couple's first child, Charles-Louis-Jules, was born.

Early in 1782 David was given a royal commission for a painting to be completed in time for the 1783 Salon. It was to be *Old Horatius Defending his Son for the Murder of his Sister Camilla*, and was to be a medium-sized work for which a fee of 4,000 livres was payable. Apart from one drawing (see 55), little progress was made, and eventually David postponed the project in order to concentrate on becoming a full Academician (*reçu)* by painting his reception piece (*morceau de réception*). This decision displeased Pierre, but d'Angiviller received the news well, approving of the decision and hoping that the painting would be ready for the coming Salon. While David's relations with Pierre seem to have slowly deteriorated, his contacts with d'Angiviller continued to be cordial. Around 1782–4 David even wrote a fable in the form of a two-verse poem dedicated to the Countess d'Angiviller, entitled 'The Field Bouquet and the Pineapple'. This was a moralizing critique of aristocratic pretensions, in which a pineapple, assuming the characteristic of an arrogant Spanish lord, resents being placed next to a common bouquet of wild flowers and field grasses on a dinner table. A humble daisy declares to the proud and haughty pineapple: 'Each condition has its own merit', and at the end of the meal, after all its posturing, the pineapple is eaten as dessert. David's message was that magnificence and display are transitory, while simpler qualities endure. Such sentiments would have found favour in the liberal and witty salons that the countess held at Versailles.

David became a full Academician with *Andromache Mourning Hector* (see 43), which he presented on 23 August 1783, again just in time for it to be shown at the Salon. The painting represents a scene from Homer's *Iliad* where Andromache grieves over the body of her husband Hector, who has been killed by Achilles in the Trojan War. The subject of a widow and a young child might have evoked personal memories for David; the fatherless Astyanax is shown trying to console his mother in the midst of her grief, and he appears to be about the same age as David was when his own father was killed. In the *Iliad* Astyanax is a baby, but, before jumping to the conclusion that this is an example of David's direct personal identification with the subject, one should remember that when Winckelmann illustrated the same scene in his *Monumenti Antichi Inediti* of 1767, the boy is shown not as a babe in arms, but at the age of eight or nine.

An appropriately dark and sombre style was used for this subject, and it is probably David's least colourful picture. To some eyes it may appear overly austere, and people at the time noted its gloomy aspect, but David was striving to match the painting's appearance with its content. The deep sorrow and tragedy of the scene is amplified by the strict geometry and the bareness of the setting. The wall behind Hector has a black curtain stretched across it, and above there is a row of fluted columns. Once again there are obvious debts to Poussin, especially his deathbed scenes such as *The Death of Germanicus* (1628) and *The Testament of Eudamidas* (1643–4). Poussin had always been dutifully respected in France, but at this time there was a genuine renewal of interest in his art; two appreciations of his work had been published in 1783. David also made extensive use of his Roman studies for the painting: the figure of Hector is derived from a funerary scene in one of his Roman sketchbooks, which is his own variation on one of the numerous antique bas-reliefs that depicted the death of

Meleager. The bier on which the body lies is taken from David's drawing of an antique bed; the immediate past is alluded to by the decorations on its side. On the left we have Hector's farewell to Andromache, and on the right the slaying of Hector. The latter scene is taken directly from David's own drawing of *The Funeral of a Hero* (see 37, 38), but both warriors now wear armour. As with the *Belisarius*, David included an inscription that would help to explain the picture. Written on the candelabra, in Greek, is the beginning of Andromache's lament from the *Iliad*: 'Husband, you died too young to leave me widowed in our home. Our son, whom you and I most unhappy brought into the world, is still so young.' While most critics appreciated and approved of David's suppression of painterly expression to achieve a sense of pathos, others failed to grasp the significance of this deliberate austerity, and complained that he had not heightened his colour since *Belisarius*.

52
Christ on the Cross,
1782.
Oil on canvas;
276 × 188 cm,
108⅝ × 74 in.
Church of St Vincent, Mâcon

In 1783, *Andromache Mourning Hector* was shown with about six other works at the Salon. One of these was the *Christ on the Cross* (52), painted for the Marshal de Noailles and his wife, Catherine Françoise Charlotte de Cossé-Brissac. Formerly a highly placed courtier with King Louis XV, and a military commander in the War of the Austrian Succession, Noailles was created a marshal of France in 1775, but had little influence at the court of the new king Louis XVI. Both he and his wife were devoutly religious, so much so that the marshal was accused of the fanatical persecution of Protestants by a fellow noble, the Marquis de Bombelles. Noailles commissioned a series of religious works for the family chapel in the Capucines church in the Place Vendôme from David, Jean Charles-Nicaise Perrin (1754–1831) and Joseph-Benoît Suvée. David found such religious subjects uncongenial, and this was the last he ever painted. Early biographers said that he had difficulty with Christ's features and so used a soldier as a model, much to the displeasure of Madame de Noailles who recognized the soldier and thought that such a borrowing detracted from the picture's holiness, and took David to court. There is, however, no proof

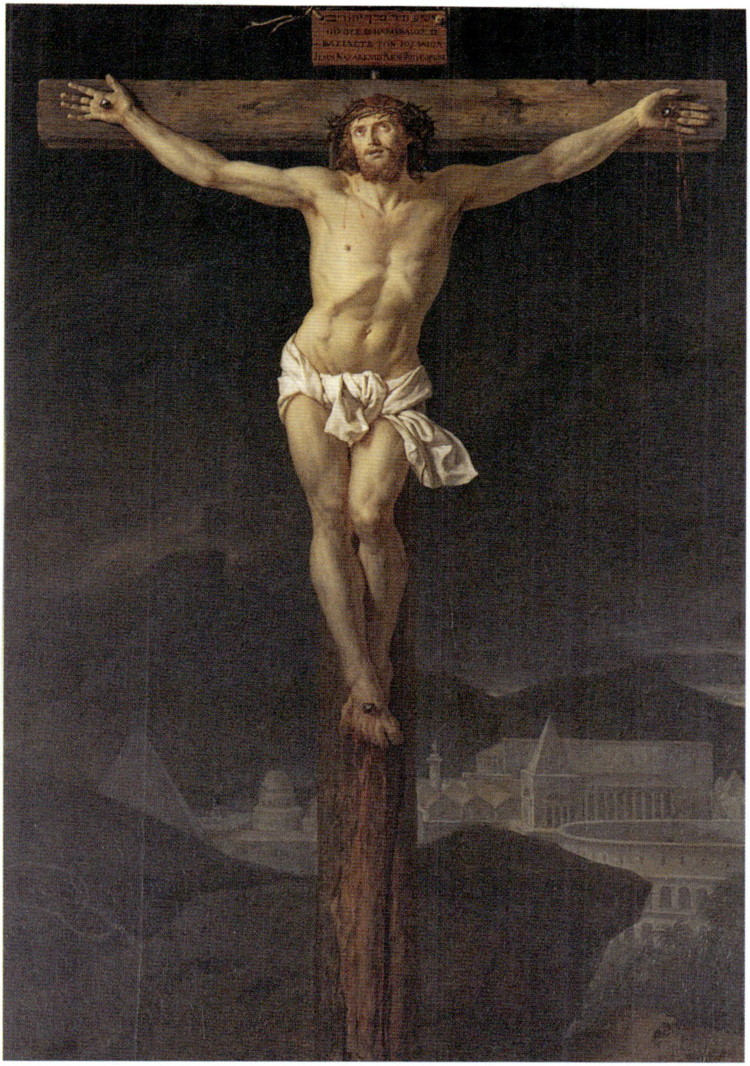

of this, and the work was such a success that the Noailles family removed it from the chapel for which it was painted and hung it in their own house. Madame de Noailles formed a particular attachment to the painting, and managed to keep it with her when most of the family's pictures were seized by the revolutionary Commission Temporaire des Arts.

David also showed two portraits at the Salon of 1783, one of his uncle Desmaisons (see 8), and the other of Doctor Alphonse

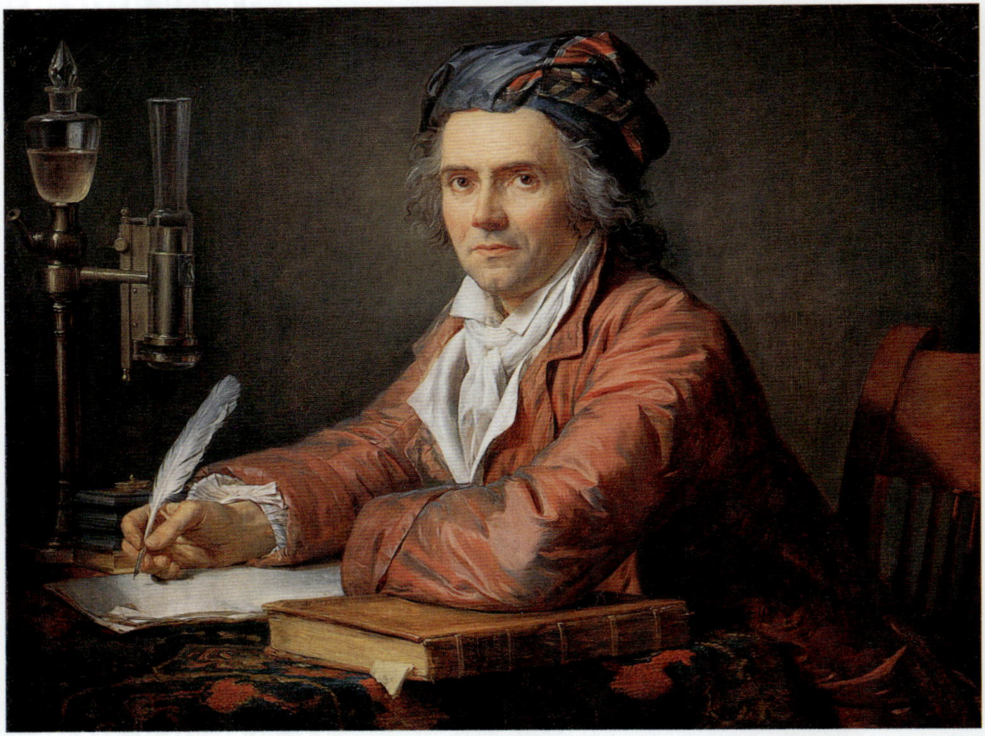

Leroy (53). Leroy was an obstetrician, and probably attended Madame David at the birth of her first child. David shows him as an intelligent and refined man, dressed in fine clothes, writing at his desk leaning on a volume of Hippocrates' *Morbi mulierum* ('The Diseases of Women'), lit by a *quinquet* lamp – a recent invention that gave illumination equal in strength to a dozen candles. The only less than successful part of the picture is the angle of the sitter's left arm that denies him a hand, and this might be partly explained by the fact that certain details were delegated by David to his pupil Jean-François Garneray (1755–1837). The sophisticated public image that David gave Leroy does not actually equate with the man himself. He was apparently irascible, held controversial medical views, was considered by some to be incompetent and negligent, and was later killed by his own servants. Yet, thanks to David, he becomes a dignified professional man of the Enlightenment.

Without a doubt David was a highly talented portrait painter, and he could have made a lucrative living from this alone. But for him, money, although very important, was not enough. He also craved fame, glory and recognition, and it was only as a history painter that his ambitions could be fulfilled. In practically the shortest time possible he had become a full Academician, joined the ranks of royally favoured artists, attracted great public attention and taken on a large number of pupils. In a world where artists were usually passive, David went out of his way to shape events and carve out his own destiny. Yet this success was not achieved without cost. Some fellow artists were jealous of his meteoric rise, and when advising David to marry Marguerite-Charlotte Pécoul, Sedaine had said, 'in an ... honourable family you must find a powerful support against your enemies; for my young friend, talent makes people envious'. His rivals were not impressed by the blatant scheming and independence of the newcomer, and his next tactical career move was to enrage them even more.

53
Portrait of Doctor Alphonse Leroy,
1783.
Oil on canvas;
72 × 91cm,
$28\frac{3}{8} \times 35\frac{7}{8}$ in.
Musée Fabre,
Montpellier

Early in 1784 David resumed work on the official commission for the Direction des Bâtiments du Roi that he had been given in 1782. He had decided to paint an episode from the story of the Horatii triplet brothers who, in the seventh century BC, had represented Rome in single combat against the Curiatii brothers of Alba. Rome and Alba were drifting into a state of war over trivial border incidents, and so, rather than embark on a destructive full-blown conflict, each kingdom elected

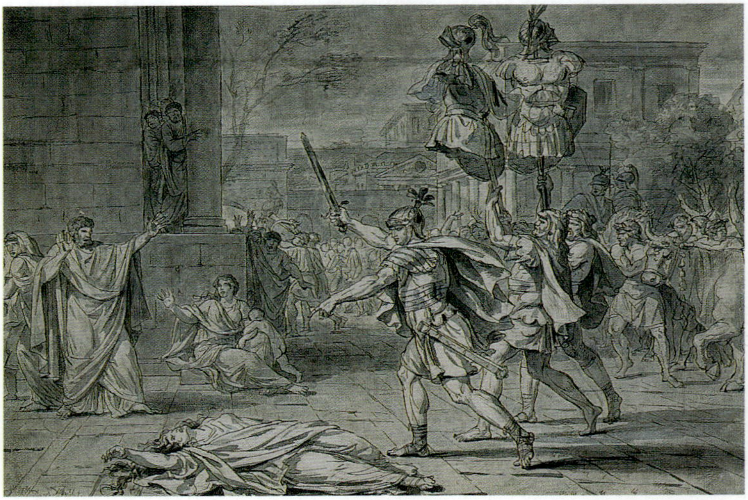

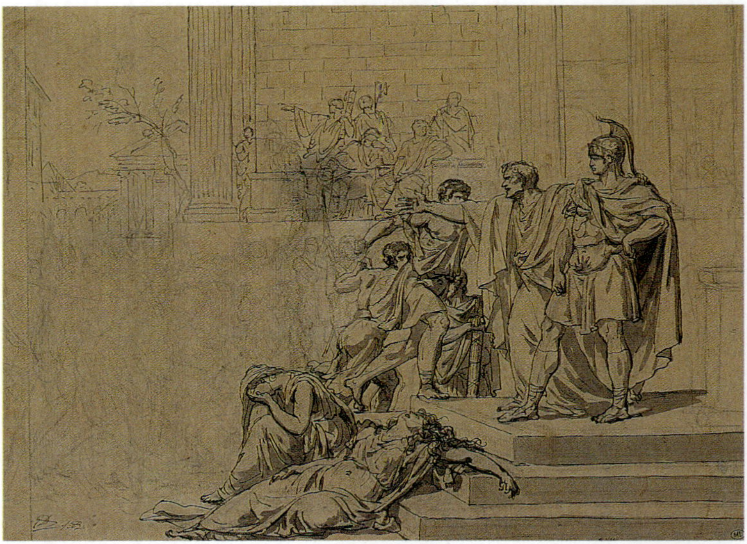

champions to do battle on their behalf. Matters were made more complicated because of the emotional ties between the Horatii and Curiatii. One of the Horatii brothers was married to Sabina, sister of the Curiatii, and Camilla, sister of the Horatii, was betrothed to one of the Curiatii. Whatever the outcome of the battle the family would suffer, and the story illustrated how duty to the homeland must come before all personal concerns. After the combat, the only survivor of the six warriors was the eldest Horatius. On his return to Rome he was cursed by Camilla for the death of her beloved, whereupon he stabbed her with his sword. Arrested for murder, young Horatius was defended by his father, who successfully pleaded for his son's life.

54
Horatius Returning Victorious to Rome (The Death of Camilla), 1781. Black chalk, pen and ink, with grey wash; 27·5 × 38·7cm, $10\frac{7}{8} \times 15\frac{1}{4}$ in. Graphische Sammlung Albertina, Vienna

55
Old Horatius Defending his Son, 1782/3. Black chalk, pen and ink; 21·6 × 28·9cm, $8\frac{1}{2} \times 11\frac{3}{8}$ in. Musée du Louvre, Paris

The subject of the Horatii and the Curiatii was rare in art, although David, after his first Roman visit, was probably aware of the fresco by the Cavaliere d'Arpino (1568–1640) in the Palazzo dei Conservatori, showing the battle between the two factions (1612). He had been thinking about painting a scene from some part of this story for about three years, and a drawing dated 1781 shows *Horatius Returning Victorious to Rome (The Death of Camilla)* (54). As recorded in an official list of February 1782, David initially proposed to paint *Old Horatius Defending his Son* (55), but he soon abandoned the subject, possibly because it illustrated a speech, and therefore had too little action and visual appeal. Instead he painted an imaginary episode: *The Oath of the Horatii* (see 62). None of the ancient or modern sources of the story – Livy, Plutarch, Dionysius of Halicarnassus or the Abbé Rollin – mentioned an oath; it was David's own inspired invention. David had taken note of the revival of interest in the plays of Pierre Corneille, the centenary of whose death had been celebrated in 1784; he is known to have attended a performance of Corneille's play at the Comédie Française late in 1782. Corneille's plays, especially *Horace* (1640; based on the subject of the Horatii), were praised for their forthright and robust language, and the celebration of masculine virtue and patriotic duty. Patriotism and duty were matters of public interest and debate, and David's work may also relate to the philosopher Jean-Jacques Rousseau's short treatise of 1762, *The Social Contract*, which contained notions of the common interest of all, civic virtue and self-sacrifice. Visually David was perhaps influenced by other paintings and engravings showing unswerving allegiance to one's country or ideals, such as *The Oath of Brutus* by Gavin Hamilton (1723–98; 56), which was available as a engraving, and the picture on the same subject by Jacques-Antoine Beaufort (1721–84) that David had seen at the 1771 Salon (57).

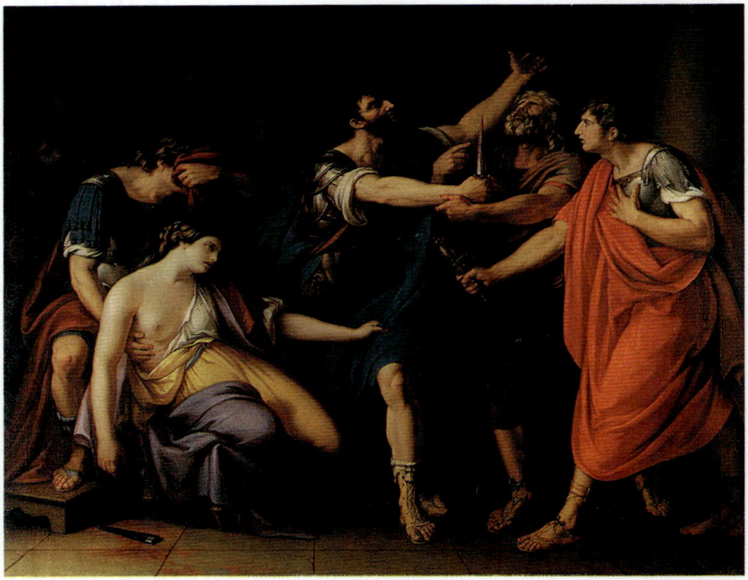

56
Gavin Hamilton, *The Oath of Brutus*, c.1763–4. Oil on canvas; 213·3 × 264 cm, 84 × 104 in. Yale Center for British Art, New Haven

57
Jacques-Antoine Beaufort, *The Oath of Brutus*, 1771. Oil on canvas; 129 × 167 cm, 50¾ × 65¾ in. Musée Municipal, Nevers

In the Brutus story, the oath was sworn as a promise of individual revenge against a corrupt monarchy, and it was somewhat inconsistent and redundant to have noble and virtuous Romans swear an oath to affirm a virtue that was beyond question – patriotism. But the motif of the oath allowed David to present a unified and memorable distillation of a highly involved story.

Like his fellow artists Greuze, Doyen, Jean-Antoine Houdon (1741–1828), Ménageot and his brother-in-law Pierre Sériziat (see 128), David was a Freemason, and so it is also possible that *The Oath of the Horatii* was in some way inspired by the rituals of the masonic lodge, where swords and the swearing of oaths played a prominent role in the proceedings (58). Though this may be the case, it is not to say that the painting is a masonic allegory of any form, as is Mozart's *The Magic Flute* (1791). David's introduction into Freemasonry is not known, perhaps it was through Sedaine or Desmaisons who, as architects, were conceivably Masons. The only record of his membership was found through the patient researches of Albert Boime in the late 1980s, who established that David

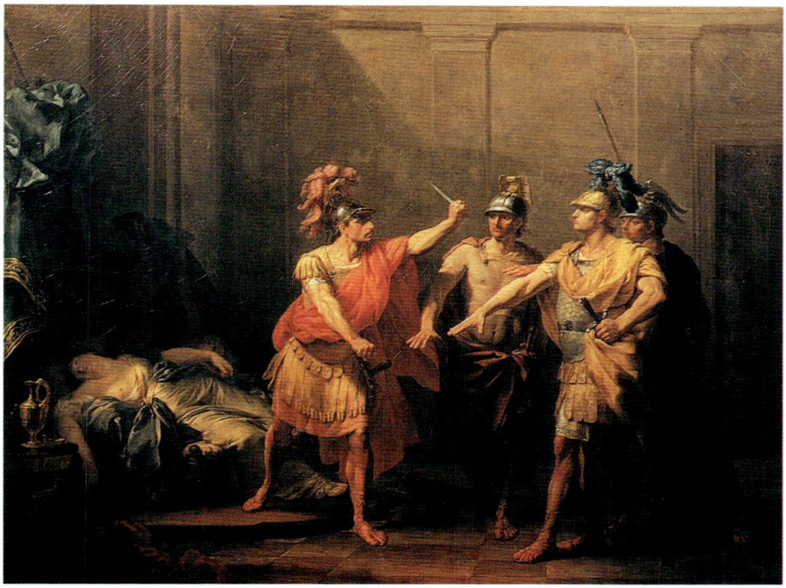

became affiliated to the Lodge of Moderation on 24 November 1787. To become an affiliate the candidate must already have been an established Mason. David had a network of masonic connections which included his pupils Jean-Baptiste Wicar and Philippe-Auguste Hennequin, Count Stanislas Potocki, the chemist Lavoisier and two of his earliest biographers, Pierre Jean Baptiste Publicola Chaussard and Alexandre Lenoir.

Although much of the preliminary work was done in Paris, David decided that to paint the *Horatii*, he should return to

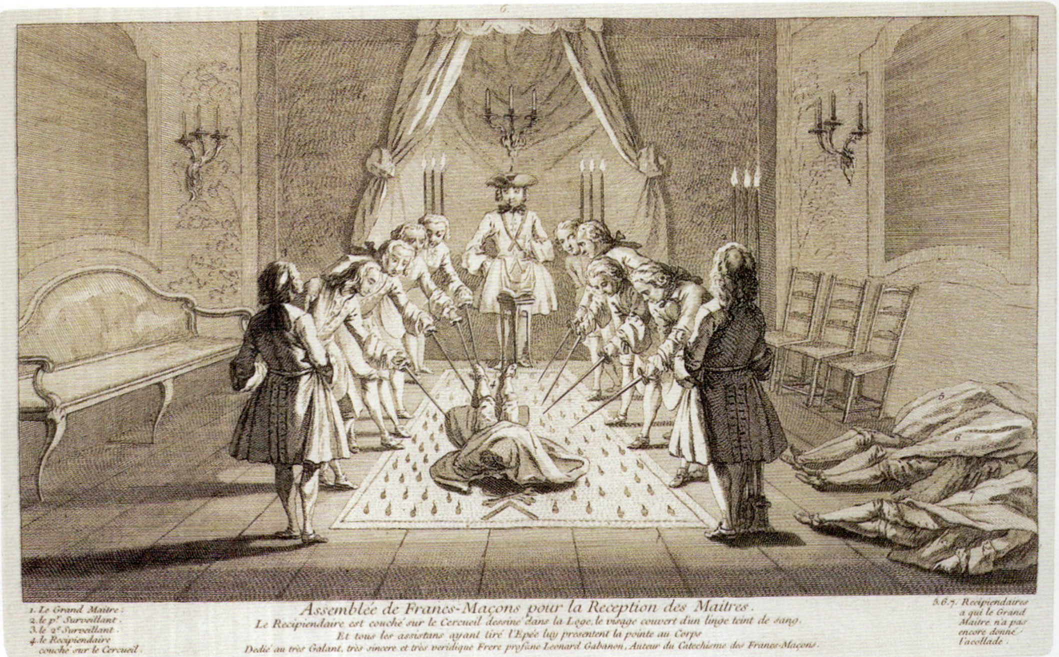

Rome. This was a very expensive undertaking, and was only made possible when David's highly supportive father-in-law offered to pay the expenses of the artist and his wife. The promise of fame and glory seems to have been the main motivation for his second trip to Rome, because the financial rewards from the sale of the picture to the king would have been far outweighed by the money spent. Such a visit, just to paint a single picture, was way beyond the means of practically any other artist of the time, and to some of his rivals David was a privileged publicity seeker for this very ostentatious expenditure.

58
Assembly of Freemasons for the Reception of a Master Mason, from Johann Martin Bernigeroth's *Les Coutumes des Francs-Maçons dans leurs assemblées, principalement pour la réception des apprentifs et des maîtres, tout nouvellement et sincerement découvertes,* 1745

Leaving their two children with their grandparents Pécoul (a second son, Eugène, had been born on 27 April 1784), the Davids left Paris at the start of September 1784. Accompanying them part of the way was David's favourite pupil, Jean-Germain Drouais, who had won the Prix de Rome in that year with the accomplished and sensationally successful painting *The Woman of Canaan at the Feet of Christ* (59). This was the first time that a pupil of David's had won this important prize, and it signalled the start of further successes and the blossoming of a true Davidian school. Not surprisingly, established Academicians were alarmed and envious of the calibre of students that David produced. At this time he had perhaps as many as forty students, and a great number of these had come to him from the studios of established masters. Leaving a teaching practice for any length of time risked losing enrolments, so David entrusted his studio to the care of the established Academician Nicolas-Guy Brenet (1728–92), who had been Drouais's first master, and was an artist in whom David must have had considerable confidence.

David is reported to have said: 'I decided to accompany him [Drouais] to Italy, for the sake of my art as well as for him. I could no longer do without him; I myself profited from giving him lessons, and the questions he addressed to me will be lifelong lessons.' Although the relationship between David and Drouais was extremely close, it is unlikely that David's well laid career plans would have revolved around the availability of a young pupil. It is more likely that the Prix de Rome success provided Drouais with the opportunity to accompany David, rather than it being the catalyst for David to leave Paris. The evidence points to Drouais being the person making hasty travel arrangements, and he left even before being issued with his passport and *brevet* (travel warrant) from the Direction des Bâtiments du Roi. Such lack of respect for the correct procedure disturbed and irritated d'Angiviller, and he pointed out that the winning of the Prix did not automatically qualify the artist concerned for the Rome pension. It was 'a grace from the King which is entirely independent'.

David arrived in Rome on 8 October and arranged to rent a studio in the Via del Babuino, between the Piazza del Popolo and the Piazza di Spagna. He worked in a very methodical manner, drawing from life models and draped mannequins, and some very detailed studies survive for many of the main figures (60). David's generous allowance also enabled him to have accessories such as the swords and helmets made by local craftsmen so that they could serve as accurate props. Some passages of the final work proved very difficult – he repainted the left foot of Old Horatius at least twenty times before he was satisfied. Drouais is supposed to have assisted David, painting the arm of the rear Horatii brother and the yellow garment of Sabina. He also urged his master to paint the heroes nude, but David rejected this idea. Drouais was also given responsibility for painting the whole of the figure of Camilla, but the result was what David called 'a figure of plaster', and he was forced to repaint it himself.

The painting was finished at the end of July 1785, and was then exhibited in David's studio. As with the *Belisarius*, David very conspicuously added the painting's place of origin to the signature and date – L David/ faciebat/ Romanae/ Anno MDCCLXXXIV – a tactic that was presumably to inform the

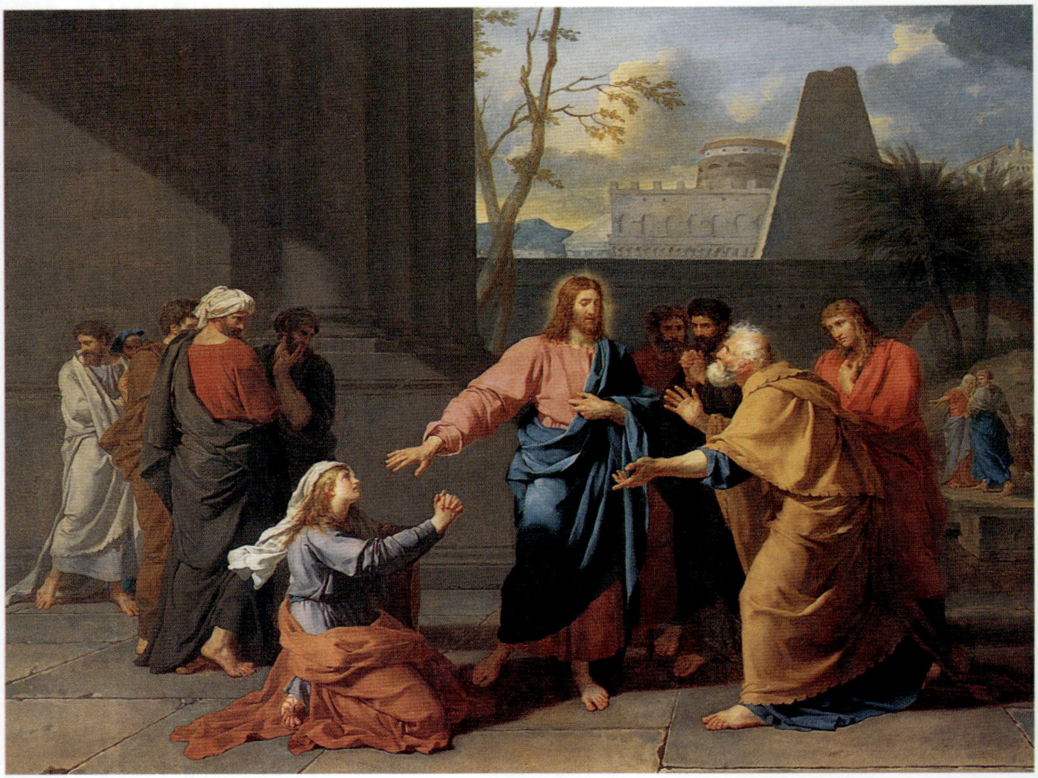

spectator of his scrupulous and dedicated search for authenticity. Newspapers and journals carried glowing reports about the work, crowds clamoured to see it, and even the Pope wanted to view the painting that had created such a sensation. In the event, this was not possible as papal protocol forbade the pontiff visiting a commoner, and it could not be brought to the Vatican. The aged Pompeo Batoni once again urged David to stay in Rome where his talent would be fully appreciated, and said: 'You and I alone are painters. The rest can be thrown into the river.' Batoni was so taken by David's talent that at his death in 1787 he bequeathed his brushes and palette to him as a mark of his esteem.

Although pleased with the success of the *Horatii* in Rome, David had always meant for it to be his grand statement at the 1785 Salon in Paris. While in Rome he wrote twice to the Marquis de Bièvre, a courtier, amateur playwright and fellow

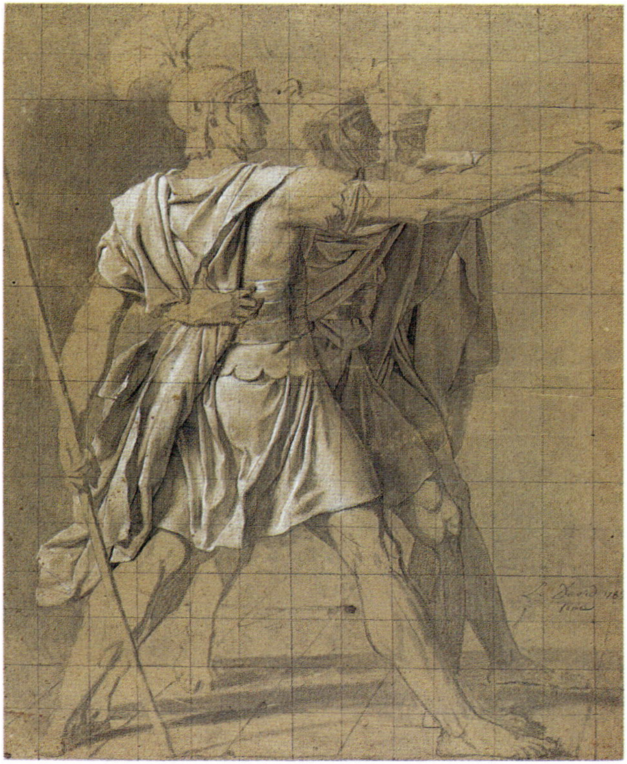

59
Jean-Germain Drouais,
The Woman of Canaan at the Feet of Christ,
1784.
Oil on canvas;
114 × 146 cm,
$44\frac{7}{8} \times 57\frac{1}{2}$ in.
Musée du Louvre, Paris

60
Drawing of the three Horatii brothers,
1785.
Black chalk, wash and white highlights;
58 × 45 cm,
$22\frac{7}{8} \times 17\frac{3}{4}$ in.
Musée Bonnat, Bayonne

Mason, who saw himself as a protector of David, asking him to use his influence to ensure that the picture was hung favourably at the Salon. David was worried that the hostile Pierre might malevolently arrange for the picture to be hung in a poor position, and said, 'It is always our Pierre that I am afraid of.' He appealed to the marquis's own theatrical talents by adding, 'Would you be content if one of your comedies were badly performed?' However, nothing could be done because the painting arrived after the Salon had opened and so it was placed high up (61), only being rehung lower when the closing date of the Salon was extended. News of the painting's great success and ecstatic reception in Rome had spread, and huge numbers of people came to view it – some of them doubtless attracted by the false rumour that the painting's author had been murdered on the way back to Paris.

61
Pietro Antonio Martini,
View of the 1785 Salon,
1785.
Engraving;
34 × 50·5 cm,
$13\frac{3}{8} \times 19\frac{7}{8}$ in

Because of its austerity and depiction of dutiful patriotism, *The Oath of the Horatii* is often considered by some writers to be the clearest expression of Neoclassicism in painting. Neoclassicism does not mean the re-creation of the style of Greek and Roman antiquity, or of paintings peopled with characters that look like coloured classical sculptures. In David's case this new style was based on scrupulous life drawing and a close study of artists such as Caravaggio and Poussin. Its association with classical antiquity came in its moral and ethical subject matter and the severe style that was stripped of all unnecessary embellishments. Of course Neoclassicism is only a shorthand term for a cultural phenomenon that was very complex, and by using it we are in danger of losing the intricacies and subtleties of individual works. Yet it is clear that to the people of the eighteenth century, the ancient authors were not remote and irrelevant – Pliny and Plutarch were used as school textbooks – and the heroic and selfless behaviour of past heroes could provide an ideal model for an imperfect present.

David gave his scene a high degree of actuality, and in doing so was highly innovative – his *Horatii* looked like no other picture

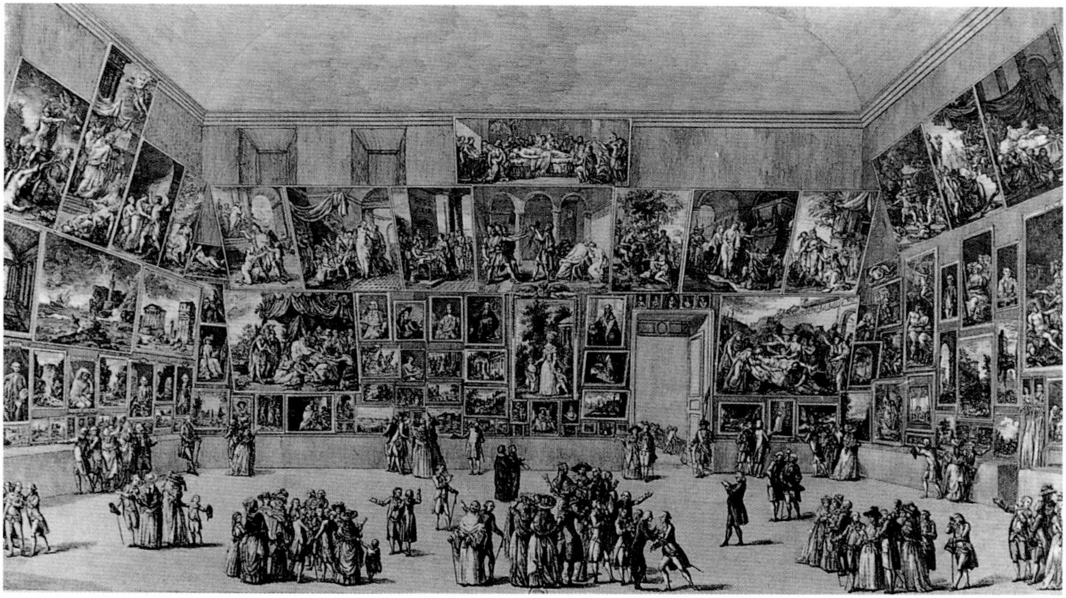

of the time (62). Its uncompromising directness, economy and tension made it instantly memorable and full of visual impact. Each of the three elements of the picture – the sons, the father and the women – is framed by a section of a Doric arcade, and the figures are located in a narrow stage-like space. David split the picture between the masculine resolve of the father and brothers and the slumped resignation of the women. Camilla in the white dress, Sabina in blue and yellow, and the nurse with the children all avert their eyes from the oath-taking, and only the young boy, whose future duty will also be to bear arms and defend the homeland, is allowed to watch (63). The focal point of the work is occupied by the swords that old Horatius is about to distribute to his sons, thus capturing a moment just prior to the passing of power and authority from one generation to the next. While the rear two brothers take the oath with their left hands, the foremost one swears with his right. Perhaps David did this simply as a way of grouping the figures together, but people at the time noticed this detail, and some supposed that this meant that the brother in the front would be the one to survive the combat.

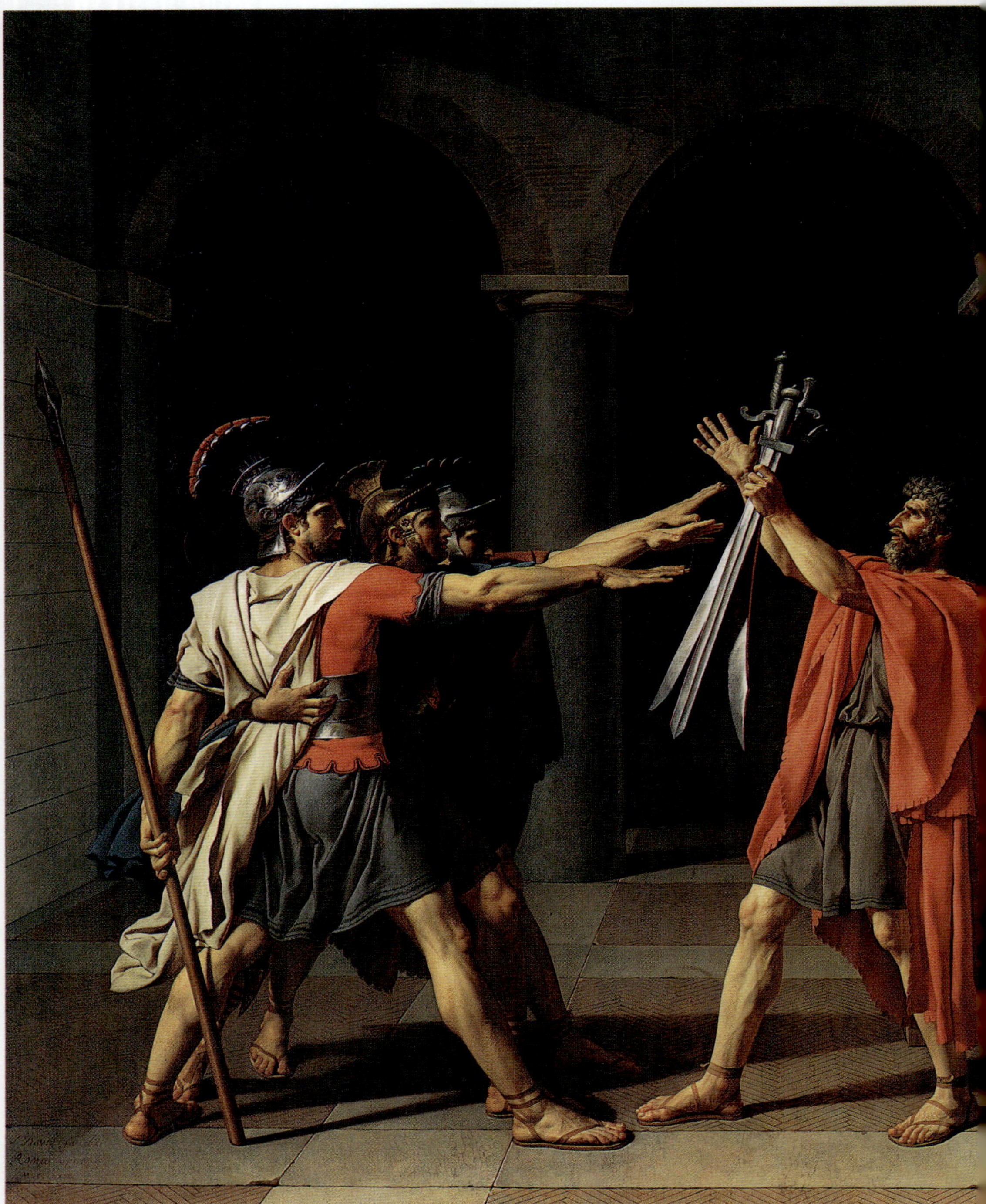

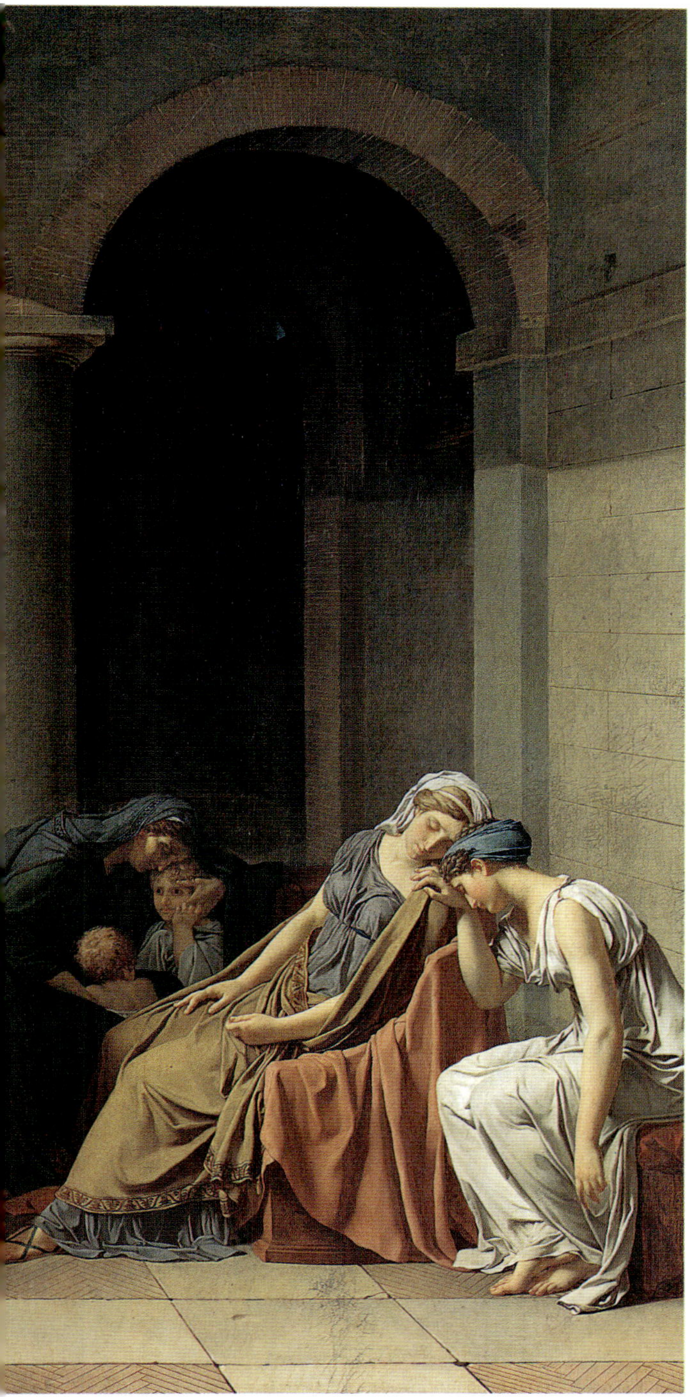

62
The Oath of the Horatii, 1784.
Oil on canvas; 330 × 425 cm, $129\frac{7}{8} \times 162\frac{3}{8}$ in.
Musée du Louvre, Paris

In creating such a picture of contrary emotions and varied figures, David broke many of the accepted rules of harmonious composition that his contemporaries took great pains to observe. By making a virtue of a display of disjunction and lack of pictorial unity, David ran counter to accepted academic methods as laid down in such manuals as Dandré Bardon's *Traité de Peinture* (1765). The *Horatii* lacked focus since the diagonal line was not used to lead the eye to the main protagonists, who were themselves split into separate groups. In his student days David had been criticized for his lack of adherence to compositional rules, so with the *Horatii* he made a bold and calculated alternative statement. Further, David's application of paint had none of the bravura effects or impasto highlights that were recommended in texts and practised by established Academicians. The surface of the *Horatii* is flat and even, and hard-edged outlines are created by the overlapping of figures and their draperies.

63
The Oath of the Horatii
(detail of 62)

Although David changed the subject of his painting from *Old Horatius Defending his Son* to *The Oath of the Horatii*, such changes were admissible by the administration and were not infrequent. However, without consulting his superiors, David increased the picture's size from 10 × 10 ft (3 × 3 m) to 10 × 13 ft (3 × 4 m), the very largest format of painting that the *Direction des Bâtiments du Roi* would sanction. David gave a lengthy explanation of his actions, saying: 'For the picture's size I have increased the dimensions given me by the King. I was told to do it 10 × 10, but having turned my composition in all ways, seeing that it would lose its energy, I ceased to make a picture for the King, and did it for myself. No one will ever make me do anything detrimental to my reputation and it now measures 13 × 10. You need not doubt my desire to please the King, as I do not know whether I shall paint another picture like it; moreover, when I offered it to M. Pierre I told him that I was not guided by self-interest and would charge as much for the 13 feet as for the 10. He said I could not do that, that it would provoke my colleagues; I did not see the matter in this light,

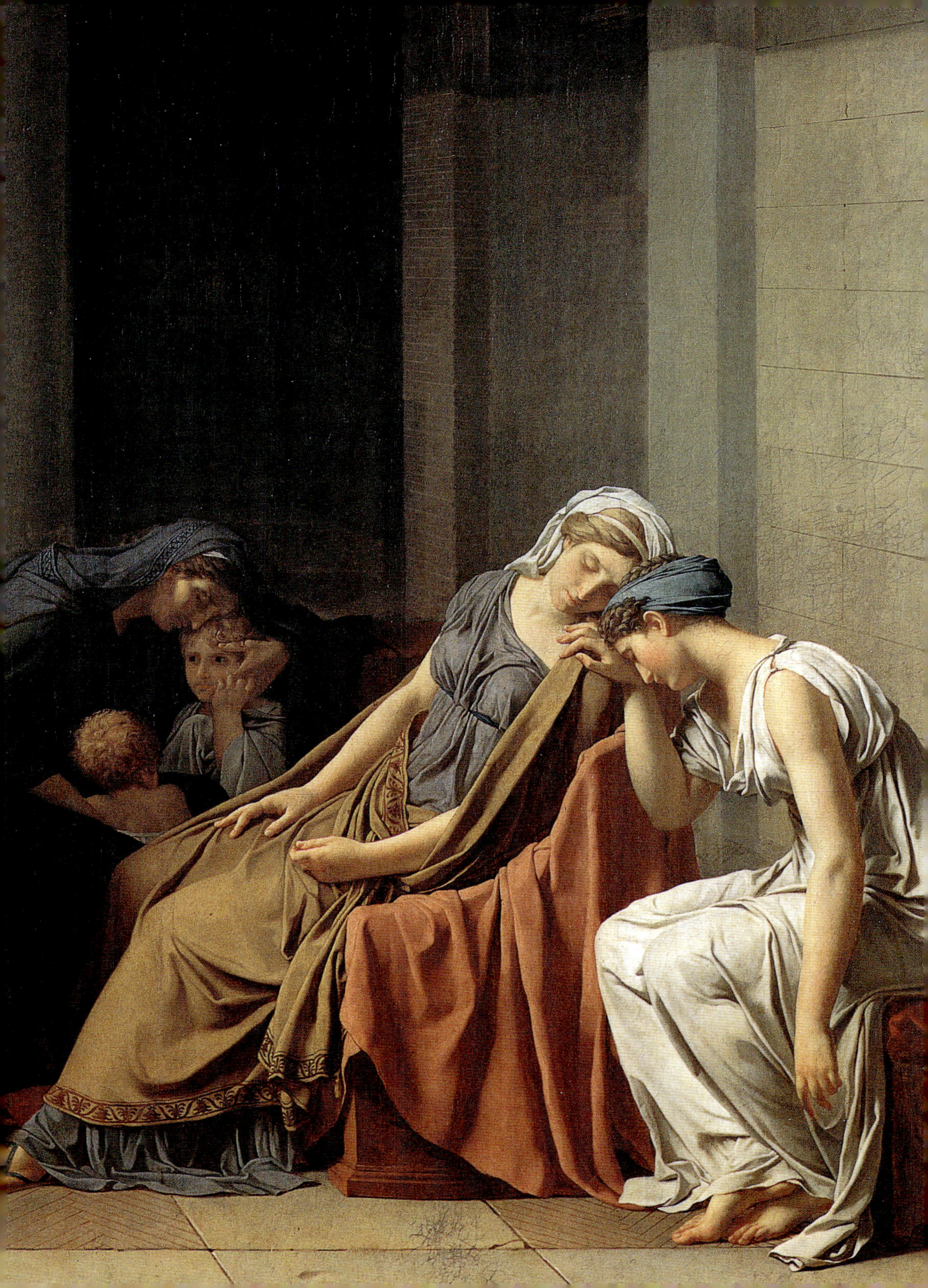

and only considered my own development.' So the *Horatii* was not simply the fulfilment of a Crown commission, but a bold assertion of David's artistic freedom and independence.

By the 1790s, *The Oath of the Horatii* had been taken up as a symbol of the French Revolution. However, it is unlikely that it was meant to be a political painting. David held no political views or allegiances at this time, and it is far-fetched to think of the painting as a call to revolt and rebellion. The Revolution was still four years away; in 1785 republicanism was not yet a force in France, and the overthrow and removal of the monarchy was unthinkable. Undoubtedly the *Horatii* was controversial and revolutionary, and had resonances with contemporary debates on virtue and patriotism, but its greatest impact was as a striking and innovative image.

With this single picture David eclipsed all of his rivals, particularly Peyron, whose sombre painting *The Death of Alcestis* (64) was in direct competition with the *Horatii* at the Salon. This was Peyron's first attempt at a large-scale work, and the increase in size and the square format – rejected by David for the *Horatii* – created problems of figure scale and focus. Peyron's dark and mournful painting, subtitled *The Heroism of Conjugal Love*, showed Alcestis, who had volunteered to commit suicide to save the life of her husband, King Admetus of Pherae, lying dead with outstretched arms between her son and daughter. Her husband turns his head in sorrow and the other members of the household display their anguish with highly stylized and overemphatic gestures. The Salon *Livret* (short catalogue) explained: 'The women, plunged in grief, fill the palace with their mourning, and the statue of Hymen [the Greek god of Marriage] is veiled for ever as it must never again witness fresh embraces.' Compared to the direct rhetoric of the *Horatii*, the painting appeared artificial and excessively gloomy.

The vast majority of critics declared David to be the unanimous victor of the Salon; he was hailed as the head of a new and vigorous French school of painting, reaching a position of supremacy that he would not relinquish for thirty years. Almost all critics wrote of the painting in terms of the action depicted, and made no reference to young Horatius' ignoble murder of his sister. It might even be argued that the Horatii story, if taken as a whole, is less of an example of Enlightenment secular virtue than it first appears, since it advances a form of patriotism where violence is seen as the ultimate solution, and the price of personal attachment and sensitivity, as paid by Camilla, is death.

The Oath of the Horatii was a personal manifesto designed to be shown on the most public of stages. It is evidence of David's refusal to be treated like a glorified craftsman – he considered his own judgement to be above that of bureaucrats and committees. Such a posture naturally antagonized the Academy, officialdom and many fellow painters, but it was very attractive to radicals and impressionable young artists. The stylistic radicalism of the painting has led Thomas Crow, in his book *Painters and Public Life in Eighteenth-Century Paris* (1985), to locate David within the milieu of pamphleteers and subversive critics who conducted a campaign against the favouritism and elitism of government institutions. Crow has maintained that the *Horatii*'s direct language of truth, that some critics found disquieting, appealed to 'a subculture of opposition'. But these interpretations have not met with universal acceptance, and other writers have noted that whereas the language employed by underground writers was colloquial and often bordered on the scandalous and obscene, for all its directness, David's production remained in the realm of 'high' art. David was effectively agitating against the Academy from within, and the financial security provided by his wife enabled him to be independent and take calculated risks.

In the arts and sciences there were also other examples of individuals pitting themselves against privilege and conservative institutions, although not always with the same success as David. In April 1784 the first performance of *The Marriage of*

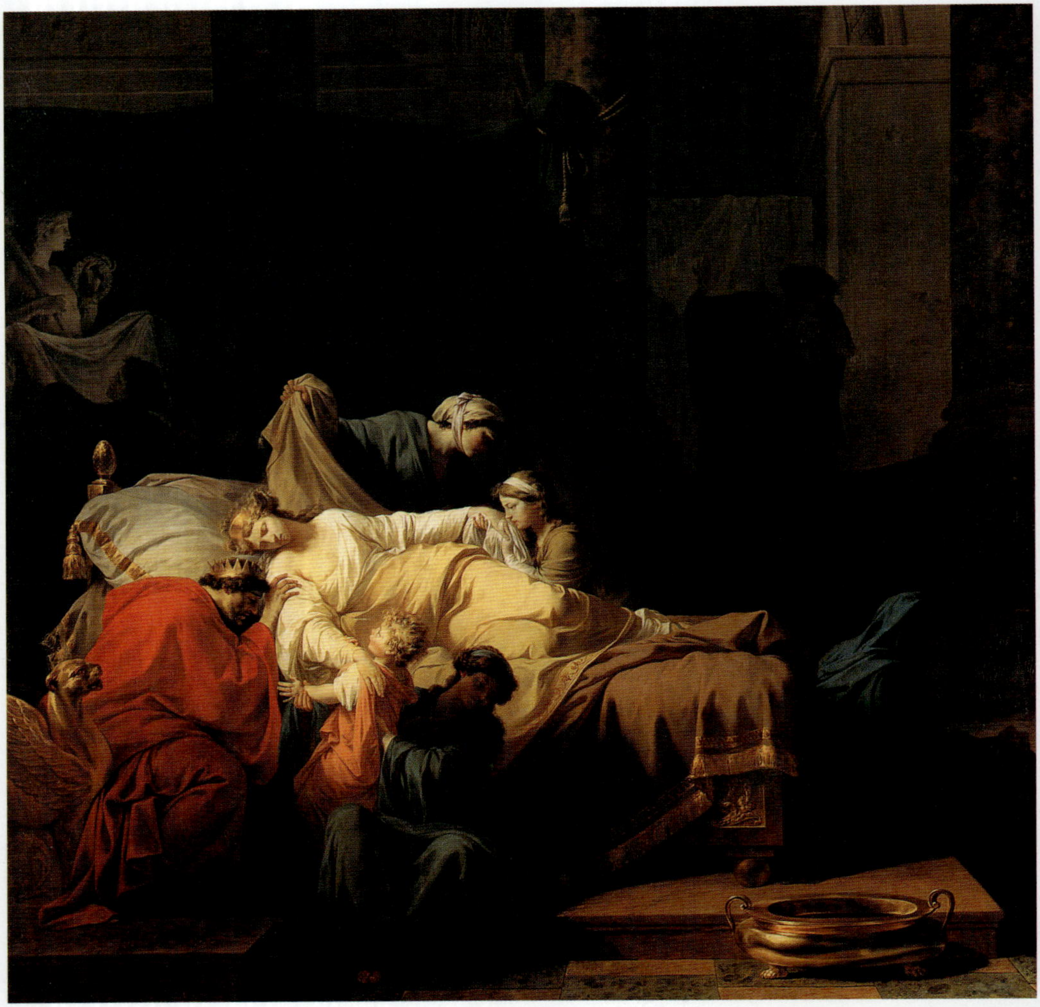

Figaro by Pierre Augustin Caron de Beaumarchais took place, a play which challenged the accepted order of absolute power and inherited privilege. For his impertinence the author was locked up with petty thieves and prostitutes in the prison of St Lazare. Later, in 1778, the Academies of Science and Medicine in Paris fiercely attacked and hounded out the Austrian physician Friedrich Anton Mesmer (founder of mesmerism), who claimed to cure disease in patients by correcting the flow of 'animal magnetism' in seance-like sessions which sometimes raised female subjects to a state of orgasm. In Paris during the Enlightenment, academies and institutions were fair game for both satirical and more openly expressed attacks from a small but energetic underground press.

David's career continued to flourish, and his pupils were also extremely successful in the Academy's competitions. It was said that: 'By a miracle that none of us fully understands, David's school has reached a degree of perfection such that his nineteen-year-old students are already fully-formed men.' But petty jealousies from established Academicians were never far away, and in 1786 the Prix de Rome competition was cancelled because all the best entrants were pupils of David's and therefore bore the clear imprint of his style. His pupils had a reputation for being clannish and aloof and disdainful of other students, but even so an atmosphere of cut-throat competition existed between them. This came to a head in the 1787 Prix de Rome, when Fabre denounced his fellow pupil Girodet for cheating, with the result that Girodet was disqualified and Fabre was awarded first prize. Meanwhile in Rome, Drouais was making rapid progress, and was proving to be an even more difficult student than David had been. He did not like the petty regulations of the Academy, and then he got into a street brawl with a local tough, after which he had to carry a pair of pistols for protection. His masterpiece, *Marius at Minturnae* (65), was shown in Rome in the summer of 1786 and in Paris the following January, and represents the first flowering of the mature Davidian school. This dramatic

64
Pierre Peyron,
The Death of Alcestis or *The Heroism of Conjugal Love*, 1785.
Oil on canvas; 327 × 325cm, 128¾ × 128in.
Musée du Louvre, Paris

and powerful work, which shows Marius turning back the Cimbrian soldier sent to kill him by the sheer force of his will, was in some ways Drouais's response to the *Horatii*. Although Drouais's painting was clearly based on David's examples, the similarities in appearance masked a fundamental difference in subject matter. While the Horatii brothers were examples of patriotism, Marius was a greedy and ambitious general who caused large numbers of innocent people to be slaughtered in his quest for power. In Paris the painting was extremely well received, and many people thought that Drouais would eventually challenge and perhaps even surpass David. Tragically this did not materialize because Drouais died in Rome in February 1788 from a combination of smallpox and overwork. David was plunged into grief, and wrote that, 'In losing him, I lost my emulation. He alone could trouble my sleep.' He even erected a small memorial to him in the garden of the Louvre, which has since disappeared.

65
Jean-Germain Drouais,
Marius at Minturnae,
1786.
Oil on canvas;
271 × 365 cm,
106$\frac{5}{8}$ × 143$\frac{3}{4}$ in.
Musée du Louvre, Paris

David now thought that his artistic triumphs qualified him for some high position in the administration of Crown art. The directorship of the French Academy in Rome was to become vacant in October 1787, and David expressed a strong wish to be chosen for the post. However, this did not happen and, much to David's disappointment, Ménageot was appointed instead. David had the support of some aristocratic patrons, and the Marquis de Bièvre wrote to d'Angiviller asking why his protégé had been overlooked for the job. He was informed that David was too young (at nearly thirty-nine) and too inexperienced for the post, but that he would be a strong candidate when the position next became vacant in six years' time. David's independent spirit was probably beginning to count against him, since his ability to teach and produce gifted students was unquestionable. Perhaps his strong-minded attitude was also a factor, because the director's duties also required considerable diplomatic skills. David's rejection from the post was yet another event in his continuing struggle with the Academy that put them on a collision course.

Because of his great impact at the 1785 Salon, David would normally have been commissioned to execute a large history painting for the following Salon. But although he received the order for a *Coriolanus Turned Back from Rome*, it was never completed. A gossipy society journal of the day, the *Mémoires Secrets*, related that David's pride prevented him from painting a subject that the autocratic Pierre wanted to impose, and that he considered unsuitable. With characteristic shrewdness,

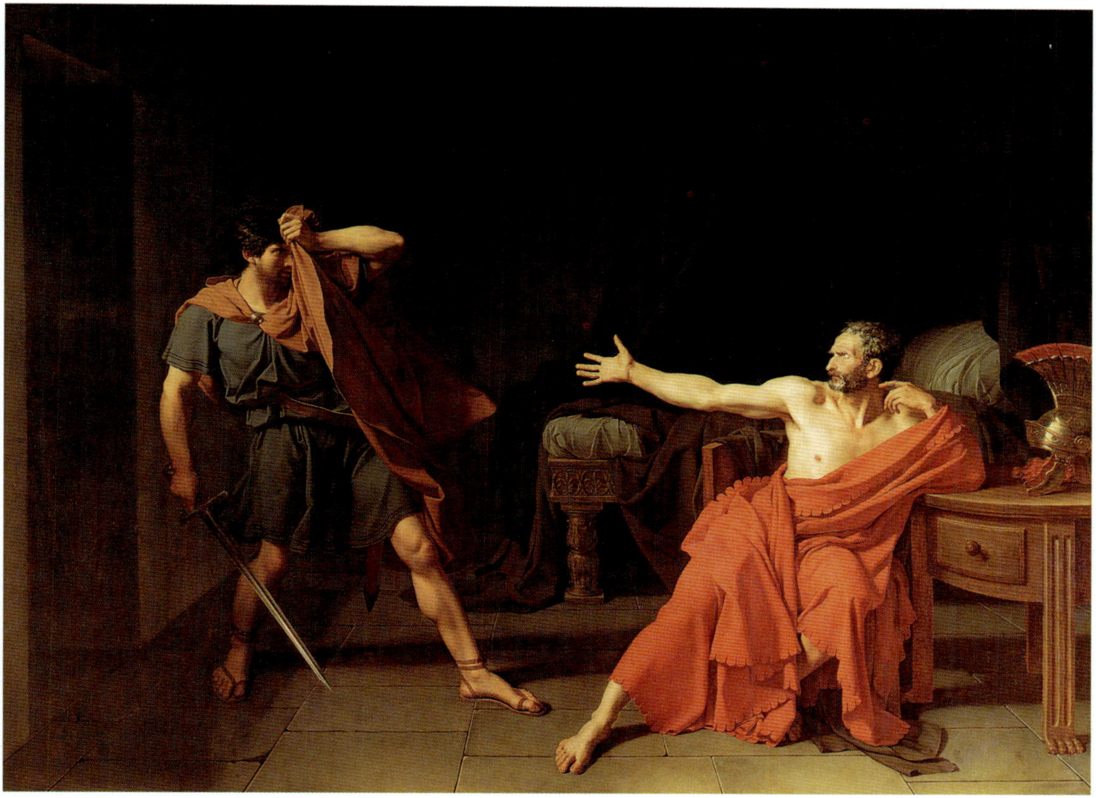

David more than compensated for the absence of an official work by securing an important private commission. This was for *The Death of Socrates* (66), paid for by the wealthy Charles-Michel Trudaine who, with his brother Charles-Louis, held a regular artistic and literary salon in their sumptuous Parisian town house in the Place Royale (now the Place de la Concorde). David's social connections had enabled him to come into

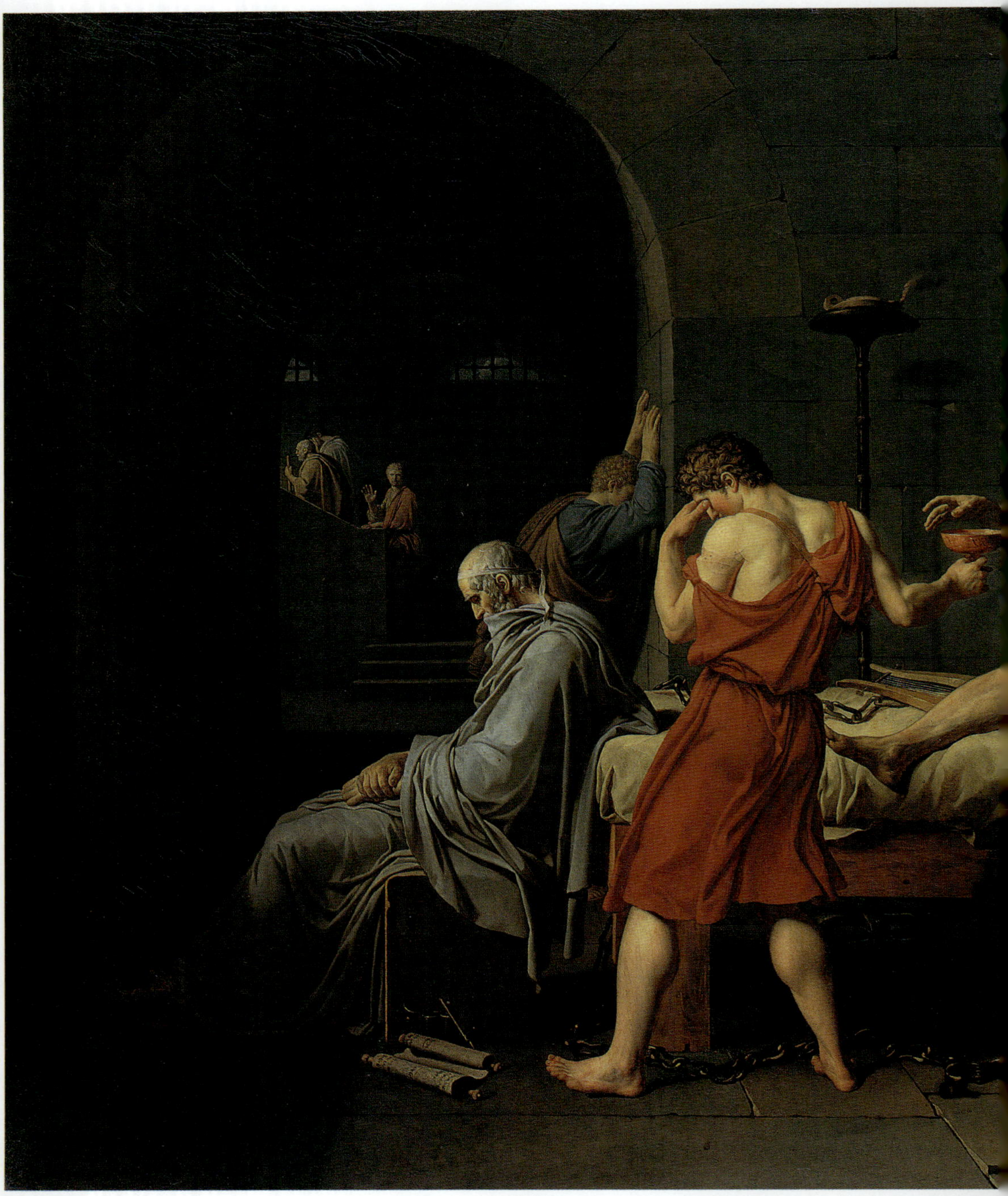

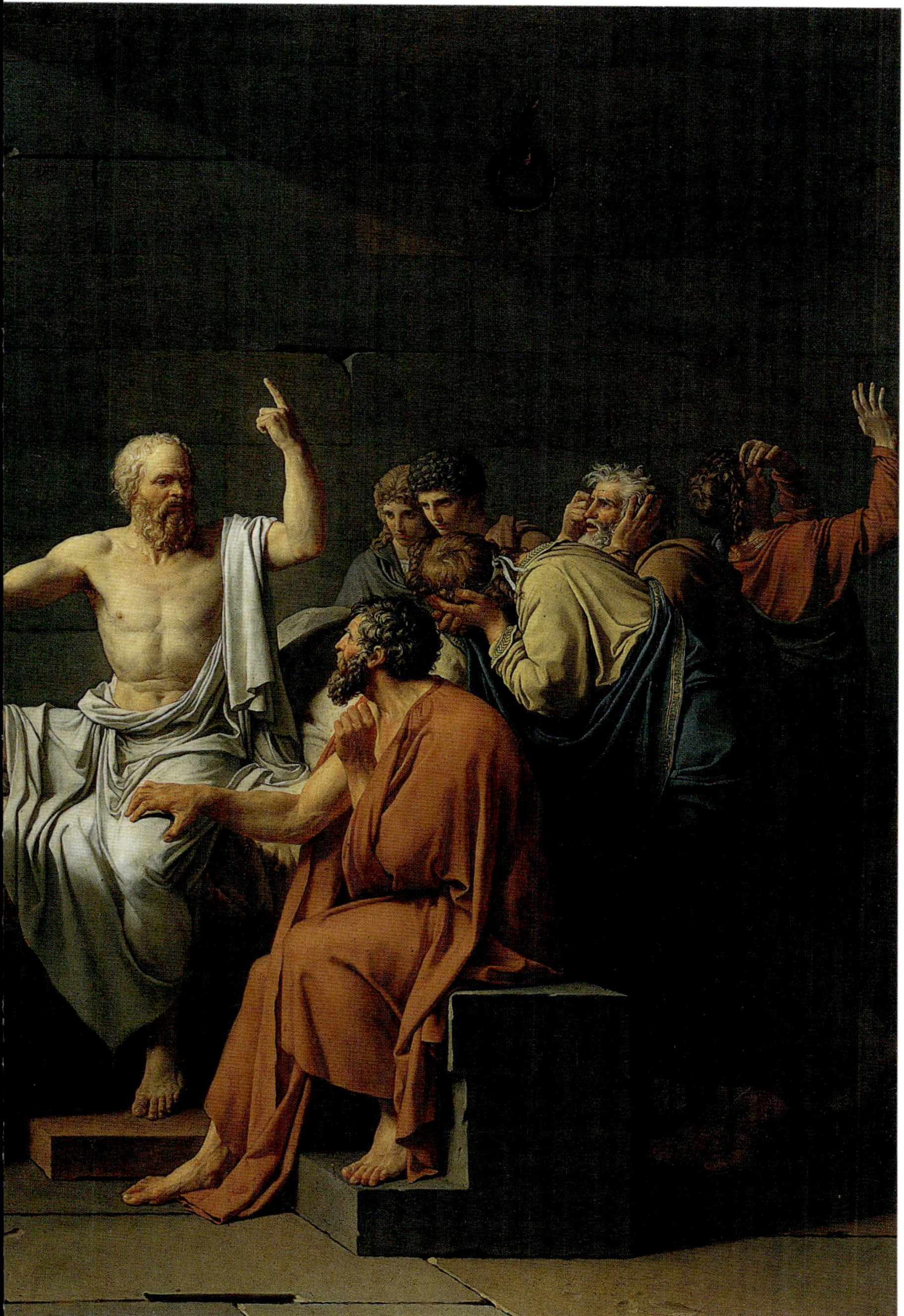

66
The Death of Socrates, 1787.
Oil on canvas; 129·5 × 196·2 cm, 51 × 77¼ in.
Metropolitan Museum of Art, New York

contact with the brothers, and attend the meetings of this so-called 'Trudaine Society'. There he mixed with the liberal nobility and Enlightenment writers and intellectuals, among them André Chénier, who was soon to become a distinguished poet and radical journalist.

The Athenian philosopher Socrates had made himself unpopular with the ruling factions by his implacable respect for the law and his desire to expose false pretensions. He was condemned to death in 399 BC on the charge of not recognizing the state's gods and of corrupting the city's youth. Socrates accepted his fate with noble resignation and died by drinking hemlock, a painless but slow-acting poison that enabled him to continue his debates and discussions with his followers until the very end. To the men of the Enlightenment, Socrates was a figure of great stature, being the embodiment of truth, moral rectitude and self-control; his evident erotic attachment to handsome young men was conveniently disregarded.

David possibly advanced the subject of Socrates himself, but it was also appealing to the Trudaine circle and provoked a great deal of discussion on how it might be depicted. Chénier gave some advice on the pose of Socrates, and David also consulted the Oratorian scholar Father Adry for details. The fullest account of Socrates' death was in Plato's *Phaedo*, but Diderot had also recommended the subject to artists in his 1758 *Treatise of Dramatic Poetry*. However, David showed Socrates reaching for the poison instead of, as Diderot suggested, 'Holding the cup in one hand and turning his eyes to Heaven.'

67
The Death of Socrates
(detail of 66)

Unlike the *Belisarius, Andromache* and *Horatii, Socrates* was a modestly sized easel painting suitable for a domestic interior. David chose to show Socrates as he is about to pick up the lethal cup of hemlock, without ceasing the flow of his wise words. Confident in the immortality of the soul, with his left hand Socrates points heavenwards, and at this sight some of his followers lose their composure and give way to grief and anguish, particularly Apollodorus at the extreme right. The

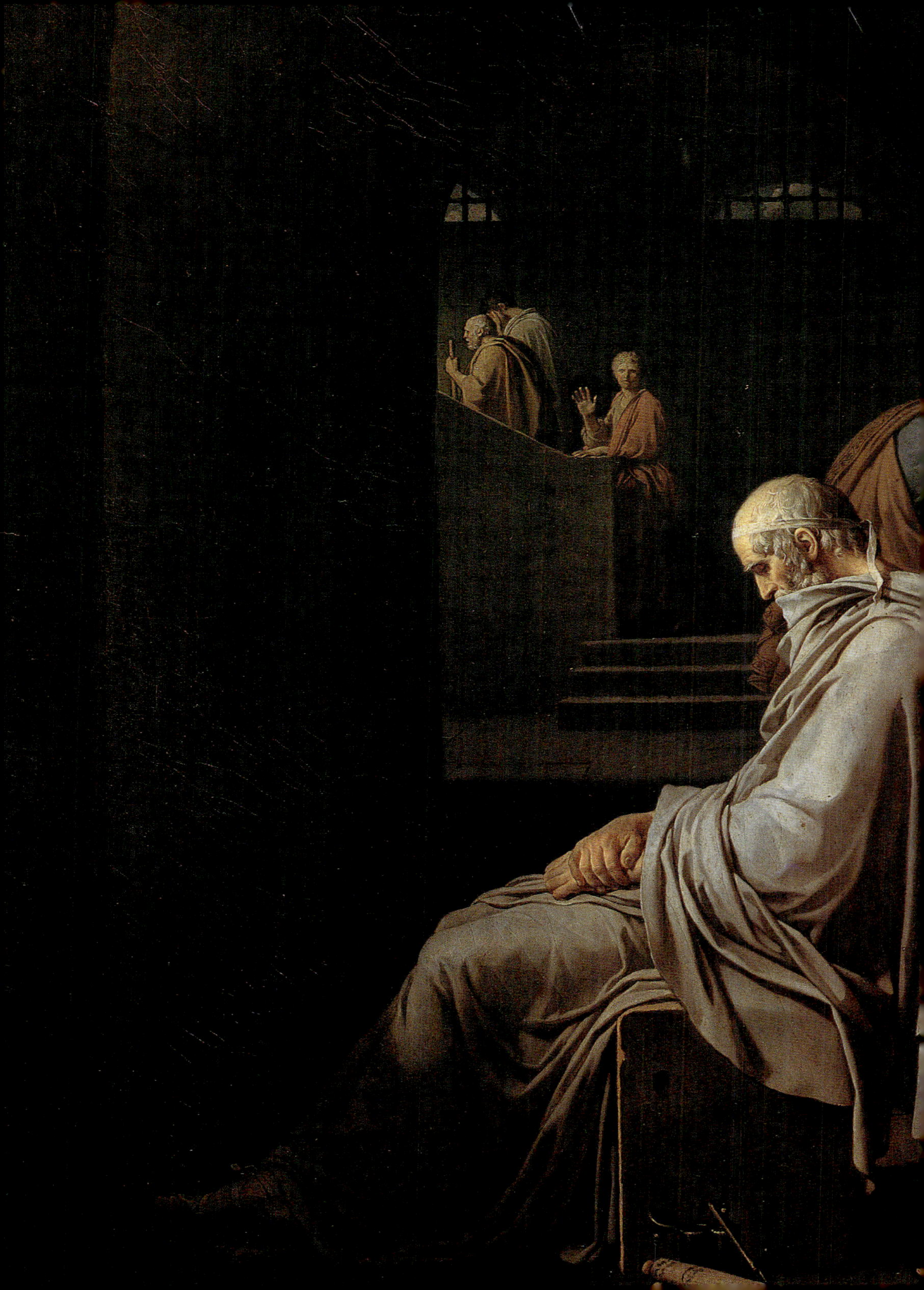

faithful Crito sits listening intently and lays his hand on his master's knee, and Plato sits impassive like a human bookend at the foot of the bed. David also used extensive artistic licence in assigning ages to his characters. Although Socrates was about seventy when he was forced to commit suicide, he is shown as a much younger man with a muscular and athletic torso. Conversely, Plato, who was considerably younger than Socrates (and not even actually present at the death), appears as an old man. According to Plato's description, about fifteen people were present, but David included twelve, to make the scene less crowded and perhaps also to suggest parallels with Christ and his Apostles. The chill setting of the cell, which seems anachronistically modern, and close to Claude-Nicolas Ledoux's (1736–1806) contemporary prison architecture, combined with the hard-edged quality of the paint, exactly match the sad dignity of the scene. On the stairway in the background, Socrates' wife, Xanthippe, who had been dismissed from the final act by her husband, casts a last wistful glance back (67).

Shown at the Salon of 1787 (68), David's work was again in competition with Peyron, who also exhibited a *Death of Socrates* (69) commissioned by d'Angiviller for the Crown. David's confidence in surpassing his rival, coupled with his aggressive and ambitious nature, make it very possible that he chose to paint his own *Socrates* when he learned of Peyron's plans. The force and clarity of David's version was thrown into even sharper relief by the lack of drama and focus in Peyron's work, and both the public and critics declared David's work to be far superior. David eclipsed his long-time rival once and for all, and from then on Peyron had to be content with a subordinate role in the art world. An English visitor to the Salon, the print publisher and art entrepreneur John Boydell, wrote that David's *Socrates* was, '(in my opinion) the most exquisite and admirable effort of art which has appeared since the Sistine Chapel and Raphael's Stanze. A picture which would have done honour to Athens in the age of Pericles; which after ten days' successive observation seems to me absolutely perfect in all its parts.' Thomas Jefferson, then in Paris as American minister to France, wrote of the Salon, 'The best thing is the *Death of Socrates* by David, and a superb one it is.' Trudaine was so satisfied with the painting that he increased David's already handsome fee of 6,000 livres to 10,000 livres.

Not only was David the most successful and talked about artist of the day, he was also a character of imposing presence. He was tall (about 1·8 m or 6 ft), dark, well-built and vigorous. He had keen and piercing eyes, slightly wavy hair, and his movements and bearing were mostly calm and distinguished. He was also something of a dandy, taking great trouble over his dress. Usually good natured, he could charm and flatter the ladies, although the increasing size of his mouth tumour must have caused some speech problems. But David was a complex character, and at times he would display a certain crudity and coarseness of manners, and could also be suspicious and vindictive. Music and the theatre were his favourite pastimes, and he fancied himself as a violinist, but his own assessment of his talent was not shared by the people who had the dubious pleasure of hearing him play. He also moved in high society and was not content with the company of other artists, whom he had little time for. As well as the Trudaine circle, he was invited to entertainments held by Queen Marie Antoinette's favourite painter Elisabeth-Louise Vigée-Lebrun (1755–1842), who was also a courtier, and by Félicité de Genlis, former mistress of the king's cousin, the Duke d'Orleans. Madame de Genlis was also the governess of the duke's three children at the country house of Saint-Leu, and David not only gave them drawing lessons but also joined in the favourite game of grouping them into *tableaux vivants* (living pictures) representing scenes from history and mythology.

Exposure to liberal intellectual thought served to increase David's dissatisfaction with the Academy and its methods. He saw it as despotic, oppressive and an obstacle to the development of natural talent. David strove to demonstrate the superiority of his own style as opposed to that of established Academicians, and sought public support for himself. He actively discouraged his pupils from attending the Academy's school, though he was of course delighted when they carried off its prizes. He eloquently summed up his attitude to the Academy in a most forthright way: 'The Academy is like a wigmaker's shop; you cannot get out of the door without getting its powder on your clothes. How much time will you waste in

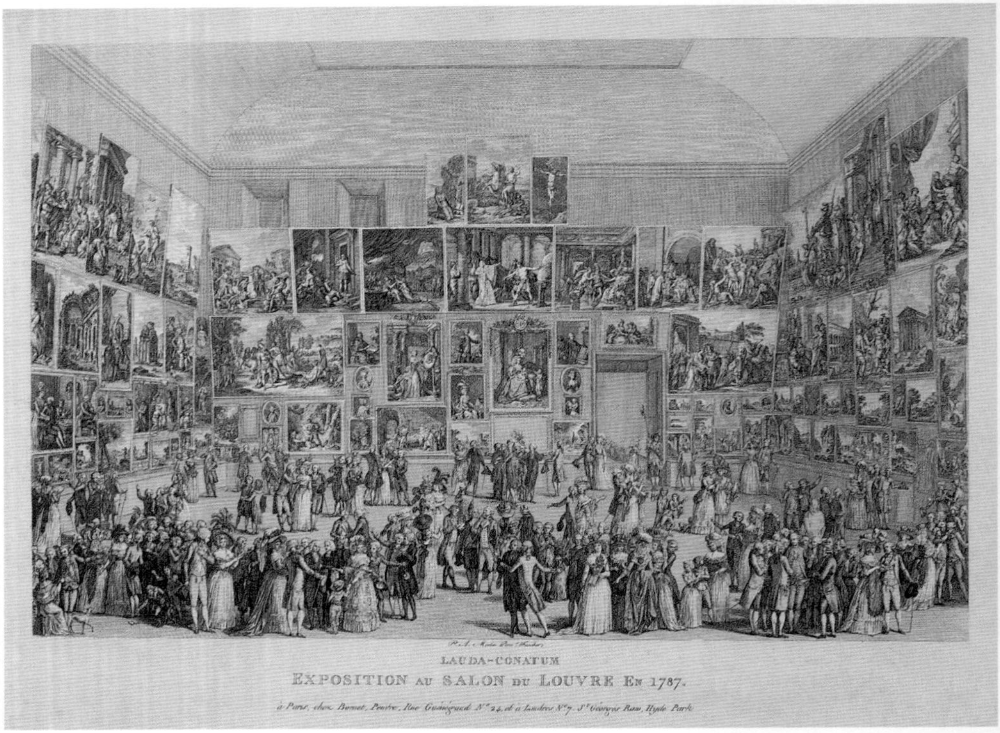

68
Pietro Antonio Martini,
View of the 1787 Salon,
1787.
Engraving

forgetting those poses, those conventional positions into which the professors force the model's torso, as if it were a plucked chicken? ... They will doubtless teach you to do your torso, teach you your trade in the end, because they make a trade out of painting. As for me I hold that trade in filthy contempt.'

David's ideas on individual liberty, both artistic and social, were clarified and developed at this time, and his friend André

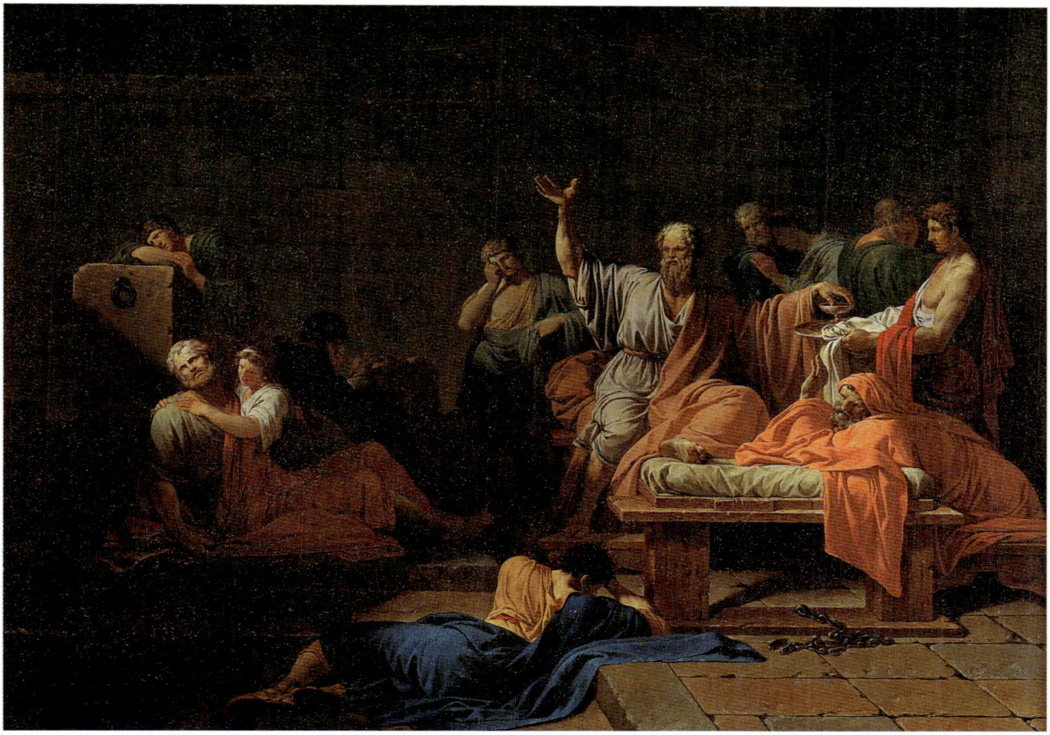

69
Pierre Peyron, *The Death of Socrates*, 1787. Oil on canvas; 98 × 133 cm, $38\frac{1}{2} \times 52\frac{3}{8}$ in. Statens Museum fur Kunst, Copenhagen

Chénier was highly influential in their formation. Contact with Americans such as the painter John Trumbull (1756–1843), who visited him in 1786, and possibly with Thomas Jefferson, with the Italian patriot Filippo Mazzei and with English people such as John Boydell and the husband and wife painters Richard (1742–1821) and Maria (1759–1838) Cosway, taught David something of democratic political systems that existed elsewhere. A significant contrast was revealed between them and the authoritarian monarchy and privileged aristocracy in France, and he began to see the necessity for change and reform. The English art world also seemed very appealing to him as he thought it to be even-handed and lacking in the prejudice and intrigue of Paris, and so a visit to London was planned, not only to renew his acquaintance with the charming Mrs Cosway, with whom he was particularly taken, but also to show either *The Oath of the Horatii* (see 62) or *The Death of Socrates* (see 66) at the Royal Academy exhibition of 1788 or 1789. However, David's plans did not materialize because of the turmoil and upheaval that surrounded the momentous events of the French Revolution.

Making a New World   David and the Revolution

3

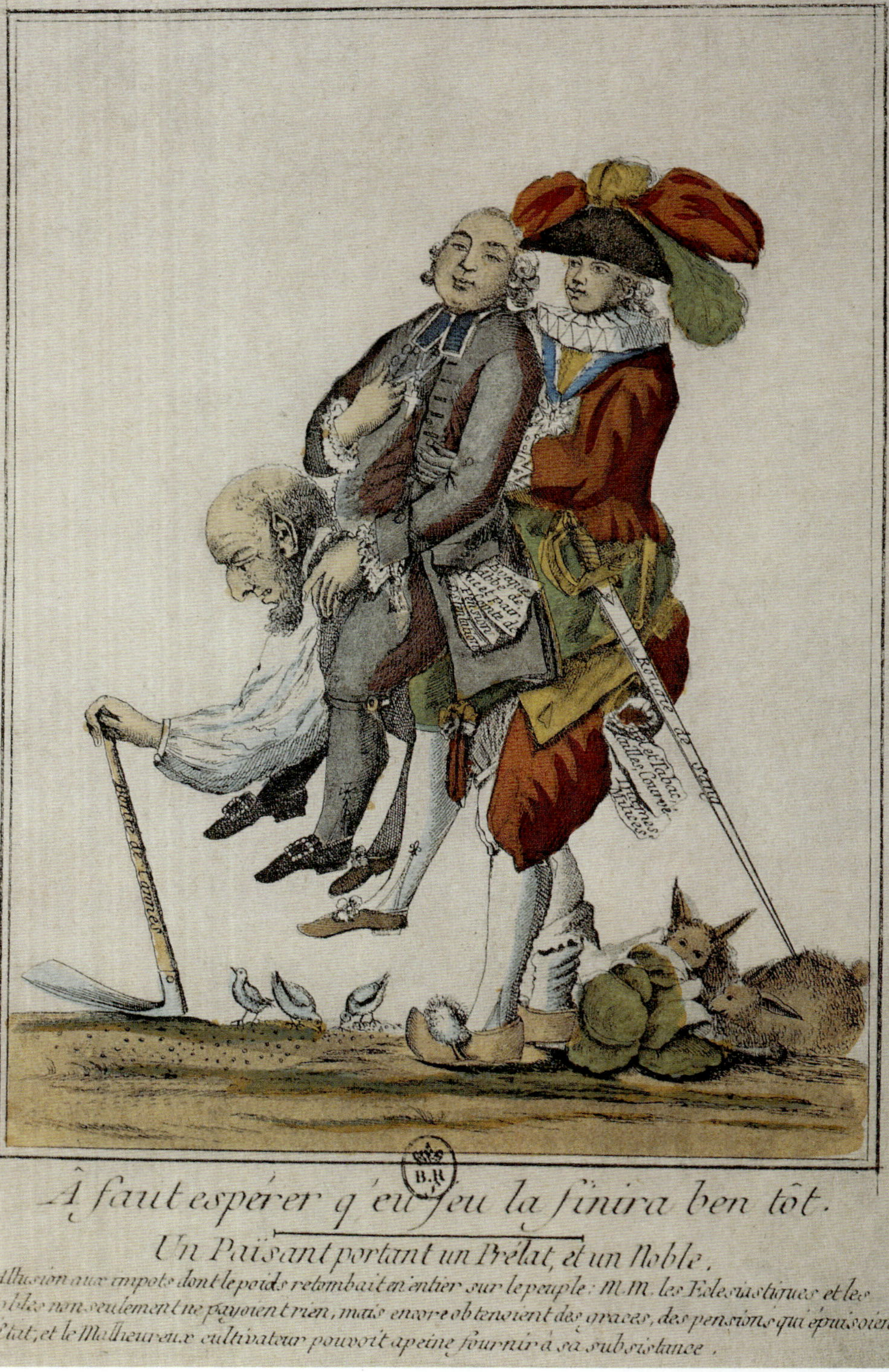

Â faut espérer q'eu jeu la finira ben tôt.

Un Païsant portant un Prélat, et un Noble.

Allusion aux impots dont le poids retombait en entier sur le peuple: M.M. les Eclesiastiques et les Nobles non seulement ne payoient rien, mais encore obtenoient des graces, des pensions qui épuisoient l'État, et le Malheureux cultivateur pouvoit apeine fournir à sa subsistance.

'Never was any such event so inevitable yet so completely unforeseen', was how the great historian Alexis de Tocqueville characterized the coming of the French Revolution. From a distance of more than two hundred years, we can see that the Revolution was the result of a series of social, economic and political pressures which, though manageable in themselves, had the cumulative effect of toppling the monarchy and changing the course of French and European history.

By the mid-1780s the whole framework of the *ancien régime* seemed close to breakdown. As a legacy of its expensive involvement in the American War of Independence (1778–83), France was facing bankruptcy and the government was forced to borrow more and more money to cover its deficits. The public was also aware of how the lavish and extravagant expenditure of the court added to the nation's debts, and they were outraged at the waste. Tensions also existed between the aristocracy and the emerging middle classes, with the latter group trying hard to gain social acceptance and a rise in their influence and status. Of course these issues of politics and class were of little importance to the poor, the vast majority of whom lived in degradation and misery trying to scratch a living from the land. They laid the blame for their misfortunes squarely at the feet of the Church and the aristocracy which claimed crippling tithes and feudal dues (70). Then, to make matters worse, the 1788 harvest was disastrous, raising bread prices and threatening the poor with starvation.

70
Let's Hope that this Game Ends Soon, 1789.
Coloured engraving;
36·5 × 24 cm,
$14^{3}/_{8} \times 9^{1}/_{2}$ in

Besides the economic and social problems, an ideological campaign was also being fought, with the democratic and liberal ideas of the Enlightenment gaining considerable currency and acceptance. In January 1789 the Abbé

Emmanuel-Joseph Sieyès, a radical clergyman, published a pamphlet entitled *What is the Third Estate?*, which was a call for a complete change in the system of government (71). The three Estates of France were the Clergy, the Nobles and the Commons, and while the first two accounted for under half a million men, the Third Estate represented about 25 million commoners. Sieyès wrote: 'What is the Third Estate? Everything. What has it been in the political order until now? Nothing. What is it asking for? To become something.'

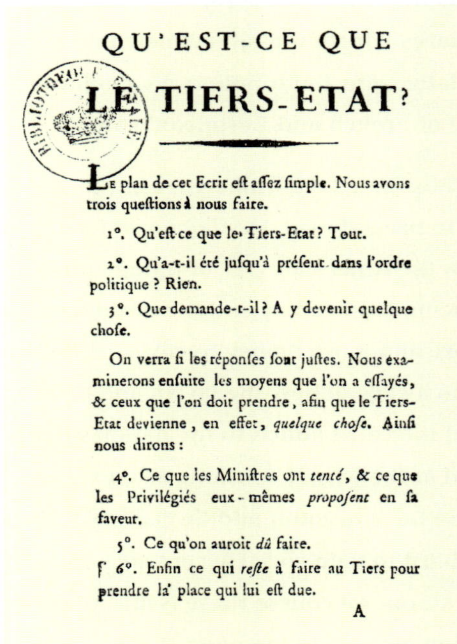
QU'EST-CE QUE

LE TIERS-ETAT?

Le plan de cet Ecrit eſt aſſez ſimple. Nous avons trois queſtions à nous faire.

1°. Qu'eſt-ce que le Tiers-Etat? Tout.

2°. Qu'a-t-il été juſqu'à préſent dans l'ordre politique? Rien.

3°. Que demande-t-il? A y devenir quelque choſe.

On verra ſi les réponſes ſont juſtes. Nous examinerons enſuite les moyens que l'on a eſſayés, & ceux que l'on doit prendre, afin que le Tiers-Etat devienne, en effet, *quelque choſe*. Ainſi nous dirons:

4°. Ce que les Miniſtres ont *tenté*, & ce que les Privilégiés eux-mêmes *propoſent* en ſa faveur.

5°. Ce qu'on auroit *dû* faire.

6°. Enfin ce qui *reſte* à faire au Tiers pour prendre la place qui lui eſt due.

A

71
Title page of Abbé Emmanuel-Joseph Sieyès's *What is the Third Estate?*, 1789

He argued that the Third Estate should become the dominant force in the government and wrestle authority away from the nobility. Following the example of Sieyès, other pamphlets and petitions on similar themes were published and distributed throughout France. An active gutter press also churned out smutty and titillating stories of sexual depravity in high places, and this socio-political pornography helped form notions of a decadent, debauched and wasteful royalty and aristocracy in the minds of the common people. The importance of the written word in creating political awareness cannot be underestimated, and it is no coincidence that the most ardent support for the Revolution came from the most literate parts of France – the Île-de-France, the North and the East.

Early in 1789 no solution to the nation's problems had been found, and so Louis XVI convened the Estates General (France's national parliament) at Versailles for the first time since 1614. Though they represented the commoners of the country, the Third Estate members who went to Versailles were far from poor peasants, they were successful men in their own right: lawyers, bureaucrats, bankers, merchants and industrialists who sought change and reform in the shape of equality, justice and liberty. The discussions reached a stalemate; on 17 June the Third Estate seized the initiative and proclaimed itself the National Assembly. On 20 June the new Assembly, now joined by some of the clergy, found itself locked out of the official meeting hall, and so, at the suggestion of the Parisian deputy Dr Joseph Guillotin, they met in the tennis court of the palace, situated just outside the complex of royal buildings. (The tennis court still stands and is now a museum.) There they swore a solemn oath not to disperse until a constitution for the nation had been established (72); this was a key event in the political course of the Revolution, with the new Assembly setting itself up as the true representatives of the people and the real power in the land.

Meanwhile, in Paris and in the provinces, popular disturbances took place with the people fearful of the king sending in troops and forcibly dissolving the Assembly. A climax was reached on 14 July 1789 when the Bastille prison was stormed by an insurrectionary mob of 800–900 people who were seeking weapons and gunpowder for future struggles with royal forces. In popular myth the Bastille was seen as a symbol of despotism and unjust imprisonment, but in reality it held only a few prisoners, kept in reasonable conditions. The majority of its conquerors were artisans – cobblers, locksmiths, joiners and shopkeepers

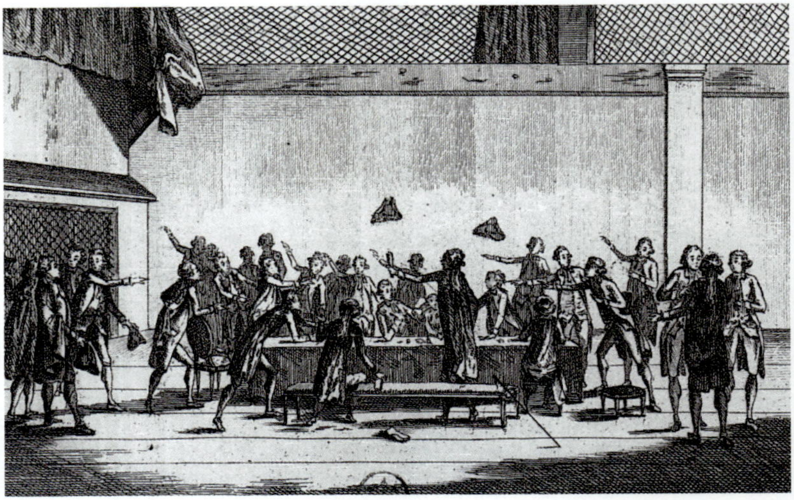

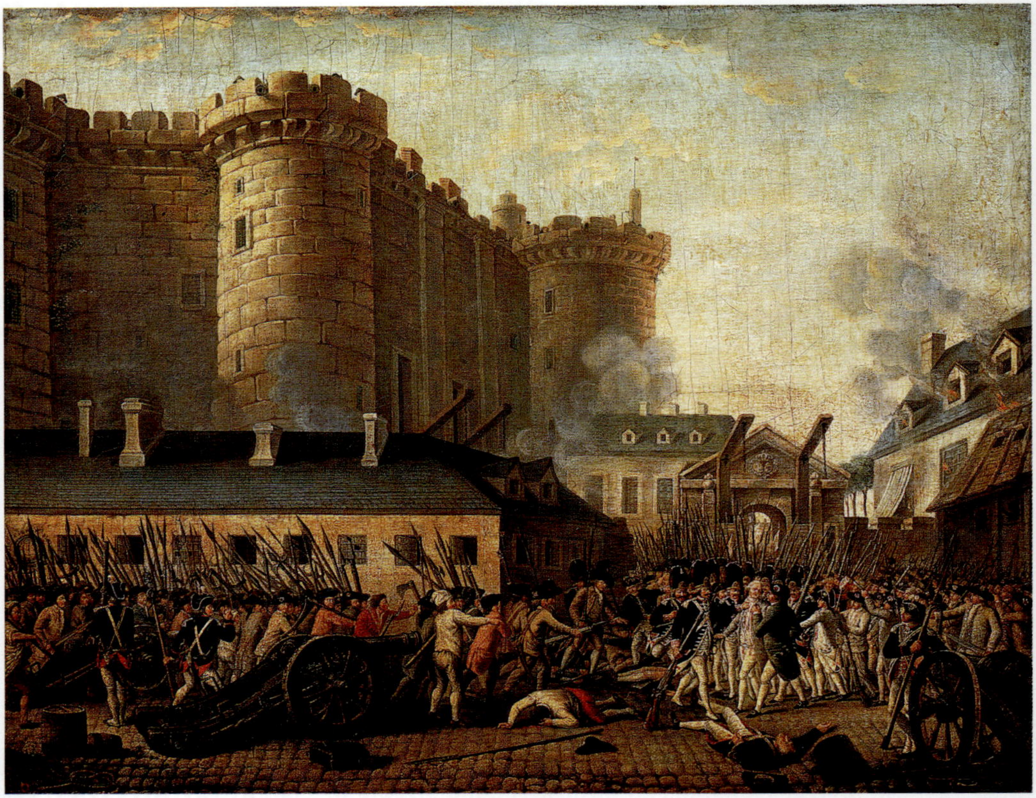

– from the nearby poor quarter of the Faubourg Saint-Antoine. Once inside, the crowd found the desired stocks of muskets and powder but no evidence for the gaol's sinister reputation; only seven prisoners – four forgers, two lunatics and an aristocrat accused of incest – were discovered. The Bastille's unfortunate governor, the Marquis de Launay, who had ordered his troops to fire on the mob, was seized and summarily butchered, and his severed head was paraded on a pike – a grim foretaste of future blood-letting (73).

The king seems to have been little disturbed by the events in Paris, as he wrote in his diary for that day 'nothing'. Similarly, the nobles and aristocrats had little inkling of the direction or speed of events that would first challenge and then sweep away their age-old privileges. However, the magnitude of the popular victory soon became clear. On 17 July the king travelled from Versailles to Paris to be greeted by cries, first of 'Long live the Nation!', then 'Long live the Nation and the National Assembly!', and finally 'Long live the King and the Nation!' He then addressed the crowd from the steps of the town hall, and his endorsement and acceptance of the Revolution was shown by his agreement to wear the tricolour cockade made up of royalist white and the blue and red heraldic colours of the city of Paris. Royal absolutism had come to an end and there was widespread rejoicing, though for the rest of the summer France was in the grip of the 'Great Fear', a hysteria fed by alarms over possible foreign or aristocratic intervention and by famine and near anarchy.

72
The Oath of the Tennis Court, 20 June 1789, 1789. Engraving

73
Artist unknown, *The Seizure of the Marquis de Launay at the Bastille, 14 July 1789*, c.1790s. Oil on canvas; 58 × 73 cm, $22\frac{7}{8} \times 28\frac{3}{4}$ in. Musée National du Château de Versailles

In 1789 David was a successful public figure of some reputation who had a vested interest in the establishment, working for both the Crown and for aristocratic patrons. Yet, like many of his liberal friends, he welcomed the Revolution as it promised reform and a greater degree of liberty. But just as the Revolution moved from optimistic ideas of national unity to repressive terror, David's political involvement changed and evolved from Enlightenment moderation to extreme radicalism. He does not, however, emerge as an active revolutionary until April 1792; although he eventually became fully committed to the cause, the process of change was, as with his art, gradual rather than sudden.

At the Salon of 1789, which took place against the backdrop of the capital's civil and social unrest, David exhibited two paintings. One was *The Loves of Paris and Helen* (74), an important private work for the Count d'Artois, the king's dissolute brother, and the other was a Crown commission, *The Lictors Returning to Brutus the Bodies of his Sons* (see 77).

David had begun work on *The Loves of Paris and Helen* in 1786, and had originally intended to have it ready for the 1787 Salon. However, due to an injury to his achilles tendon sustained in October 1786, and a long illness in 1787, the work was not completed until 1788. *The Loves of Paris and Helen* was a work on a new theme, and to express the amorous nature of the subject, David greatly modified the uncompromising and severe style of his previous paintings. The two figures are smooth and sculptural and are bathed in subtle light, a clear move away from the dramatically lit and sinewy characters of the *Horatii* (see 62) and *Socrates* (see 66). David took great trouble over the details in this painting of courtship and physical attraction. A statue of Venus, goddess of love, is placed on a column at the left, and we also see two wreaths of myrtle, an evergreen sacred to Venus and an emblem of conjugal fidelity. The painting examines the differing emotions that Helen feels towards Paris because, according to Homer's account in the *Iliad*, Paris won Helen over even though he had been defeated in combat by her husband Menelaus. This seduction had the tragic consequence of starting the Trojan War, when Paris took Helen back to Troy as his wife and the incensed Greeks laid siege to the city for ten years. Helen stands, her head inclined, attracted by the handsome Paris yet still harbouring doubts. Paris' passion is understated and simply suggested by the gentle grasping of Helen's arm. For

74
The Loves of Paris and Helen, 1788.
Oil on canvas; 147 × 180 cm, $57\frac{7}{8} \times 70\frac{7}{8}$ in.
Musée du Louvre, Paris

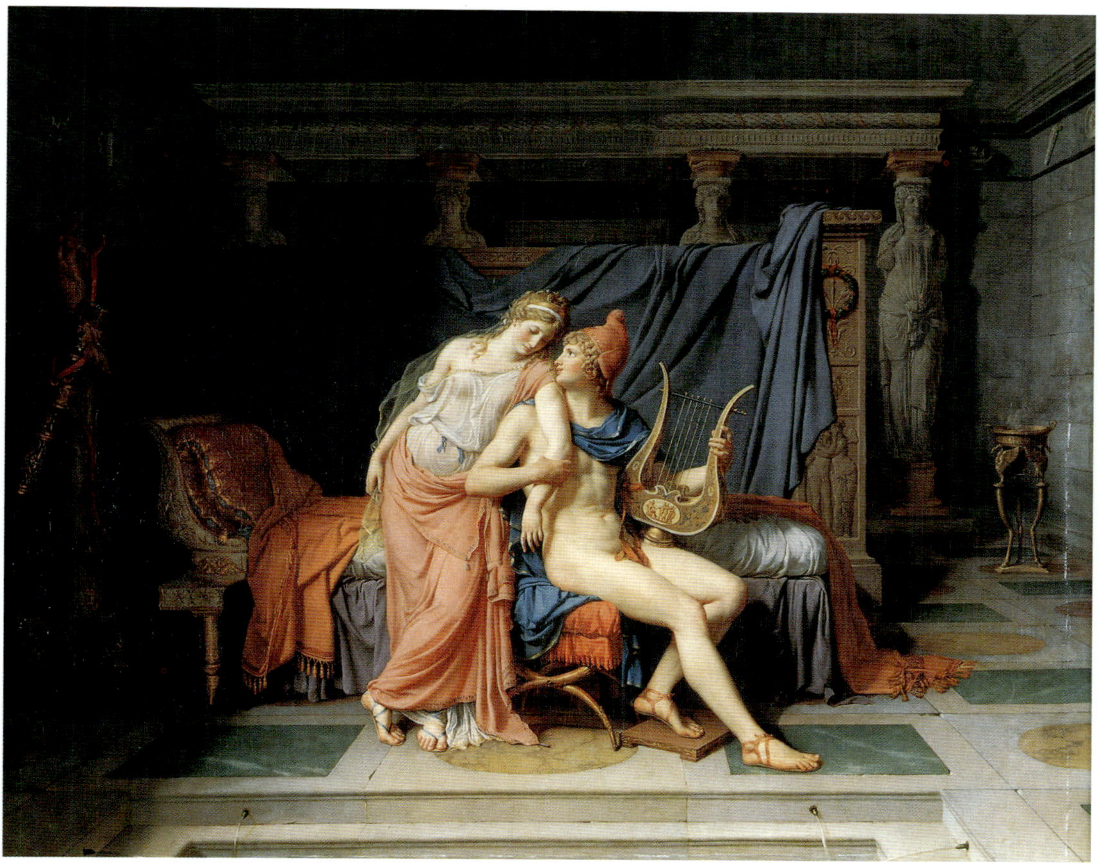

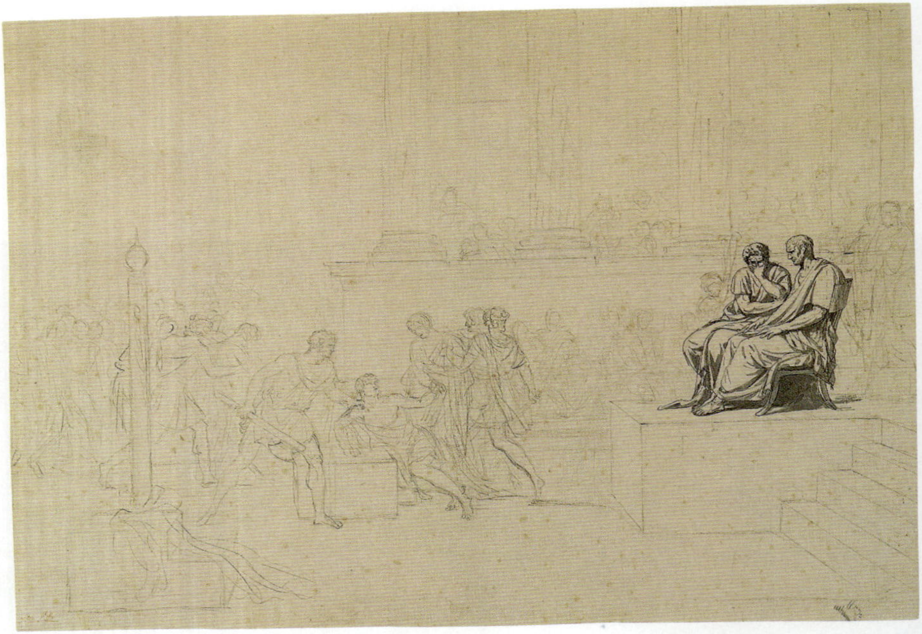

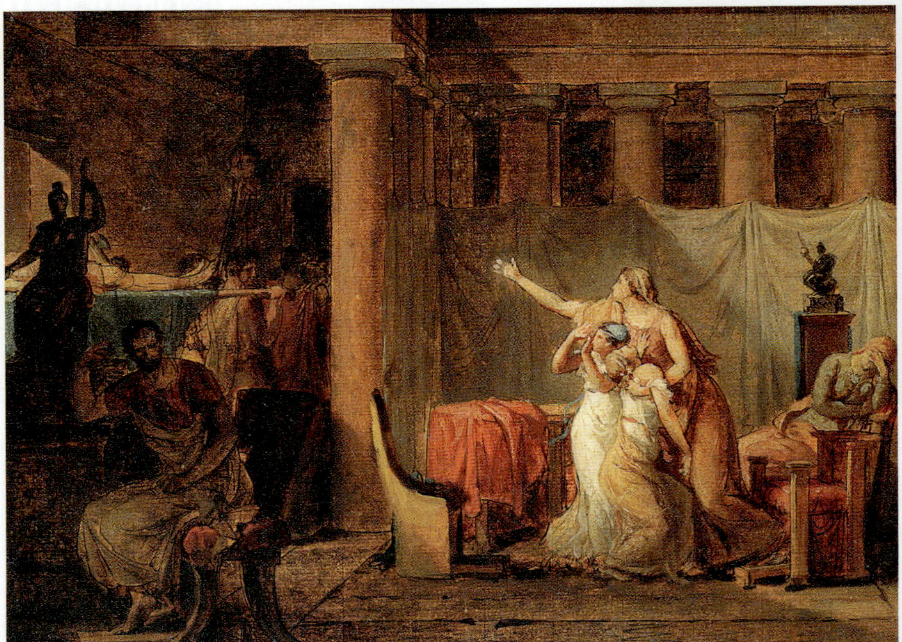

added, although incorrect, detail in the background, David included four caryatids (columns in the shape of female figures) copied from the Salle des Cent-Suisses in the Louvre.

In *The Loves of Paris and Helen*, David went to great lengths to show his versatility and to demonstrate that he was not just a painter of heroic and masculine scenes. He described the painting as 'in the Greek and thoroughly antique manner', and the subject matter determined the elegant and refined treatment. It has been suggested that *The Loves of Paris and Helen* was a satire on the well-known scandalous and licentious behaviour of the Count d'Artois, and was thus a condemnation of royalty, although the count happily accepted the painting and nobody at the time detected anything political or subversive in it. But with the delicate political situation in Paris at the time, the fact that the painting belonged to the king's brother was omitted from the exhibition catalogue.

75
Brutus Attending the Execution of his Sons, c.1788. Graphite, pen and wash; 61 × 77·5cm, 24 × 30½ in. Private collection

76
Sketch for *Brutus*, 1789. Oil on canvas; 27·5 × 35cm, 10⅞ × 13¾ in. Nationalmuseum, Stockholm

David's second exhibit of 1789, *The Lictors Bringing Brutus the Bodies of his Sons* (77), was much more controversial from the start. Its full title was *J Brutus, First Consul, returned to his house after having condemned his two sons who had allied themselves with the Tarquins and conspired against Roman liberty; the lictors return their bodies so that they may be given burial*. This was the fulfilment of the Crown commission for the 1787 Salon that had not been delivered, and it seems likely that as a disciplinary measure Pierre attempted to have David excluded from carrying the work forward to the next Salon. But the order stood and David changed the subject from Coriolanus to Brutus, although it is not known whether or not this was done with the permission of the *Direction des Bâtiments du Roi*.

Lucius Junius Brutus (not to be confused with Julius Caesar's assassin Marcus Brutus, who lived some 500 years later), had helped to rid Rome of the last of its kings, the tyrannical Tarquin the Proud. This came about because Tarquin's son Sextus had raped the virtuous Lucretia. She then committed

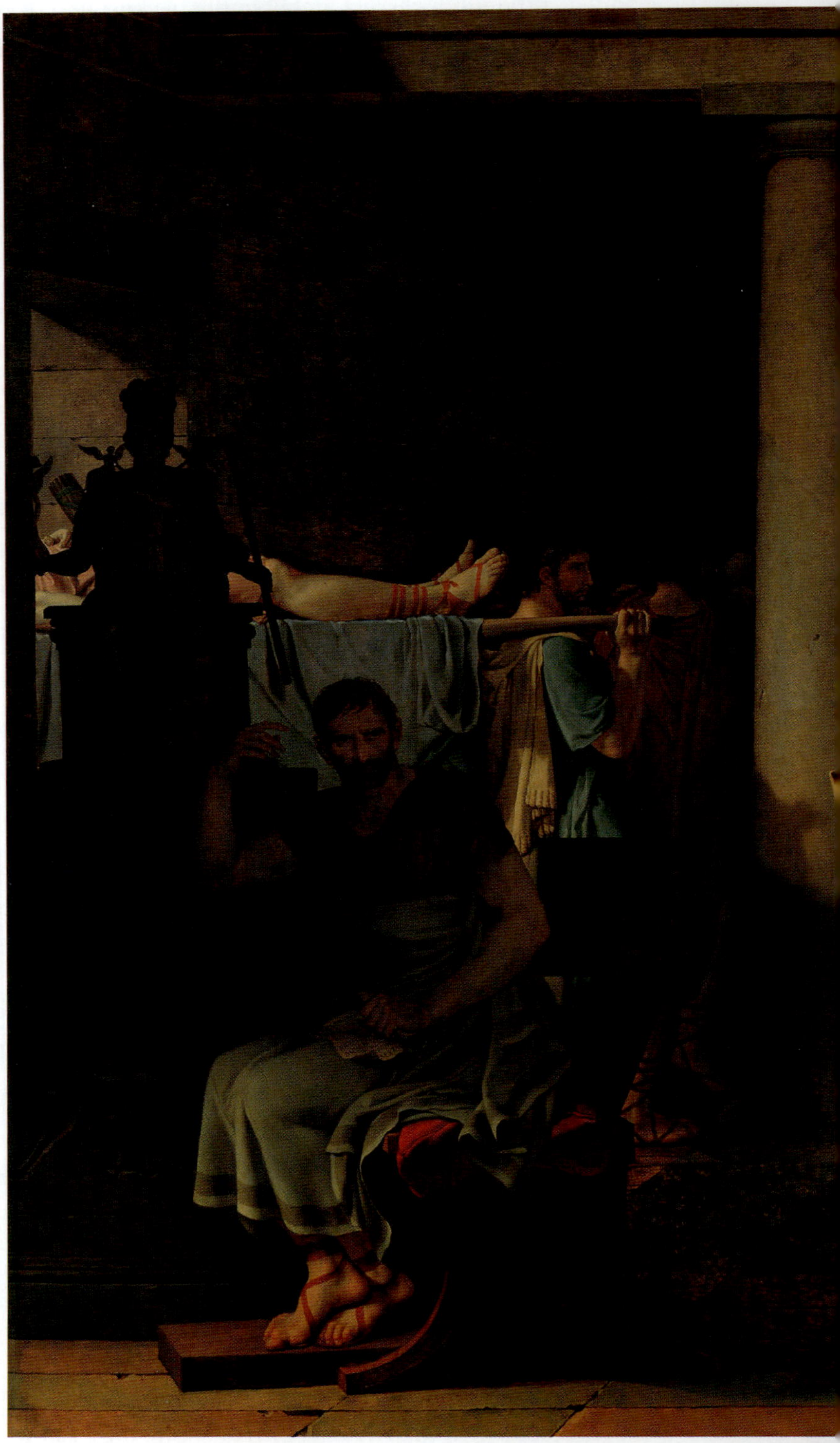

77
The Lictors Returning to Brutus the Bodies of his Sons,
1789.
Oil on canvas;
323 × 422 cm,
$127\frac{1}{8} \times 166\frac{1}{8}$ in.
Musée du Louvre, Paris

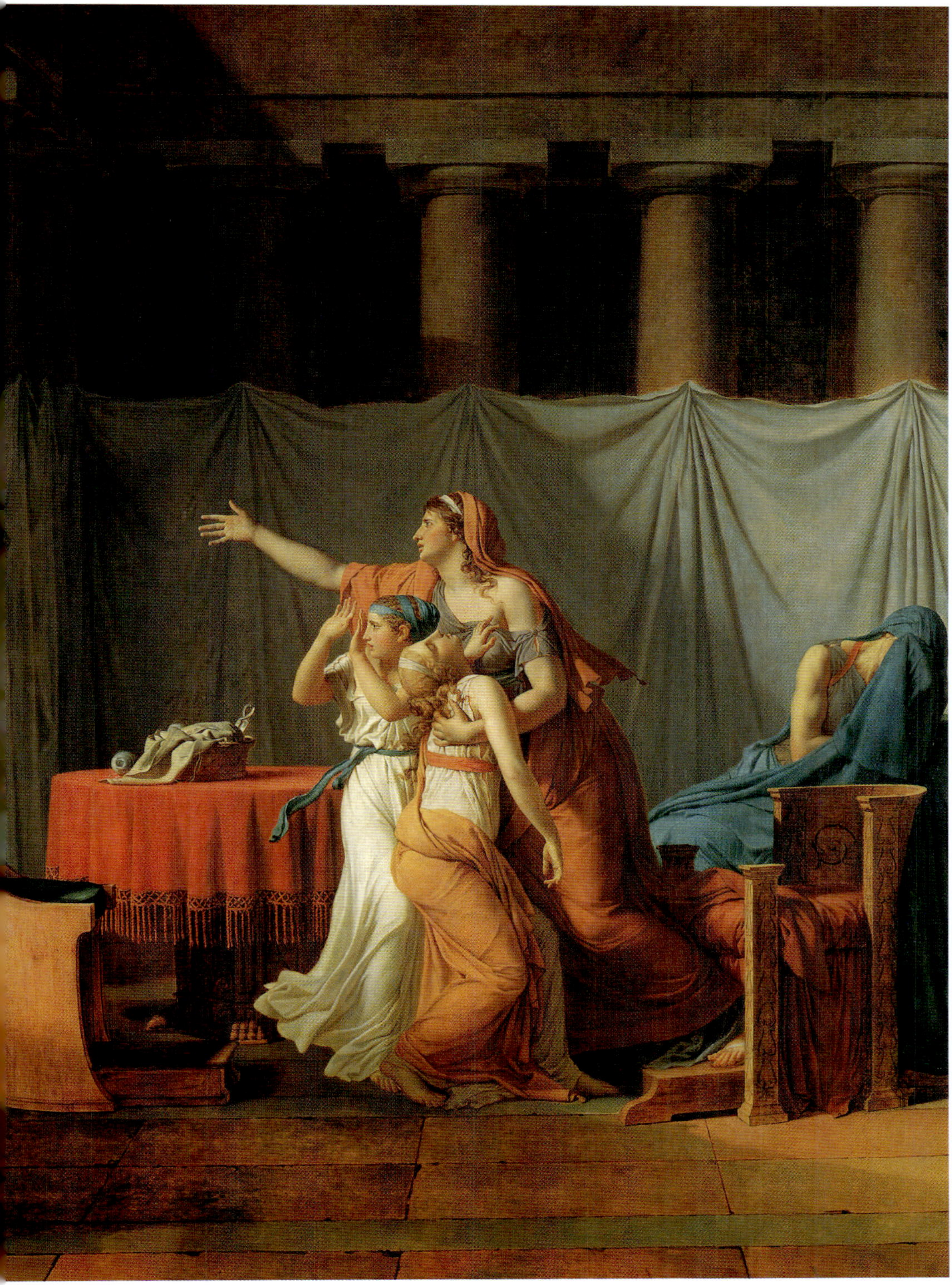

suicide in the presence of both her husband Collatinus and Brutus, who withdrew the knife from the fatal wound and swore on Lucretia's blood to avenge her death and destroy the corrupt monarchy. Tarquin was exiled, and the first Roman Republic was established in 508 BC, with Brutus and Collatinus elected as co-consuls. As the picture's title tells us, Brutus' two sons, Titus and Tiberius, were drawn into a royalist conspiracy to return Tarquin, and their father condemned them to death. This was another picture about Roman patriotism, and David's

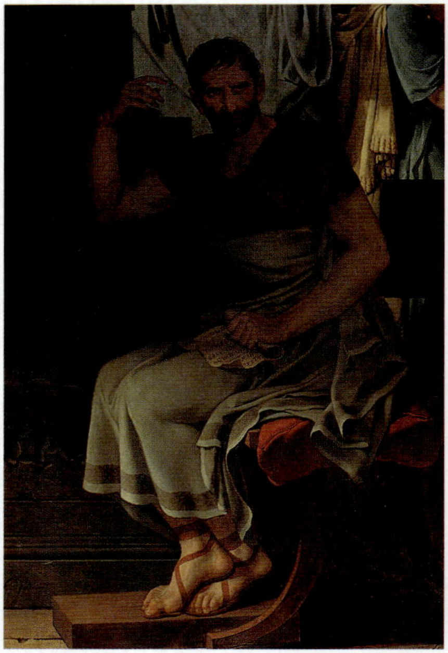

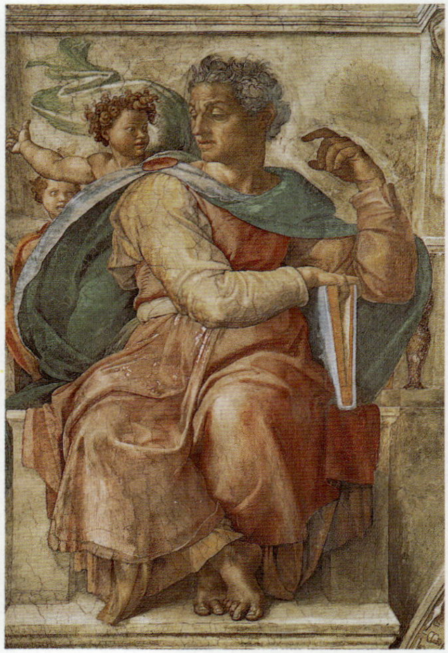

first idea had been to show Brutus dispassionately witnessing the execution of his two sons (75), but he then decided to shift the scene from the public to the private and show Brutus in his own home. So the *Brutus*, like the *Horatii*, became a painting about the conflict between duty to the nation and the love of the family, and also about how men and women respond differently to such a dilemma. Brutus' extreme patriotism had long been a recommended subject for painters, and he provided a very potent symbol of unflinching devotion to the state. Yet when looking at David's painting today, we should be careful of using a knowledge of the future course of the Revolution to colour our view of it. Although Brutus was instrumental in ridding Rome of the last of the kings, the Tarquins, and Louis XVI was sent to the guillotine in 1793, such a course of events was not envisaged by even the most ardent revolutionary in 1789. The removal of Louis came only as a last resort after all efforts at a constitutional monarchy, as in Britain, had failed. It should also be remembered that David had actually thought about painting the subject as early as 1786.

78
The Lictors Returning to Brutus the Bodies of his Sons (detail of 77)

79
Michelangelo, The prophet Isaiah from the Sistine Chapel Ceiling, Rome, 1508–12. Fresco

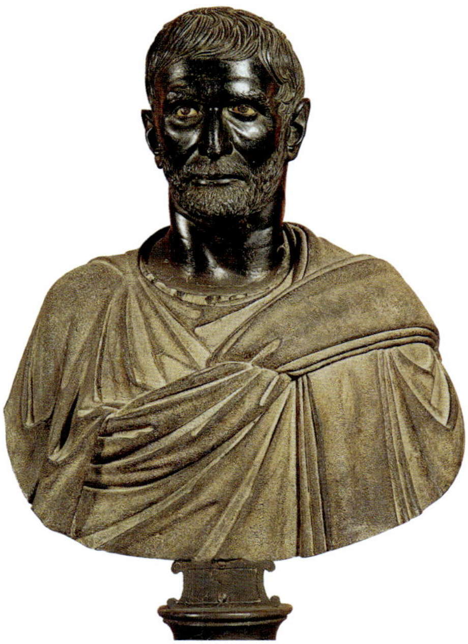

80
Capitoline Brutus, 3rd century BC. Bronze. Capitoline Museum, Rome

But although the *Brutus* was not a call for the abolition of the monarchy, this does not mean that it was entirely without a political dimension. David would have been fully aware of the capacity of the Brutus story to provoke controversy. In the crisis years of 1788–9 patriotism and the national good became even more topical, and any painting on those subjects was likely to attract attention. In fact some attempt was made by the *Direction des Bâtiments du Roi* to prevent the painting being shown at the Salon, but when news of this leaked out, the popular outcry made such an action impossible. In all likelihood one detail alone made the authorities uncomfortable. In his sketch (76) David had shown the severed heads of the two sons carried in on pikes, something that was painfully reminiscent of recent events in Paris, and so for the sake of decorum and good taste he omitted them in the final painting.

In a letter of 14 June 1789 to his former pupil Wicar, David gave his own explanation of the work: 'I am doing a painting of my own invention. It is Brutus, man and father, who has deprived himself of his children and who has returned to his home, where are brought to him the bodies of his two sons for burial. He is interrupted in his distress, at the foot of the statue of Rome, by the cries of his wife, the fear and the fainting of his eldest daughter.' For this grim and terrible event David adopted a compositional format that was even more radical than that of the *Horatii*. The main character, Brutus, is placed at the extreme left, plunged into deep shadow (78). His body is tense and knotted as he broods over the consequences of his act, he grasps the death warrant and clenches his feet one across the other. This last detail, in addition to the position of his arms, was probably taken from the figure of the prophet Isaiah on the Sistine Chapel Ceiling by Michelangelo (1475–1564; 79). David said that 'there is something Florentine in the rendering of my Brutus' by which he meant a shared feeling of sombre and grim power with Michelangelo. The pose of Brutus was possibly inspired by an engraving after the painting *Count Ugolino* of 1771 by Sir Joshua Reynolds (1723–92), one of his rare excursions into history painting. In a story taken from Dante, Ugolino, his sons and grandsons were imprisoned, and it gradually dawned on the old man that they were to be starved to death. The painting shows the terrible moment of Ugolino's realization that he will have to resort to cannibalism to survive. Ugolino and Brutus thus had much in common and both are represented as isolated, withdrawn and reflective. For the sake of accuracy David based the features of Brutus on a famous antique bust, the so-called Capitoline Brutus (80), of which he owned a copy. On the other side of the image

81
The Lictors Returning to Brutus the Bodies of his Sons
(detail of 77)

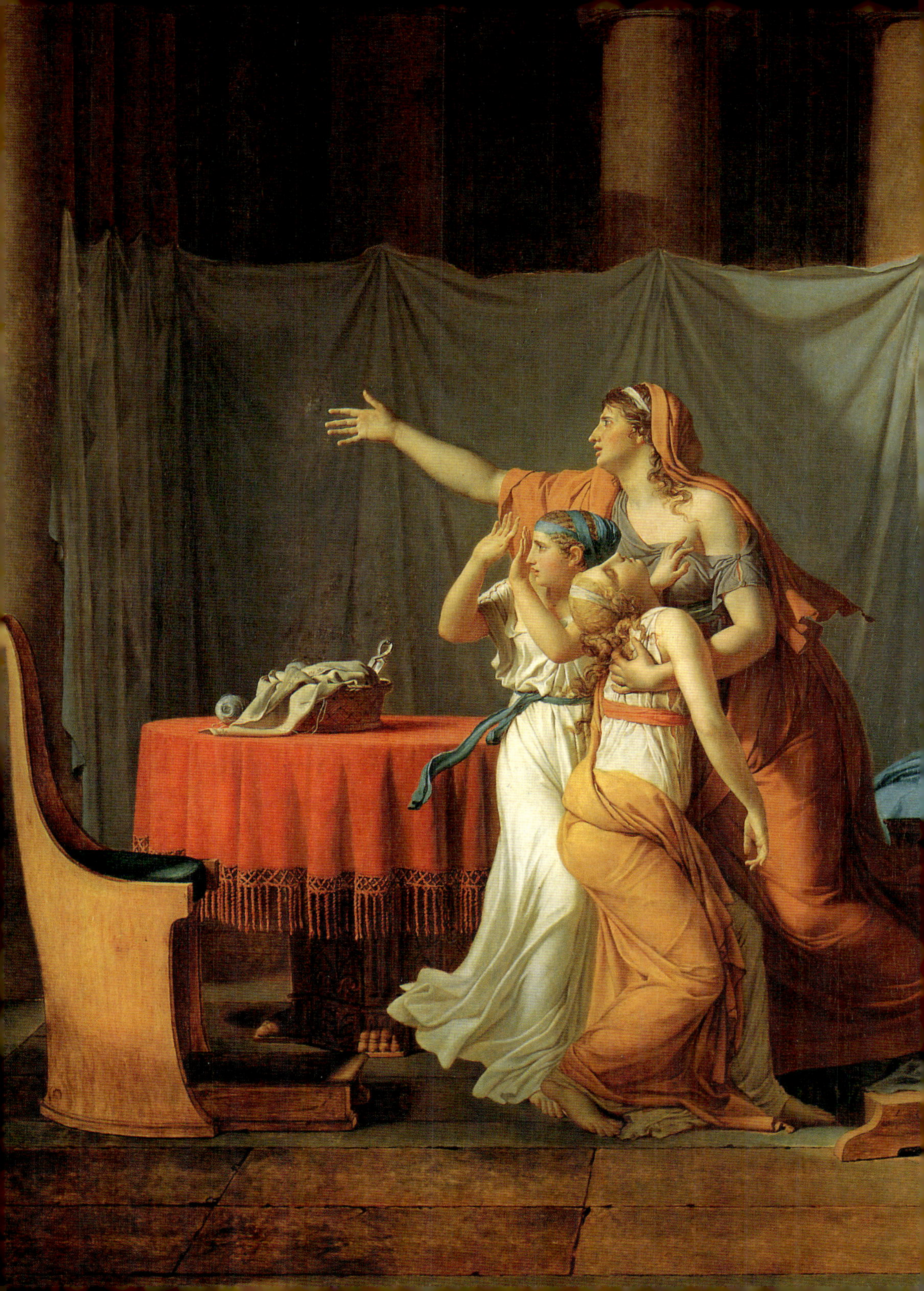

the inconsolable women are brightly illuminated and one could be forgiven for thinking that they are the picture's main subject (81). The centre of the picture is taken up by a still life of a sewing basket, an emblem of domesticity, which is rendered in stark clarity. As well as using his past Roman sketchbooks for details, David also produced drawings for antique style furniture which were then made by the famous cabinet-maker Jacob for him to copy from and incorporate into the picture. He also asked Wicar in Rome for help with the hairstyle of the fainting daughter and posted a drawing of her to him requesting that he fill in the correct details from a sculpture of the Bacchantes. In the ancient world the Bacchantes were roused into ecstatic frenzy by the god Bacchus and their poses were often used in Roman art to suggest hysterical and unrestrained grief. David must have been thinking about such figures when planning the pose of the daughter who collapses in sorrow.

David invites the spectator to judge Brutus. Is he the ultimate patriot who does not shrink from sacrificing his own sons, or is he an unfeeling monster who tears his family apart? Plutarch wrote that Brutus' action was 'open alike to the highest commendation or the strongest censure', and that his character was 'at one and the same time that of a god and that of a beast'. Even more so than in the *Horatii*, the picture is fragmented and broken up by the reactions of the figures to the arrival of the bodies. Pierre is supposed to have said to David: 'You have in your *Horatii* given us three personages in the same plane, something never seen before! Here you have put your principal actor in shadow ... but where have you seen that a composition can be made without using the pyramidal line?' In reality Pierre could never have seen the finished work as it was not completed until late August, and he had died on 15 May – it is possible that he saw the sketch or examined the work in progress. Critics seeing the work remarked upon its novelty and used such adjectives as 'noble', 'severe' and 'virile' to describe it, and almost all of them considered David once again to be the Salon's victor. As the Revolution proceeded

David's picture acquired a topicality that he could not have foreseen and its dreadful subject and memorable image entered the public's consciousness. At the end of a performance of Voltaire's play *Brutus* at the National Theatre on 19 November 1790, to the thunderous applause of the audience, the actors and actresses grouped themselves into a living representation of David's famous picture.

Politics had a more direct effect on another of David's works which should have been shown in 1789, the *Portrait of Antoine-Laurent and Marie-Anne Lavoisier* (82), painted in the previous year. Lavoisier was an eminent experimental physicist and chemist, a very wealthy tax farmer (an investor in a company hired by the government to collect duties on commodities – something for which he was later guillotined) and a member of the liberal intellectual élite that advocated moderate reform. He was also a Freemason which was possibly his point of contact with David. As a scientist he was also Commissioner for Gunpowder and had nearly been lynched on 6 August in a riot at the Paris arsenal when it was thought that gunpowder stocks were being removed from the city. With the supply of arms and munitions such a sensitive concern at the time, it was thought imprudent to allow a portrait of the commissioner to be shown and so it was suppressed. The portrait is strongly reminiscent of *The Loves of Paris and Helen* (see 74), the main difference being that while Lavoisier's wife, Marie-Anne, engages the viewer, Helen averts her gaze. Madame Lavoisier leans like an inspirational muse against her husband's shoulder, almost like a decorative addition, though this was far from the role she actually occupied. In reality she was an indispensable assistant who studied drawing with David in order to illustrate and record her husband's experiments and learned English so that she could translate the work of British scientists. Her drawing portfolio rests on the chair and she probably also gave David drawings of the experimental apparatus on the right. These expensive items, custom-made for Lavoisier, are given great prominence both for their unusual visual appeal

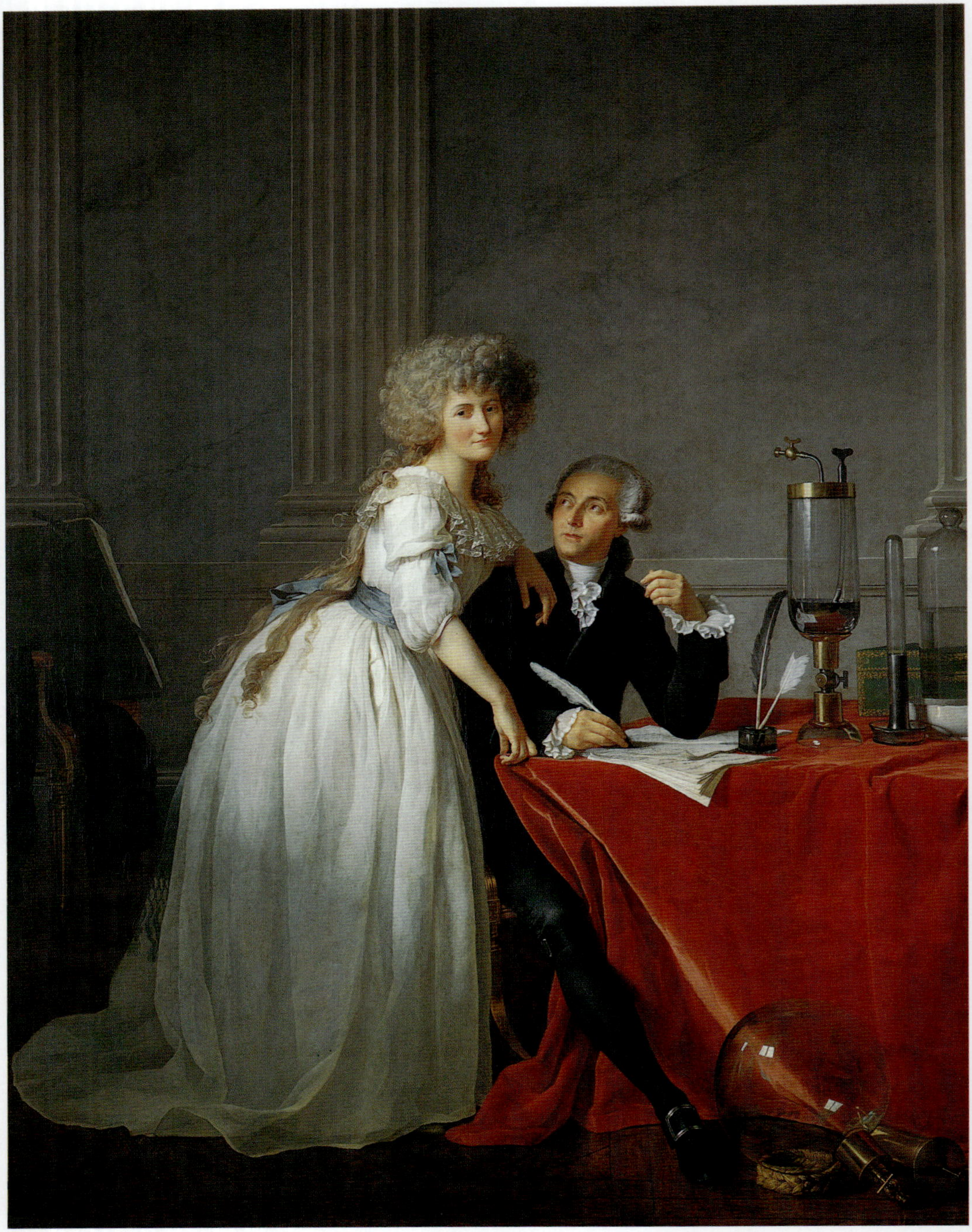

and to locate the couple in their working environment. In the centre of the table is a gasometer, and to the right a simple barometer and a pneumatic trough, while at Lavoisier's feet is a glass flask with a stopcock. For this very grand full-length work David was paid the considerable sum of 7,000 livres – more than he had received from the king for the *Horatii*. The precise observation present in the portrait is worthy of Lavoisier's own meticulous recording of scientific data, and although painted as a commercial transaction, it appears almost like the tribute of one enlightened and cultivated individual to a couple of equal rank and intelligence.

On 26 August 1789, shortly before the *Brutus* reached the walls of the Salon, the National Assembly adopted the *Declaration of the Rights of Man and Citizen* (83) which had as its first principle: 'Men are born and remain free and equal in rights'. For some little time David had been agitating against the Academy, and the Revolution gave him the opportunity to mount a sustained attack against it. Years of discontent and brooding malice against the Academy meant that David felt a disgust for its officers and their undemocratic privileges, and for its blinkered and repetitive teaching methods. He was joined in his attacks by a few dissatisfied fellow Academicians and by rebellious students, and his apartments in the Louvre became the regular meeting place for the dissidents. David first demanded that his lamented pupil Drouais should be made a posthumous Academician, so that his works could be shown as a memorial at the next Salon. This was refused and the Academy's officers presented such stubborn opposition that David and his colleagues had to call on the sympathetic politicians of the Paris Commune, the National Assembly and later the radical Jacobin Club, a political pressure group so called because they held their meetings in the former monastery of the Dominicans of St James (Jacobus in Latin), for leverage. But David gradually moved from pushing for reform to demanding the complete abolition of the Academy, and he clearly saw himself as the head of a new artistic order.

82
Portrait of Antoine-Laurent and Marie-Anne Lavoisier, 1788.
Oil on canvas; 259·7 × 194·6 cm, $102\frac{3}{8} \times 76\frac{5}{8}$ in.
Metropolitan Museum of Art, New York

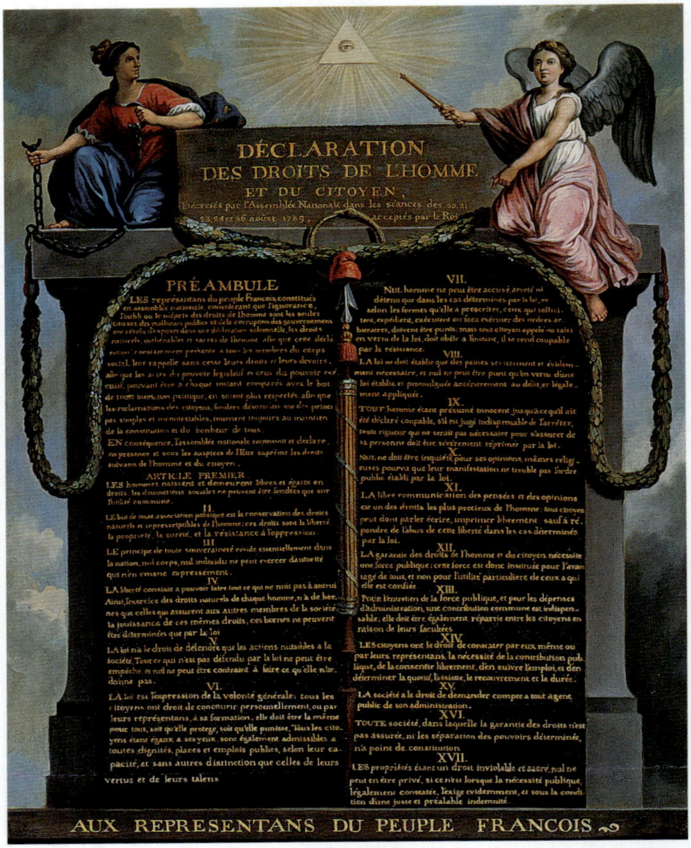

83
Declaration of the Rights of Man and Citizen,
1789.
Musée Carnavalet, Paris

On 27 September 1790 a new democratic art society was founded, the Commune des Arts, with 300 members and David as its leader. Perhaps in an effort to placate him, in July 1792 the Academy appointed David an associate professor, but when in April 1793 he was called to exercise his duties of posing the model in the life class, David wrote a terse note which read: 'I was formerly of the Academy.' Finally, in his role as deputy of the National Convention (the successor to the Assembly), he delivered a speech to his fellow deputies on 8 August 1793 which signalled the end of the Academy and his total victory. This speech contained a multitude of personal details and observations and was the summation of over twenty years of dissatisfaction with the Academy. It ended: 'In the name of humanity, in the name of justice for those who love art, and, above all, in the name of your love for youth, let us destroy, let us annihilate those sinister Academies. They must not be allowed to exist in the reign of liberty.' On 12 August the Convention decreed that all Academies should be suppressed, their buildings sealed and their property and equipment sequestered. David was appointed to the committee charged with overseeing this operation. But although he was a very active figure in denouncing the iniquities of the Academy, his actions alone did not achieve its closure. Since 1791 the Convention had required the wholesale reform of all learned academies as well as guilds and corporations of craftsmen, and this process was concluded by the August 1793 decree that rid the nation of these exclusive and privileged bodies. Ironically, though, the Academy came to be replaced in 1795 by an even more élite body, the Institute, and David had no qualms about being a founding member.

Personal vengeance and dissatisfaction were the prime motives for his attacks on the Academy; a disinterested concern for the training of young students and the professional development of colleagues were only marginal issues. Some alleged that David was frustrated by his lack of promotion within the official system and that he wanted to be an artistic dictator. His direct adversary in the battles over the Academy, its secretary Antoine Renou, gave a shrewd, if biased, opinion: 'Apart from his talent Monsieur David is a negligible man. Moreover he is full of pride and contempt for his colleagues; he wants to destroy the Academy by force of slander because the King has not made him Director of the French Academy in Rome, a position he is quite incapable of filling, because it is almost a diplomatic post ... Such a post could not go to a man who, outside the limits of his talent, does not know how to comport himself and cannot speak properly.'

Inevitably David's activities against the Academy led to the sacrifice of personal friendships. A permanent rupture took place between David and Madame Vigée-Lebrun because his

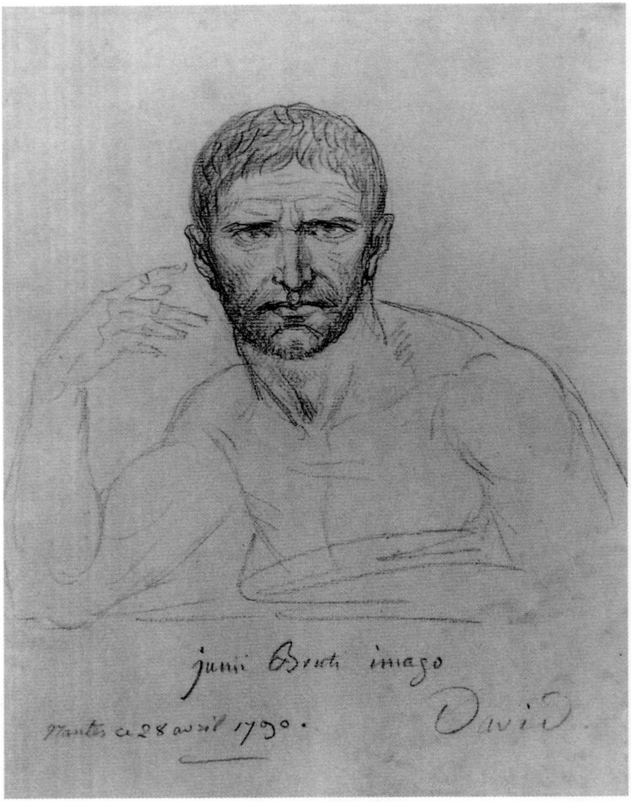

84
Brutus,
1790.
Black chalk;
22·3 × 18·6 cm,
$8\frac{3}{4} \times 7\frac{3}{8}$ in.
Private collection

85
Drawing for *Nantes Allegory* (Study after Michelangelo),
1790.
Black chalk;
18 × 11 cm,
$7 \times 4\frac{3}{8}$ in.
Album 7, folio 8 recto.
Musée du Louvre, Paris

stance against privilege irrevocably alienated him from this royal favourite. As director of the Academy and the king's First Painter, his former master Vien also had to endure many attacks, mostly directed at his position rather than at his person, and though estranged for a while, they were later reconciled. Perhaps most importantly, these struggles with the Academy had a longer lasting significance and were David's political training ground, providing a platform for his entry into politics proper.

From 1789 to 1791 David, although supportive of the Revolution, played no active part in it and was concerned only with artistic matters. In December 1789 he was approached by two former fellow students in Rome, the architect Mathurin Crucy (1749–1826) and the sculptor Jacques Lamarie, to create an allegory commemorating the role played by the city of

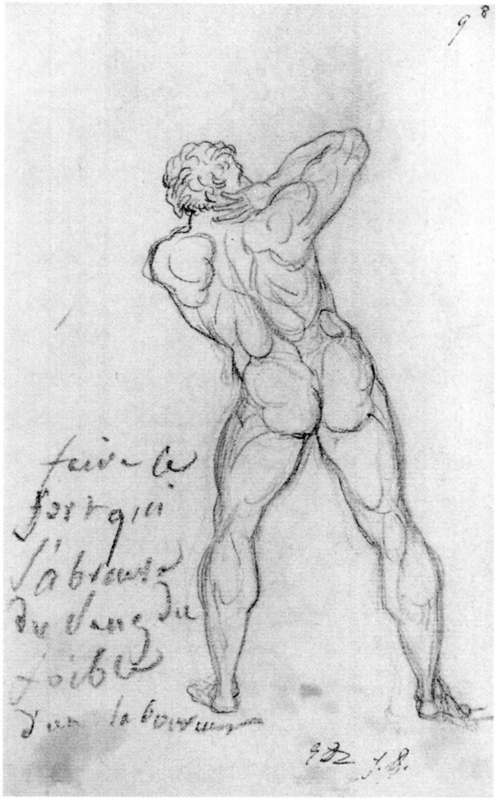

Nantes in the events leading up to the Revolution. Since allegory was unfamiliar territory for David, he had some reservations about how such a subject might be approached but he agreed to go to Nantes in March 1790 and stayed a month. There he was warmly welcomed and feted as France's leading painter and at one reception drew the head of Brutus to give his hosts an idea of his recent Salon success (84). But the Nantes authorities never gave him a formal commission and the project was abandoned with just a few figure drawings completed (85). But although nothing came of the Nantes allegory, it made David aware of the opportunities that the Revolution gave to history painters and he wrote: 'I am making it my duty to answer the noble invitations of patriotism and of glory that will consecrate the history of the most felicitous and most astonishing Revolution.'

At the time that he was starting work on the Nantes painting, David undertook a project for an even more important and prestigious commemoration of a revolutionary event – *The Oath of the Tennis Court*. The first anniversary of this event had recently been celebrated and great significance was already attached to it as the real start of the Revolution. The painting was proposed by the Paris Jacobin Club, of which David was a member from September 1790, and it was to be paid for by 3,000 subscriptions of twenty-four livres, with every subscriber receiving a print of the finished work. But this method proved unsuccessful and the government stepped in to guarantee the project. David considered this to be a good business venture as well as a piece of committed revolutionary painting, particularly because the political upheaval meant that work for the king had dried up.

David planned an epic depiction of the event, with the 600 deputies gathered together experiencing the emotion, drama and exhilaration of their momentous decision to remain in session until France was given a constitution. The painting was to be immense, about 7×10 m (23×33 ft), a size in keeping with the importance of an event that gave birth to a new France, and it was to be prominently displayed in the meeting room of the Assembly. David showed a highly finished drawing of *The Oath of the Tennis Court* (86) at the 1791 Salon, where it was actually one of the few depictions of the Revolution. Perhaps in order to emphasize the unified actions of the deputies as a collective body, the Salon *Livret* stated: 'The author has not intended to show a true likeness of the members of the Assembly.' But David had prepared lists of the most prominent foreground figures and many of them are recognizable. The central figure of the work is the Assembly President Jean-Sylvestre Bailly, who turns to address the spectator and gazes out impassively. This was an obvious piece of artistic licence because Bailly, as one might expect, actually faced his fellow deputies; he is turned around as a direct appeal to the spectator. Just below him appear a group of three ecclesiastics who joined the members of the Third Estate and welcomed the Revolution. On the left, in his Carthusian monastic habit, is Dom Gerle (who was not actually present), the Abbé Grégoire and Rabaut Saint-Etienne. They represent the regular clergy, the secular clergy and the Protestant church respectively. Their fraternal embrace symbolizes the creation of a new order, where division and factionalism are a thing of the past. All around, the massed ranks of the deputies raise their arms to swear the oath and also raise their hats into the air. To the right of Bailly, Maximilien Robespierre places both hands on his chest to signify his unbridled devotion. The very opposite to this committed action is seen in the right corner where Martin Dauch, the one deputy who refused to take the oath, sits with his head lowered and his arms folded obstinately across his chest. At the extreme left, the elderly Maupetit de la Mayenne is carried in from his sickbed to join the momentous event and to his right the priests Thiebault and Rewbell repeat the fraternal embrace of the ecclesiastics. On the window ledges and at the entrance on the left a variety of ordinary people hang onto vantage points and even climb up ladders eager to see what is happening and to witness this great event. Parents bring their children to see history taking place: on the left a mother supports her young daughter, while on the right the group in the first window is said to include David's two sons, Charles and Eugène. Beyond them, on the tiny balcony, is a group that includes a Royal Guard raising his sword, and a journalist, perhaps Jean-Paul Marat, writing his report. Although it was actually a hot summer's day, a storm is depicted to heighten the drama; a powerful wind blows the curtain, turns an umbrella inside out and causes onlookers to hold onto their hats. The violence of the weather is suggestive of an act of cleansing from which the land emerges renewed and invigorated. While some aristocratic critics saw this detail as indicative of a desire to destroy the royal family, David said that it represented the destruction of despotism. His Freemasonry may again have played some part in the

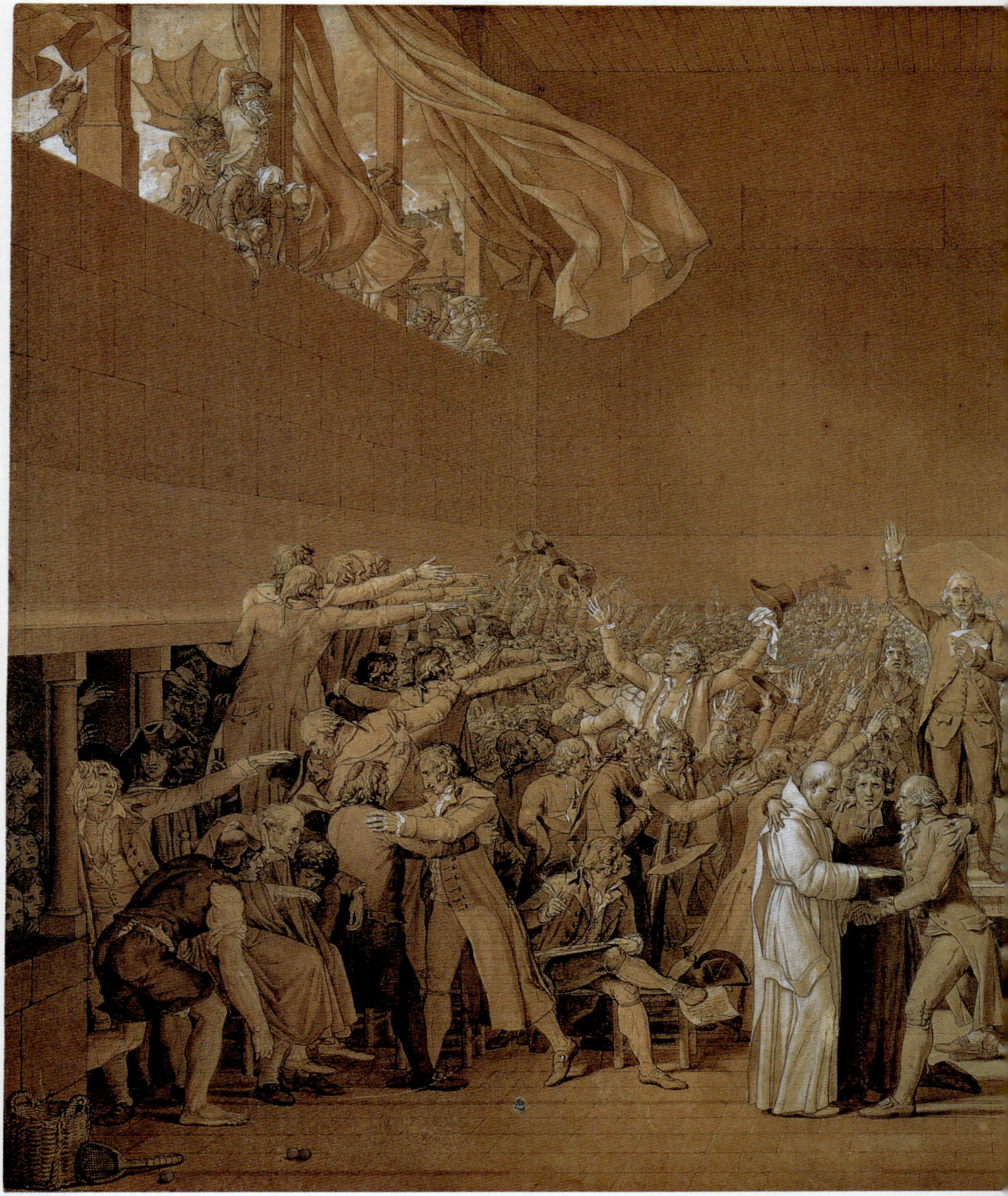

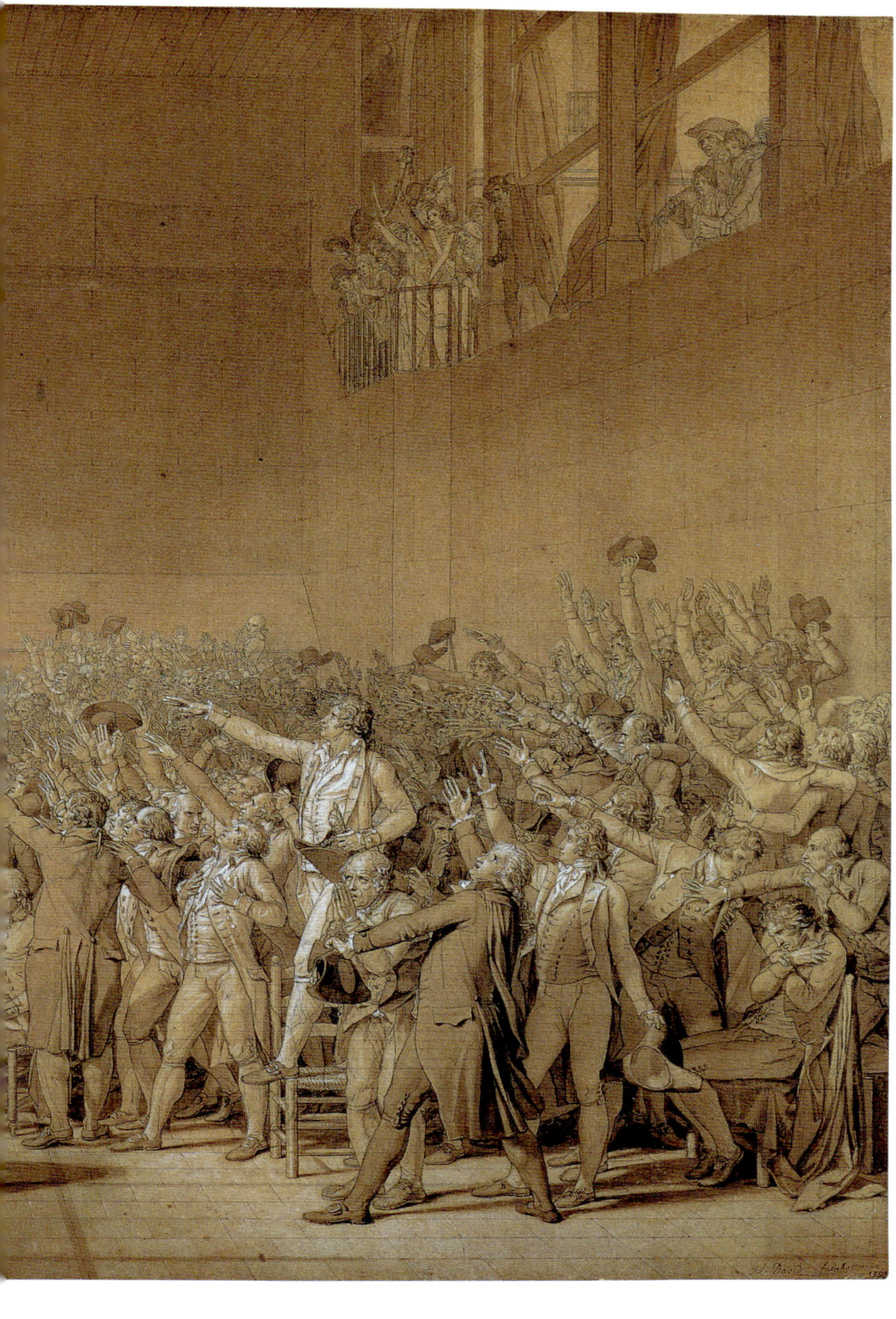

86
The Oath of the Tennis Court,
1791.
Pen and brown ink, brown wash with white highlights;
66 × 101·2 cm,
26 × 39⅞ in.
Musée National du Château de Versailles

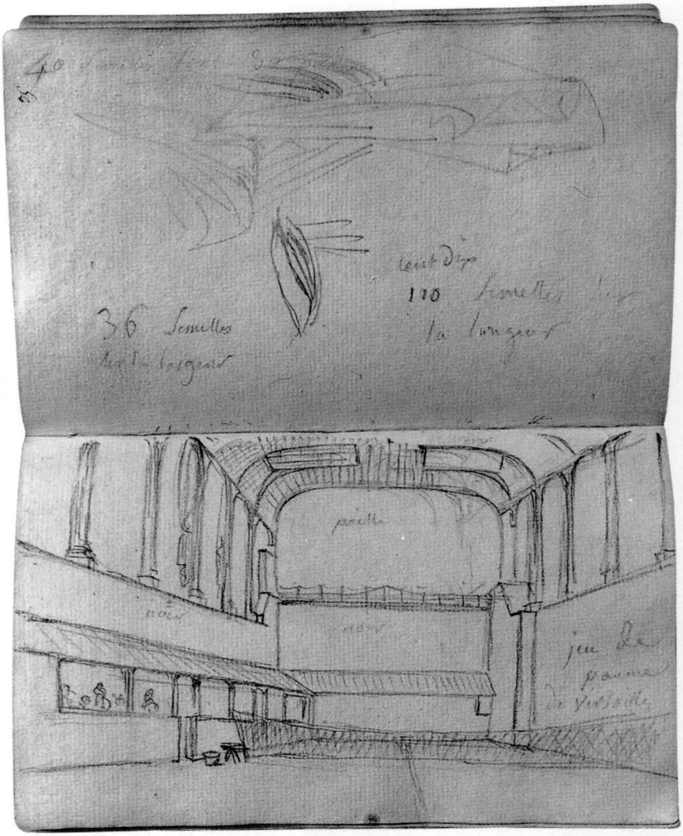

87
View of the interior of the tennis court, 1790/1.
Black chalk; each page: 12·5 × 19·2 cm, $4\frac{7}{8} \times 7\frac{1}{2}$ in.
Album, folio 33 verso.
Musée National du Château de Versailles

88
Studies of deputies swearing oaths, 1791.
Pen and ink and wash with black chalk; 49 × 60 cm, $19\frac{3}{8} \times 23\frac{5}{8}$ in.
Musée National du Château de Versailles

visualization of the event, and indeed some of the deputies, including Bailly, were Masons. Masonic lodges, meeting places combining business and philanthropic undertakings, helped spread the liberal ideas that fuelled the Revolution and the symbols of Freemasonry, especially the all-seeing eye (symbolizing vigilance) and the square or level (symbolizing equality) became part of revolutionary imagery.

David's drawing was warmly greeted by the popular press and by his friend André Chénier who dedicated an ode entitled 'The Tennis Court' to him. Chénier called David 'the King of the learned brush', and thought that the artist had done a great service to the Revolution by commemorating the creation of the nation's newly won liberty. Royalist critics, on the other hand, strongly objected to the work and accused David of treason.

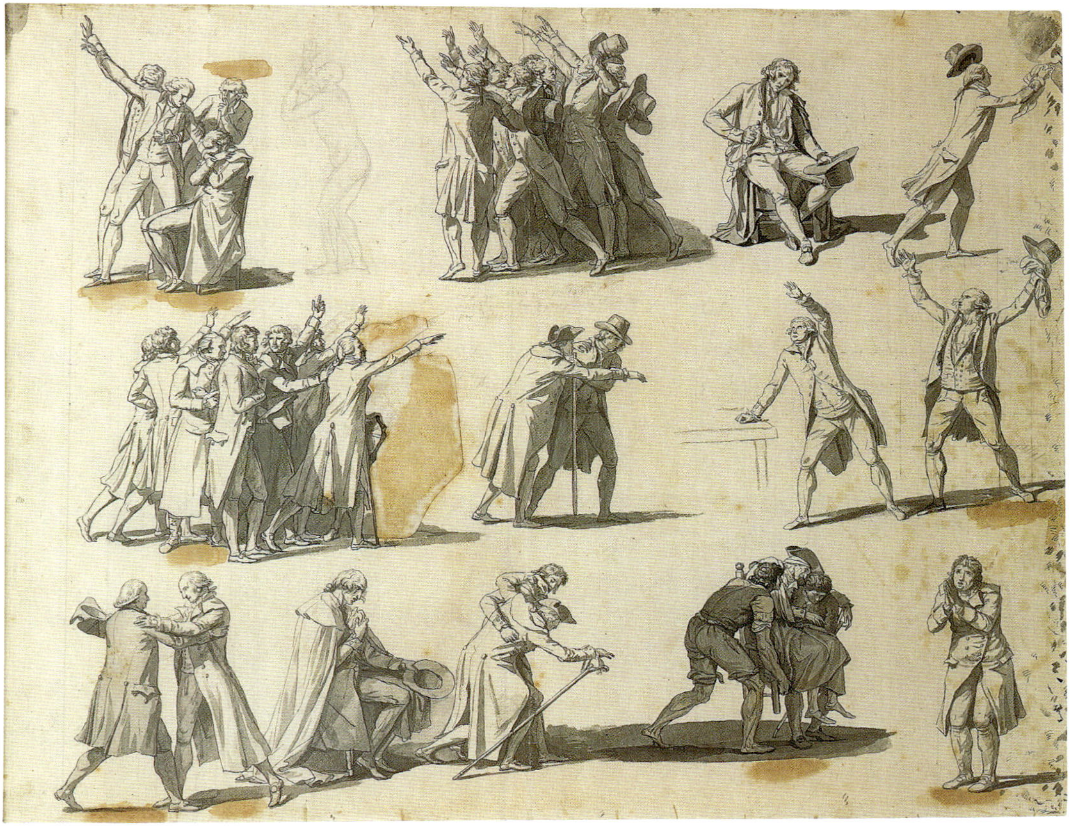

Such an ambitious project as *The Oath of the Tennis Court* required an enormous amount of preliminary work and David filled two sketchbooks and many individual sheets with details and figure studies. He went to Versailles and drew the empty tennis court (87), and experimented with the poses of the deputies (88). As he hadn't witnessed the oath, he wrote little notes on his sketches to remind himself of how characters should appear, and which small but telling details to include: 'do not forget to show the deputies moved to tears and holding their hands to their eyes', 'remember to show the dust that was raised by the movement of the action' and 'remember the bell' (used not very successfully by Bailly to call the noisy and animated deputies to order). David saw the oath as a modern and greatly expanded version of the *Horatii* and the deputies became the equivalents of the heroes of antiquity.

After showing the drawing, David moved on to the full-size canvas, and for this massive undertaking he was allocated a large studio in the nave of the deconsecrated church of the Feuillants, conveniently next door to the Tuileries Palace where the National Assembly met. On 4 October 1791 the following notice was published in the newspaper *Le Moniteur Universel*: 'Monsieur David requests the deputies who were present at Versailles for the Oath of the Tennis Court, and whose likenesses he has not been able to paint, to send him their engraved portraits; unless of course, they are able to make the journey to Paris during the time when he will be working on

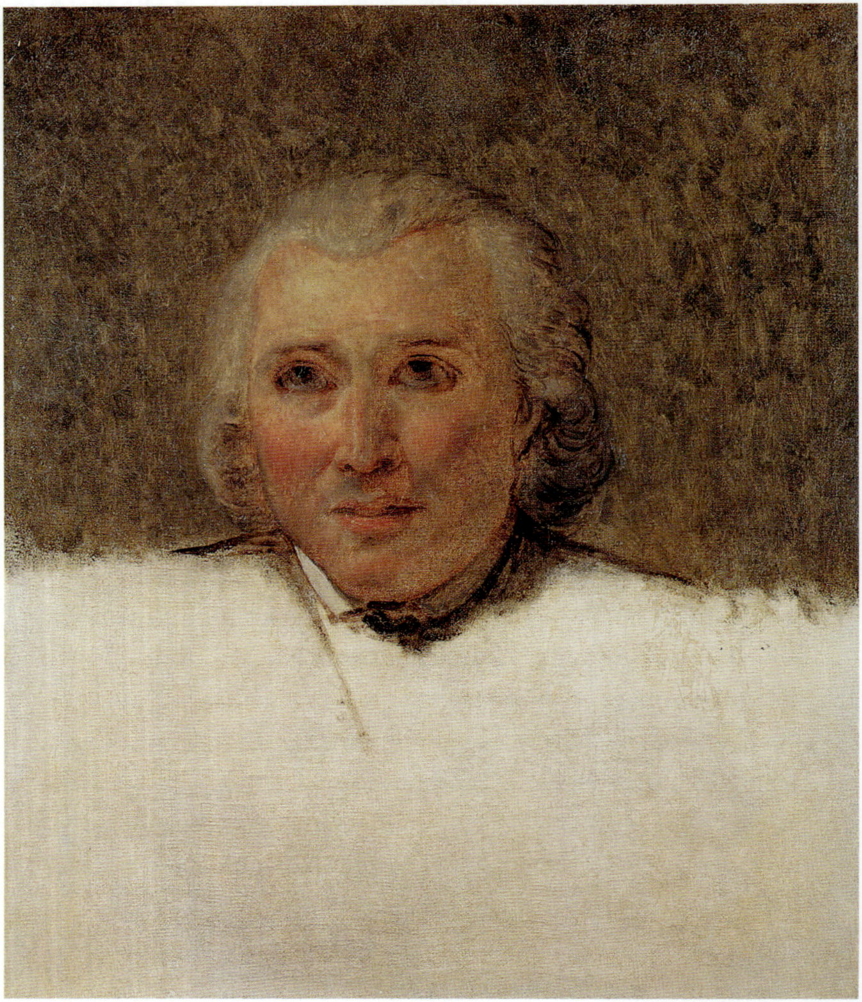

the painting, which he supposes will be about two years. In that case would they kindly come to his studio at the Feuillants.' He also wrote to individual deputies and on 20 November asked the Abbé Grégoire to come to pose with three other priests. Grégoire's portrait sketch (89) has survived, along with three or four others. As well as working from the deputies themselves, David and his three assistants employed a model to study poses. As a legacy of his training, David frequently first drew or painted his figures nude and then clothed them with the final paint layer. For help with the perspective drawing of the architecture of the tennis court, the architect and painter Charles Moreau (1762–1810) was drafted in.

The painting of *The Oath of the Tennis Court* was never completed and today only an unfinished fragment remains with the clergy and other figures outlined and the heads of four deputies finished (90). From the left these are Edmond-Louis-Alexis Dubois-Crancé, Père Gérard, the Comte de Mirabeau and Antoine Pierre Barnave. The painting had to be abandoned in the winter of 1791–2 because events had overtaken it. By then David's rather naïve vision of the Revolution which stressed fraternity and national unity was out of date. Some of those swearing the oath were now discredited and later went to the guillotine – Bailly had to resign as the Mayor of Paris in July 1791 after using the army to disperse a crowd and was guillotined in November 1793; Mirabeau had died in April 1791 just before his dealings with the king to establish a constitutional monarchy with himself as prime minister were discovered; Barnave was in the midst of converting to support the monarchy and was imprisoned in August 1792 and executed ten days before Bailly. Moreover, all the deputies that David had planned to commemorate were part of an élite middle class and by 1792 the Revolution had moved on to embrace 'the people' – those whom David confined to the position of excluded spectators in his version of the event. To continue might have been dangerous and led to awkward questions about David's loyalties and associations, and so he stopped work.

89
The Abbé Henri Grégoire, 1791.
Oil on canvas; 56 × 47 cm, 22 × 18½ in.
Musée des Beaux-Arts et d'Archéologie, Besançon

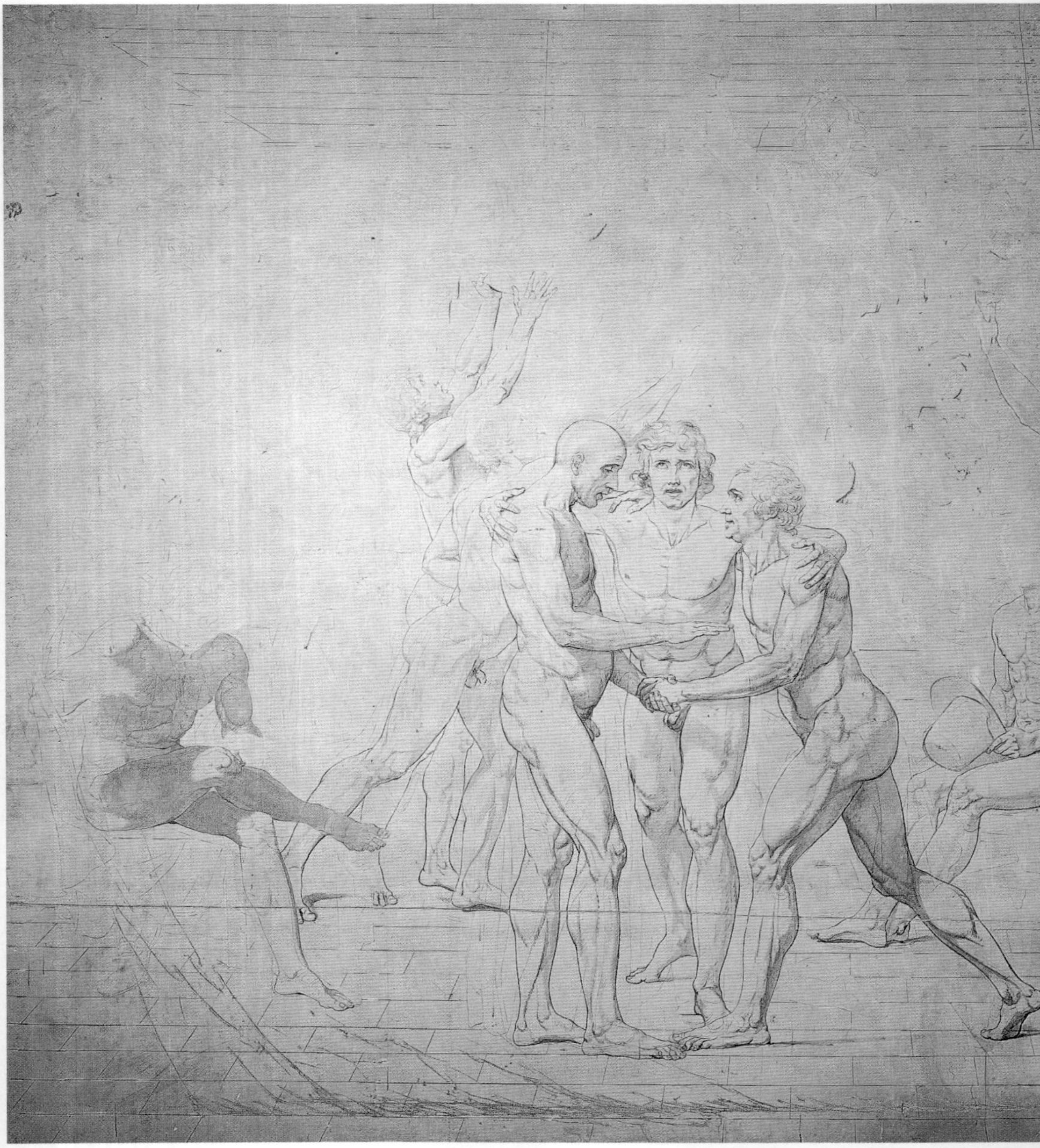

90
The Oath of the Tennis Court (unfinished), 1791–2.
Oil on canvas; 358 × 648 cm, 141 × 255⅛ in.
Musée National du Château de Versailles

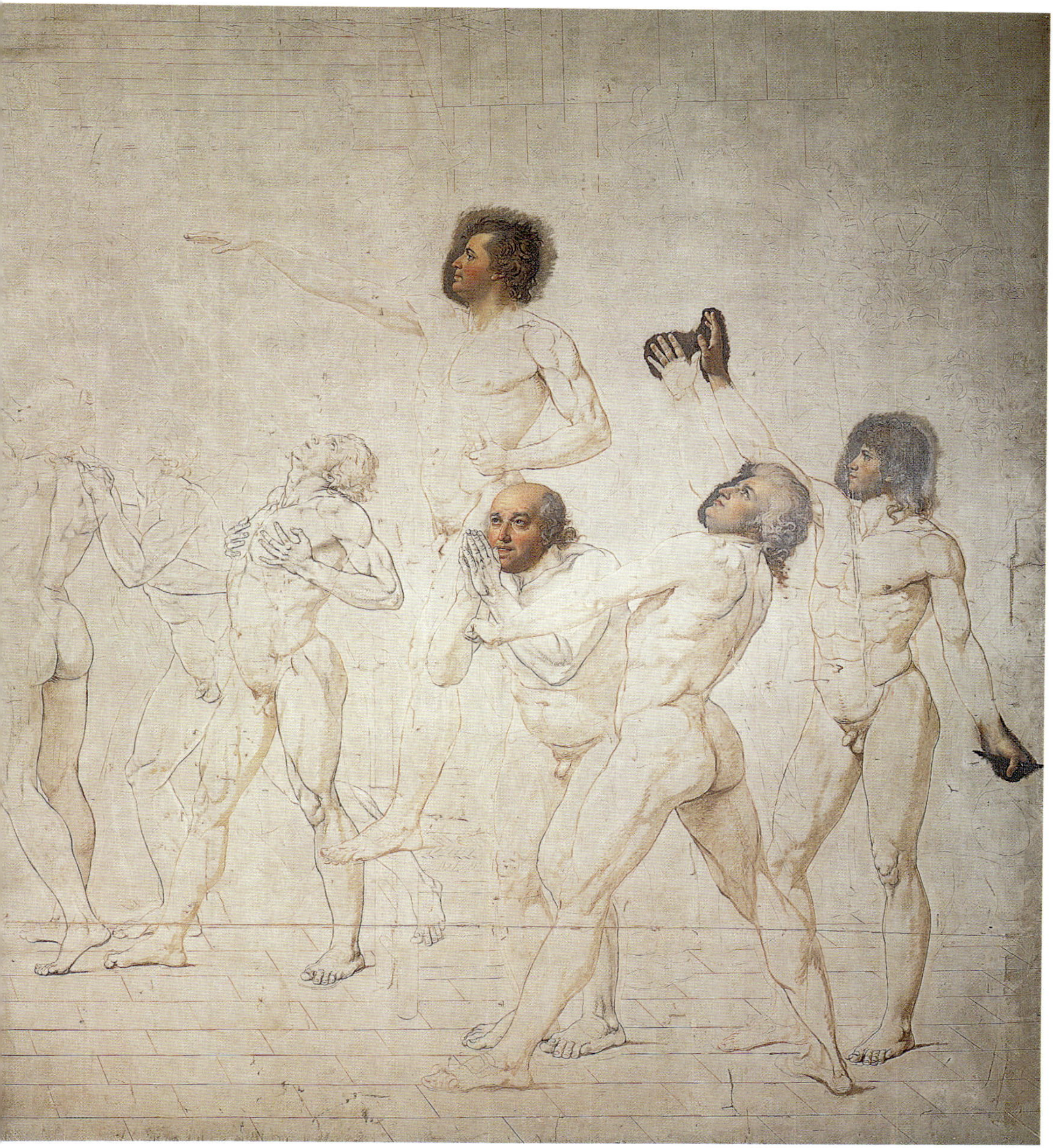

David's unfinished fragment stands as a reminder of the vicissitudes of both the Revolution and of his own career and reputation. He kept the huge canvas in the Feuillants studio where it was damaged on 10 August 1792 when the Royal Swiss Guards took refuge there and were slaughtered by the revolutionary National Guard – six bayonet holes have been found in it. David planned to complete the work around 1799–1800, but could not attract sufficient financial support from the government. It was rolled up and deposited in the Louvre in 1803, David retrieved it in 1819 and put it into the studio of Antoine-Jean Gros (1771–1835) for safe keeping. Just before the posthumous sale of the contents of David's studio in 1826 it was cut down to its present size, but still remained unsold. It was bought by the French state in 1836 when it was suggested that the four painted heads should be cut out. Finally, the canvas was placed in the Château of Versailles in 1921.

To David and many people in France it must have appeared that the excitement of real life was surpassing all the deeds of the heroic past. History was being made and they were part of it. People could see themselves as the equals of the noble and patriotic Romans, and antiquity, along with Freemasonry, provided the example for much revolutionary rhetoric and symbolism. As early as 7 September 1789, a delegation of twenty-one women artists and artists' wives, including Madame David, went to Versailles and handed the president of the Assembly a casket containing their jewels which they were donating for the benefit of the nation. This was a conscious re-enactment of a famous incident from Roman history when the noble ladies offered up their jewellery in a sacrifice to Apollo.

The Revolution brought David's paintings many new admirers. When the 1791 Salon was declared open to all artists, David decided not only to show the *Oath of the Tennis Court* drawing, but also to re-exhibit the *Horatii, Socrates* and *Brutus*. In the moral and patriotic climate of the Revolution, their direct and heroic messages seemed even more compelling and topical

91
Portrait of the Marquise d'Orvilliers,
1790.
Oil on canvas;
131 × 98cm,
$51\frac{1}{2} \times 38\frac{5}{8}$ in.
Musée du Louvre, Paris

92
Portrait of the Countess de Sorcy,
1790.
Oil on canvas;
129 × 97cm,
$50\frac{3}{4} \times 38\frac{1}{8}$ in.
Neue Pinakothek, Munich

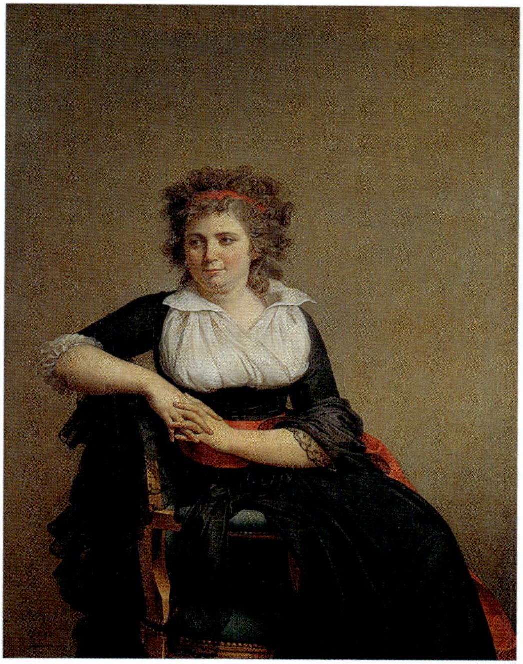

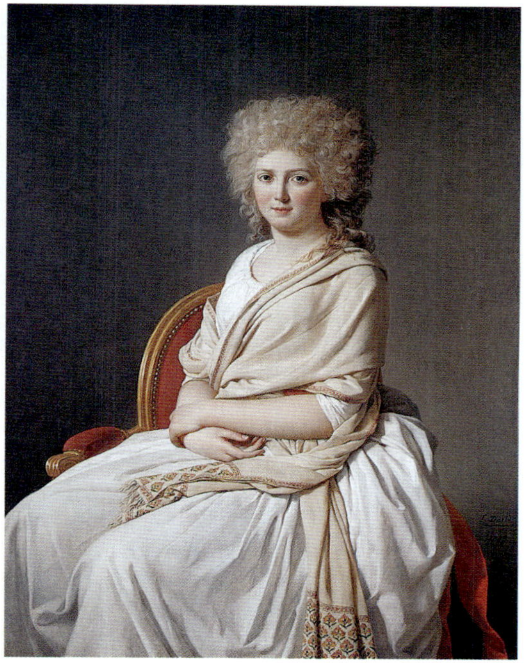

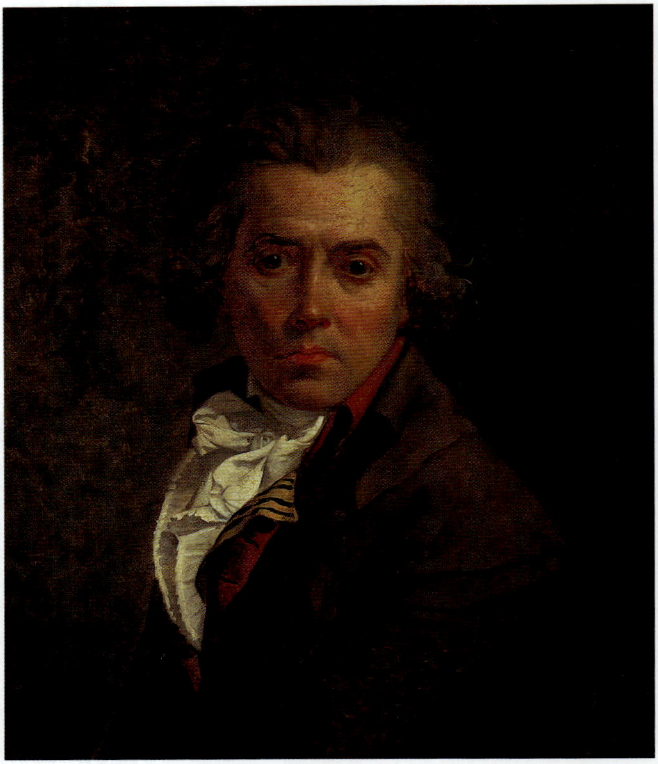

93
Self-Portrait,
1791.
Oil on canvas;
64 × 53cm,
$25^1{}_4 \times 20^7{}_8$in.
Galleria
degli Uffizi,
Florence

94
Portrait of Madame Adélaide Pastoret,
1791–2.
Oil on canvas;
129·9 × 96·6cm,
$51^1{}_8 \times 38$in.
The Art
Institute of
Chicago

than before and it was even said that 'they inflamed more souls for liberty than the best books'. David was rapidly becoming a public figure of some influence and no little ambition, but he was still some way away from being a political activist and continued to paint portraits of the cultivated upper classes and aristocracy. In 1790, a year of social calm, he had painted the Marquise d'Orvilliers (91) and the Countess de Sorcy (92). These two women were the Rilliet sisters, Robertine and Anne-Marie-Louise, who had both married rich and titled husbands, and David shows them dignified and at ease, wearing the simple fashions of the day.

In 1791 the pressures of the Revolution began to tell. David painted a *Self-Portrait* in that year (93), looking slightly dishevelled and with a piercing gaze, very different from the normally relaxed pose of his sitters and perhaps an indication of the internal conflicts that eventually led him to become a fully

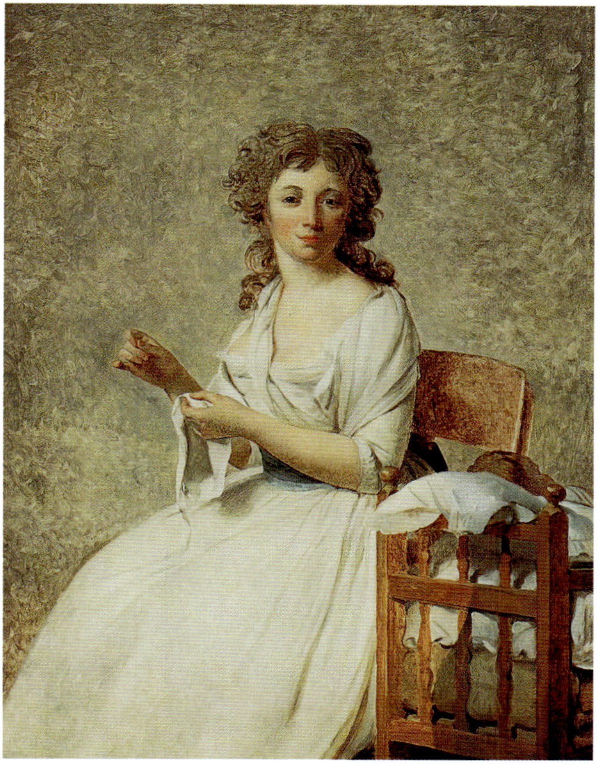

committed Republican. Around this time he also painted Madame Adélaide Pastoret (94), who, although of the upper class, is shown as a wife and mother without display of finery. The politics of the day called for homely virtues to be emphasized and any display of rank or status would have been considered suspect. Like so many of David's paintings of the Revolution, this work was not finished, as we can see from the incomplete quickly brushed shimmering background (*frottis*) and the absence of a sewing needle in Madame's hand. In all probability there was a split between the Pastorets and David over the latter's increasingly extreme politics, which meant that the portrait was left in its present state.

In the spring of 1792 David received a most unexpected commission. This was to paint the king in the act of showing the constitution to his heir, the Dauphin. David was certainly no royalist and the fact that he actually started work on the picture meant that he thought that it could be a positive contribution to the course of the moderate Revolution and also reminds us of the intrigues and complexities of the time. As well as studies for *Louis XVI Showing the Constitution to his Son, the Dauphin* (95), David also made drawings for an *Allegory of the French People Offering the Crown and Sceptre to the King* (96). The implication of the image was that power could be withdrawn if the king did not respect the constitution. But this work, too, was never completed, this time because of

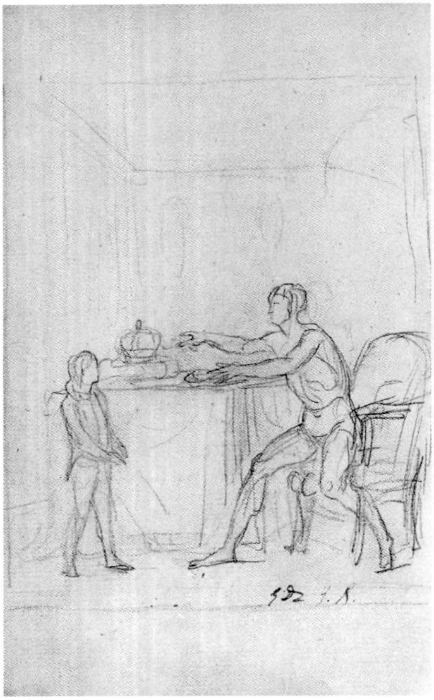

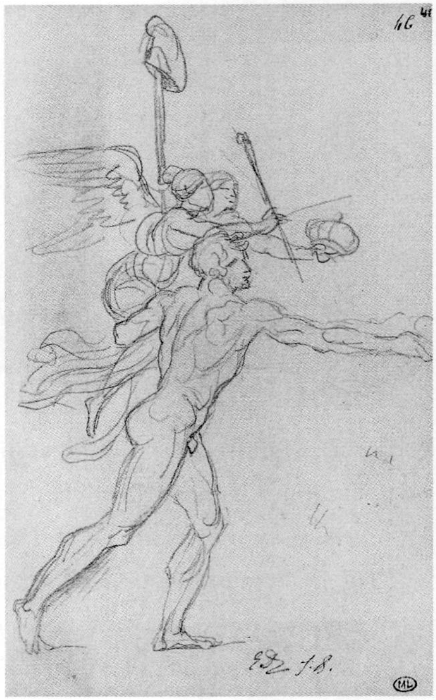

Louis's refusal to co-operate with the constitution which led to the creation of a Republic. Later, when the political climate turned against David, he vehemently denied that he had ever been involved with such a project and declared, 'the painter of Brutus was not made to paint kings'. The plans of many other artists of the time suffered the same fate as David's projects simply because the course of the Revolution was so rapid and so convoluted that paintings were out of date before they could be completed.

David's decisive intervention in politics came in September 1792 when he was elected as deputy for Paris at the National Convention. In April of that year he had helped to arrange a successful revolutionary festival in favour of the soldiers of Châteauvieux who had mutinied against their officers in 1789, been condemned as galley slaves, but who were now rescued and honoured as heroes of the Revolution. This show of commitment perhaps made David an acceptable political candidate, although it began a final and irrevocable split with André

95
Louis XVI Showing the Constitution to his Son, the Dauphin, 1792. Graphite; 18 × 11cm, $7 \times 4\frac{3}{8}$ in. Album 7, folio 38 verso. Musée du Louvre, Paris

96
Allegory of the French People Offering the Crown and Sceptre to the King, 1792. Graphite; 18 × 11cm, $7 \times 4\frac{3}{8}$ in. Album 7, folio 41 recto. Musée du Louvre, Paris

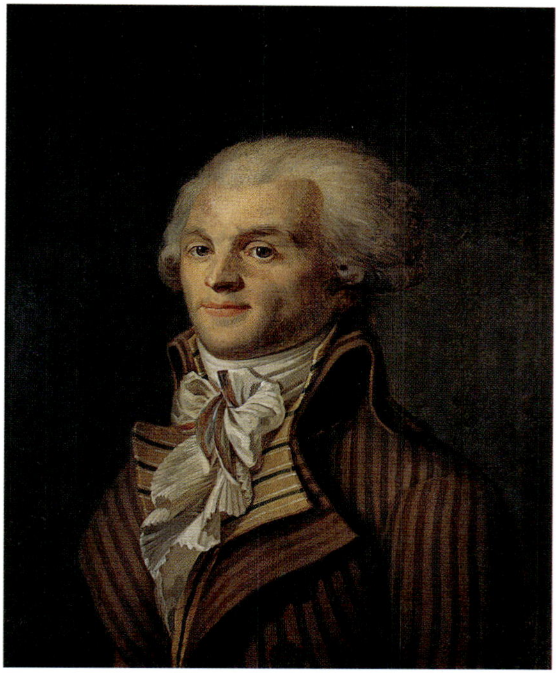

97
Anonymous, *Portrait of Maximilien Robespierre*, c.1790. Oil on canvas; 60 × 49cm, $23\frac{5}{8} \times 19\frac{3}{8}$ in. Musée Carnavalet, Paris

Chénier who thought the soldiers were rebellious murderers and public enemies. David probably first sought elected office as a way of sharpening his attack on the Academy, but once a member of the Convention, he took a radical stance on practically all matters and aligned himself very closely with the Mountain group whose members included Maximilien Robespierre, Jean-Paul Marat and Georges Jacques Danton. Of these the most prominent was Robespierre (97), a lawyer from Arras in northern France who was serious, possessed great intellectual clarity and whose fervour for scrupulous democracy and refusal to compromise with the royal court earned him the nickname of 'The Incorruptible'. Though ten years younger than David he was a figure with whom the artist increasingly identified as the course of the Revolution turned towards violent repression. Following his election to the Convention David became extremely active in politics. He was President of the Convention for a month, Nîvose Year II (January–February 1794), served a term as President of the Jacobin Club, and was a member of the Committee of General Security and the Committee of Public Instruction. On the floor of the Convention David made many impassioned speeches, although the increasing size of his mouth tumour made him very difficult to be understood, so much so that many people were forced to read them later when they were printed in *Le Moniteur*, the official journal of record. An unsympathetic account of 1797 described David thus:

Nature, or rather disease has incapacitated David from being an orator. A frightful tumified cheek has not only distorted his features to a great degree, but, at the same time, disqualified the organs of speech from uttering ten words in the same tone of voice; so that a grave subject, in his mouth, notwithstanding the sensibility of the man, loses its dignity: at best he is only able to give a silent vote.

Although his other duties meant that he could not attend all of the sessions on the Committee of General Security (he attended 134 out of 315), some of David's work was mundane bureaucracy, but he also signed many arrest warrants with the consequence that people had their property confiscated, were imprisoned or even sent to the guillotine. David's avid desire to rid the Republic of its actual or perceived enemies meant that former patrons such as the Marshal de Noailles and his wife and the Count de Sorcy were the subjects of his attention. But although the Noailles were later executed, it seems far-fetched to think that David had been nursing a grievance ever since the 1783 *Christ on the Cross* commission (see 52); it is more probable that their arrest and condemnation were part of the relentless and severe revolutionary legal process rather than the result of his vindictiveness. Doubtless David and his former protector, the Marquis de Bièvre, would also have found themselves on opposite sides of the political divide, had not the marquis died at the age of forty-two in 1789.

David the politician was a highly complex and volatile mixture of personal grudges, private insecurities, artistic ambition and democratic righteousness. He was said to be in a state of near delirium as he tackled his duties with the vigorous intensity of a zealous convert. The American artist John Trumbull recorded that he was 'a naturally kind and warm hearted man, but ardent, sometimes even violent in his feelings, an enthusiastic admirer of the Roman republic', and, 'This gave to his public life the imprint of a ferocious monster while, as a private individual, his primitive character of kindliness resumed its sway.' As with many people in times of crisis, the Revolution seems to have brought out the best and the worst in him. On one hand he was generous, anxious to help the unfortunate, and capable of tolerance and leniency. Yet he could also be a fanatic, an inflexible patriot and able to ignore pleas for help. Some stories, perhaps apocryphal, tell of his rabid and extreme antimonarchical sentiments. He is reported to have drawn a sketch of the king at the guillotine, his head severed, with the inscription, 'The head of the tyrant will soon fall like this', and once at dinner he said he hoped that Queen Marie Antoinette would either be strangled or cut to pieces by the mob. Then, in June 1794, the horse and battle painter Carle Vernet (1758–1836) approached him to intervene on behalf of his sister Emilie Chalgrin who had been arrested for possessing items stolen from the royal château of La Muette, and which now belonged to the Republic. David categorically refused to act, though it is possible that the affair was too far advanced for anything to be done, and Madame Chalgrin went to the guillotine. Thereafter Vernet blamed David and held him responsible for his sister's death. David was, however, particularly sympathetic towards his fellow artist Fragonard who was experiencing hard times because artistic taste had moved away from the charming, decorative and delicate Rococo to weightier and more noble subjects – a change that David had been instrumental in effecting. David remembered Fragonard's kindness over the 1773 Guimard commission and, although their art was by now poles apart, David still held the older artist in high regard. In October 1792 he intervened with the Minister of the Interior, Roland, to get Fragonard lodgings in the Louvre, and a year later helped him become one of the first curators of the newly established Musée du Louvre.

On 21 September 1792 the Convention (the new republican assembly) abolished the monarchy, and from November debates took place concerning the king's fate. Although no court in the land had legal jurisdiction over him, from 11 December Louis XVI was put on trial as a tyrant and a traitor. In fact Louis's rule in France was by no means the most oppressive in Europe and he was actually a sensitive, kindly, though ineffectual man. His crimes, if crimes they were, amounted to indecision, evasion and the refusal to become a constitutional monarch. He was, however, considered a dangerous and unreliable double-dealer because of his ill-judged attempt to flee the country with the royal family – the so-called 'Flight to Varennes' of 20–25 June 1791 – to seek foreign support and rally exiled royalists. On 16 January 1793 the deputies of the Convention unanimously found the king guilty and immediately turned to the sentence. Each deputy had to make a statement before his peers concerning his decision and this voting occupied twenty-four hours from the evening of 16 January. The hardline Mountain group, which included David, insisted on the death penalty, while more moderate alliances, such as the Girondins, favoured imprisonment or exile. Finally, by a majority of 387 to 334, the Convention decreed that the king should be executed. A subsequent motion asking for a reprieve was denied. Louis was executed on 21 January 1793, the day after the announcement

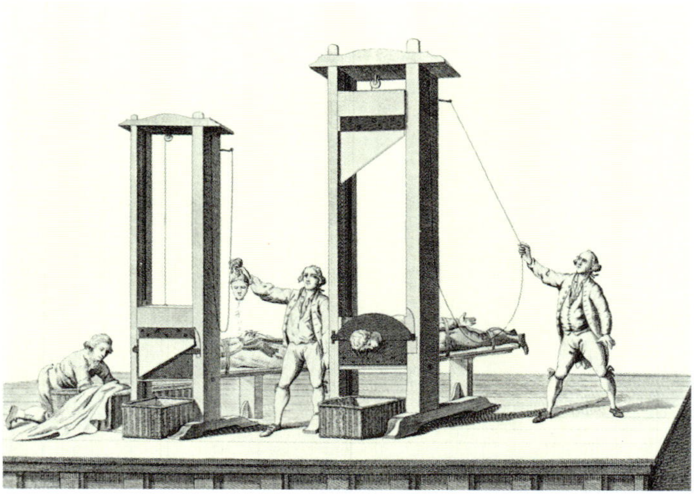

98
Explanation of the function of the guillotine in Paris

of the formal verdict. By now the official method of execution was beheading by the guillotine, a new invention to give all of the condemned, no matter what their status, an equally swift death. Though Dr Guillotin had suggested a machine to 'separate the head from the body in less time than it takes to wink', it was actually constructed by a piano maker and engineer called Tobias Schmidt and it was much to the shame and embarrassment of the well intentioned doctor that his name became forever associated with this feared instrument of death (98). For the king's execution the guillotine was set up in the Place de la Révolution (formerly the Place Louis XV and today the Place de la Concorde) and Louis was accompanied to the scaffold by his priest and confessor the Irish-born Abbé Henry Edgeworth. As the king mounted the steps (99) the Abbé delivered his famous phrase: 'Son of Saint Louis ascend into heaven' and Louis XVI approached his death with uncharacteristic fortitude and nobility. He addressed the crowd and forgave his executioners, but a drum roll cut short his speech. At the fall of the blade he was heard to scream, his fat neck had prevented decapitation at a single stroke. One of the young guards picked up the severed head and showed it to the crowd (100), while some onlookers rushed forward to dip handkerchiefs or pieces of paper into the newly spilled royal blood.

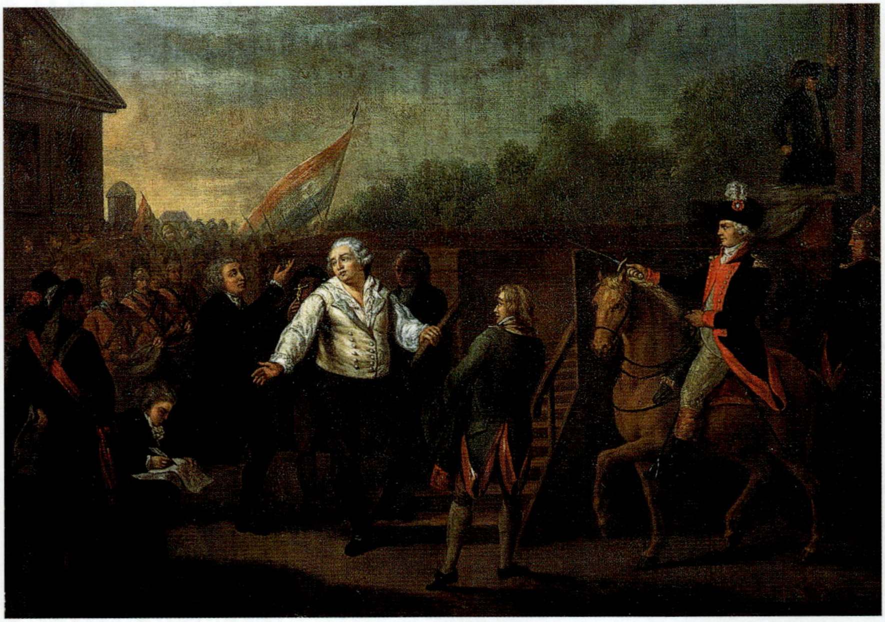

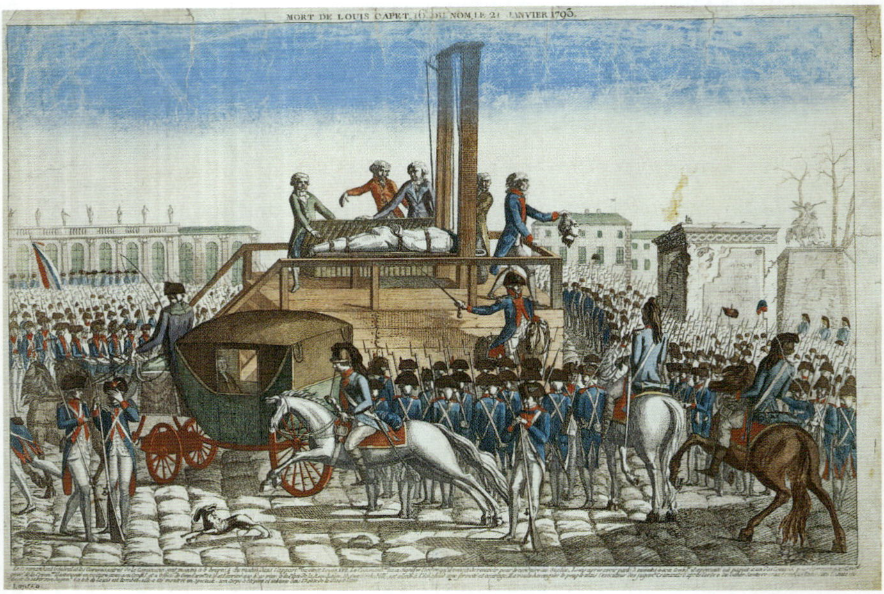

99
Charles Bénazech, *Louis XVI at the Foot of the Scaffold*, 1793/4. Oil on canvas; 42 × 56 cm, 16½ × 22 in. Musée National du Château de Versailles

100
The Death of Louis XVI, 21st January 1793, 1793. Coloured etching; 30·3 × 45·2 cm, 11⅞ × 17¾ in. Musée Carnavalet, Paris

101
James Gillray, *The Blood of the Murdered Crying for Vengeance*, 1793. Etching. New College, Oxford University

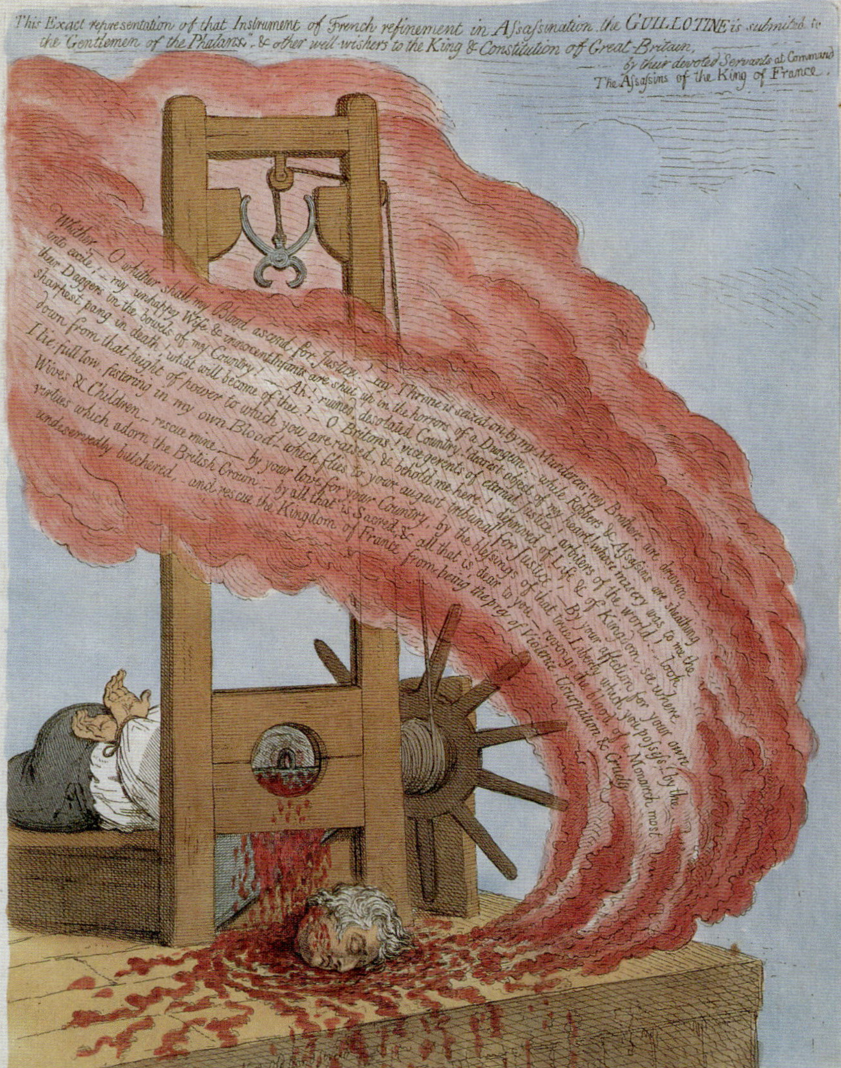

The Blood of the Murdered crying for Vengeance. J. Gy. des. et fect. pro bono publico.

The crowned heads of Europe were plunged into shock, horror and fright when news arrived of Louis's bloody end, and even liberal supporters of the Revolution outside France changed their opinions and felt that anarchy and violence had replaced the ideals of freedom and equality (101). As the king had always proclaimed that he was the state and ruled by divine right, it was as if France had turned on and executed herself. For fear of an export of radicalism from France, both England and Spain introduced severely repressive measures.

In Paris the guillotine soon became a familiar sight, although many of the crowd were disappointed because everything was over so soon when compared to the spectacle of former methods of public execution. Local residents and shopkeepers disliked the unpleasant smell and the packs of dogs drinking from the pools of spilt blood, and so the guillotine was periodically moved around the city. The black humour of guillotine jokes also surfaced, and ladies of fashion could even wear earrings in the shape of the 'philanthropic decapitating machine' from which the decapitated heads of the executed hung down.

102
Tributes Paid to the Memory of Le Pelletier, 1793. Engraving; 11·5 × 18·6 cm, $4\frac{1}{2} \times 7\frac{3}{8}$ in

The execution of the king had great repercussions for David's private life. His wife was appalled at her husband for having voted in favour of the death penalty and instituted divorce proceedings, the final decree being granted in March 1794. Tensions within the marriage had been present for some time and although Madame David had supported the Revolution in its early stages, she neither shared nor approved of her husband's extremist stance. As early as August 1790 David had authorized his wife to enter a convent, a contemporary euphemism for a separation. Without his wife's money David's finances were very limited and the blow of these reduced circumstances may have given greater impetus to his already intense behaviour and extremism.

By this time David had pledged his brush to the republican cause and he came to commemorate three martyrs of the

Revolution in a group of extraordinary pictures. A prelude to the king's execution gave him his first subject. On the eve of the execution a deputy of the Convention, Louis Michel Le Pelletier de Saint-Fargeau, had been assassinated by one of the king's former bodyguards named Pâris while at dinner. Le Pelletier was a former aristocrat and something of a political opportunist and had voted for the death of the king. After his death he was hailed as a martyr of liberty and given an impressive state funeral. His body was displayed in the Place Vendôme, a laurel crown placed on his head and his torso uncovered so that the fatal wound could be seen (102). Le Pelletier's torn and bloodstained clothes and the sword used

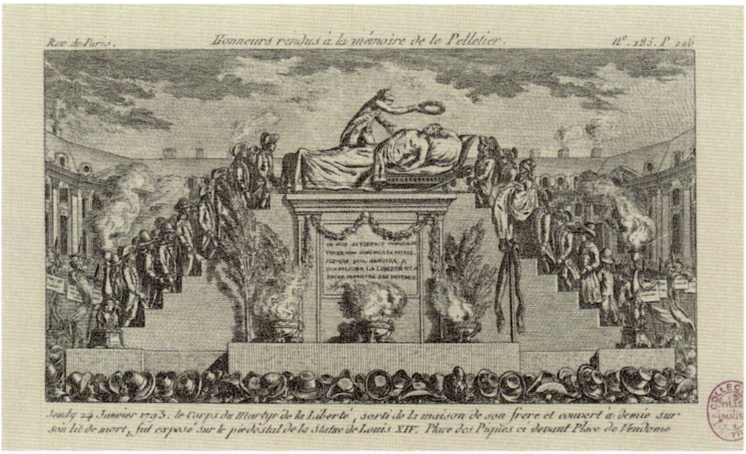

by Pâris were also included in the spectacle. David originally proposed a marble monument, but then decided to produce a painting. In a speech to the Convention on 29 March 1792 he explained his intentions:

> the true patriot must seize any opportunity of enlightening his fellow citizens and must constantly show them the sublime face of heroism and virtue ... I shall have done my duty if one day I cause an old father surrounded by his large family to say: 'Children come and see the first of your representatives to die for your freedom. See how peaceful his face is – when you die for your country, you

die with a clear conscience. Do you see the sword hanging over his head by just a hair? Well, children, that shows how much courage Michel Le Pelletier and his noble companions needed to rout the evil tyrant who had oppressed us for so long, for, had they set a foot wrong, the hair would have broken and they would all have been killed. Do you see that deep wound? You are crying, children, and turning your heads away! Just look at the crown; it is the crown of immortality. The nation can confer it on any of its children; be worthy of it.'

The painting was finished in time for the 1793 Salon which opened on 10 August. Le Pelletier appeared like a nobly dead ancient warrior, not unlike Hector in *Andromache Mourning Hector* (see 43), and for a nation still experiencing the guilt of having executed their king, here was a republican saint and martyr to make amends for their sins. The assassin's sword, with its pommel shaped like the Gallic Cock and decorated

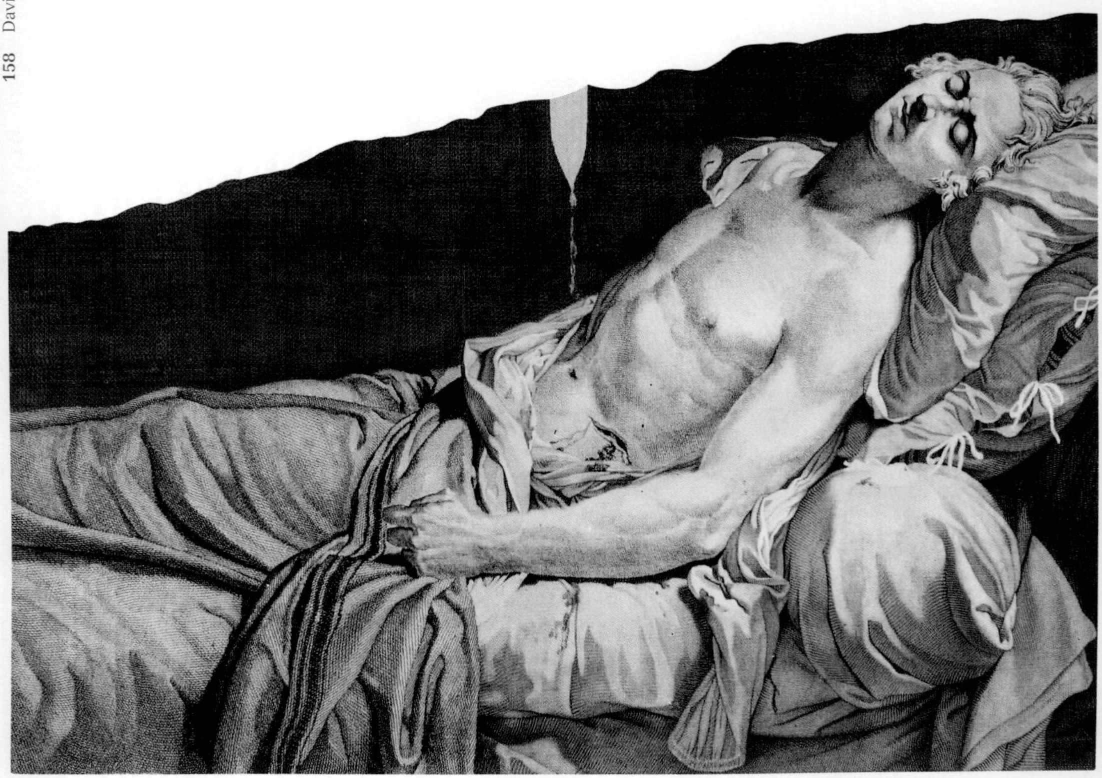

with the royal fleur-de-lys, is hung by a single strand of hair above Le Pelletier's gaping wound, inspired by the proverbial ancient tale of the sword of Damocles which illustrated the insecurity of power and position. This sword pierces a piece of paper on which is written 'I vote the death of the tyrant', and as a tribute at the bottom right of the picture David placed the inscription 'David to Le Pelletier. 20 January 1793'. The picture combined the ideas of heroic sacrifice and the precarious realities of the revolutionary process – the deputies who voted for the king's death knew that they endangered their own lives from the vengeance of royalists and here was an example of how devotion to duty exacted the ultimate cost. David, in his first fragmentary autobiography, written in April 1793, said that the work showed Le Pelletier expiring after his dying words: 'I am content to spill blood for my country; I hope it will be a lesson to her enemies.' Unfortunately this powerful painting has not survived. Le Pelletier's daughter Suzanne grew up

103
Pierre-Alexandre Tardieu, Engraving after David's *Le Pelletier de Saint-Fargeau on his Deathbed*, 1793

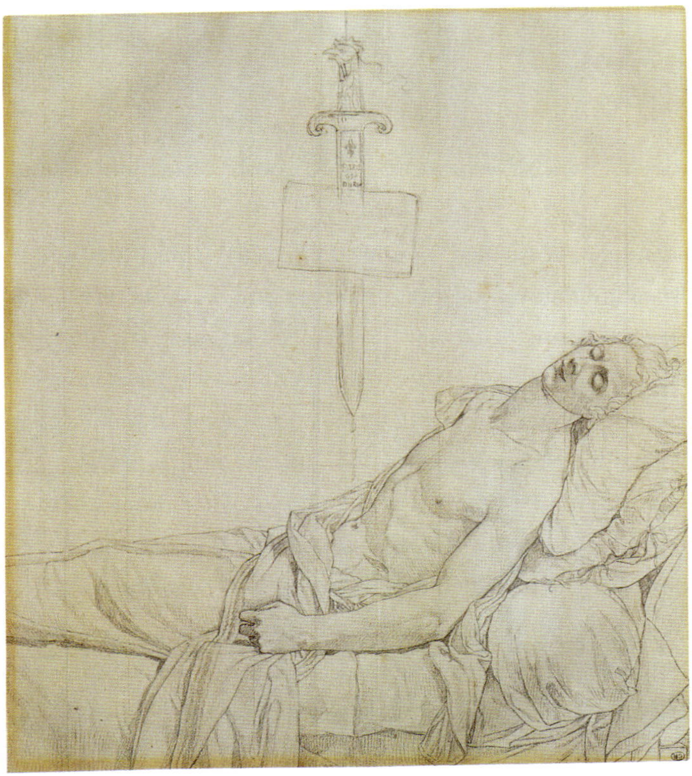

104
Anatole Devosge, Drawing after David's *Le Pelletier de Saint-Fargeau on his Deathbed*, 1793. Black chalk; 38 × 33cm, 15 × 13in. Musée des Beaux-Arts, Dijon

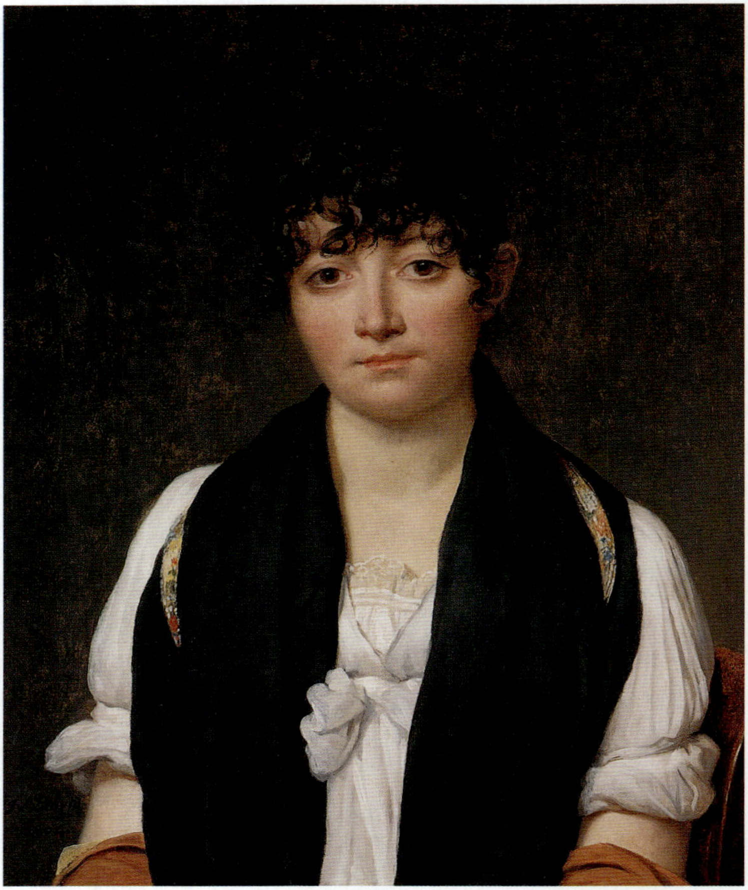

105
Portrait of Suzanne Le Pelletier de Saint-Fargeau, 1804. Oil on canvas; 60·5 × 49·5 cm, $23\frac{7}{8} \times 19\frac{1}{2}$ in. J Paul Getty Museum, Los Angeles

106
Joseph Boze, *Portrait of Jean-Paul Marat*, 1792. Oil on canvas; 44·5 × 36·5 cm, $17\frac{1}{2} \times 14\frac{3}{8}$ in. Musée Carnavalet, Paris

to be an ardent royalist, bought the picture from David's heirs for the massive sum of 100,000 francs and had it burnt shortly before her death. Such was her determination to rid the world of this image that she also gathered copies of the engraving by Pierre-Alexandre Tardieu (b.1756) and destroyed them as well as the original plate. Our best reminders of the work are a torn engraving (103) and a drawing by David's pupil Anatole Devosge (1770–1850; 104). Although removing the visual evidence of David's memorial to her father, Suzanne had her portrait painted by David in 1804 to commemorate her engagement to her second husband (105). This work was acquired by the J Paul Getty Museum in Los Angeles in 1997.

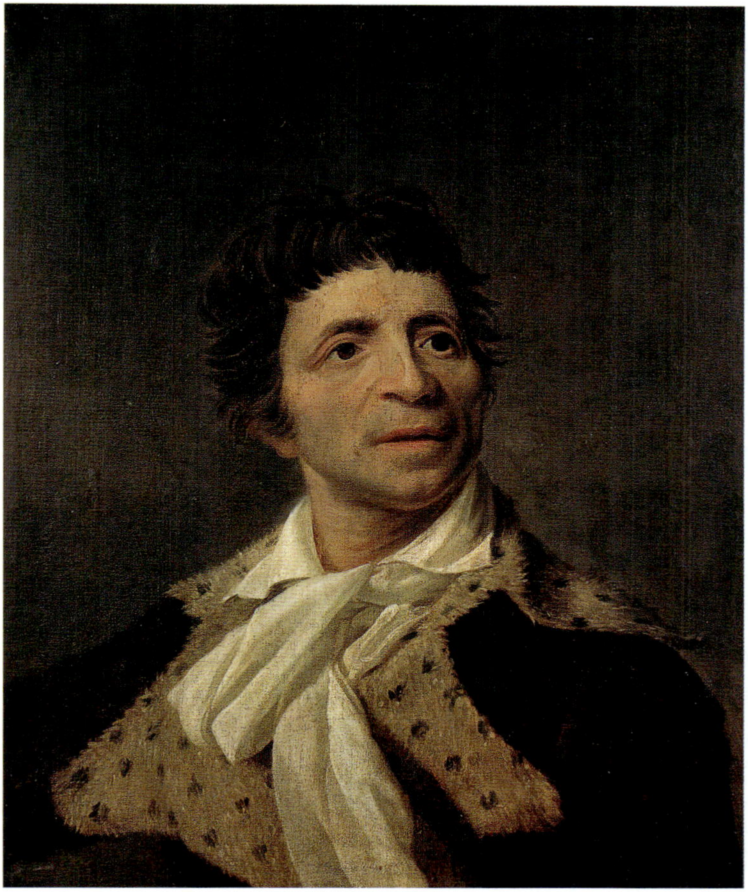

Just over three and a half months after presenting the Le Pelletier painting, David was called upon to depict another assassinated deputy of the Convention, the radical journalist Jean-Paul Marat (106). Formerly a physician, Marat had practised in Harley Street in London and on returning to France attended the guards of the king's brother, the Count d'Artois. Before the Revolution Marat had sought recognition of his scientific credentials but his ambitions had continually been thwarted by the officers of the Royal Academy of Science who denied him admission to their élite body. Such rebuffs made him bitter and self-righteous. Like David he attacked and condemned privilege, and in the early days of the Revolution he published and edited a newspaper called *The Friend of the*

People. Within its pages the deeply suspicious Marat detected and denounced royalist plots and called for even more radical reforms than those already carried out. Marat was often a fierce government critic; his entry into official politics in 1792 was arranged as a method of enlisting his support, and that of the volatile ranks of the *sans-culottes* that formed his power base. The *sans-culottes* (literally 'without knee-breeches') were radical and committed small property owners and artisans who took part in many of the most extreme acts. Indeed so popular and influential was Marat that he became known as 'The Friend of the People'. France was moving towards the bloody period of the Reign of Terror that was instigated by Jacobin activists, notably Robespierre, who called for the preservation of the Revolution and the creation of a 'Republic of Virtue'. The atmosphere of war, treachery and internal conflict required the ruthless purging of all hostile elements (even including fellow Convention members) and the ends were seen to justify the extreme means. Marat was also one of the leading figures in these events, saying that 'Liberty must be established by violence', and his strident and vigorous attacks also included denunciations of speculators and hoarders for causing high food prices. In April 1793 he was arrested after calling for the forcible removal of the moderate Girondins from their position of power in the Convention. He was acquitted by the Revolutionary Tribunal and two months later the Girondins were indeed arrested and control of the Convention passed to the radical Mountain group of which he was a member.

Marat was assassinated on 13 July 1793 by the 24-year-old Charlotte Corday from Normandy (107), who decided that he was a mad and dangerous fanatic who had diverted the Revolution on to a murderous course. Travelling from Caen to Paris, she saw his removal as both a patriotic duty and a quasi-religious act. Considering herself a modern Judith (slayer of the Assyrian general Holofernes), she wrote: 'I expected to sacrifice him on the summit of the Mountain of the National Convention', and she intended to do so on the fourth anniversary of the Revolution so that the significance of her deed would be immediately recognized. Finding out that Marat was too ill to attend the Convention and thus forced to change her plan, she tried to gain access to his home in the rue des Cordeliers, but was at first turned away by his common-law wife, Simone Evrard. Very astutely Charlotte Corday then wrote him a note with news of counter-revolutionary activity in Caen, just the thing to excite his curiosity. All of this plotting was done with an extraordinary degree of calm calculation and sense of purpose – she even had her hair done in the afternoon before returning to Marat's apartment. Again refused entry, she slipped inside when Simone Evrard's attention was distracted by a newspaper seller. Marat heard the raised voices and called out for her to be admitted. She found him working in his bath, where he was obliged to soak to gain relief from a painfully irritating skin disease, with a vinegar soaked turban wrapped around his head. He asked for more information about the traitors whom she had written about in her letter and took down their names, saying that 'they would all soon be guillotined in Paris'. At that point she took out a newly purchased five-inch butcher's knife from her dress and plunged it through his right side next to the collarbone, severing the aorta and piercing the heart. Marat cried out for Simone Evrard and died in a matter of minutes. Her mission accomplished, Charlotte Corday then made no attempt to escape, knowing that her punishment would be death.

The following day, at the Convention, the deputy Guirault, after demanding a torture worse than death for Charlotte Corday, spoke out, saying: 'A patricidal hand has robbed us of the most courageous defender of the people. His only crime was that he always sacrificed himself for the sake of freedom. Our eyes are still seeking him among us ... Where are you, David? You have transmitted to posterity the picture of Le Pelletier dying for the nation, and here is another painting for you to do' – 'And I shall do it', the artist replied. David knew Marat personally (both were Freemasons) and had previously defended him

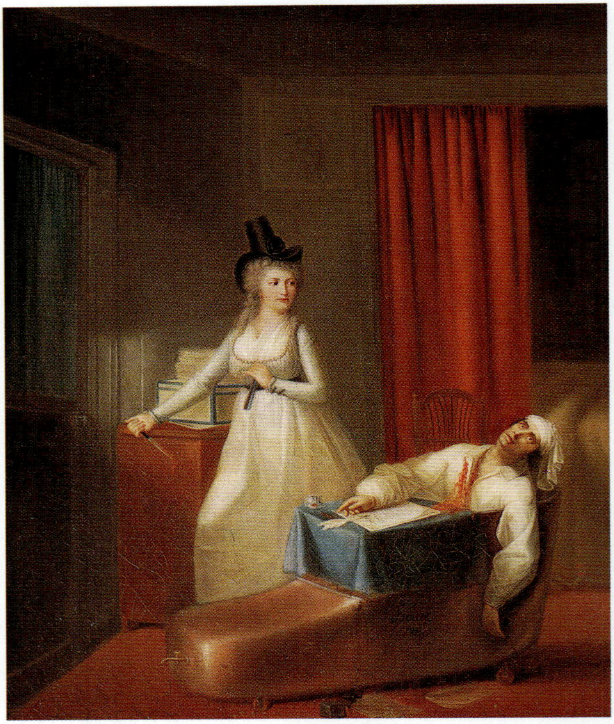

107
Jean-Jacques Hauer,
The Assassination of Marat,
1794.
Oil on canvas;
60 × 49cm,
23⅝ × 19¾in.
Musée Lambinet,
Versailles

108
Head of the Dead Marat,
1793.
Pen and black and brown ink;
27 × 21cm,
10⅝ × 8¼in.
Musée National du Château de Versailles

from the hostile criticisms of moderate Girondin deputies at the Convention. David also recounted that: 'On the eve of Marat's death the Jacobin Society sent us, Maure [a fellow deputy at the Convention] and me, to hear how he was. I was struck by the circumstances in which I found him. He had a wooden block beside him with ink and paper upon it, and his hand, stretched out of the bath, was writing down his latest thoughts on the salvation of the People ... I thought it would be appropriate to show him in the attitude in which I saw him that day, writing for the greater good of the People.'

David also made plans for an elaborate funeral, but these had to be cancelled because the corpse had begun to decompose rapidly in the summer heat. Instead it was briefly exhibited, in the manner of Le Pelletier, draped with a damp cloth and the wound exposed, and flanked by the bathtub and his bloody shirt at the deconsecrated Cordeliers church between 14 and 16 July. The odour of putrefaction was disguised by aromatics

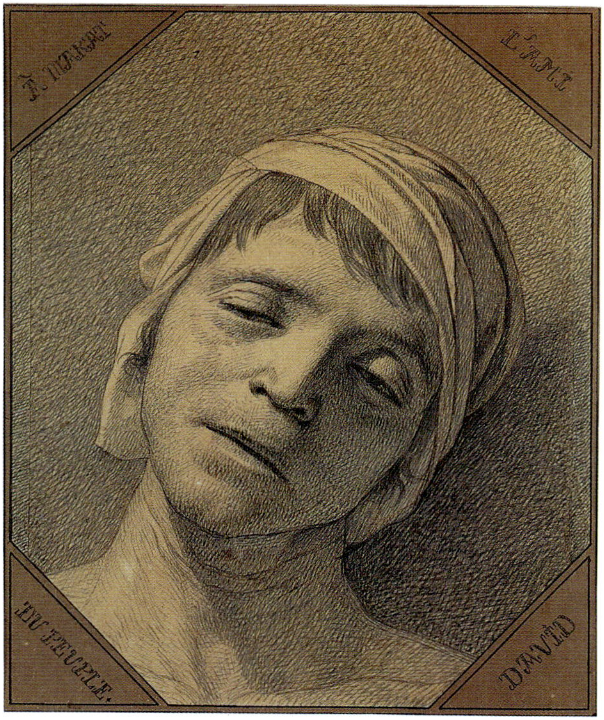

and vinegar. David had intended for a very moving spectacle to be created by placing the body upright as if at work, but this proved impossible because of the effects of decomposition and rigor mortis on the body. Neither Marat's eyes nor mouth could be closed and the lolling tongue had to be cut out. Both the head and torso had become so green that white make-up had to be applied. The Marquis de Créqui, admittedly an unsympathetic witness, described a grisly scene and claimed that the right arm had so stiffened that it was removed and replaced with another from the local morgue that then had Marat's quill pen placed in it. One mourner was horrified and alarmed to find that it came away as he rushed to kiss the hand of 'The Friend of the People'.

David probably drew Marat while the body was on display (108) and this drawing, with its network of crosshatching in the manner of an engraving, isolates the head and produces a macabre yet powerful portrait of the deceased. As with the final painting there is no suggestion of the violent act that had taken place, and in the four corners David wrote À MARAT/ L'AMI/ DU PEUPLE./ DAVID (To Marat, the Friend of the People, David), retaining this tribute in the final canvas. In the following year this image became widely available thanks to a very faithful engraving by Jacques-Louis Copia (1764–99).

After the body had been displayed, Marat's funeral took place by torchlight on the evening of 16 July. A cortège processed

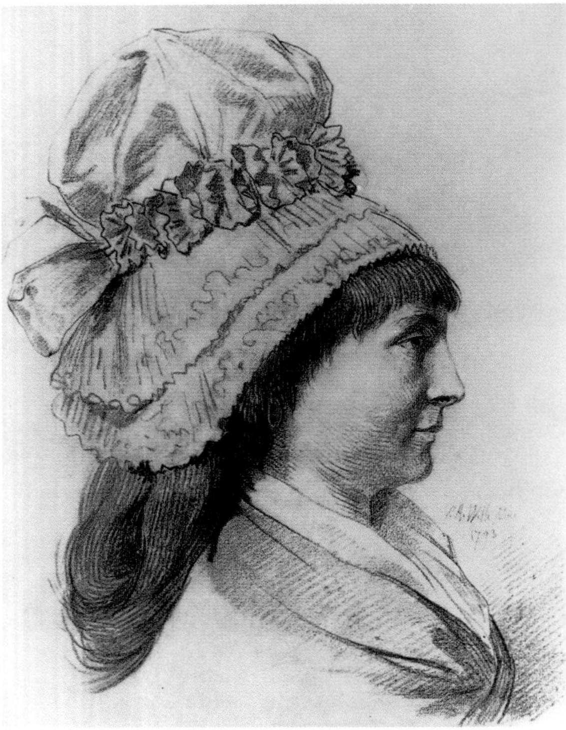

109
Pierre-Alexandre Wille,
Charlotte Corday in Prison,
1793.
Red chalk;
43·3 × 33·4 cm,
17 × 13⅛ in.
Private collection

around Paris for six hours, and then arrived back at the Cordeliers. The main oration ran: 'O heart of Jesus! O heart of Marat! ... Like Jesus Marat loved the people ardently ... Like Jesus, Marat detested nobles, priests, the rich, the scoundrels. Like Jesus, he led a poor and frugal life.' His body was then interred in the garden of the Cordeliers under, as David said, 'the trees where he used to take pleasure from instructing his fellow citizens'; his heart was taken out and placed in a porphyry urn that was suspended from the ceiling of the Cordeliers. Though much was made of Marat's poverty in life, in death his funeral cost the huge sum of 5,000 francs, the embalming of the body 7,500 francs, and his tomb, by the sculptor Jacques-François Martin, 2,400 francs.

The following day Charlotte Corday was sent to the guillotine; all through her ordeal she retained the composure that she had so steadfastly exhibited during her arrest and trial, even sitting for her portrait in prison (109). It was a bitter irony that even without her intervention, Marat would probably have died anyway, so serious was his illness, and his murder, calculated to save France from bloodthirsty anarchy, only created a popular martyr, assured the political victory of the Mountain faction and brought forth even more death and violence. On 5 September 1793 the chilling declaration was made that 'Terror is the order of the day', and on 17 September the 'Law of Suspects' was passed which gave the Committee of Public Safety sweeping powers of arrest and punishment against any person suspected of counter-revolutionary activity. If not demonstrably supportive of the Revolution, people came under suspicion and an even more intense period of violent repression began that did not end until July 1794.

David completed the *Marat* on 14 October 1793 and immediately asked permission to loan the work and the *Le Pelletier* to the Section of the Museum for a ceremonial procession in honour of the two martyrs. Significantly this was to take place two days later, the same day as the execution of Queen Marie Antoinette, and it seems clear that the afternoon ceremony was meant to rival the morning execution. In Paris there were forty-eight Sections, or units of self-government, and that of the Museum, the neighbourhood of the Louvre, was at that time seeking to become affiliated to the Jacobin Club. It is likely that by honouring the memory of Marat and Le Pelletier they were seeking to prove their revolutionary credentials at a time when proofs of orthodoxy were needed. The procession consisted of drummers, a marching band, members of the Section with banners, deputies of the Convention, conscripts carrying busts of Marat and Le Pelletier with oak crowns held over their heads, and bouquet-carrying mothers dressed in white leading their children by the hand. Throughout the parade the army were heavily represented. At the end of the route, in the courtyard of the Louvre, David's *Le Pelletier* and *Marat* were set up on two sarcophagi under a temporary covering, perhaps made of branches and tricolour drapery. Witnesses said that the effect was like a funerary crypt. The two paintings were not displayed out of doors for long and were then put on public view in David's studio in the Louvre, before being given to the Convention. To an even greater degree than the *Le Pelletier*, the *Marat* was a kind of republican altarpiece, since the citizens of Paris were encouraged to bring themselves and their children to gaze at the image and be instilled with a mixture of awe, reverence and revolutionary fervour.

110
Marat Breathing his Last, 1793.
Oil on canvas; 165 × 128 cm, 65 × 50⅜ in.
Musées Royaux des Beaux-Arts, Brussels

David's painting of Marat (110) represents the peak of his involvement in the Revolution where invention, style, fervent belief and devotion combine to produce one of the most perfect examples of political painting. David presented the painting to the Convention on 14 November and said:

Citizens, the people ask for their friend again, their sorrowful voice wished itself heard – my talent is roused, they want to see again the features of their faithful friend: David! they cry, seize your brushes, avenge our friend, avenge Marat; let his vanquished enemies grow pale again at the sight of those disfigured features, reduce them to such a state that they could envy the fate of him whom they were cowardly enough to have killed when they could not succeed in corrupting him. I heard the voice of the people; I have obeyed.

Gather round! mother, widow, orphan, oppressed soldier; all you whom he [Marat] defended at the peril of his life approach! and contemplate your friend; he who watched over you is no more; his pen, the terror of traitors, his pen falls from his hands. Oh despair! our tireless friend is dead.

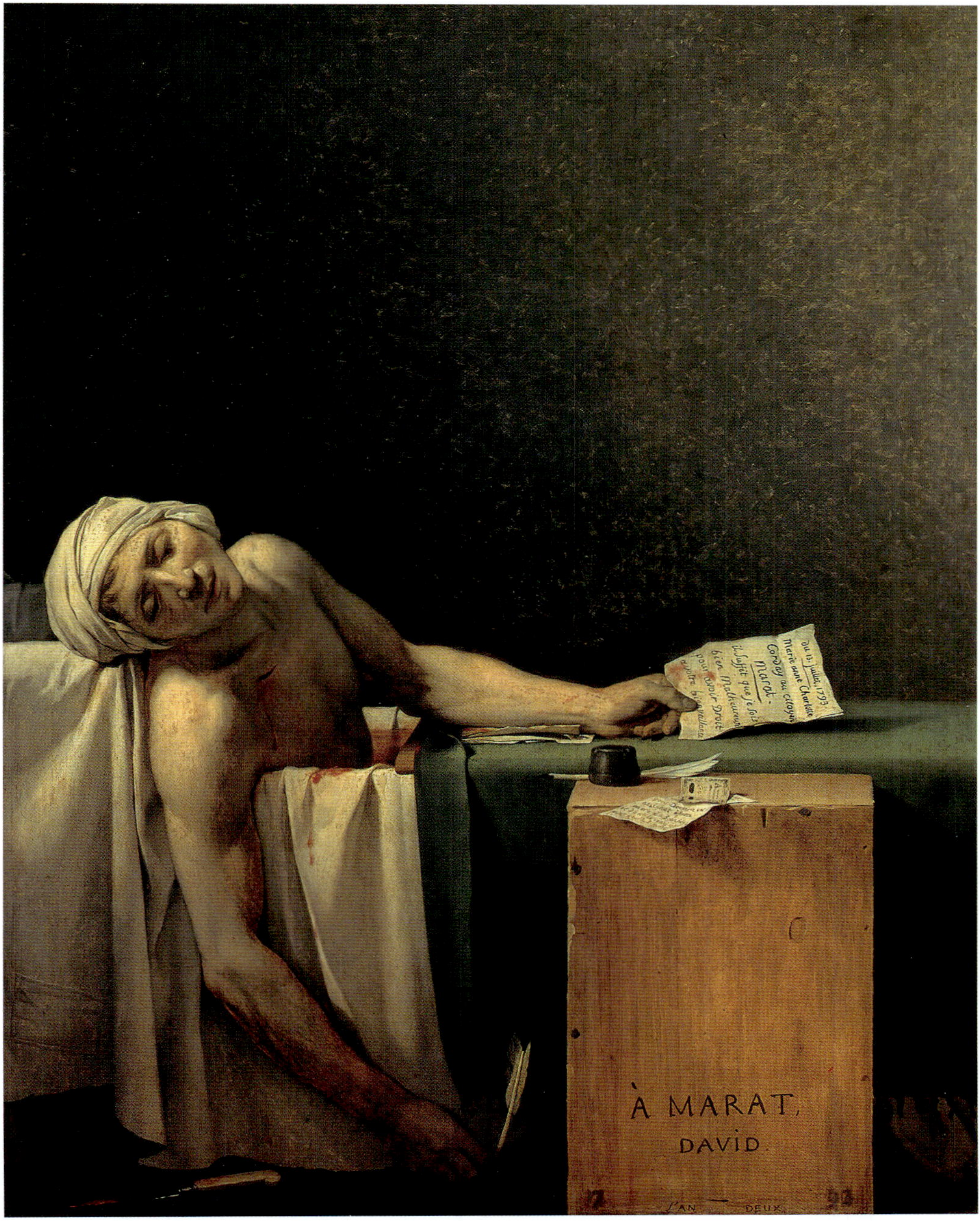
À MARAT,
DAVID.
L'AN DEUX

He is dead, your friend, giving you his last morsel of bread; he is dead without having even enough to have himself buried. Posterity, you will avenge him; you will say to our descendants how many riches he could have possessed, if he had not preferred virtue to fortune ...

It is to you my colleagues, that I offer the tribute of my brushes; when gazing at his livid and blood-soaked features you will recall his virtues, which must never cease to be your own.

Never a natural orator, David resorted to melodramatic and sentimental appeals to his audience and such a long-winded and overblown speech was the complete opposite to the eloquent and poignant simplicity of his painting. David called the painting *Marat Breathing his Last*, and the painting is clearly not of a dead but of a dying man. Even more obviously than with the *Le Pelletier*, in the *Marat* David turned to religious art to consecrate this second republican martyr. The pose recalls the Deposition or Entombment of Christ and the chill and silent void of the background, animated only by the shimmering brushwork, is reminiscent of Caravaggio's religious works (see 34). Marat had already been compared to Jesus at his funeral oration and David, who was perhaps present, seized on this association. Marat's nudity also brought

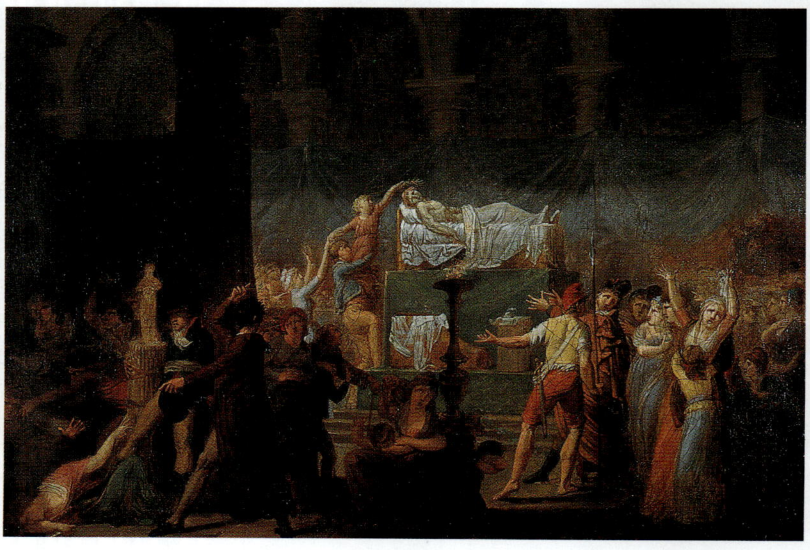

to mind the dying heroes and philosophers of antiquity. The lighting, from a high and invisible source, has a supernatural quality which suggests Marat's assumption into a Jacobin hereafter. Some elements of the body's exposition at the Cordeliers are also included and a contemporary painting of the lying in state, attributed to Fougeat (111), has light effects similar to the *Marat* as well as showing the bath and the wooden case exhibited on a step below the body.

In common with most propaganda images, David's *Marat* is less to do with facts than with the creation of an accessible, credible and persuasive image. Marat's room actually had white wall-paper decorated with illusionistic pilasters on which hung a map of France and a pair of crossed pistols, but such mundane and insignificant details were suppressed to create a spiritual realm far removed from Marat's sordid and brutal death. Bathroom murders are inevitably gruesome and, as exploited by makers of sensationalist prints and later by many makers of horror films, the mixture of blood and water creates a messy and disturbing aftermath. But in David's *Marat* a supreme calm reigns which dissipates the violence of the attack.

Marat's ugly face was considerably improved and rejuvenated, and a reading of the picture's accessories leaves the viewer in no doubt as to Marat's virtue, humanity and generosity. The sheets that protected his fragile scaly skin from the copper lining of the wooden bath have patches on them, indicating his frugality, a virtue that was also much emphasized at his funeral. In his left hand he holds Charlotte Corday's deceitful note that reads (in David's own handwriting): 'July 13 1793: Marie-Anne-Charlotte Corday to citizen Marat/ It is enough for me to be truly wretched to have a right to your kindness' (112). Corday's actual note to Marat had ended: 'I am being persecuted for the sake of Liberty; I am unhappy, that is sufficient to give me the right to your protection', and the change in wording suggests that she accomplished her murderous deed by appealing to Marat's kind-hearted

111
Attributed to Fougeat,
The Funeral of Marat in the Cordeliers Church,
1793.
Oil on canvas;
59 × 73 cm,
23¼ × 28¾ in.
Musée Carnavalet, Paris

sympathy. On top of the packing case or crate is another short letter and a bank note. The letter, from Marat, reads: 'you are to give this *assignat* [a bill issued as currency during the Revolution] to this mother of five whose husband died for his country', and is yet further proof of his concern for others. Apart from the two letters, David placed the words TO MARAT, DAVID. YEAR TWO, on the packing case and thus transformed it into a form of tombstone. The new revolutionary calendar, which counted its years from the proclamation of the Republic in 1792 and also renamed the months (reflecting the progress of the seasons), had only been officially adopted on 6 October 1793, when the work was nearing completion, and the smudged arabic numerals of 17 and 93 can also be seen in the corners of the packing case. By definition Marat's assassin must have been abnormal and a traitor to the Revolution, and the two notes help shape this perception of her. She dates her note using the old royalist calendar, and instead of employing the more egalitarian 'tu' form of address, uses the 'vous' form with its associations of feudalism and deference. Corday's letter is placed in close proximity to Marat's own generous and benevolent note to the widow and children. Corday was a spinster; therefore, at a time when the family unit and the birth rate were much promoted in revolutionary rhetoric, in more ways than one, she was considered an 'unnatural woman'. The culmination of this negation of Charlotte Corday was to banish her from the scene altogether and to turn the picture into a whodunit. As well as her treacherous note, the bloodstained knife of the assassin lies on the floor and her traces are revealed by the blood stains on the white handle – in reality the handle had been black but David changed it to make the blood clearly visible. Thus Corday's recent presence is indicated by these metonyms, though she herself is not seen. All these accessories are rendered in high detail and serve as the equivalents of the attributes of a Christian martyr. If St Catherine had her wheel and St Lawrence had his gridiron, then Marat had his butcher's knife, quill and inkwell.

112
Marat Breathing his Last
(detail of 110)

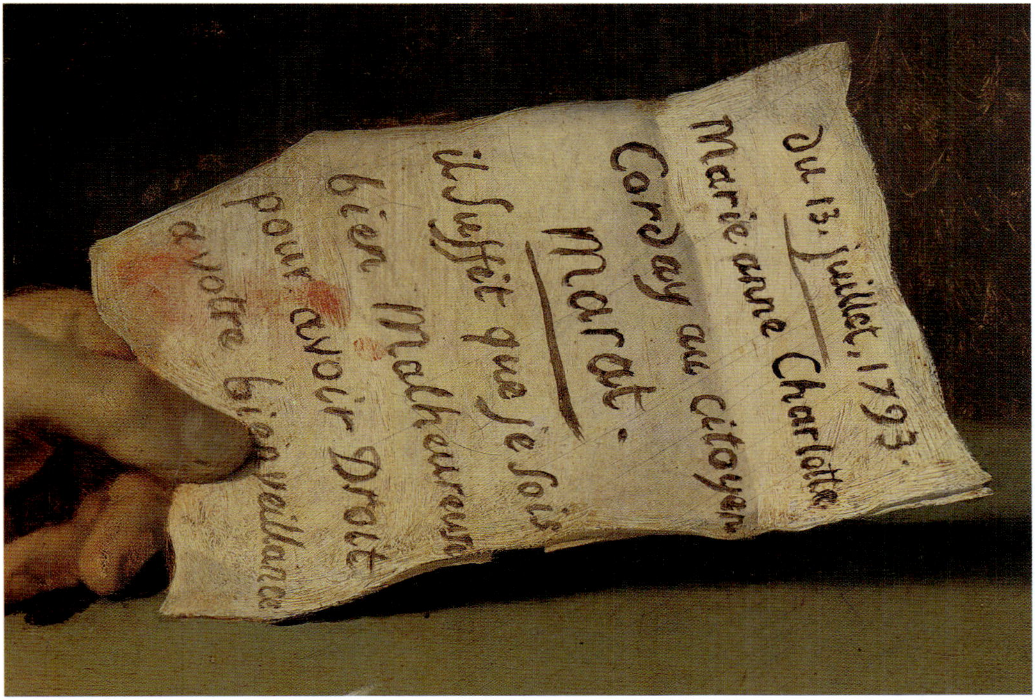

In *Marat*, as with *Belisarius* (see 45), *Andromache Mourning Hector* (see 43), *Le Pelletier* (see 104) and the later *Bonaparte Crossing the St Bernard Pass* (see 144), *Sappho and Phaon* (see 173) and *Leonidas at Thermopylae* (see 177), David used the written word to provide the viewer with telling extra pictorial information. David's use of words to complement and amplify the image was a legitimate tactic according to late eighteenth-century artistic theory. In his entry on 'Inscriptions', P C Lévesque wrote in his *Encyclopédie Méthodique* of 1788–91: 'We praise the artist when he uses plausible means to make known his subject, his main character ... which then makes easier the understanding of the actions or feelings represented. This may be achieved by a short inscription on a portico, on the base of a column, on a rock, by the title of a book or by a few words on the page of an open book.' In the case of his paintings of revolutionary martyrs, which were to reach all levels of society, David only used French, but in the histories and mythologies a more learned viewer was presupposed and Latin and Greek were employed.

The Convention decreed that both *Marat* and *Le Pelletier* should be engraved and afterwards placed on either side of the president's chair in the hall of the Convention. There they hung until 9 February 1795, and on 27 October David was given permission to take them back. Once again David had proved himself adept and tenacious at regaining possession of works that had been painted for others – by this time he had also managed to retrieve the *Horatii* and *Brutus*.

As a political loose cannon, Marat was actually much less of an acceptable martyr to the Mountain than Le Pelletier, and Robespierre had been anxious to avoid a public funeral that might give the assassinated deputy cult status and attract and inspire a populace that was not easily controlled. But events moved so rapidly that 'The Friend of the People' became 'The Martyr of the People'. Processions, speeches and apotheoses of Marat were enacted all over France, towns and villages were renamed after him, and Marat became popular as an anti-Christian name for children. David's painting both reflected and helped shape this transition.

113
The Heroic Death of the Young Bara, 1793. Engraving

The third and last of David's republican martyrs was not an established politician but a youth of thirteen whom the artist had never seen. Joseph Bara had been killed in the civil war in the Vendée on the Atlantic coast on 7 December 1793 (17 Frimaire Year II) after refusing to hand over two horses to royalist soldiers (113), shouting 'up yours, you fucking crook'. The Convention, and Robespierre in particular, anxious for a young martyr to inspire the nation, made up an official account of the event whereby Bara met his death for refusing to shout 'Long live the King', and died exclaiming 'Long live the Republic' – defiant and patriotic gestures much more in keeping with the creation of a national legend. This third martyr painting was never completed, and the unfinished *Death of Bara* (114) is possibly the most puzzling of all David's works, its incomplete state only adding to the mystery. A nude Bara lies on the ground holding a letter and a revolutionary cockade.

Although it was often David's working practice to draw and sketch figures nude and then clothe them, it seems that it was his intention for Bara to remain nude. David probably had in mind the beautiful youths of antique sculpture such as the *Apollo Belvedere* (115), and Bara appears androgynous, almost feminine, a sinuous figure far removed from any conventional image of a soldier-patriot. Isolated on the canvas, and with no other figures from which to draw a comparison, the undeveloped body of Bara evokes the image of a slightly older figure – an ephebe (a Greek youth of seventeen or eighteen). Perhaps David was aware that such youths were taken away

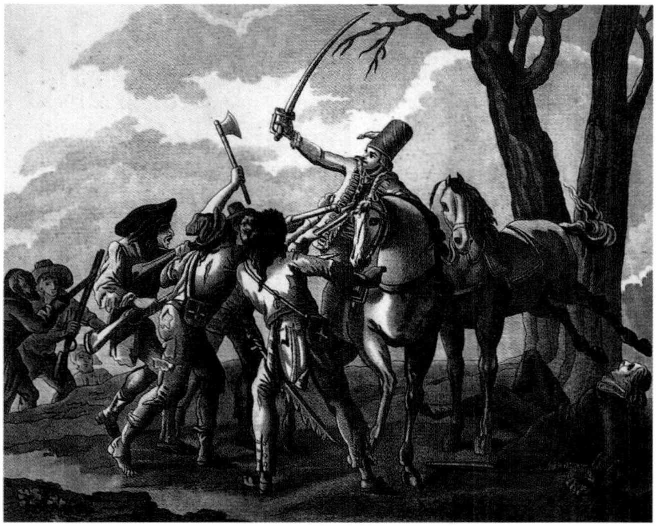

for military training as a kind of rite of passage into manhood and civic responsibility. Although Bara's body has none of the imperfections of the mature male body, great liberties have been taken with his anatomy – the lower half of his body has been turned in and twisted at the hips and knees to an impossible degree to conceal his genitalia. At the left there is the suggestion of a group of soldiers with a banner – perhaps his murderers – and this, coupled with his nudity, also gives a hint that Bara was not only killed, but stripped and violated as well. As with the *Marat,* the details are telling – the tricolour cockade denoted love of *La Patrie* (the Fatherland), and is clutched to the breast as is the letter, which would probably have had some phrases of filial devotion to his mother. Although David had both the factual and fabricated details of Bara's death available, he decided not to follow them and by eliminating practically all of the historical details and depicting a nude hero, the overall effect of the painting was to be timeless, spiritual and even ecstatic. The beauty and purity of *Bara* are all the more extraordinary when one considers that David was working on the painting when the Reign of Terror was at its height. All three of his revolutionary martyrs are deliberately distanced from the violence of their deaths, and painted either 'at their last breath' (Marat and Bara) or in peaceful repose (Le Pelletier) to suggest a consoling afterlife. Beauty and tranquillity were associated with immortality and rebirth.

David's art could also display a ruthless and fanatical streak that was in marked contrast to the heroism and patriotism of his revolutionary martyrs. David at his most savage is seen in his rapid drawing of *Marie Antoinette on the Way to the Guillotine*, done on 16 October 1793 (116). He observed the queen from an upper window and his profile drawing is brutally frank.

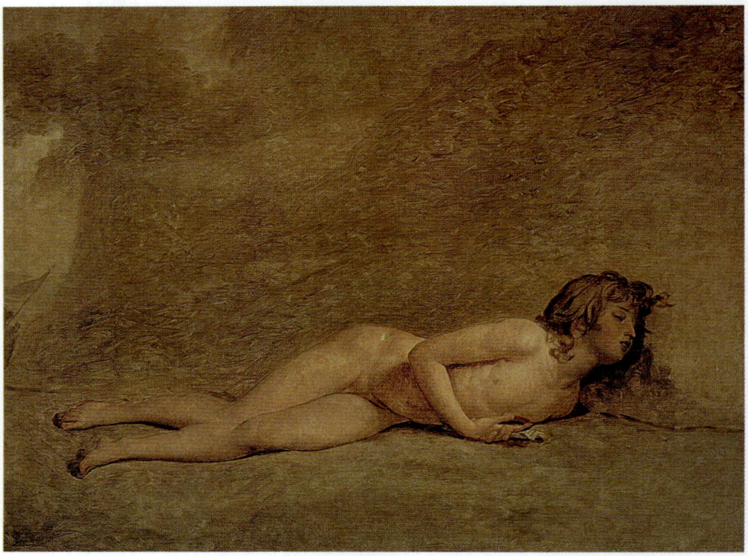

Marie Antoinette was only thirty-seven, but a year's imprisonment had made her look much older. Her hair was prematurely grey and, robbed of her false teeth, wig and corset and seated on a wooden plank on the back of a tumbrel, she looked a pathetic figure. After a brief loss of composure she met her end with great fortitude, dignity and calm, even apologizing to the executioner for having accidentally stepped on his foot.

Painting actually occupied only a fraction of David's time during the Revolution. He wanted the arts to reach all levels of society and so was also occupied with projects for the embellishment of Paris. David also made designs for civic uniforms (117), for money and official seals and even produced two crudely drawn and vulgar caricatures that mocked the English (118). Since the Revolution his views on the English had clearly changed and he no longer felt them to be the epitome of a free nation. According to the print's caption the English government 'is personified by the figure of a Devil skinned alive, monopolizing commerce and covered with all the Royal decorations. The portrait of the king is located at the rear end of the government which vomits on its people a myriad of taxes which overwhelm them.' David also saw himself as the artistic

114
The Death of Bara,
1794.
Oil on canvas;
119 × 156 cm,
$44\frac{7}{8} \times 61\frac{1}{2}$ in.
Musée Calvet,
Avignon

115
Apollo Belvedere,
Roman copy of a Greek original made c.330 BC.
Marble;
h.224 cm,
$88\frac{1}{4}$ in.
Vatican Museums,
Rome

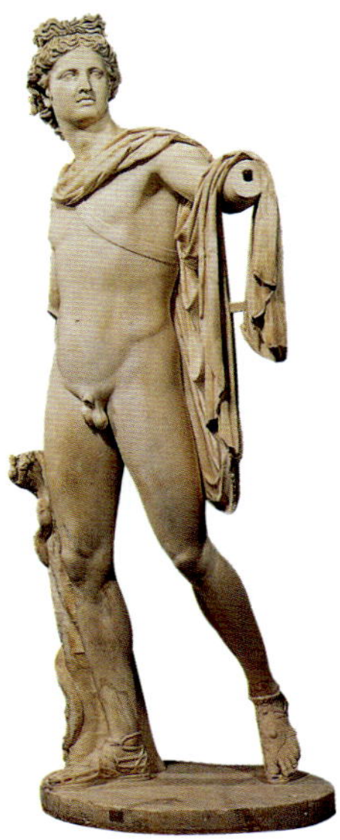

patriarch of the nation, and on 14 January 1792, with great pomp and seriousness he undertook the training of twin brothers, Joseph-Boniface (1774–1833) and Jean-Pierre Franque (1774–1860), shepherd boys from the Drôme department in southeast France who had shown great natural gifts. Their precocious talent, like the tale of Cimabue finding Giotto, had been discovered by a passing nobleman, who was impressed by the figures and landscapes they had engraved onto the rocks. From 1786 they studied in Grenoble, and during the Revolution the department assumed responsibility for their

116
Below left
Marie Antoinette on the Way to the Guillotine,
1793.
Pen and ink;
15×10cm,
$5\frac{7}{8} \times 4$in.
Musée du Louvre, Paris

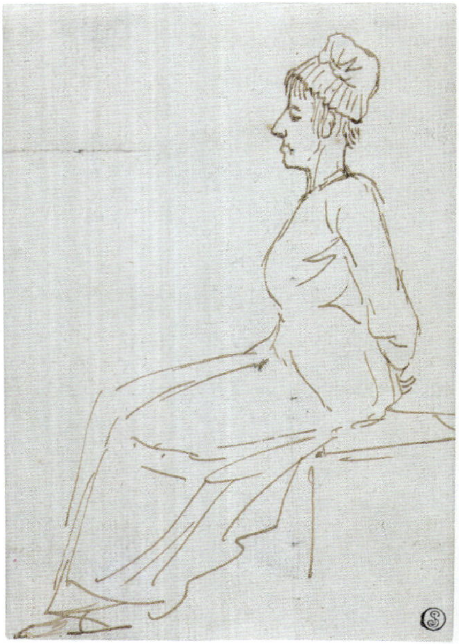

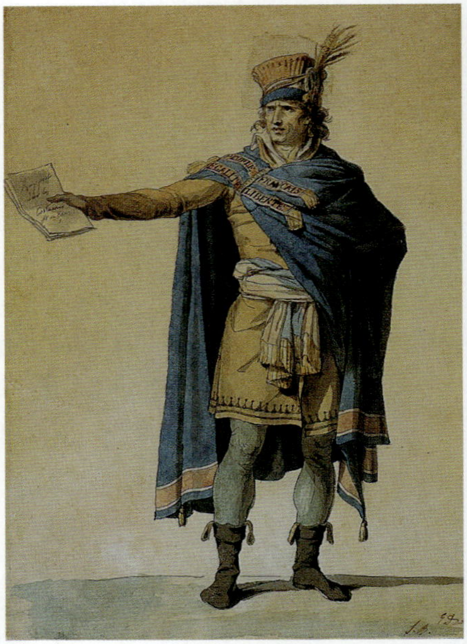

education and brought their case to the attention of the National Assembly. They were then placed with David who was proud to have been chosen as, 'the first teacher of these young men who can be justly called the children of the nation since they owe everything to it'. Refusing payment for tuition, he virtuously declared: 'The love of money has never troubled in my soul the love of glory which I value above all else.' Both the brothers went on to enjoy moderate success in painting and Jean-Pierre was briefly a studio assistant to David.

117
Above right
The Representative of the People on Duty,
1794.
Pen, ink and watercolour;
$31{\cdot}5 \times 22$cm,
$12\frac{3}{8} \times 8\frac{5}{8}$in.
Musée Carnavalet, Paris

The aspect of David's work that reached the most people was his organization of the great festivals or feasts which involved hundreds of thousands of the populus of Paris. As the 'Pageant Master of the Republic', he was responsible for four of these and contributed to two others. Such popular spectacles, which were themselves based on traditional Catholic festivals, were meticulously planned and choreographed and meant to be both socially unifying and celebrations of key revolutionary events. They were also calculated to bring order and control to the chaotic masses by overawing them with the

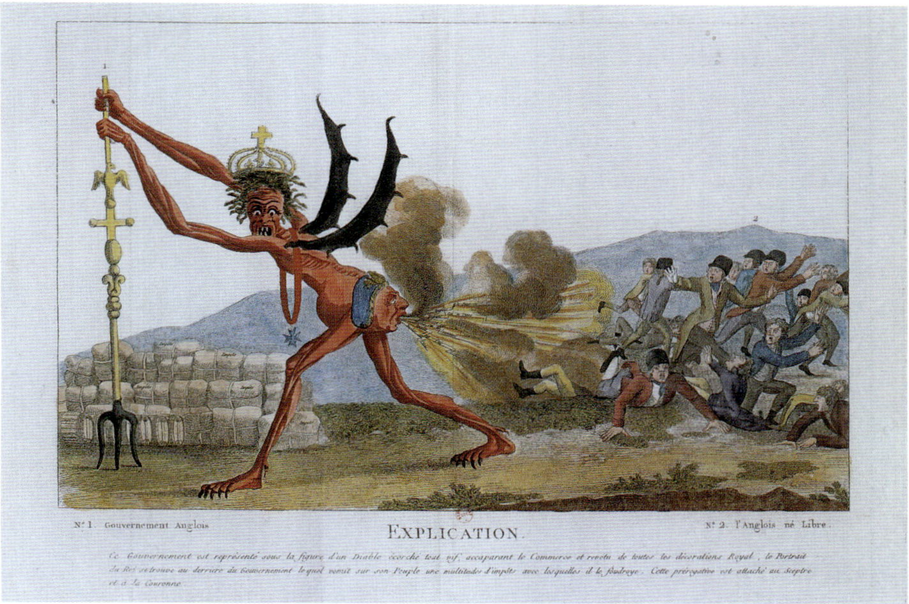

118
The English Government, 1794. Hand coloured etching; 24·8 × 39·2 cm, $9\frac{3}{4} \times 15\frac{1}{2}$ in. Bibliothèque Nationale, Paris

sheer scale and strict organization of the operation. David was the head of a group of workers that included his pupil Gioacchino Giuseppe Serangeli (1768–1852), the architects Auguste Cheval Hubert (1755–98) and Jean-Nicolas-Louis Durand (1760–1834), the carpenter Duplay and the musicians Bruni, Sarette and Méhul. He made designs for the costumes, the ceremonial architecture and the props which were then made by this very capable team. These festivals took the form of great processions which went from one place to another where speeches were made and symbolic dramatizations enacted. The whole procession would then meet for a grand finale at a large open space. In 1793, to celebrate the first anniversary of the overthrow of the monarchy (10 August 1792), David planned the Festival of Reunion or the Festival of Unity and Indivisibility. In this festival the history of the Revolution was turned into an allegorical pageant. The enormous crowd met at the site of the Bastille where a huge statue of an Egyptian-looking goddess of nature was seated at the top of a flight of white steps. Her hands cupped breasts from which water spouted into a sarcophagus-like basin below. The president of the Convention, Hérault de Séchelles, stepped forward holding an antique chalice and after filling it, poured it on to the ground to re-baptize the soil in the name of Liberty. This was then repeated by eighty-six old men, each representing a department of France. The second station was a triumphal arch dedicated to the women of 5 October 1789 who had brought the king back from Versailles to Paris. At the third station in the Place de la Révolution, a great statue of Liberty stood where once the statue of Louis XV had been placed, and at its feet were piled the debris of monarchical despotism – busts of past kings, flags and trophies etc. As this symbolic heap was set alight, a great cloud of three thousand white doves was released into the air. The fourth station was a huge statue of Hercules, representing the French people, crushing the hydra of federalism. The fifth and final station was an altar to the Fatherland. The whole was thus a mixture of Christian ritual, masonic imagery, patriotism and popular theatre. David's propaganda techniques were highly thought of, but this festival marked the final rupture with André Chénier who called the whole thing, 'the atrocious madness of the stupid David whom I once praised'.

The greatest of David's revolutionary pageants was the Festival of the Supreme Being, which took place on 8 June 1794 (or 20 Prairial Year II, according to the revolutionary calendar). France had become de-Christianized in 1793, mainly because of the age-old association between the Crown and the Church, but it was recognized that some form of religion was needed for social cohesion and to promise hope of salvation after death. Therefore a civic religion, the cult of the 'Supreme Being', was instituted with a deity that was rational, beneficent and wise. The festival began in the Tuileries gardens when 100,000 people saw Robespierre deliver the opening oration and then set light to a huge papier mâché statue representing Atheism, which burned away to reveal a statue of Wisdom (119). Robespierre then spoke again saying: 'It has vanished into dust, this monster which the evil genius of Kings once vomited over France, let it disappear and with it all the evils and misery of this world.' The procession then departed for the Champ de la Réunion (the revolutionary name for the Champ des Mars, where the Eiffel Tower now stands) where an amphitheatre, triumphal arches and a huge artificial mound, complete with grottoes, a statue of Hercules and a Tree of Liberty had been erected (120). The crowd, now swollen to about 200,000, sang a hymn to the divinity, the orchestra played a symphony and youths and old men swore oaths of allegiance inspired by the figures from David's *Horatii*. In each of these festivals, memorably called 'an immense living fresco' by David Dowd, David gave the political authority of the day a visible and tangible cultural framework and succeeded in mobilizing, uniting and controlling a disparate and hitherto disorderly populace.

David also considered how to represent the people to themselves, and to do so he turned to the figure of Hercules that had been used in the Festival of Unity and Indivisibility. Early in November 1793 he suggested that a colossal statue of Hercules, representing the French people, be erected on the Pont Neuf in Paris. In selecting Hercules, David avoided all references to the Convention and its deputies, intending a simple and memorable image embodying collective popular power instead. The bronze statue was to be made from captured enemy cannons and its base was to incorporate smashed statues of saints and kings from royal monuments and Notre Dame (which was then

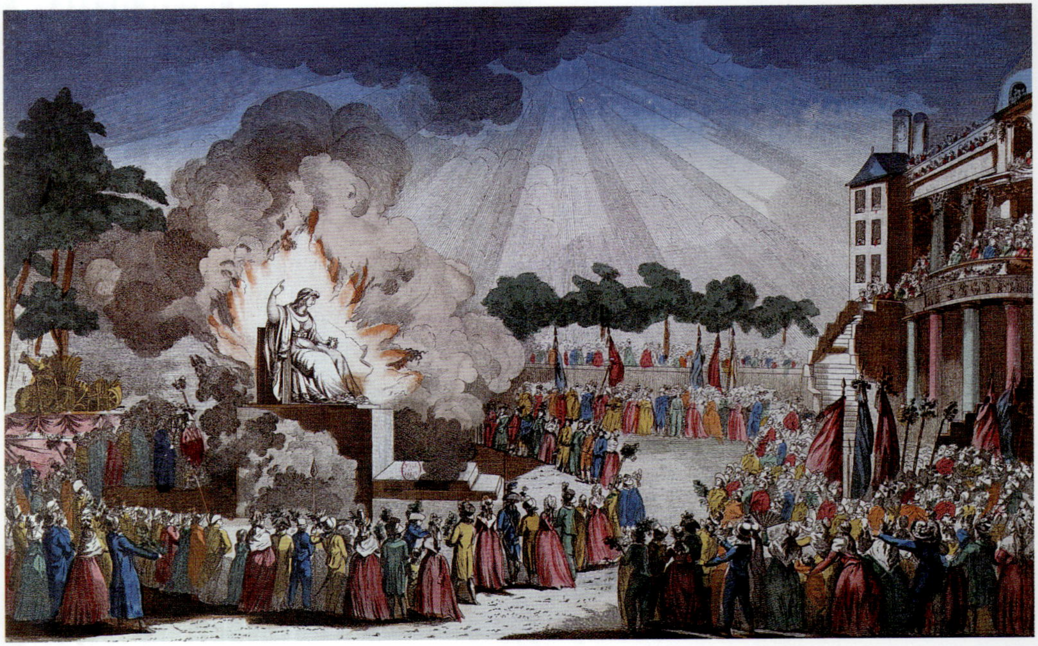

called the Temple of Reason). According to David, the Hercules would perpetuate the triumph of Reason and citizens would be further instructed by the engraving of key words on the body. On his forehead the word 'light' would be inscribed (a rather obtuse way of referring to intelligence); 'nature' and 'truth' would be placed on his chest, 'strength' on his arms and 'work' on his hands. In one of his hands Hercules would hold small figures of Liberty and Equality, while in the other, his deadly club would be carried. Two competitions for the figure were suggested but such a huge and costly project, extravagant even under a stable regime, had little chance of success in a country whose industry and manufacturing was geared towards war production.

119
The Statue of Atheism Burnt and Replaced by that of Wisdom during the Festival of the Supreme Being,
1794.
Engraving

To David, Hercules was a very potent revolutionary symbol; he is the principal figure in two designs made by him for *The Triumph of the French People* (121). These were probably part of a project for the curtain to a five-act *sans-culottes* play, *The Meeting of the Tenth August* or *The Inauguration of the French Republic*. This entertainment, by Gabriel Bouquier (1739–1810),

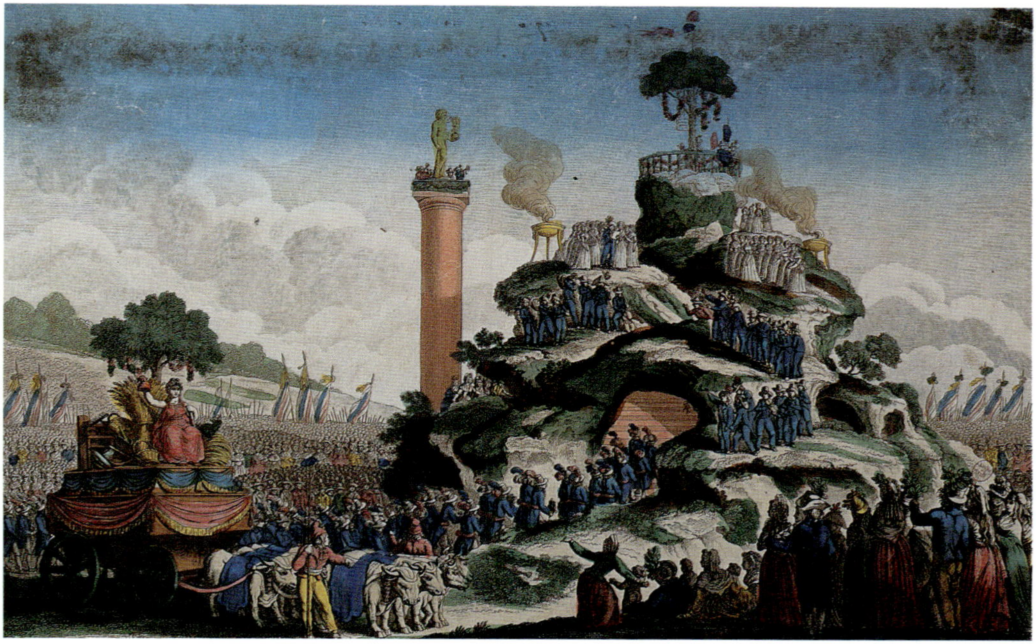

120
The Mound Erected on the Champ de la Réunion for the Festival of the Supreme Being,
1794.
Engraving

a painter and deputy to the Convention, and by P L Moline, its registrar, had its first performance at the Paris Opéra on 5 April 1794. The play's content and sets relied heavily on David's creations for his festivals, and his own curtain designs both show how some of his processional floats would have looked and reveal his own pantheon of revolutionary actors. Hercules sits atop a triumphal chariot with Liberty and Equality on his knees and personifications of Science, Art, Business and Plenty in front of him. A team of four oxen draw the chariot which crushes symbols of royalty and feudalism beneath its wheels. Victory holding a spear flies above the oxen and in front two patriots stab a fallen king. Behind come ancient, medieval and modern political heroes. These include Cornelia, the Roman woman who referred to her own children as her jewels, who holds their hands as an example of patriotic motherhood; and then Brutus; William Tell with his son on his shoulders; Marat displaying his wound; Le Pelletier placing his hand over his bleeding side; and behind them are Pierre Bayle (or Baille) and Charles Beauvais de Préau, both Girondins in

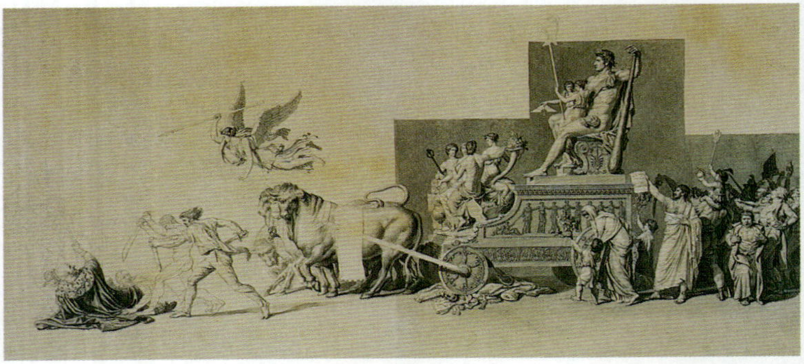

121
The Triumph of the French People,
1794.
Graphite, pen and ink wash;
38·6 × 71cm,
15¼ × 28in.
Musée Carnavalet, Paris

Toulon who had been handed over to the English by royalists when the city fell in the summer of 1793. Bayle had hung himself on the night of 1–2 September 1793 and is shown pulling at his neckcloth. Although released from prison in December 1793 after the recapture of Toulon by republican troops, Beauvais de Préau died, it was said, as a result of his harsh treatment and thus rattles the chains that once held him. Created at a time when the Reign of Terror was at its height, these drawings show David at his most radical and extreme, and are perfectly in tune with the current inflexible and violent phase of the Revolution. The creation of Robespierre's 'Republic of Virtue' would be achieved by the spilling of blood to consecrate martyrs and to purge the enemy within. Due to the Opéra moving premises and decisive changes in the political climate, like so much of David's revolutionary work, the curtain was never painted.

Seven weeks after the highly successful Festival of the Supreme Being, on 9 Thermidor (27 July), Robespierre and his closest supporters were overthrown by a temporary coalition of both left- and right-wing dissidents in the Convention, and they were sent to the guillotine in the days following. It soon became clear that it was a victory for the conservative deputies such as Jean Lambert Tallien and Louis-Stanislas Fréron. The Reign of Terror, which had lasted nearly ten months and had seen between 30,000 and 40,000 people killed, was over. So too was David's political career.

Close to the Edge   Prison, Recovery and Change

4

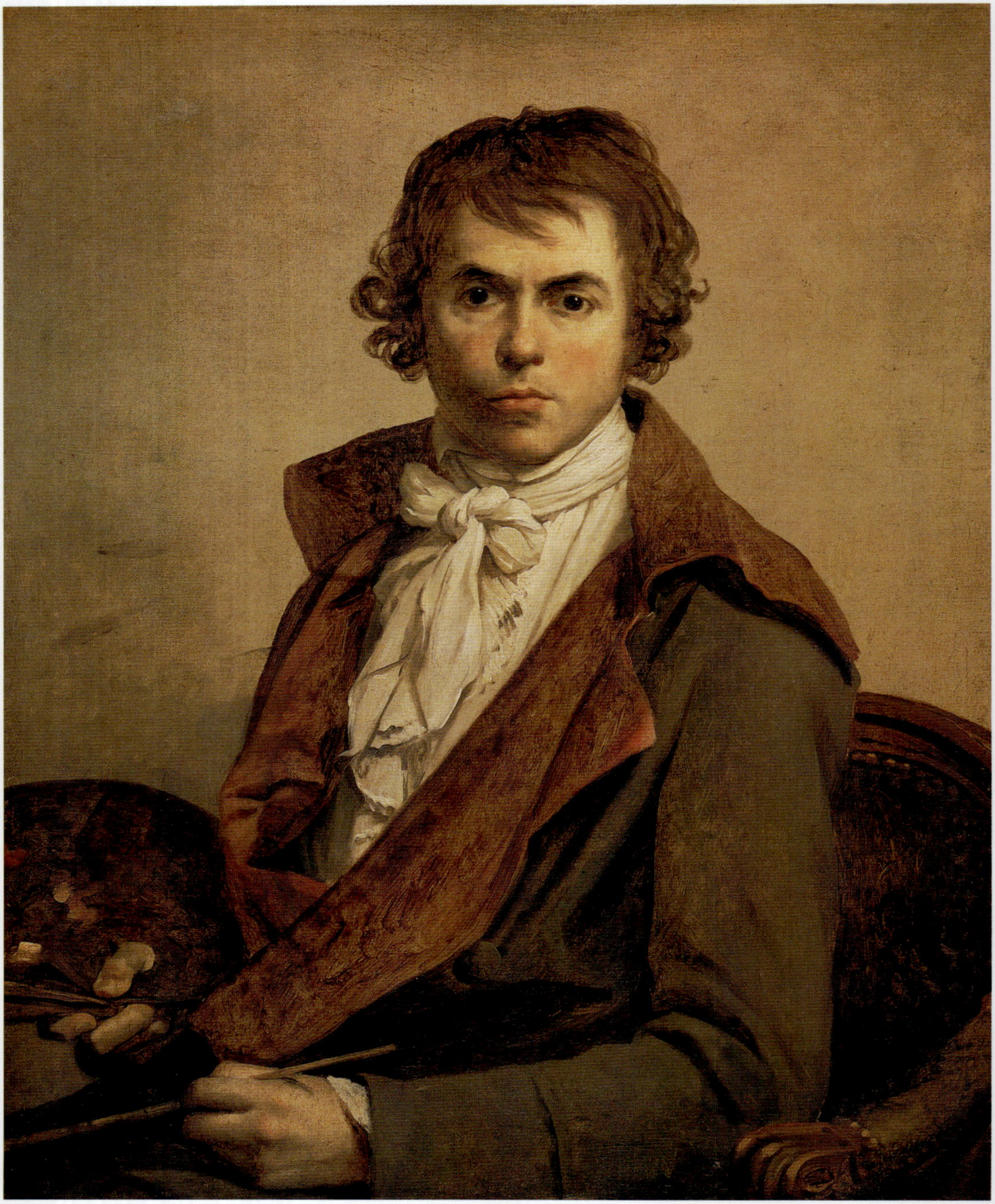

As David was so closely linked with Robespierre, he too might easily have been executed after the events of 9 Thermidor. But on the day of Robespierre's arrest David did not attend the Convention. He claimed that he was ill, even though he had been well enough the day before to have declared his support for the beleaguered Robespierre by saying, 'If you drink the hemlock, I will drink it with you.' This absence probably saved his life, and it seems very likely that he had been forewarned. At the Convention on 13 Thermidor (31 July) David was denounced as a 'traitor', 'usurper' and 'tyrant of the arts'. He sweated and stammered to defend himself from his political enemies and survived the onslaught but was still arrested two days later. The former artistic dictator of the most revolutionary nation on earth was now on trial for his life. The first charges related to his support of Robespierre and his activities for the Committee of General Security, which had involved the signing of arrest warrants. Called to account for his past actions and allegiances, he wrote that he had been duped by Robespierre's powerful personality and revolutionary ardour – 'My heart is pure, only my head was wrong', he declared. Later, on 2 May 1795, further charges were brought against him alleging abuses of power and the persecution of rival artists who did not share his political views. In this second indictment there were seventeen charges – what David called 'a malicious slander' – and he prepared a lengthy and closely argued reply. 'I explicitly testify that I have never caused any artists' arrest, on the contrary ... I busied myself helping a number of those who had sided with my enemies.' All of the charges against him were somewhat contrived and related more to hearsay and to passages from his melodramatic and rhetorical speeches rather than to any specific deeds.

122
Self-Portrait, 1794. Oil on canvas; 81 × 64 cm, $31\frac{7}{8} \times 25\frac{1}{4}$ in. Musée du Louvre, Paris

At his arrest on 15 Thermidor (2 August 1794) David was initially held in reasonably comfortable conditions in the Hôtel des Fermes Générales, formerly the administration building of the tax farmers. After a month he was transferred to the Luxembourg Palace from which he was released on 28 December when the Convention found that he had no case to answer. However, when the new accusations were brought against him, he was re-arrested on 28 May and imprisoned in the Collège des Quatre Nations for just over two months until 3 August. Towards the end of July he had been very ill, and special precautions were taken when it was feared that he might attempt suicide. Released on parole due to delicate health, David's ordeal only ended on 26 October 1795 when all revolutionary detainees were amnestied following the abolition of the Convention. A new constitution was passed which created the Directory – a group of five 'Directors' who had central executive authority and who were responsible to two legislative bodies.

123
Woman in a Turban, 1794. Pen and brown ink; 37 × 26 cm, 14½ × 10¼ in. Private collection

Having painted relatively few works during the Revolution, David worked with great energy while in prison, possibly using painting both as an escape and as tangible evidence that he was a painter and not a politician. In the Hôtel des Fermes Générales, David's room had been the painting studio of the former concierge's son, one of his ex-pupils, F A Légé (1779–1837), who was then away in the army. Another pupil, Pierre-Maximilien Delafontaine (*c*.1774–1860) brought painting equipment and materials as well as a mirror which enabled David to paint his second self-portrait (122). Less agitated than his first effort (see 93), in this painting David stares out with a mixture of bewilderment and candour, brush and palette in hand, the tumour in his left cheek very prominent. (Because it was painted with the aid of a mirror, the swollen cheek appears on the right due to the inversion that accompanies a mirror image.) This picture is David's powerful and persuasive visual plea that he be judged for what he is – an artist. He also appears younger than his forty-six years – a characteristic of not only his self-portraits but also of some of his portraits. When he was moved to the Luxembourg Palace David continued to work, producing a now lost portrait of his mother (who perhaps visited him in prison), and a drawing, in the style of an engraving, of a *Woman in a Turban* (123), which he very pointedly inscribed 'J L David did this in chains' [*ie* in prison]. Additionally he painted his one and only landscape, a *View of the Luxembourg Gardens*, painted from his prison window, which is possibly the picture now in the Louvre (124). David

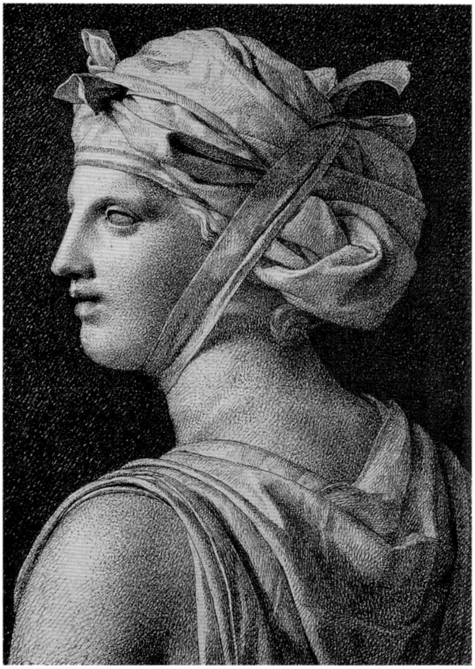

always needed to paint from either life or nature and in the confined conditions of prison he had to use those limited subjects that presented themselves. However, both the subject and the authorship of the Louvre painting have been doubted. To some scholars the view seems more Mediterranean than northern European, and the paint handling is unlike David's other works of the time. So although it is known that David painted his prison view, not all authorities are convinced that this is the landscape in the Louvre.

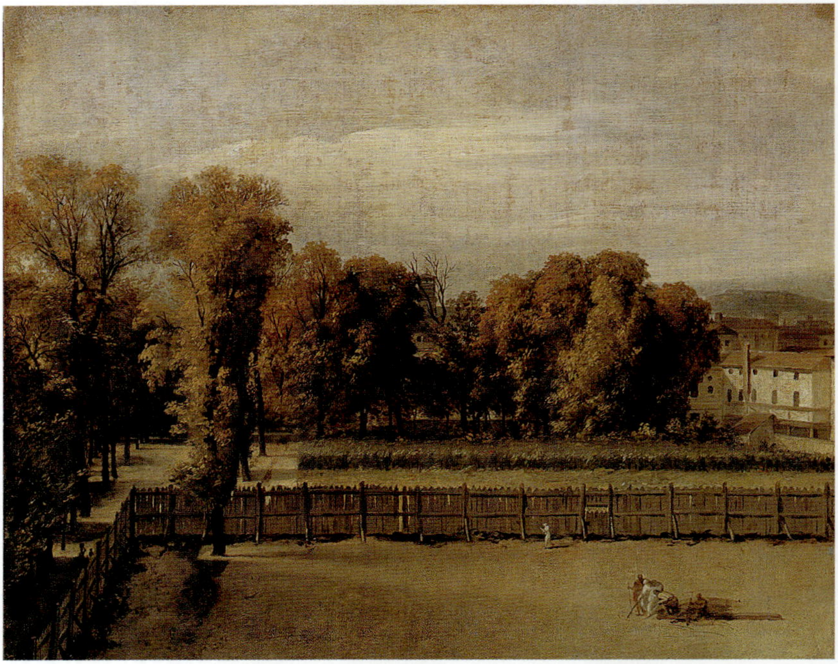

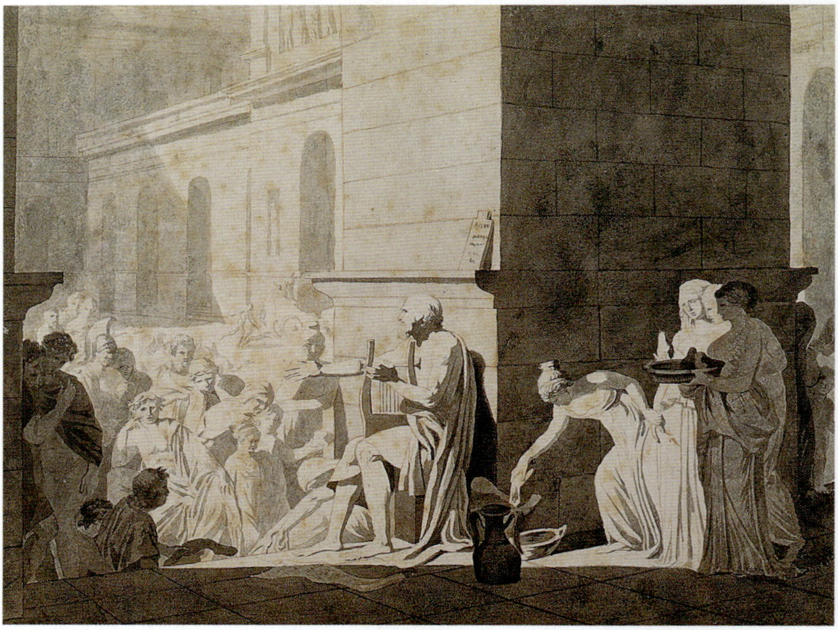

David also began work on a history painting on the theme of *Homer Reciting his Verses to the Greeks* (125); he closely identified with the blind poet of antiquity because of a shared sense of solitude and victimization. When in the Collège des Quatre Nations, David drew an oval portrait of a fellow detainee, the former Protestant minister, Jeanbon Saint-André (126). Politically Saint-André had much in common with David. He too had sat on the Mountain, had voted for the death of the king and had been president of the Convention. He had also been a member of the Committee of Public Safety, the group of twelve that virtually ruled France during the Reign of Terror. David's portrait shows him as upright and determined,

124
View of the Luxembourg Gardens,
1794.
Oil on canvas;
55 × 65cm,
$21\frac{5}{8} \times 25\frac{5}{8}$ in.
Musée du Louvre, Paris

125
Homer Reciting his Verses to the Greeks,
1794.
Black and red chalk, pen, ink and wash;
27·2 × 34·5cm,
$10\frac{3}{4} \times 13\frac{5}{8}$ in.
Musée du Louvre, Paris

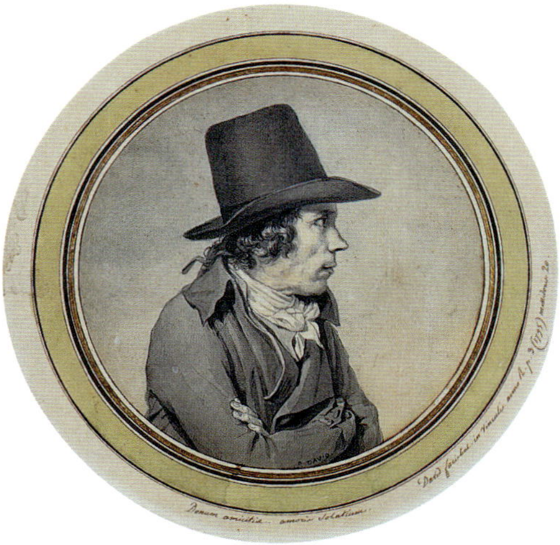

126
Portrait of Jeanbon Saint-André,
1795.
Pen, black ink, wash and white highlights;
diam.18·2cm,
$7\frac{1}{8}$ in.
The Art Institute of Chicago

with no hint of a man subdued by imprisonment. David, however, revealed his personal sense of injustice in an inscription in Latin at the bottom of the drawing: 'A gift of friendship. Solace of affection. David made in chains Year III of the French Republic (1795) Messidor 20.'

David's letters from his first and longest period of captivity, not surprisingly, reveal a considerable degree of mental anguish and torment. His prison ordeal was perhaps made worse by the first real signs of ageing – his eyesight began to weaken and he had to start wearing spectacles to work. He also had time to reflect on his political involvement – 'I am prevented from returning to my studio, which alas, I should never have left. I believed in accepting the honourable, but extremely difficult, task of legislator, that a righteous heart would suffice, but I lacked the second quality, understanding.' His tendency towards paranoia also resurfaced, and he attributed his continuing incarceration to the work of a 'secret enemy'. While in the Luxembourg, David and his wife also became reconciled. By now she was even more financially independent after receiving a considerable inheritance at her father's recent death, and their reconciliation suggests that genuine affection had been rekindled as she now had even less need of a troublesome husband. David wrote that, 'my wife with her four children presented themselves before the Concierge who, softened by their tears, brought them to me. She threw herself around my neck in his presence. "Citizen," she told him, "do not believe that you are guarding a bad person. He is the most honest man I know; believe a devoted wife." In tears she and my four children held me longingly in their arms, my tears flowed abundantly and we mingled souls in tender and unexpected embrace.' The couple eventually remarried on 12 November 1796.

David's faithful students campaigned on his behalf and on 30 November 1794 seventeen of them delivered a petition to the Convention requesting their master's release. When he was eventually released from the Luxembourg prison at the end of December 1794, David became ill and so requested permission from the Convention to visit his wife's sister and her husband, Emilie and Pierre Sériziat, at their country house in Saint Ouen, near Tournan-en-Brie, about 32 km (20 miles) east of Paris. This visit was cut short by the accusations of May 1795 and arrest, but he returned there, accompanied by a guard, to recuperate after his second and final release in August. He then painted the portraits of his hosts. Madame Sériziat (127) is shown in an interior setting with her young son, having just returned from a walk. Her cheeks are ruddy and she carries a recently picked bunch of wild flowers which are painted in a lively but meticulous manner. Unusually for David, the lawyer Pierre Sériziat (128) is posed out of doors seated on his coat spread over a rock, an elegant and leisured country gentleman and reminiscent of English portraits by Reynolds and George Romney (1734–1802). These two portraits were testaments of friendship and, by showing them at the 1795 Salon, he could prove that he was still able to paint after his ordeals. He wrote: 'Here is fodder for my enemies. I believe they will be forced to admit that at least I have not yet lost my talent.' Portraits, of course, were ideal vehicles for David at this time because they were politically neutral subject matter and free from the possible controversies of interpretation that history paintings could bring.

The Paris that David returned to was a changed place. The spectres of Robespierre and the Reign of Terror had gone, and had been replaced by the relaxation and frivolity of the Directory. Although there was raging inflation, the dance halls, cafés and theatres did a roaring trade and clothes and fashion returned to their former prominence in the lives of privileged society. In the autumn of 1795 David painted two further important portraits, those of Jacobus Blauw and Gaspar Mayer. Both men were in Paris as representatives of the new revolutionary government of the Netherlands, now renamed the Batavian Republic. David placed Jacobus Blauw (129) at his desk, with quill in hand, looking out with an expression of alertness and enthusiasm. He seems very fresh-faced and boyish for a man of thirty-nine, and perhaps this was done to give a sense of his energetic political conviction. David took great care over the details in the painting, scrupulously observing the still-life of the papers, snuff-box, ink well and handkerchief. As was common for him, David set the figure in a shallow space against a plain background. Blauw was delighted with his portrait and wrote to David, 'My wishes are at last satisfied, my dear David. You have brought me to life again on the canvas; you have, in a way, immortalized me with your sublime brush.' The image of Gaspar Mayer (130) is more

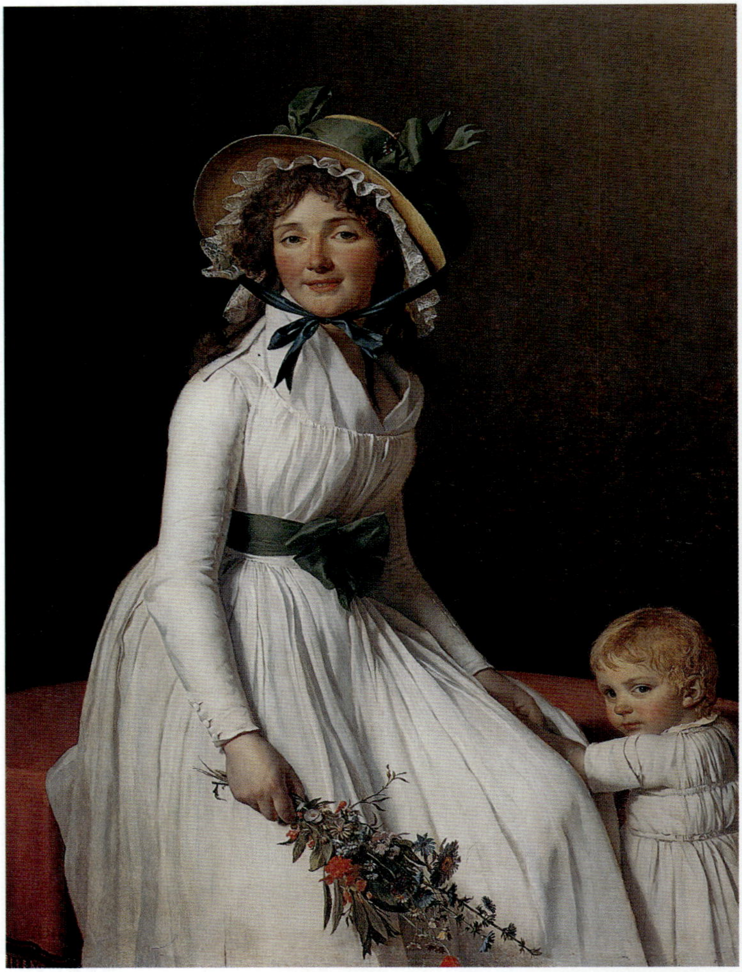

127
Portrait of Emilie Sériziat and her Son, 1795. Oil on canvas; 131 × 96 cm, $51^{5}/_{8} \times 37^{3}/_{4}$ in. Musée du Louvre, Paris

sedate, formal and distant. Evidently he was a shrewder and more circumspect diplomat than Blauw and David placed him in a much more self-conscious pose. One question that these two pictures raise is why two foreign representatives should have requested their portraits from a disgraced Jacobin only recently released from prison. For Blauw's part it appears that he admired both David's art and his politics, and the commission for a portrait might have been a minor act of defiance by Blauw because he was disappointed with the moderate direction that the French Revolution had taken. Mayer, on the other hand, probably doubted the political wisdom of having his

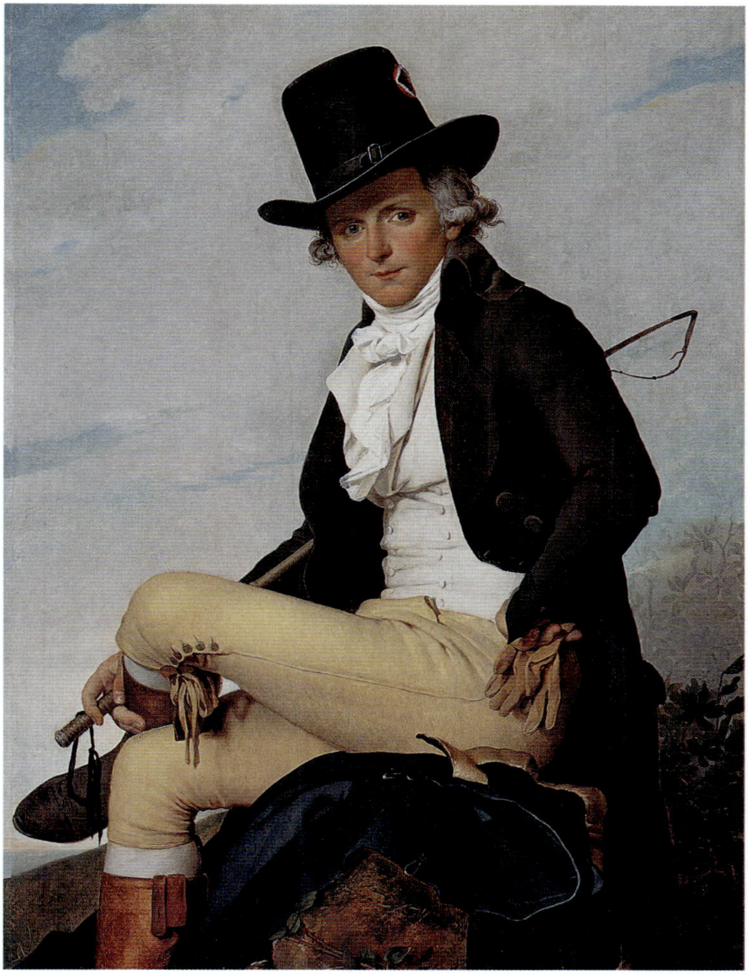

128
Portrait of Pierre Sériziat,
1795.
Oil on canvas;
129 × 95 cm,
$50\frac{3}{4} \times 37\frac{3}{8}$ in.
Musée du Louvre, Paris

portrait painted by David and found the whole episode highly embarrassing, and never bothered to collect it from David's studio, where it remained until the artist's death.

David was gradually regaining his reputation, and proof of this came in December 1795 when he was one of six artists nominated to the painting section of the Institute, the body that replaced the Academy. As the Directory had some say in the election of members, it seems that David's former actions were not being held against him – he was, after all, still France's premier painter. Ironically, membership of the Institute was even more restricted than that of the old Academy, but

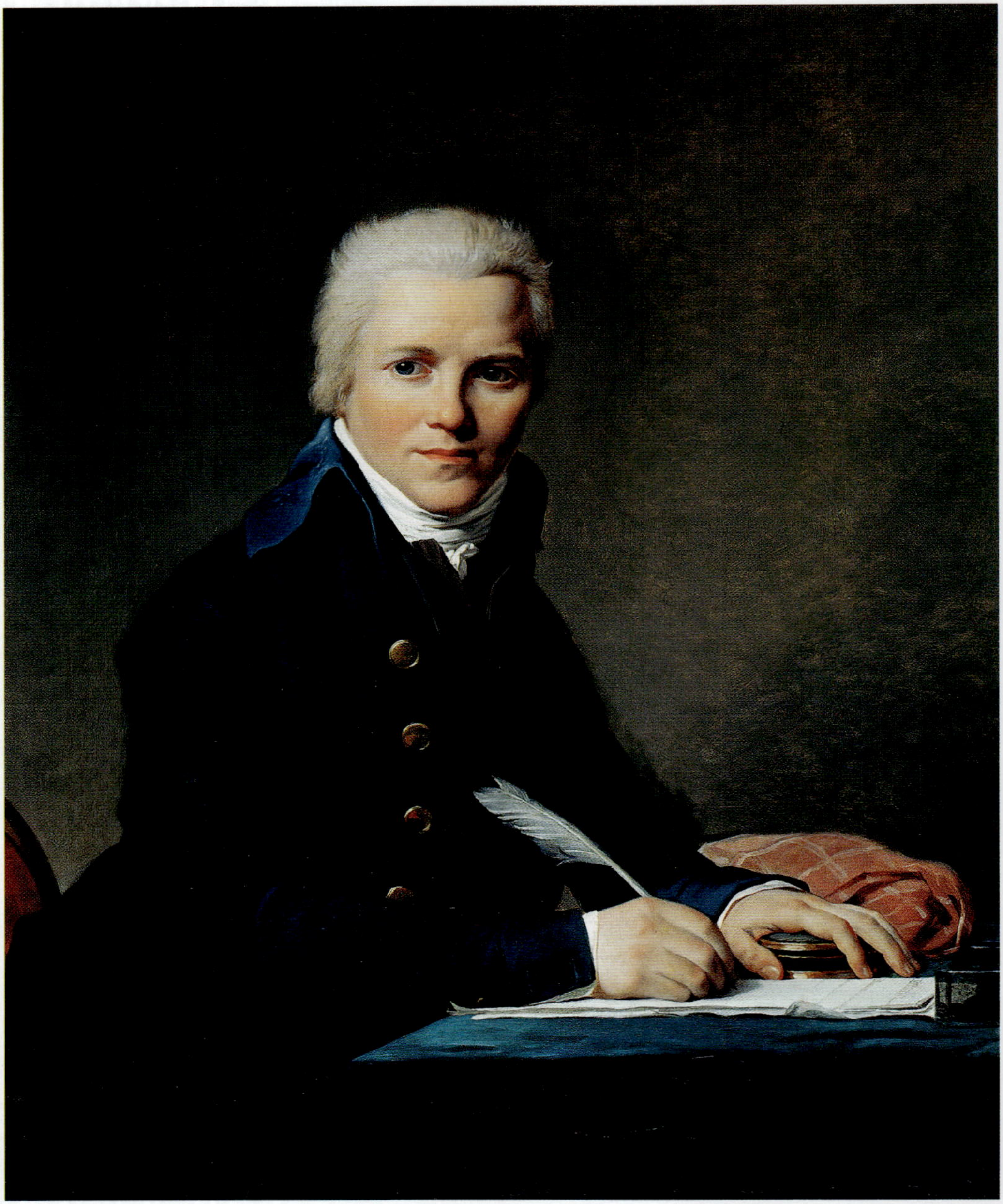

129
Portrait of Jacobus Blauw,
1795.
Oil on canvas;
92 × 73 cm,
36¼ × 28¾ in.
National Gallery, London

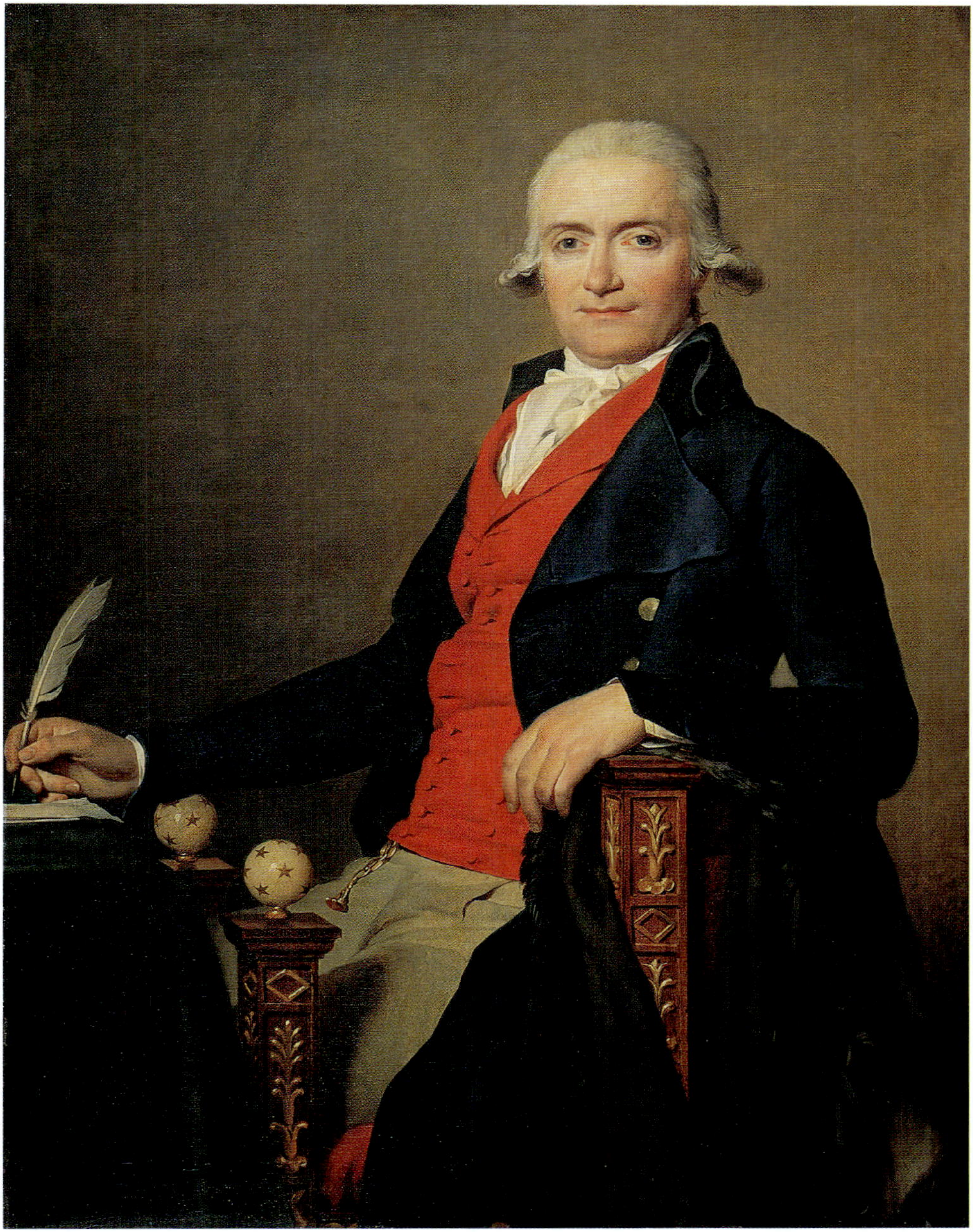

130
Portrait of Gaspar Mayer,
1795.
Oil on canvas;
116 × 89·5cm,
$45\frac{5}{8} \times 35\frac{1}{5}$ in.
Musée du Louvre, Paris

David happily accepted the nomination. His former grievances against authority had mainly been personal or else concerned with the dull and repetitive student tuition, and teaching was not to be part of the Institute's functions.

While in prison David had planned a return to history painting, as the drawings for the *Homer* project (see 125) prove. However, he soon abandoned that subject and instead started work on *The Intervention of the Sabine Women* (131), a project that was to occupy him until 1799. This subject, from ancient Rome, was the aftermath of the rape of the Sabines when, to ensure the population growth of their city, Romulus and his Romans abducted the womenfolk of their neighbours, the Sabines. Three years passed before the Sabine men, led by Tatius, mounted a counterattack. David himself described what happened next in the brochure he wrote to accompany the painting's exhibition.

Battle was joined; both sides attacked. The two chiefs [Romulus and Tatius] met in the centre of the mêlée and made ready for the single combat according to the custom of these heroic days. But what may not conjugal and maternal love together accomplish? The Sabine women, who had been kidnapped by the Romans, suddenly rushed upon the scene of battle; their hair streaming in the wind, carrying their naked children at their breasts, they passed the piles of the dead and the horses frenzied in their combat. They called loudly to their fathers, their brothers, their husbands, addressing themselves now to the Romans, now to the Sabines, calling them by the sweetest names known to man. The combatants, softened by pity, gave place to them. One of them, Hersilia, wife to Romulus, to whom she had borne two children, came forward between the two chiefs. 'Sabines, what are you doing below the walls of Rome?' she cried. 'These are no longer daughters whom you would restore to their parents, nor ravishers whom you would punish. We should have been dragged from their arms while we were still strangers, but now we are bound to them by the most sacred ties; you would tear wives from husbands, mothers from their children' … Some of the women who accompanied her laid their children at the feet of the soldiers, who let their bloody swords fall from their hands. Others lifted up their nurslings in their arms and held them like shields against the forest of lances which dropped when confronted by them. Romulus holds back the javelin which he is about to hurl at Tatius. The general of the cavalry puts his sword back into its sheath. The soldiers raise their helmets as a sign of peace. The feelings of conjugal, fatherly and brotherly love spread through the ranks of both armies. Soon the Romans and the Sabines embrace to form a single people.

Such a subject was somewhat rare in painting; it was much more usual for artists to depict the drama and action of the rape. Poussin had painted two versions of the subject (*c.*1635 and *c.*1637), one of which was in the Louvre. David decided to contrast the violence of the rape with the pacification of the intervention. The image of family conflict in the *Sabines* was a metaphor of the revolutionary process which had now culminated in peace and reconciliation, and the subject had both a general and a personal relevance to him. France itself was returning to normality and recovering from the shock of the Reign of Terror, factional strife had diminished and political refugees were returning from exile. The painting was also a tribute to Madame David, and a recognition of the power of women as peacemakers. For the first time in a history painting by David, the central figure is a woman, Hersilia (132), who forces herself between Romulus, her husband, on the right and the Sabine Tatius, her father, on the left. Other women cling to the warriors and place themselves and their children between the opposing groups. The passive and recumbent females, so prominent in the *Horatii* and *Brutus*, are nowhere to be seen. But although women play a central role, when considering the work contemporary (male) critics spent more time discussing the suspended action and idealized nude forms of Romulus and Tatius. To a contemporary male audience Hersilia was not so much an independent free-thinking and free-acting individual, but one whose actions were determined by her identity that

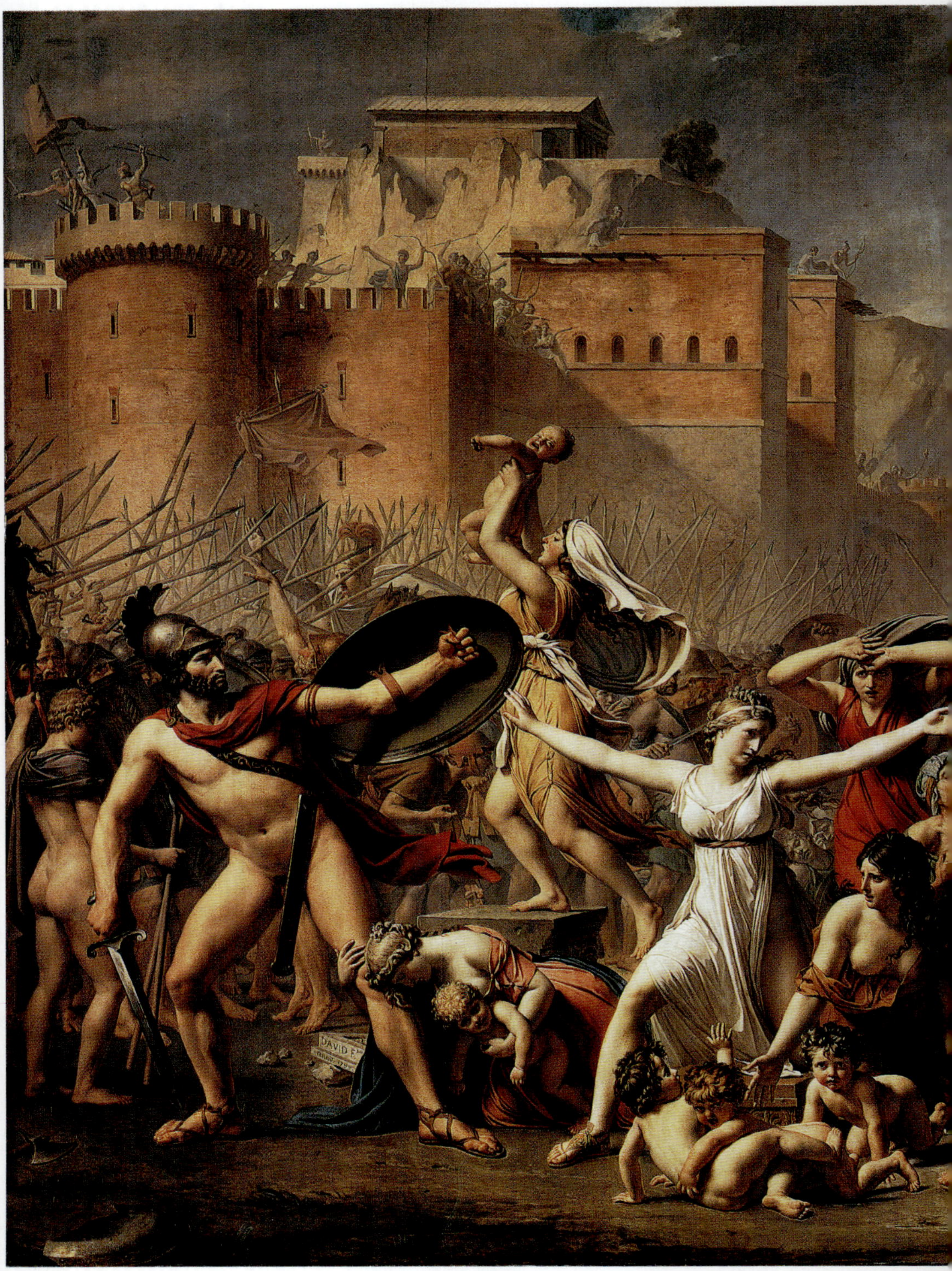

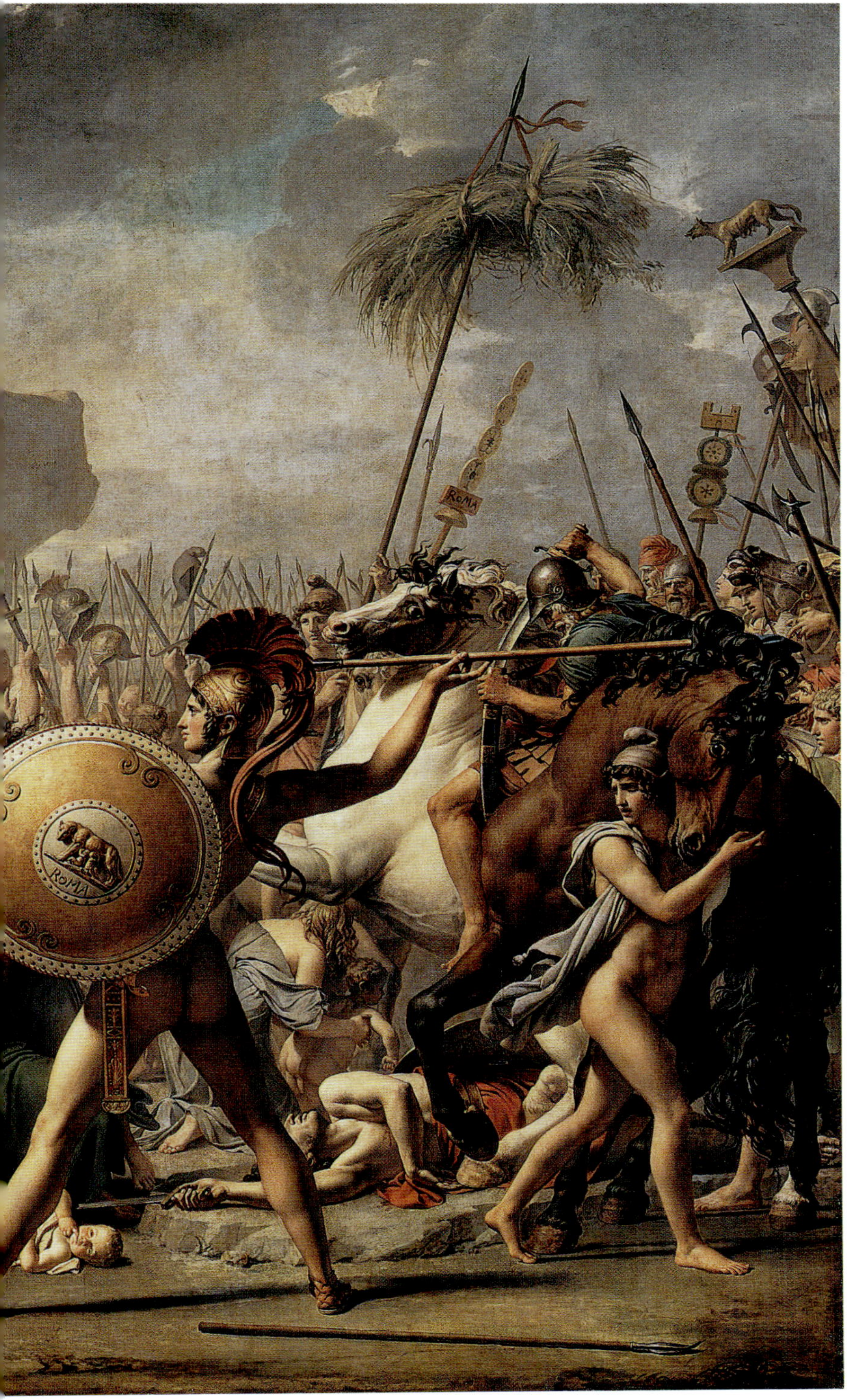

131
The Intervention of the Sabine Women,
1799.
Oil on canvas;
385 × 522 cm,
$151\frac{5}{8} \times 205\frac{1}{2}$ in.
Musée du Louvre, Paris

was shaped by her relationship to the two male protagonists – her father Tatius and her husband Romulus. Intervention and the cessation of fighting was the only solution to the dilemma of divided family loyalties. Present-day scholars, notably Ewa Lajer-Burcharth, have seen the work as being concerned with the relations between men and women in the course of the Revolution. While the men could be related to the dignity and authority of the antique, the women were seen as creatures of nature, subject to their emotions, and their actions were welcome but nevertheless spontaneous, disorderly incursions into the male spheres of war and politics. The only adult figure that looks out and directly engages with the spectator is the woman in red, behind Hersilia, with her arms raised to her forehead. Of the women she alone has neither child nor participates in the action, and by the colour of her dress and her pose she appears as a powerfully charged representative of frenzy, an uncomfortable reminiscence that, unchecked, such forces can lead to the outrages of the Reign of Terror.

132
The Intervention of the Sabine Women
(detail of 131)

David painted *The Intervention of the Sabine* on a huge scale, 3·9 × 5·2 m (nearly 13 × 18 ft), and he worked in a newly acquired and larger studio on the Seine side of the Louvre. When looking at the *Sabines* a change in David's style is immediately obvious. The tension, drama and austere economy of the *Horatii* or *Marat* is replaced by an evenly lit and crowded composition that contains a number of different actions. Whereas the *Horatii* focuses on a single, highly memorable image, the *Sabines* has to be read serially, incident by incident. In the course of fifteen years David's ideas about art had changed and he said that he wanted the *Sabines* to be 'more Greek', meaning that he aimed at a form of heroic simplicity that corresponded to the ritualized representations of warfare in ancient Greek art. In place of the sinew and muscle of the Horatii men, which came from close observation of the life model, Romulus and Tatius have smooth bodies, based on a study of sculpture (133). David said, 'Perhaps I have shown too much anatomy in my painting of the Horatii; in this one, the

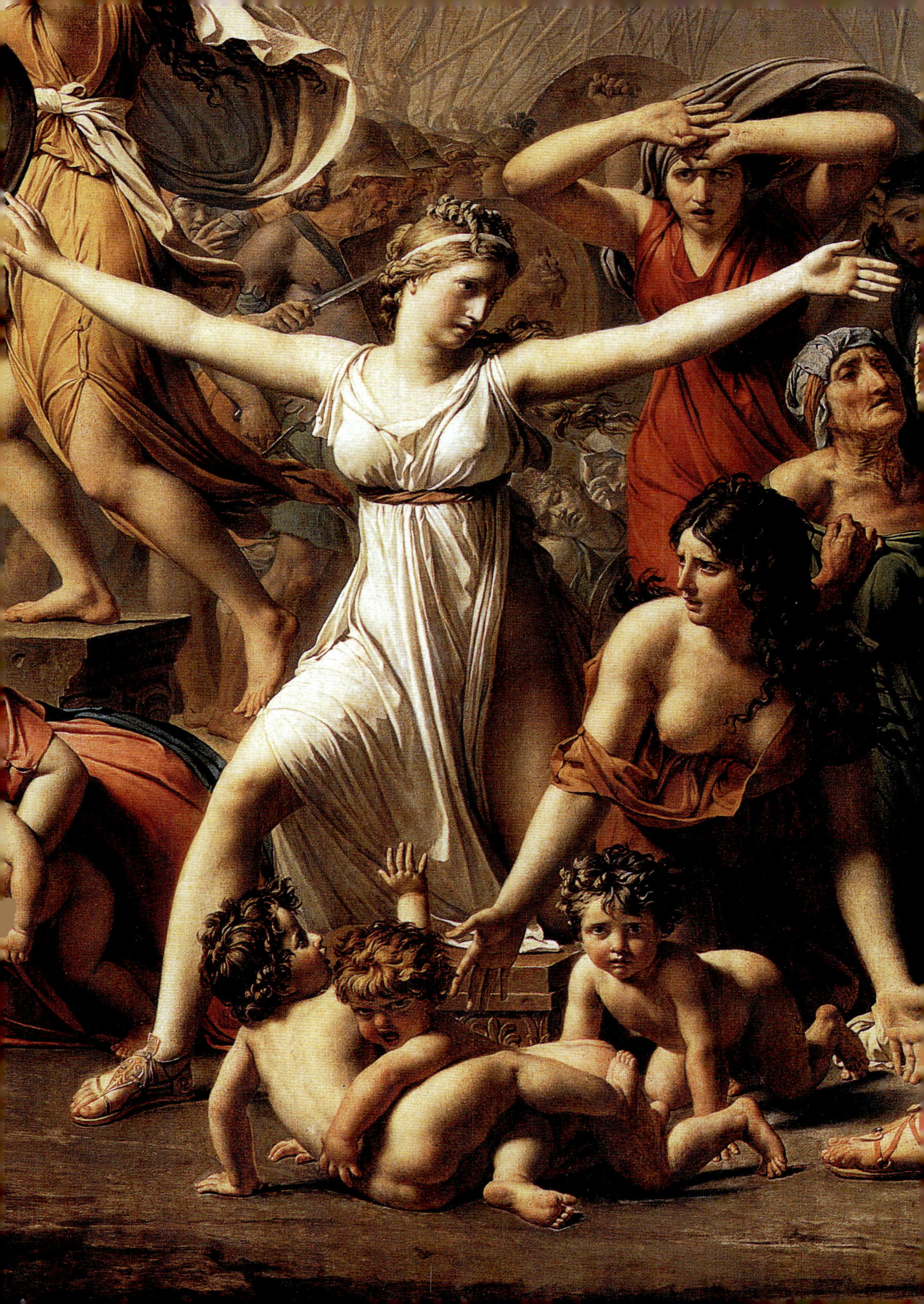

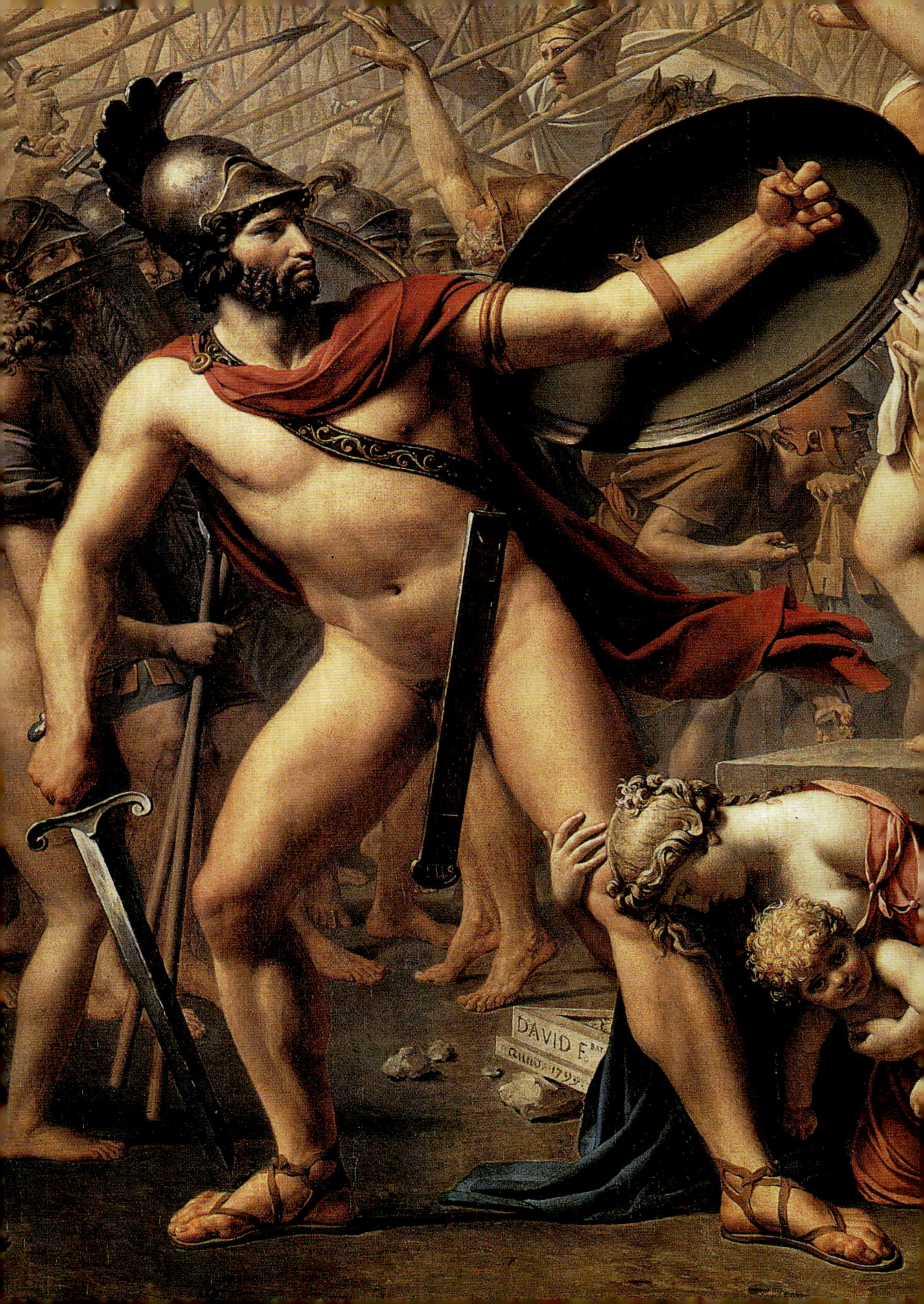
DAVID F

133
The Intervention of the Sabine Women
(detail of 131)

134
John Flaxman,
Illustration to Homer's *Iliad*, *The Fight for the Body of Patroclus*,
1793.
Engraving;
15·2 × 26·6 cm,
6 × 10½ in

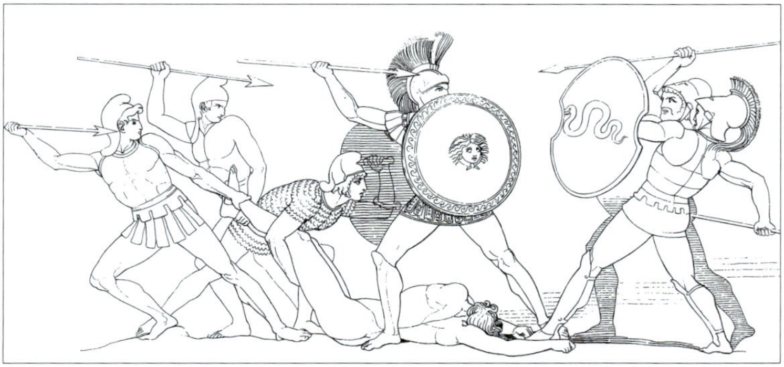

135
James Gillray,
Sin, Death and the Devil,
1792.
Etching;
31·9 × 39·9 cm,
12½ × 15¾ in

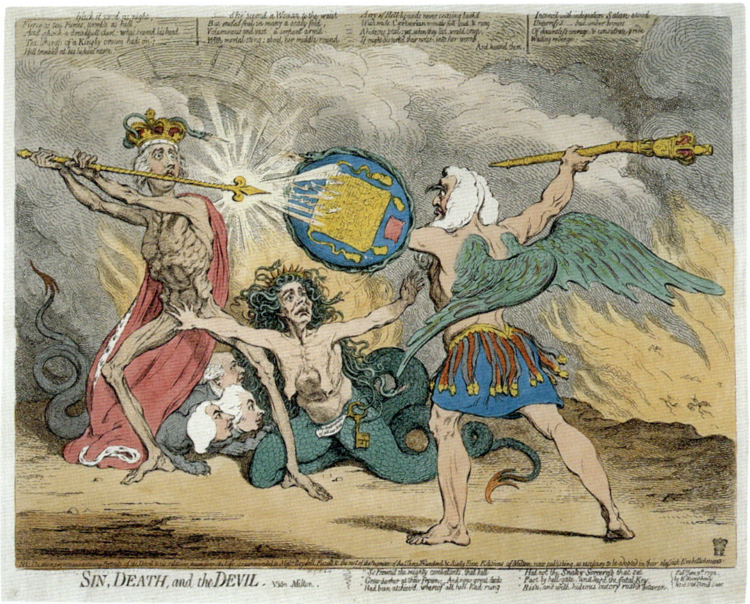

Sabines, I will hide it with more care and more taste.' As with all of his major projects, David made detailed preparations for the work. Research was done in libraries, and engravings by Old Masters and other artists were consulted. Most particularly David borrowed from two English sources: engravings by John Flaxman (1755–1826) of two illustrations to Homer's *Iliad – The Fight for the Body of Patroclus* (134) and *Diomedes Casting his Spear against Mars* – and James Gillray's (1756–1815) satirical print *Sin, Death and the Devil* of 1792 (135). He also wanted to be as accurate as possible in the setting and details of the drama. The background is dominated by the brooding presence of the Tarpeian rock, situated at the southwest corner of Rome's Capitoline Hill. At the time of the intervention it was occupied by the Sabines, who had captured it thanks to the treachery of a Roman woman, Tarpeia. She was the daughter of the commander of the Capitol, and she offered to betray the citadel if the Sabines gave her what they wore on their left arms, which were gold bracelets. However, on entering and taking the Capitol, the Sabines crushed her to death with their shields – which they also wore on their left arms. Therefore the rock was named after her, and became traditionally associated with treachery – it was later used as a place of execution, where murderers and traitors would be hurled from the top. Thus the heroic intervention of the Sabine women is played out against a backdrop associated with an infamous dimension of the female character – base greed.

In his desire for archaeological accuracy, David showed the horses in the foreground without bits and bridles, an omission that caused critics to question exactly how these Romans controlled their steeds. Since none was found on the ancient sculpture he knew, David thought he was being faithful to the evidence, but it is now known that the ancient bits and bridles had been made out of metal and had simply decayed and not survived. His pupils and friends posed for the warriors and his children's nurse posed for the old woman tearing her clothes who is willing to suffer the humiliation of exposing her elderly breasts to assist the ending of the conflict. Two famous beauties, Aurore and Adèle Bellegarde, approached David and, much to his embarrassment, disrobed so that he might better judge their suitability. The dark-haired Adèle posed for the bare breasted kneeling Sabine mother in the foreground and later, to attract public attention, she vainly made a point of wearing her hair in the same way when attending the theatre. The fact that the sisters offered to pose for David at all is somewhat surprising, and signifies the healing of old wounds and the forgiveness of past actions – during the Revolution he had signed warrants for their arrest.

The 'Greek' purity of the *Sabines*, when contrasted with the Roman drama and theatricality of the *Horatii*, shows us that David's art continued to evolve and was by no means static. His style reflected changes both in himself and in the society around him and as such was neither cold nor detached. Although it may seem odd that David chose to paint a Roman subject in a 'Greek' style, this was a time when a return to simplicity pervaded both art and fashion. Ancient Greek art was seen to be genuine and unaffected, giving it a moral and aesthetic superiority over more sophisticated Roman art. Within his own studio there was a breakaway sect which was known by four names – the *Barbus* (Bearded ones), *Penseurs* (Thinkers), *Méditateurs* (Meditators) or *Primitifs* (Primitives). Led by an enigmatic and bizarre figure called Pierre-Maurice Quay (*c*.1779–1802/3), who liked to be called Agamemnon (136), this small group called for paintings based on the unadorned purity of the linear designs on ancient Greek pottery and on the simple and direct compositions of the early Italian Renaissance. Quay and his followers wore outlandish clothes (often imitating ancient Greek garb) in the street, attracting catcalls and abuse, practised vegetarianism and consciously distanced themselves from the everyday world. In terms of painting they produced very little, their best-known work being the moonlit and crystalline *Death of Hyacinth* by Jean Broc (1771–1850) of 1801 (137), and with the death of Quay in

1802 or 1803 the sect dispersed. But while the *Barbus* may have contributed to David's desire to return to Greek-inspired art, he also found them a disruptive influence, especially as one of their number, Jean-Pierre Franque, was his assistant on the *Sabines* and used his room above one of David's studios as a meeting place for the group. David was therefore obliged to remove Franque and replaced him with more compliant Jérôme-Martin Langlois (1779–1838), but this was not the end

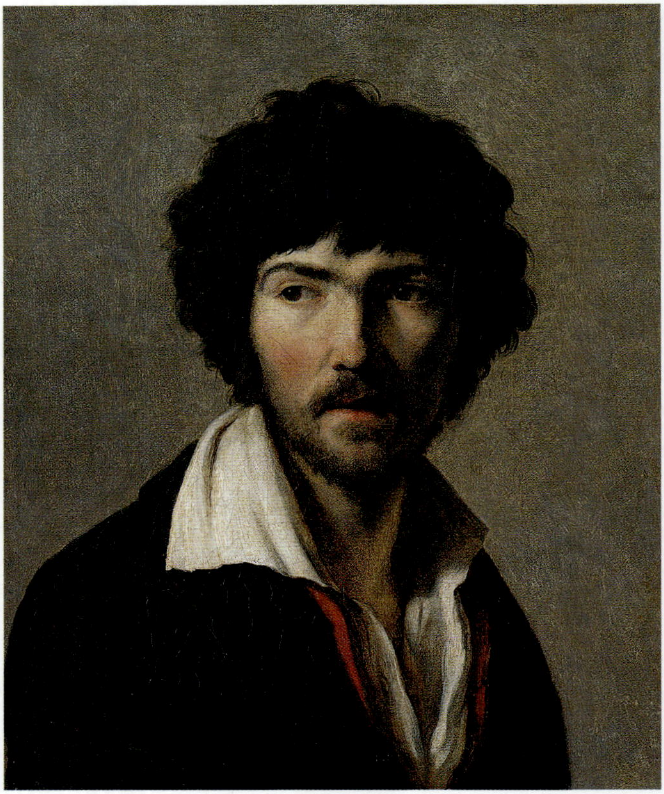

136
Henri-François Riesener, *Portrait of Pierre-Maurice Quay,* c.1800. Oil on canvas; 56 × 46 cm, 22 × 18⅛ in. Musée du Louvre, Paris

137
Jean Broc, *The Death of Hyacinth,* 1801. Oil on canvas; 175 × 120 cm, 68⅞ × 47¼ in. Musée de Poitiers

of the matter. When the *Sabines* was exhibited the *Barbus* condemned David for not going far enough in his purity of outline and called the picture, 'Vanloo, Pompadour, Rococo' – terms that stigmatized David as still painting in a florid and artificial style. Such provocative and irritating criticisms could not be tolerated and, without causing a fuss, David asked the sect members to leave his studio.

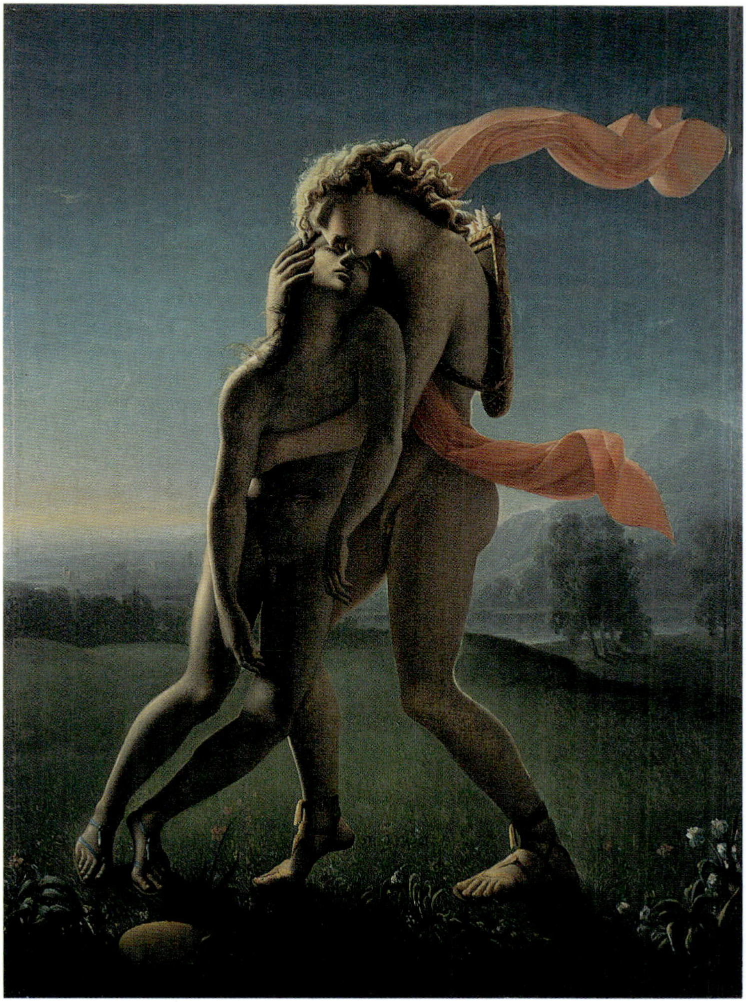

Although many considered the *Sabines* to be a masterpiece, much was made of David's decision to paint the warriors nude, a detail that some critics thought ridiculous and implausible – there is indeed something both comic and absurd about Tatius' strategically placed scabbard. This detail was only added in 1808 when David hoped to sell the work to Napoleon – originally Tatius was totally nude. David defended this heroic nudity in the

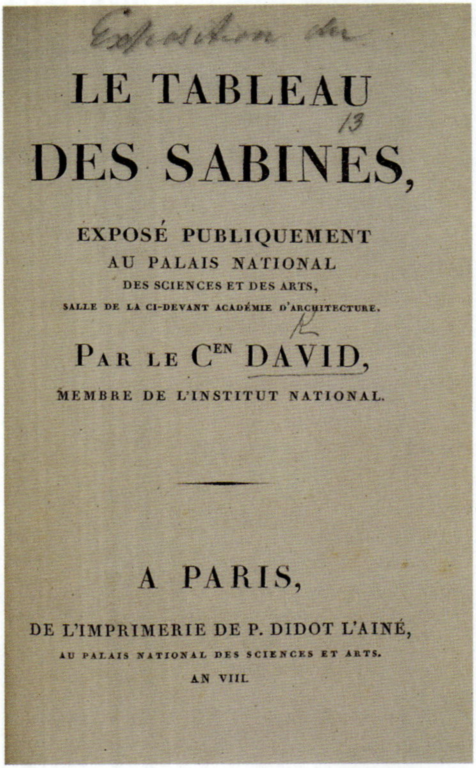
Exposition du

LE TABLEAU

DES SABINES,

EXPOSÉ PUBLIQUEMENT

AU PALAIS NATIONAL

DES SCIENCES ET DES ARTS,

SALLE DE LA CI-DEVANT ACADÉMIE D'ARCHITECTURE.

PAR LE C^EN DAVID,

MEMBRE DE L'INSTITUT NATIONAL.

A PARIS,

DE L'IMPRIMERIE DE P. DIDOT L'AINÉ,

AU PALAIS NATIONAL DES SCIENCES ET ARTS.

AN VIII.

138
Title page of the descriptive brochure to accompany the exhibition of *The Intervention of the Sabine Women*, 1800

pamphlet he wrote to accompany the picture's exhibition (138):

One criticism which has been made to me, and will without doubt be repeated, deals with the nudity of my heroes. The examples to be noted are so numerous in what remains to us of ancient art, that the only difficulty I find is to make a choice. This is what I would answer: It was a recognized custom among the painters, sculptors and poets of antiquity to portray gods, heroes and in general the men whom they wished to represent, in the nude.

Were they painting a philosopher? He was nude, with a mantle on his shoulders and the emblems of his character. Were they painting a warrior? He was nude, a helmet on his head, a shield on his arm and his buskins on his feet. Sometimes a drapery was added if they judged that it would add to the grace of the figure, as may be seen in my painting of Tatius; or still better as one may observe displayed at the Central Museum of the Arts [the recently opened Louvre], the figure of Phocion, newly come from Rome. Are not the sons of Jupiter, Castor and Pollux, the works of Pheidias and Praxiteles at Monte Cavallo, nude? The Achilles of the Villa Borghese is likewise nude. At Versailles, on the so-called Medici vase, a bas-relief may be seen representing the sacrifice of Iphigenia; Achilles is here again nude, as are the majority of the other warriors around the vase. In the Museum of the sculptor Giraud [Pierre François Giraud (1783–1836)] in the Place Vendôme, a bas-relief of Perseus and Andromeda may be seen. The hero there is nude, although he has just ended his battle with a monster who spits forth poison. In the National Library in the book of prints of Herculaneum, one can find the same thing in the subject of the departure of Hippolytus for the hunt in the presence of Phaedra; he is nude. How many other authorities could I mention? Those that I have just spoken of will without doubt be enough, so that the public will not be surprised that I should have tried to imitate the great models in my Romulus, who is himself the son of a god. Here is one example that I have kept until the last, because it is the sum of all of the others: it is Romulus himself, represented nude on a medal, at the moment when, after having killed Acron, King of the Cenineens, he brings on his shoulders a trophy made of the royal arms, which he afterwards places in the Temple of Jupiter Feretrien; this was the first rich booty to enter there. I believe now that I have satisfactorily answered the criticism which has been made of me – or may be made – on the nudity of my heroes: such an answer permits me to appeal to the artists. They know better than anyone else how much easier it would have been for me to paint my figures clothed; let them say how much draperies would have helped me to find easier ways to make my figures stand out on my canvas. I think, on the contrary that they will be satisfied with the difficult task I imposed on myself, convinced of the truth that he who may accomplish the most could have done the least. In a word, in painting the picture my desire was to represent the customs of antiquity with such an exactitude that the Greeks and the Romans, had they seen my work, would not have found me a stranger to their customs.

This explanation failed to convince many people and David's idea that the physical perfection of Tatius and Romulus signified their moral perfection was not universally understood. Whatever his argument, the fact was that nude figures were not part of the everyday experience of public life at that time. The Opéra Comique put on a one-act burlesque called *The Painting of the Sabines* and humorous poems and epigrams were penned. The most famous of these ran:

See dressed in naturalibus
here's Tatius and Romulus
and lovely girls, no kerchiefs or petticoats.
David now teaches us what well we knew;
for Paris has long proclaimed him what we view;
the Raphael of the Sans-Culottes

The last line is a pun on the words 'sans-culottes' ('without knee-breeches') which mocked David both for his revolutionary activities and for the absence of clothes on his ancient warriors.

David painted the *Sabines* without a commission, so in order to recoup his money and also make a profit, he exhibited the painting and charged an entry fee. To do so, the government lent him the assembly room of the former Academy of Architecture, situated in the Louvre. A paying exhibition was unheard of in Paris and previously artists had been forbidden to take such action by the Academy. David therefore encountered considerable criticism and resistance from those who were used to seeing art for free. The cost of entry was not cheap at 1 franc 80 centimes and thus made the exhibition accessible mostly to polite society and visiting foreigners.

At this time the average daily wage of a skilled labourer was less than one franc and the entrance fee to the *Sabines* was roughly the cost of such luxury food items as 450 g (1 lb) of butter, a bunch of asparagus or 700 g (1½ lb) of ham. Each visitor was given the sixteen-page brochure in which David explained that such exhibitions were common in England and cited the examples of Benjamin West (1738–1820) exhibiting *The Death of General Wolfe* in 1770 and John Singleton Copley (1738–1815) showing *The Death of Lord Chatham* in 1781. David also argued that such a commercial venture was not without risk, that the fee-paying public would be the ultimate judges of a work, and that the artist, 'If his work is mediocre, public opinion will soon mete out justice to it. The author, acquiring neither glory nor material reward, would learn by hard experience ways of mending his faults and of capturing the attention of the spectators by more happy conceptions.' The fee-paying exhibition might also allow history painters to pursue noble and moral subjects and not compromise in painting subjects that just pleased individual patrons. David further argued for the social utility of this practice because art was thus endowed with a sense of purpose far beyond that which the patronage of private clients could offer. Many people would have the opportunity of seeing an instructional painting that would otherwise have been sold to an individual collector and kept out of reach of the public gaze, or even taken abroad. It was therefore a legitimate way for an artist to receive a just reward for the fruits of his labour and for art to reach a larger audience. He concluded this section of the brochure: 'I shall have received a most flattering reward if, by the public having come to enjoy my picture, I may have been able to point a useful road to the artist, and, by giving him encouragement, contribute to the advancement of art and to the perfecting of a righteous spirit which we should, without doubt, have for our aim.'

David also introduced a novel way of viewing the painting by placing a large mirror directly opposite the painting on the other side of the exhibition room. By turning and looking into the mirror, the distancing effect of the reflection intensified the painted illusion, and the visitors could imagine themselves among the crowded throng of Romans and Sabines. To some the whole exhibition seemed more of an entertainment than a display of art, and David may even have felt that he was in direct competition with Paris' first panorama or cyclorama – a circular room, the walls of which were painted with an illusionistic and perspectivally correct view of the city – which had opened a few months before, and which charged an entry fee of 1 franc 50 centimes.

Contemporary reports, notably Pierre Chaussard's *On the Painting of the Sabine Women* (1800), thought that the people attending the exhibition were similar to a theatre audience: 'The crowd rushes around it to find new and vivid sensations. This is for them only a spectacle ... That profound contemplation which I constantly observe on the faces of the spectators has probably flattered the artist more than the loudest applause.' It is of course worth remembering that this was the same crowd that had taken part in the great revolutionary festivals of 1792–4, and therefore spectator involvement, though a novelty, was not a totally alien experience. The mirror may also have evoked more complex associations and contributed to a sense of the reshaping and reunification of a formerly divided society. After the Reign of Terror, the Directory promoted itself as the culmination and accomplishment of the Revolution, and a sense of resolution was sought. The alert spectator, by looking into the mirror, could not only participate in the painting but also cast themselves as part of the newly reconciled, enlarged and coherent 'family' that was created by the eventual union of the Romans and the Sabines. The mirror was not the only aid to the inspection of the work and every square centimetre of the vast canvas was scrutinized by a curious public. The gentlemen used opera glasses and the ladies employed specially made fans with a built-in lens so that they might observe the painted nude bodies without fear of embarrassment. In the past David had manoeuvred to ensure

139
View of Ozouer-le-Voulgis, 1801. Black chalk and ink wash; 15 × 23 cm, $5^7\!/\!_8$ × 9 in. Private collection

prime positions at the Salon for his pictures, but the *Sabines* exhibition was the first time that he had managed to make his own decisions over the display of his work. His was a very public art and it is no wonder that he sought to have control over where, when and under what conditions it was seen. This was yet another example of David's independence and his example was soon followed, rather less successfully, in 1800 by Jean-Baptiste Regnault (1754–1829), Jean-Baptiste Isabey (1767–1855) and Vernet. Much later, in 1855, Gustave Courbet (1819–77) revived the practice for his one-man show (held in the Pavilion of Realism) that was in direct competition to the painting section of the Universal Exposition.

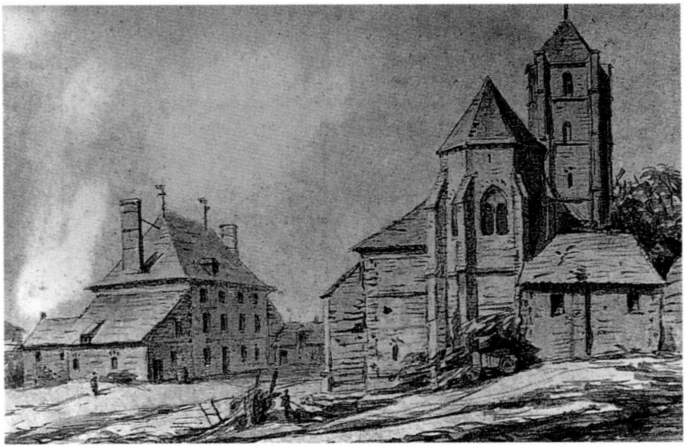

As well as presenting his new style to the public, the exhibition was a very shrewd piece of business and was the supreme example of David's entrepreneurship and financial acumen. He even managed to avoid having the exhibition classified as a public spectacle (a category which then included plays, balls, firework displays and balloon ascents) and thereby was exempt from the twenty-five per cent charitable tax on entrance fees. This achievement was due to the enthusiastic intervention of the government commissioner N E Lemaire, and such special treatment indicates the appreciation of David by the new regime of the Consulate, which had been established following

Napoleon Bonaparte's seizure of power at the Coup of 18–19 Brumaire (9–10 November 1799). Thanks to the pleading of his wife he also managed to get the government to pay for some of the exhibition's expenses, including the security guards, but his claim for reimbursement for the cost of installing a new window in the roof of the exhibition room for improved lighting was turned down. The *Sabines* was exhibited from 21 December 1799 and remained on show for five years, with an estimated 50,000 people paying to see it. David promised his pupils that he would treat them to dinner each time the exhibition receipts reached 24,000 francs and these dinners took place three times. Although David had initially proposed to give the painting to the nation when the exhibition receipts equalled what a buyer might have paid for it, he never did. In October 1801, from the proceeds of the exhibition, he bought the country property of Marcoussis at Ozouer-le-Voulgis, 48 km (30 miles) southeast of Paris, near the Forest of Fontainebleau (139).

David's major history paintings from *Belisarius* to *The Intervention of the Sabine Women* all had a marked theatrical element to them. Throughout his life David maintained contacts with the theatre and regularly attended performances. Both his 'uncle' Sedaine and one of his earliest patrons, the Marquis de Bièvre, were playwrights and his circle of friends included critics, actors, dancers, opera singers, composers and set designers. David had first become involved in the theatre around 1782 when he was approached by the actor Jean Maudit Larive to design an authentic costume for the role of the Spartan king Agis at the Théâtre Français. Later in the 1780s he was introduced, by Girodet, to François-Joseph Talma, who went on to become the greatest tragic actor of the age, and David also designed costumes for his productions. French tragedy and David's history paintings of the 1780s shared a common concern for historical accuracy of setting, didacticism and expression. In the theatre the latter two demands were met by a revival of emphatic but naturalistic gestures. Accordingly, not only the face, but the whole body could articulate the narrative, the passions and the emotional response. David's works have often been likened to theatrical scenes due to their stage-like settings, the rhetorical gestural exchanges and the posing of the characters. The visualization of a significant moment, charged with pathos and emotion, has clear parallels with contemporary theatrical conventions. During the Revolution David's paintings were re-enacted as *tableaux vivants* or living pictures on the Paris stage – the *Horatii* and *Socrates* on 31 October 1789 and the *Brutus* on 19 November 1790 following a performance of Voltaire's play of the same name (see Chapter 3). But whereas the paintings of the 1780s may be related to acting styles to intensify climactic moments, the *Sabines* has a feeling of suspended rather than frozen action that it would be difficult to sustain as a *tableau vivant* – though it was performed as one, in modern dress, in a vaudeville on 30 March 1800. With its different form of action, concentration on the formal call and response between the figures of Romulus and Tatius, and even illumination, the *Sabines* is less reminiscent of a staged play than David's other history paintings. Its theatricality lay in the way that it was presented to the public: the involvement of the spectator was closer to a performance than to the passive act of standing in front of a canvas.

David's desire to keep a low profile, and his work on portraits and on a theme of reconciliation, may have been related to his membership of the short-lived cult of Theophilanthropy. It was an all-embracing religion for the people which proclaimed the existence of god and the immortality of the soul and preached tolerance and the importance of one's duty to one's fellow man. Theophilanthropy had its origins in Freemasonry, which unfortunately meant that it was held in some suspicion because of the links between Freemasonry and the Jacobins. A number of its adherents were Masons who gravitated towards the cult when the majority of lodges were closed during and after the Reign of Terror. It was an eclectic and utopian creed that called for an examination of one's conscience and little formal worship, although David and his fellow members did request to share the use of the church of Notre Dame des Champs with those who remained faithful to Catholicism.

Even if he was no longer directly involved in politics, David still retained an active interest; he subscribed to a radical newsletter and signed petitions and in private could still hold extreme views. At the end of October 1797 the American painter John Trumbull approached him to help him obtain a passport to leave France for England. Though Trumbull liked David, he found his involvement with the Reign of Terror repugnant and felt moved to ask David about that horrific episode in recent French history. The artist's reply was that of an unrepentant advocate of the Revolution. 'True,' said David, 'much blood has been shed, but it would have been well for the Republic if five hundred thousand more heads had passed under the guillotine.' But more important than any such opinions, David still considered his art to be of both political and national value. For a time he considered completing *The Oath of the Tennis Court*, but found that the necessary expenditure was beyond his means and there was no possibility of government support. The *Sabines*, although a great financial success, was also seen as a public-minded project that was painted to allow the people to share and participate in an experience reminiscent of the reconciliation of the nation following the fall of Robespierre.

As part of the process of promoting himself as a dedicated artist, David increased the number of students that he had, and some of these, especially Etienne-Jean Delécluze (1781–1863), wrote valuable accounts of his studio and teaching methods. David was very fortunate (and astute) in having acquired studios in the Louvre both for his own work and in which to teach. His teaching premises consisted of a large room lit by a single window linked to another of his studios above by a wooden staircase. Beneath the staircase the youngest and least experienced pupils drew from plaster casts of ancient sculpture. There was a cast-iron stove in a recess and the dominating feature of the room was a raised platform where the life model was posed and drawn from. There was also space for student painters to place their easels. For storage there were shelves some distance above the ground where canvases and paints were put when not in use. The busy atmosphere of the studio is best captured in a drawing of 1804 by Jean-Henri Cless (see 1) which shows David in the background wearing a hat and correcting the life drawing of one of his pupils. About forty students, from backgrounds both aristocratic and revolutionary, studied with David, and they paid a monthly fee of twelve francs with an extra three francs to pay for a model, although especially poor students had their fees waived. Before the financial success of the *Sabines*, money was as tight for David as for his pupils and to save on expenses a well-built student might pose for free and the master would join his students in the life class. David encouraged his pupils to develop in their own directions, urging them to study from nature, to obey their own instincts and to copy from whichever past artists they admired. He did not want to impose his own style on them and preferred them not to copy from his successful works, though some of course did. However, he had little time for his rivals and fellow history painters Vincent and Regnault, and was contemptuous of their teaching abilities. David gave his pupils regular critiques and advice, although his stammer sometimes got in the way of what he wanted to say. His opinions on art were neither highly theoretical nor greatly intellectual, and he confined himself to general observations, saying that an artist must always paint with feeling and that the resulting work should 'deeply stir the soul of the spectator'. He also wanted his students to be well educated and neat of habit and appearance – 'a painter should be a man of order', he said. There was also a social dimension to the studio and sometimes the students were received in David's own apartments or else clubbed together to invite him out to dine at a country inn. A sense of camaraderie existed and David derived a great deal of satisfaction from his teaching responsibilities, although he could become jealous when a pupil progressed so far as to become a potential rival.

By the time of the *Sabines* exhibition David's rehabilitation was complete. He had demonstrated his capacity for self-preservation and survival and had won back the public with a grand painting on an ancient subject that touched a chord in the modern viewer. Once again he was part of the establishment, although old rivalries were not completely forgotten and some tensions still existed. He continued to prepare projects for epic history paintings, but these plans had not allowed for the rise of an ambitious, dashing and charismatic young Corsican general, Napoleon Bonaparte.

5

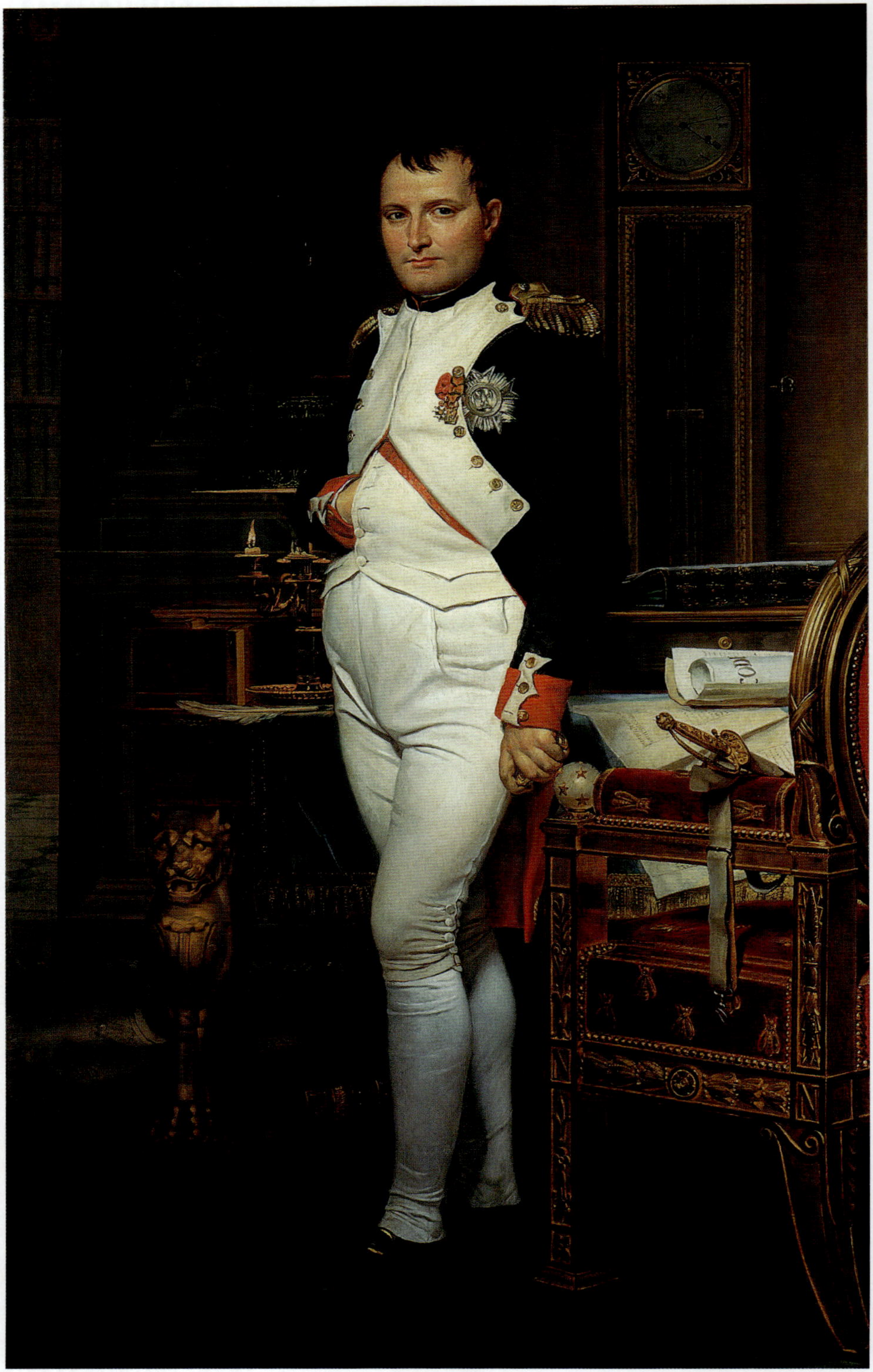

On his release from prison David had declared with some certainty that, 'I will no longer attach myself to men but to principles', and in the immediate aftermath of his imprisonment he did just that. Yet, like the rest of France, he became entirely captivated by Napoleon Bonaparte, who rapidly rose from a lieutenant to a general in the revolutionary army, staged a *coup d'état* to become the First Consul of France, and finally proclaimed himself emperor in 1804.

140
Napoleon in his Study, 1812.
Oil on canvas; 204 × 125 cm, $80^3\!/\!_8 \times 49^1\!/\!_4$ in.
National Gallery of Art, Washington, DC

Napoleon, born in Corsica in 1769, had attended military college in France from the age of nine, and graduated from the élite École Militaire in 1785. He joined an artillery regiment at Valence and when the Revolution came he approved of it in principle, though he was alarmed by the violence and disorder of the popular uprisings. During the Revolution the army was short of trained leaders as many officers had joined the royalist cause, and Napoleon made the most of the opportunities for swift promotion. In 1793 he distinguished himself at the siege of Toulon, France's principal Mediterranean naval base, which was then held by the English. His brilliantly executed plan had forced the enemy to evacuate the port and, at the age of twenty-four, he was made a brigadier general. Napoleon's Jacobin sympathies also meant that he was looked on favourably by the revolutionary government, but with the fall of Robespierre he, like David, only narrowly avoided the guillotine. Fortunately, he was far away from Paris at the time and his case was investigated by a friend and fellow Corsican, Jean-Christophe Saliceti, who found there to be no evidence against him. Consequently Napoleon spent just two weeks imprisoned in the fortress of Antibes. By August 1795 he was the government's chief military adviser, and on 5 October he put down a popular royalist revolt in Paris by firing on the

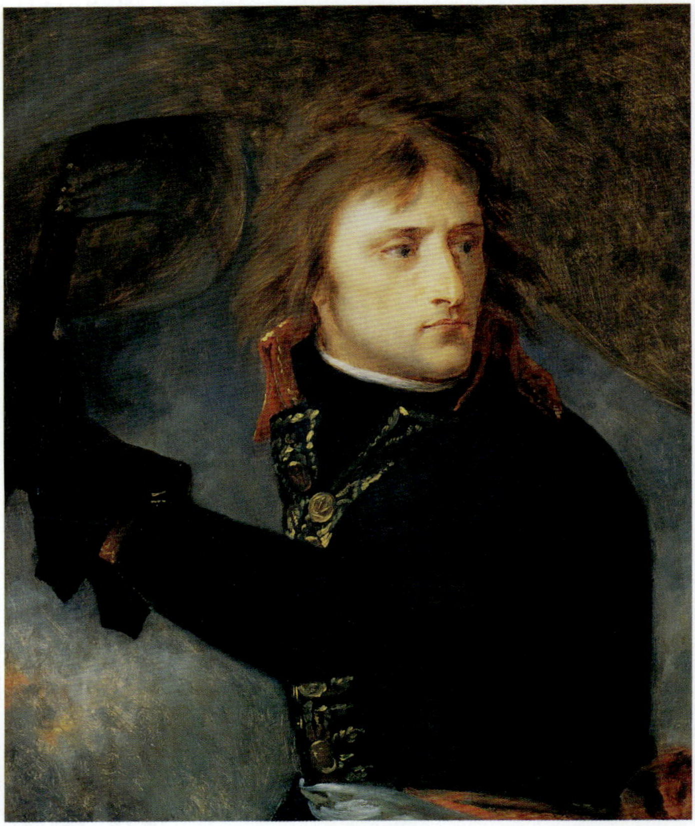

141
Antoine-Jean Gros,
General Bonaparte at Arcola,
1796.
Oil on canvas;
73 × 59cm,
28¾ × 23¼ in.
Musée du Louvre, Paris

mob with cannons – what he referred to as a 'whiff of grapeshot', but which, in reality, killed about a hundred people. Further promotion followed and he was made a major-general and given command of the Army of the Interior. In the next year he married a beautiful 32-year-old widow from the French territory of Martinique, Josephine de Beauharnais, whose husband had been guillotined during the Reign of Terror. Under the newly established Directory, Napoleon was appointed general commanding the Army of Italy and two days after his wedding he set off to invade the peninsula. The Italian campaigns of 1796–7 contained a series of dazzling victories – at Lodi, Castiglione, Arcola and Rivoli – and culminated in the advantageous Treaty of Campo Formio whereby France made peace with continental Europe, gained possession of Belgium and had its rule in several Italian states

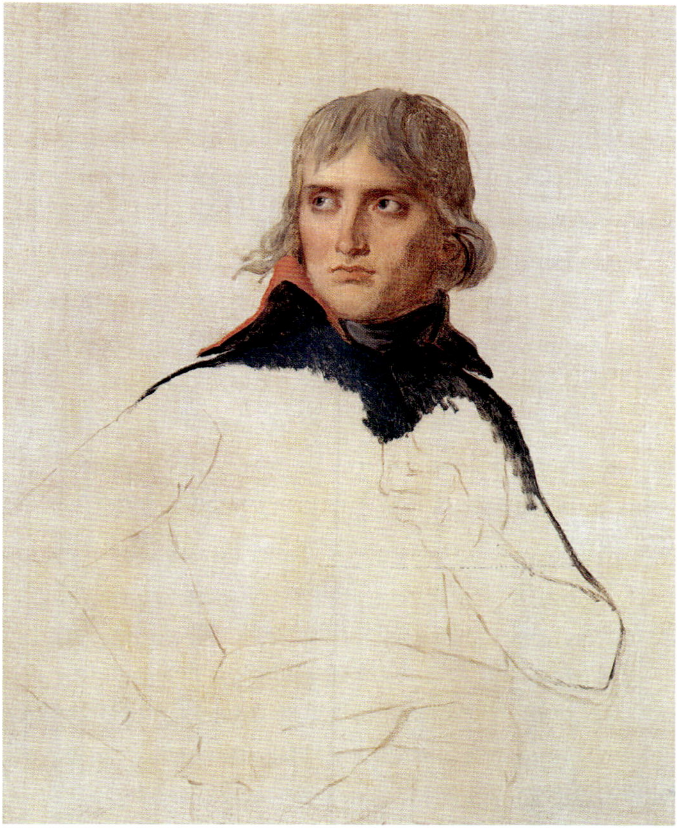

142
Portrait of General Bonaparte (unfinished), 1797. Oil on canvas; 81 × 65cm, $31\frac{7}{8} \times 25\frac{5}{8}$ in. Musée du Louvre, Paris

recognized by Austria. These successes, coupled with Napoleon's great gift for self-promotion, ensured that he was hailed as a national hero upon his triumphant return to Paris in December 1797.

David was perhaps in contact with Napoleon in the spring and summer of 1797, when the general is supposed to have asked the painter to join him in Italy to paint his battles. David declined the offer and it was his pupil Antoine-Jean Gros, already travelling as part of the body set up to select and transport Italian art treasures back to France, who captured the likeness of Napoleon on the battlefield (141). David first met Napoleon in Paris on 10 December 1797, at one of the public receptions given to honour the victorious general. Napoleon was anxious to make the acquaintance of the famous painter and arranged for them both to attend a dinner given by the secretary of the Directory, Joseph-Jean Lagarde. He was so keen to talk to David that he is supposed to have switched the place cards around so that they could sit next to each other. It was during the course of this dinner that David asked to paint Napoleon's portrait, a request that was soon granted. Napoleon came to David's studio in the Louvre, granting him only a single sitting of three hours, during which he was fidgety, impatient and eager to leave. From this sitting David only managed to paint the head and collar (142) but he still managed to capture the confidence and vitality of the nation's hero. Three hours of direct contact with Napoleon was enough to have completely won over David and he responded with an enthusiasm close to the fervour that he had displayed for the painting of *Marat*. He very excitedly told his pupils: 'Oh my friends, what a fine head he has! It's pure, it's great, it's as beautiful as the Antique! Here is a man to whom altars would have been erected in Ancient times; yes my friends ... Bonaparte is my hero!' The portrait was to have been very large, 2·3 × 2·9 m (7 × 9 ft), and David intended to show Napoleon victorious after the battle of either Lodi or

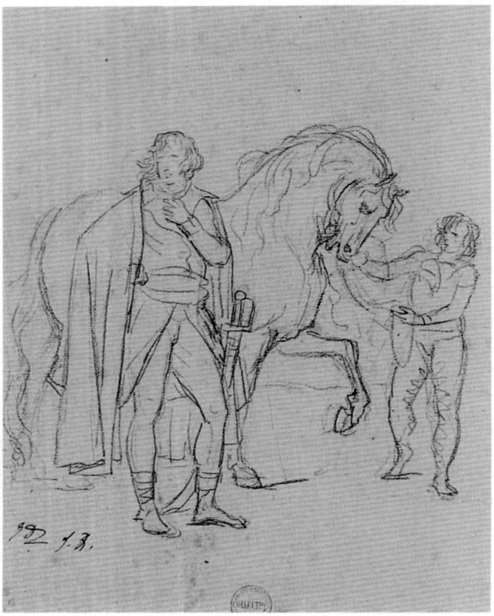

143
Study of General Bonaparte, 1797. Black crayon; 23·5 × 19 cm, $9\frac{1}{4} \times 7\frac{1}{2}$ in. Private collection

Castiglione, standing beside a horse held by a groom (143), but it was never completed. No more sittings took place and on 19 May 1798 Napoleon embarked from Toulon as general-in-chief of the Army of the Orient, leading the campaign to invade Egypt and drive out the English. David was once again invited to go along as a battle painter, and once again refused, pleading ill health. He was also approaching fifty and was thus ill-suited to either the privations of war or the extreme climate of the Middle East. David did, however, say that he would be willing to accompany an invasionary army to England 'to fight', but for the present Napoleon had decided that the best way to destroy the enemy was to seize Egypt. Though David did not go with him, Napoleon was accompanied by 150 writers, scientists and artists whose job it was to study and record the archaeological riches of Egypt; from their work the new discipline of Egyptology was created. Among the party was Dominique Vivant Denon (1747–1825). An engraver and later a Bourbon diplomat, during the Revolution Denon was saved from the guillotine by David. Following the Egyptian expedition, he produced a two-volume illustrated work, *Voyages dans la Haute et Basse Egypte* (1802). In that same year Napoleon appointed him general director of museums, and he energetically set about reorganizing the Louvre, integrating the captured works of art into the collection.

Napoleon's Middle Eastern campaign was only partially successful. Although victories were gained at the battles of the Pyramids and Aboukir, the occupation of Egypt was a strategic dead end and did not prove to be the desired stepping stone for an assault on India, the source of much of England's wealth. The local inhabitants remained hostile, and when Cairo rose in revolt in October 1798, Napoleon crushed the rioters with ruthless brutality, giving orders to 'cut the throats of all prisoners taken with arms in hand. They will be conducted to the banks of the Nile ... their corpses without heads will be thrown into the Nile.' In August 1799 news reached him of a succession of defeats for the French army and the loss of Italy. A new political crisis was at hand and, without waiting for orders, Napoleon left his army and returned to France.

To many of his countrymen Napoleon was the only man who could impose strong government and save the Republic from extremism at home and its enemies abroad. Political manoeuvrings took place and, with the support of the army, Napoleon staged the Coup of 18–19 Brumaire (9–10 November 1799), overthrowing the Directory and its two Councils. Under a new constitution Napoleon became First Consul and, at the age of thirty and enjoying massive popularity, all real power was in his hands. Although promising peace, Napoleon resolved to attack the Austrians in Italy and in April and May 1800 a newly formed army crossed over the St Bernard Pass. At the Battle of Marengo on 14 June 1800 a hard-fought victory was won, but further victories in Italy and in Germany were necessary before the signing of the favourable Treaty of Lunéville in February 1801. A year later in March 1802 the Peace of Amiens ended hostilities with England. These settlements gave Napoleon such enormous prestige in France that all opposition was silenced and he was able to declare himself Consul for life and extend his powers still further. Effectively, Napoleon was a dictator and all notions of a democratic Republic were merely cosmetic.

During his successful Italian campaign of 1797, Napoleon had seized a huge array of art works as trophies of conquest, much as the ancient Roman generals had plundered Athens. While he was engaged in the conquest of Egypt, these treasures were brought back to Paris and paraded with great ceremony through the capital on 9 Thermidor (27 July 1798). Eighty wagons were laden with war booty consisting of paintings, sculptures, precious books and manuscripts. Prominent among these were Raphael's *Transfiguration* (1517–20) and *Madonna della Sedia* (*c*.1518), as well as some of the most famous statues of antiquity, including the *Apollo Belvedere* (see 115) and the *Laocoön* (see 28). David seems to have been one of the very few witnesses who lacked enthusiasm for this triumphant procession and the prospect of such works entering the Louvre. He observed that, 'the arts are not naturally loved in France; the taste for them is artificial. You can be sure that, in spite of all the enthusiasm which we see these days, the masterworks from Italy will soon be regarded only as curiosities ... The sight of these masterpieces will perhaps produce scholars, men like Winckelmann, but artists – no!' David's pessimism was doubly inaccurate in underestimating both the contemporary (and continuing) enthusiasm for the arts and the enormous influence that the Louvre collections had on future generations of artists.

On his return to Paris from Egypt, Napoleon sought out David as he was finishing the *Sabines*. After examining the picture Bonaparte remarked, 'I have never seen our soldiers fight as yours do ... this is how ours fight', and immediately imitated a bayonet charge. David replied that he had painted ancient warriors and not modern French soldiers, only to be met with, 'Believe me dear David, change it; all the world will be of my opinion.' David's regard for Napoleon meant that he was upset by such criticisms but consoled himself by complaining to his students that, 'These generals know nothing of painting.'

Napoleon's artistic taste and understanding was indeed very limited and his own minister of the interior, Jean-Antoine Chaptal, could later write: 'Napoleon did not care for the arts probably because nature had denied him the sensibility to appreciate their merit ... Nevertheless ... he always appeared to interest himself in the arts ... He did this for political reasons in order to demonstrate his broadmindedness ... [he] gave commissions but was indifferent as to the manner of execution, because he lacked the taste to judge for himself, and being unable to appreciate any particular artist, he was disposed to believe the one he trusted was the best.' More than anything else, Napoleon liked paintings in which he was the main character, and his brother Lucien told David, 'You must understand my dear David that my brother Napoleon takes an interest only in pictures in which he counts for something. It is his weakness and he has no objections at all to being in the limelight.' But Napoleon also saw that the visual arts were valuable propaganda and was prepared to spend large amounts on them. The Consulate and the Empire became a boom-time for artists; commissions were not only distributed by the government and later the imperial household, but speculative works were also produced featuring Napoleon in the hope that they would be noticed and bought.

After the Coup of Brumaire Napoleon had offered David a seat in the council of state, but David refused and explained that he wanted to devote himself solely to painting and that his place was at work in his studio – he added: 'Moreover, positions will pass: I hope my works will endure.' But this refusal did not mean that David was uninterested in occupying a position of power under Napoleon. In fact his ambition was as great, perhaps greater, than ever, and he became the artistic adviser to Napoleon and his brother Lucien, who was minister of the interior from the time of the coup until November 1800. Proposals were made to improve and embellish Paris by refurbishing existing buildings and constructing monuments and memorials to the heroic dead of the Republic. David formed part of an advisory team, though little was actually achieved. Over and above this, thanks to his relationship with Napoleon, David saw an opportunity to play a central and dominant role in the arts. The disgrace and misfortune of his imprisonment was behind him and, urged on by his wife, David pushed for a prime appointment in overall control of the fine arts. He proposed a total reorganization of the arts administration and recommended that a 'Conservator of National Monuments, Manufactures and Arts' be appointed with responsibilities for art education, design-based industries (mainly textiles), official commissions and public buildings. David obviously thought that he was the only person capable of fulfilling such a demanding and wide-ranging post and felt confident that such an appointment would be his. Others at the time also thought that he was destined to become the artistic supremo of the

Consulate, and on 27 January 1800 twenty-five established artists sent him a letter of goodwill and requested his future support and protection. Yet David had badly miscalculated his position and instead of being appointed as minister of fine arts he was simply made 'Painter to the Government' on 7 February. This much humbler position with its limited responsibilities fell a long way short of what David had wanted for himself and was a humiliating rebuff. Consequently, he declined to accept the appointment; his refusal, printed in the *Journal de Paris* on 27 February, was calculated to be face-saving and to deflect any accusations of self-interest. David thanked Lucien Bonaparte for the nomination but asked him to receive, 'my resignation from a post which seemed to be only profitable to myself, not to art and artists, the sole objects of my concerns'. This setback, however, only temporarily dampened David's ambitions – they would resurface four years later when Napoleon became emperor.

David's first piece of work associated with the new First Consul was not commissioned by Napoleon himself, but by King Charles IV of Spain, who had been impressed by the young commander's notable victories and rise to power. Fresh from his second conquest of Italy, Napoleon was asked by David to pose, but he refused, saying that the most important feature of a portrait was character not likeness, and added that Alexander the Great had certainly not posed for the ancient Greek artist Apelles. Bonaparte also observed that 'No one knows if portraits of great men are likenesses: it suffices that genius lives.' David was forced to agree and so had to make do with dressing up a mannequin, one of his sons or his student François Gérard (1770–1837) in the uniform that Napoleon had worn at Marengo with the added accessories of his coat, riding boots, bicorn hat and an ornate mameluke sword. Having the uniform of the famous general in the studio almost inevitably led to some horseplay: David was surprised and amused to find that Napoleon's head was much larger than his own; when he tried his hat on, it fell over his eyes.

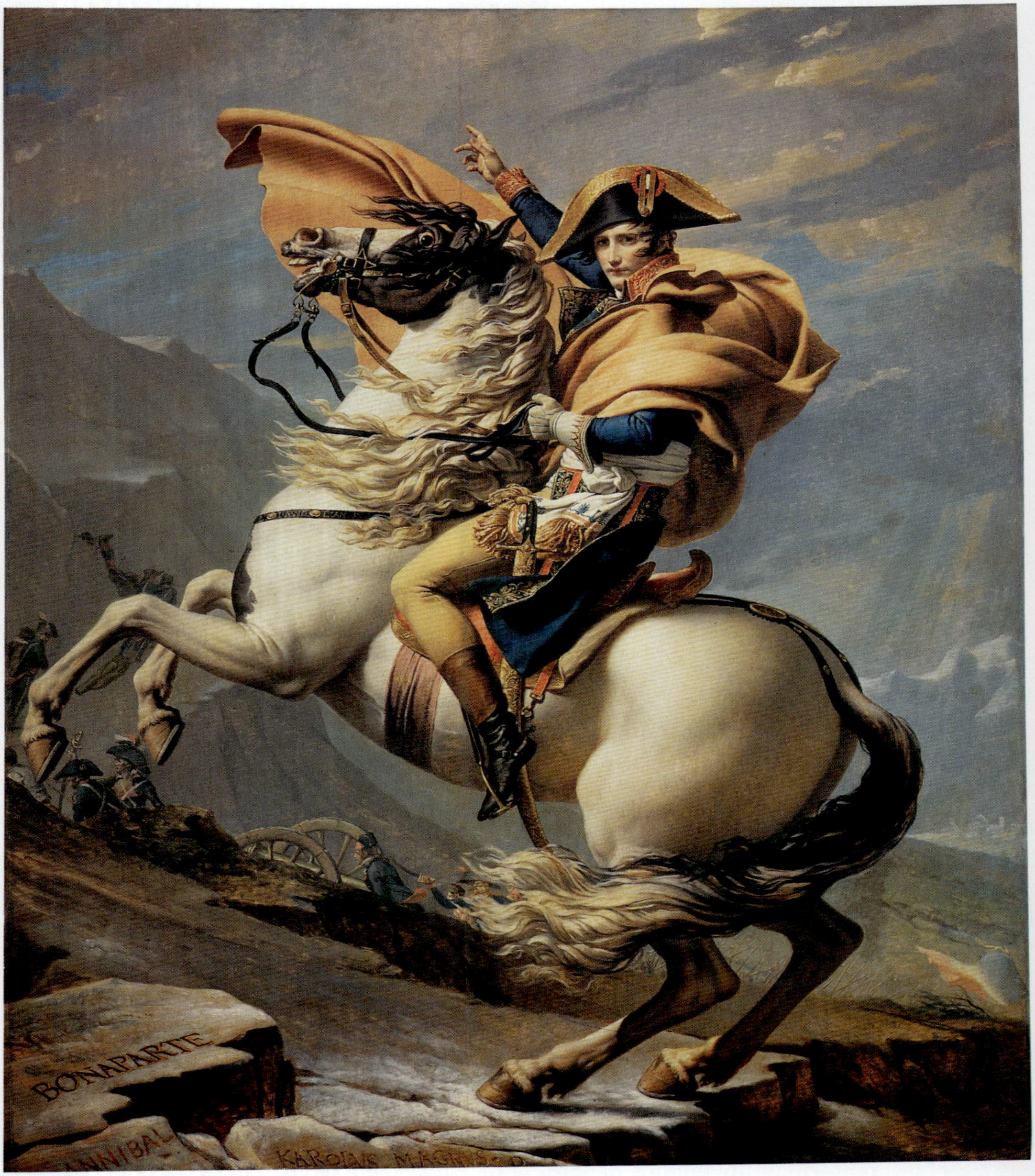
BONAPARTE

For the painting David's idea was to show Napoleon, sword in hand, in the midst of battle, but Napoleon replied that battles were no longer fought in that way and announced that he wanted to be shown 'calm on a fiery horse'. David duly obliged, choosing the subject of Napoleon crossing the St Bernard Pass (144). The long-established tradition of the equestrian portrait was drawn upon to glorify the victorious First Consul, and on the rocks below the horse Napoleon's name is inscribed with

144
Bonaparte Crossing the St Bernard Pass,
1800.
Oil on canvas;
260 × 221 cm,
$102^{3}/_{8}$ × 87 in.
Musée National de Malmaison

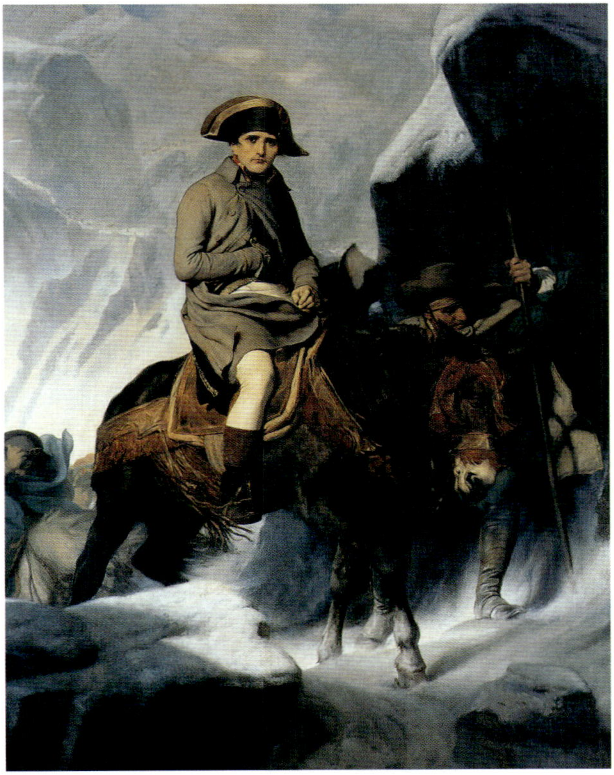

145
Paul Delaroche,
Bonaparte Crossing the St Bernard Pass,
1848.
Oil on canvas;
289 × 222 cm,
$113^{3}/_{4}$ × $87^{3}/_{8}$ in.
Musée du Louvre, Paris

those of two earlier transalpine conquerors, Hannibal and Karolus Magnus (Charlemagne). But like many images of power, *Napoleon Crossing the St Bernard Pass* is economical with the truth. Napoleon did not lead his army over the Alps riding on 'a fiery horse' – he actually crossed a few days after the main advance and was led along a narrow track seated on a mule, a less than heroic scene that was depicted later in 1848 by Paul Delaroche (1797–1856; 145). For the first time David was painting a living hero – his other subjects had been from ancient history or were revolutionary martyrs such as Marat – but, because Napoleon refused to pose, the end result was remote and impersonal and lacked the immediacy and vitality of direct contact that can be seen in the earlier unfinished portrait (see 142). However, Napoleon was so taken by the final work that he ordered a replica and David painted this and two other versions for him with the assistance of his pupils. When completed in 1801, Charles IV's painting and Napoleon's first copy were added to the *Sabines* exhibition so that the public would have the opportunity of seeing them. David charged a little less for the replicas than for the original and his wife was very active and persistent in pursuing Napoleon's ministers for payment. Since their remarriage, Madame David played an increasingly assertive role in her husband's business affairs and was eager for him to cash in on his fame and talent.

Though disappointed by the swing towards absolutism, marked by Napoleon's seizure of power, exactly what David thought of the march towards dictatorship is not known. When informed of the coup David said, 'I have always thought that we are not virtuous enough to be republicans', and quoted from the Roman poet Lucan's epic *Pharsalia*, on the civil war between Caesar and Pompey: 'The victors had their cause approved by the gods, the vanquished by Cato.' He then puffed on his pipe while comparing himself to Cato the Younger, who had a reputation for fairness, had been uncompromising in his opposition to Caesar and who committed suicide as a political martyr. The cherished ideals of liberty, intellectual freedom and the abolition of privilege were swept aside as Napoleon dismantled the Republic, violently suppressed all forms of opposition and turned France into a police state. One of David's favourite pupils, a Jacobin and political activist, François Jean-Baptiste Topino-Lebrun (1764–1801) was guillotined on 30 January 1801 following an unsuccessful assassination attempt on Napoleon on 24 December 1800, even though there was no evidence to implicate him in what later proved to be a royalist plot. David's testimony on his behalf was somewhat lukewarm, but as a known agitator Topino-Lebrun's fate had been sealed at the time of his arrest. But if David had misgivings or criticisms of Napoleon's regime he kept them to himself or within the confines of his studio, and outwardly he gave his full support.

After completing the *Sabines*, David had immediately planned a companion piece, *Leonidas at Thermopylae*, but his work for Napoleon meant that this project could not be taken up for over a decade. But from the time of painting the *Sabines* until Napoleon became emperor in 1804, David still found time for portrait work which was a valuable source of income during the period of high inflation and financial troubles of the Consulate. Early in 1800 David was approached by one of the foremost society beauties of the day, the 22-year-old Juliette Récamier, to paint her portrait. Daughter of a banker from Lyon, in 1793 at the age of sixteen she had married a 43-year-old banker, a business acquaintance of her father's. Unfortunately, her sitting for the portrait (146) proved problematic and, although it reached an advanced stage, it was never finished. Progress was slow because David found the lighting too dark in the room where Madame Récamier was posing and decided that a new location must be found. His client was also wilful, spoilt and habitually late for sittings, which severely tried his patience. David set her in a cold and bare studio reclining on a chaise-longue with an antique-style lamp – painted by his newest pupil Jean-Auguste-Dominique Ingres (1780–1867) – at her side. But David's picture of her as a distant yet fragile and vulnerable young woman did not match Madame Récamier's image of herself as a confident and sophisticated society figure, and so she was to turn instead to David's pupil Gérard to satisfy her wishes (147). David finally informed her: 'Madame, ladies have their caprices; so do painters. Allow me to satisfy mine; I shall keep your portrait in its present state.' Though attempts were made to bring about a reconciliation, it never

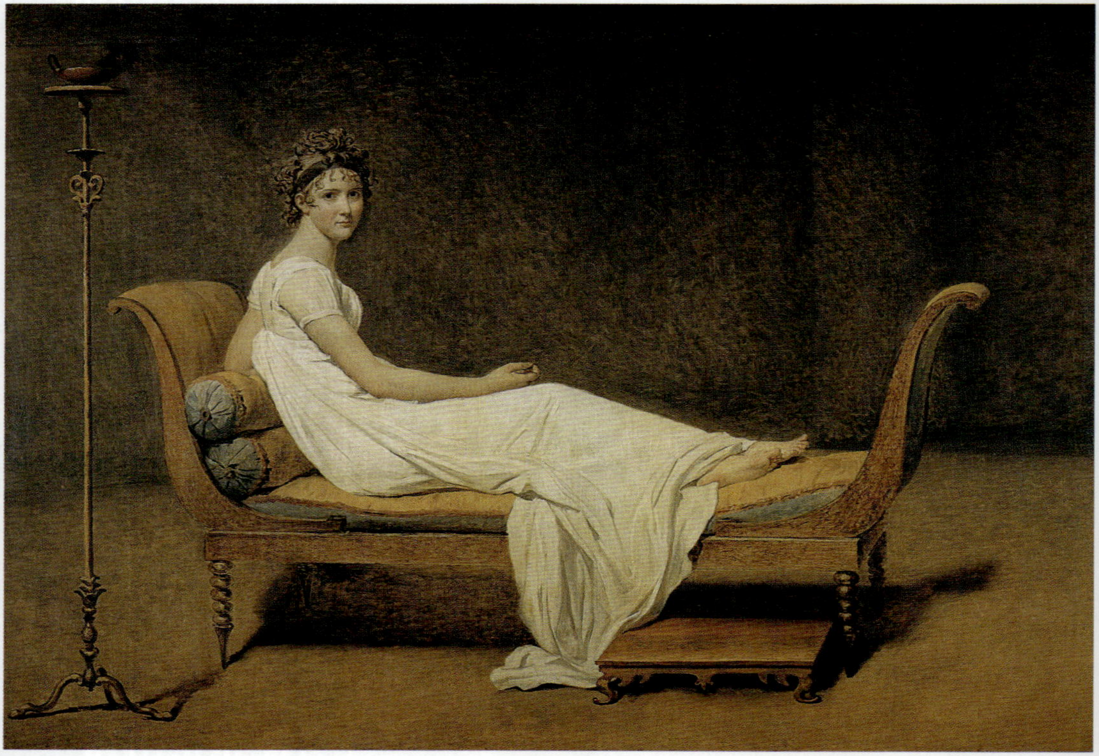

146
Portrait of Juliette Récamier,
1800.
Oil on canvas;
174 × 224 cm,
$68\frac{1}{2} \times 88\frac{1}{8}$ in.
Musée du Louvre, Paris

147
François Gérard,
Portrait of Juliette Récamier,
1805.
Oil on canvas;
225 × 148 cm,
$88\frac{5}{8} \times 58\frac{1}{4}$ in.
Musée Carnavalet, Paris

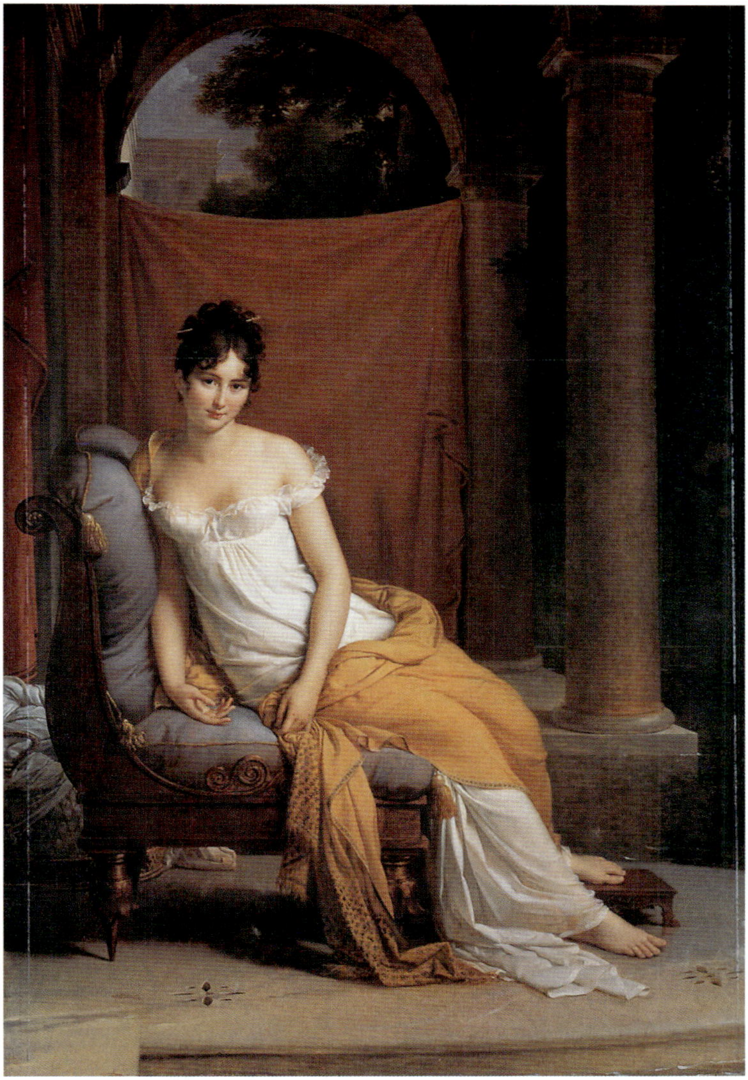

occurred; David's decision to forego the payment and prestige of his most important portrait since the Lavoisiers (see 82) must have been reached after considerable thought and was not the result of any single petty incident or quarrel. Financial compensation, at least, came with the portrait of *Cooper Penrose* of 1802 (148). Penrose was an elderly Irish Quaker on a visit to Paris; David not only charged a hefty fee for the work (5,000 francs) but, as with the Blauw and Meyer portraits, insisted on being paid in gold, a safe haven in times of inflation. He often charged foreigners inflated prices for his works and he had no qualms about this mercenary aspect of his business practice. But sound financial sense demanded that the client be reassured that such great expenditure was justified, and David soothingly declared, 'Let Mr Penrose have complete confidence in me ... I will represent him in a manner worthy of us both. This painting will be a monument which will attest to Ireland the virtues of a good family man, and the talents of the painter who has painted it.' For his money Penrose received a very sombre treatment and the whole image suggests Quaker plainness and sobriety with even a hint of dullness.

Although thwarted in his attempt to become minister of fine arts, David received other honours from Napoleon. In 1802 Napoleon founded the Legion of Honour, an order of knighthood, and David was created a Knight of the Legion (the first of the five ranks of the order) in December 1803. Napoleon was turning himself into a monarch and reviving the privileges and institutions of royalty that had been so painfully abolished in 1792–3; it therefore came as no surprise that in May 1804 the Senate proclaimed him Emperor of the French. David was soon appointed 'First Painter to the Emperor' (18 December 1804) and so now held a post similar to that of the king's First Painter under the old regime, a position which he had variously coveted and agitated against. In an unusual outburst of altruism, he briefly shared his good fortune with the public, granting free admission to the *Sabines* exhibition for a few days.

Napoleon was crowned emperor in a grand ceremony in Notre Dame on 2 December 1804 and David was asked to commemorate the events. Exactly what he was going to paint remained unclear, as no written order existed, but eventually, in June 1806, David replied to the minister of the interior's inquiry that he was to paint *The Coronation of the Emperor and Empress, The Enthronement, The Arrival of the Emperor and Empress at the Hôtel de Ville* and *The Distribution of the Eagle Standards*. These four subjects documented and celebrated the arrival and acceptance of the new imperial order, and Napoleon planned to create a special room in which to display them. However, only *The Coronation* and *The Distribution of the Eagle Standards* were completed. *The Arrival of the Emperor and Empress at the Hôtel de Ville* only got as far as a detailed drawing and *The Enthronement* seems never to have been started.

It was first suggested that the coronation should take place outdoors on the Champ de Mars, the site of many of the great revolutionary festivals. Napoleon dismissed this by saying that the spectacle was not for the benefit of the 'ignoble and corrupt populace', and that an indoor location was required to be certain that the winter weather did not turn the event into a cold and muddy farce. The church of the Invalides was then put forward, but it was rejected in favour of Notre Dame which would give, as Napoleon said, 'a more august character to the solemnity'. With the location fixed, the ceremony could be planned. Napoleon had decided that the crowning and anointing should be performed by Pope Pius VII. He and Napoleon had already been in negotiations over the Concordat, an agreement signed in 1801 which re-established the Church (albeit with limited powers) in France following the de-Christianization of the Revolution. Arrangements were made for the Pope and his retinue and they arrived in Paris on 28 November. It was to be a frustrating time for the Pope because Napoleon had very strong and fixed ideas about which aspects of the religious ceremony he would accept and which he would not. Practically the only concession that the Pope won came when he found out that Napoleon and Josephine had only undergone a civil ceremony of marriage. He insisted that they be remarried in church and this took place quietly, with no witnesses, on the eve of the coronation.

An imperial court was quickly created with titles showered on Napoleon's relations, friends and loyal army generals, and for the first time in European history important positions were held by non-nobles. Care was taken that the new court should not

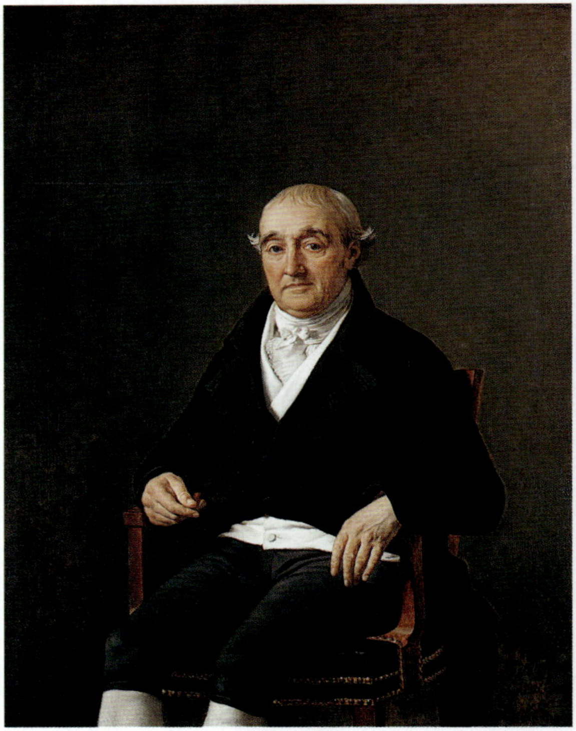

148
Portrait of Cooper Penrose, 1802.
Oil on canvas; 130·5 × 97·5 cm, $51^3/_8 \times 38^3/_8$ in.
Timken Museum of Art, San Diego

resemble that of the old regime too closely and indeed that was a determining factor in the decision to carry out the coronation in Paris – traditionally the kings of France had been crowned in Rheims Cathedral. Rather than being an extension or replacement of the previous Bourbon dynasty, Napoleon saw himself as the modern equivalent of the Frankish emperor Charlemagne. To further emphasize the links with the Carolingian Empire, for his coronation he ordered the repair and/or recreation of three items of regalia that were said to have belonged to Charlemagne – the sword, the sceptre and the crown. These were supplied by the workshop of the jeweller Étienne Nitot (active 1783–1809). The most visible indication of the relationship between the new empire and that of the Franks was at the main entrance to Notre Dame where a huge temporary porch in the form of a triumphal arch had been erected with colossal statues of Clovis (as the founder of the Merovingian dynasty) and Charlemagne (as the founder of the Carolingian dynasty) placed on two of the four supporting pillars. The painter Jean-Baptiste Isabey, a former pupil of David's, and the architects Charles Percier (1764–1838) and Pierre François-Léonard Fontaine (1762–1853) were given the task of the design of the costumes for the coronation and of transforming the Gothic exterior and interior of Notre Dame into a splendid and sumptuous auditorium. Velvet draperies and carpets were placed everywhere and stands were erected along the nave and in the choir. Beneath another enormous temporary triumphal arch Napoleon and Josephine had magnificent thrones placed on a platform at the top of twenty-four steps, and nearer the altar they had smaller thrones and prayer stools.

The day of 2 December had begun with icy rain but, as if preordained, blue skies appeared when the imperial cortège began the journey from the Tuileries Palace to Notre Dame. On arrival, Napoleon and Josephine put on their heavy coronation robes of crimson velvet, lined with ermine and embroidered in gold with the emperor's emblems of bees and eagles and interlaced branches of laurel, olive and oak surrounding the letter 'N'. On his head Napoleon wore a simple gold circlet of laurels, reminiscent of those worn by the Roman Caesars, made by the goldsmith Martin-Guillaume Biennais, and Josephine wore a diamond diadem. She also had her yellowish face made up by Isabey. The ceremony took over three hours but the whole ritual was considerably altered in comparison to that of previous French kings. Instead of swearing a devout religious oath, this particular part of the ritual consisted of the Pope asking

Napoleon if he would uphold the rights of the Church, to which he merely replied 'Profiteor' (I promise). Napoleon then submitted, with some displeasure, to the anointing with holy oil by the Pope, although he chose a simplified triple unction – forehead and both hands – in preference to the sevenfold anointing given to past kings. Breaking with tradition, Josephine was also anointed in the same way. Napoleon was bareheaded at the anointing, and his laurel crown had been placed on the altar along with the rest of his own personal coronation regalia. This consisted of the ring, the collar, the sword, the orb, the sceptre, the mantle and the Hand of Justice. Charlemagne's regalia was not used in the ceremony and its value was mostly symbolic. The Pope blessed all of the items on the altar, and at the moment that he raised the laurel crown, Napoleon took it from him and crowned himself (149).

Napoleon had not wished to appear subservient or reliant on the authority of the Church, and although some people thought that the crown was taken on the spur of the moment, this alteration to the liturgy had been agreed beforehand. In fact, the Pope was forced to give in on many matters by Napoleon, who also refused to take communion. Once he had crowned himself, the new emperor crowned the kneeling Josephine

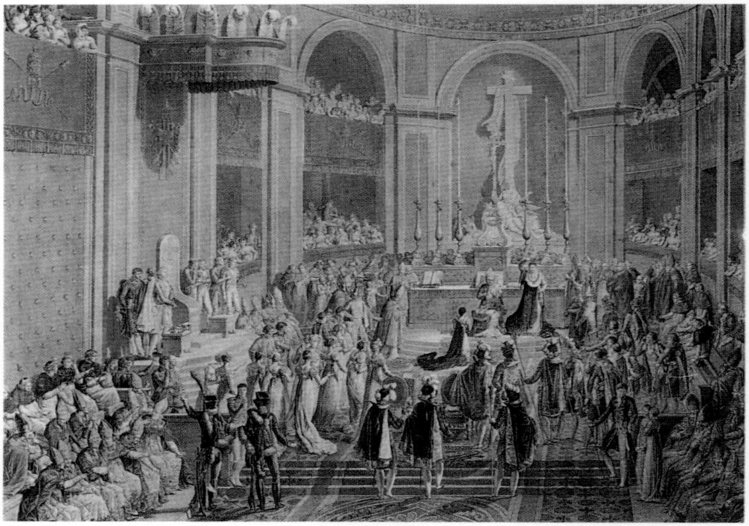

who, according to the Duchess d'Abrantès, seemed to be praying to Napoleon rather than to God. Taking place at the far end of the cathedral, these religious aspects of the ceremony were difficult for the majority of the spectators to make out. This was deliberate, and Napoleon stated that this first part was only to be seen in detail by 'the priest and such men whose superior intellects have bestowed upon them the faith equal to that of the eighth century'. The imperial couple then moved back to their official seats to be enthroned and blessed by the Pope, who kissed Napoleon on the cheek and exclaimed 'Vivat Imperator in Aeternum'. A mass followed and a seated Napoleon then took the constitutional oath wearing his crown and with his right hand on the Bible. 'I swear to maintain the territory of the Republic in its integrity; to respect and enforce the laws of the Concordat and the freedom of worship; to respect and enforce equality before the law, political and civil liberty and the irreversibility of the sales of national property; to lay on no duty, to impose no tax except according to law; to maintain the institution of the Legion of Honour; and to govern only in accordance with the interests, the happiness and the glory of the French people.' At the conclusion of the ceremony the imperial party processed in carriages around the centre of Paris before returning to the Tuileries Palace. From the grand balcony of the palace the emperor and empress received the homage of the army, detachments of which marched past to the sound of trumpets.

149 *The Coronation (Napoleon Crowning Himself)*, 1807. Engraving by Lavalé after Jean-Baptiste Isabey and Charles Percier, from Percier and Fontaine, *Le Livre du Sacre de S M l'Empereur*, Paris

David had been present both at the dress rehearsal held the day before in the Gallery of Diana at the Tuileries Palace, and at the coronation proper, and he made some drawings on the spot. In all likelihood he sat in a stand on the left of the choir: the preliminary drawings and the painting itself indicate such a position. One story relates that the day before the event David had a violent disagreement with the master of ceremonies, Count Ségur, who had tried to reseat him with a restricted view of the proceedings. Tempers were raised and blows were nearly exchanged with one of Ségur's sons, but

David's determined insistence ensured that he kept his original place. David said that 'I drew the whole from life and I did all the principal groups separately. I made notes on everything that I did not have time to draw.'

Napoleon had said that 'nothing is beautiful unless it is large', and, sensing his requirements, David sought to create one of the world's largest paintings. *The Wedding at Cana* of 1562–3 (150) by Paolo Veronese (1528–88), then, as now, in the Louvre,

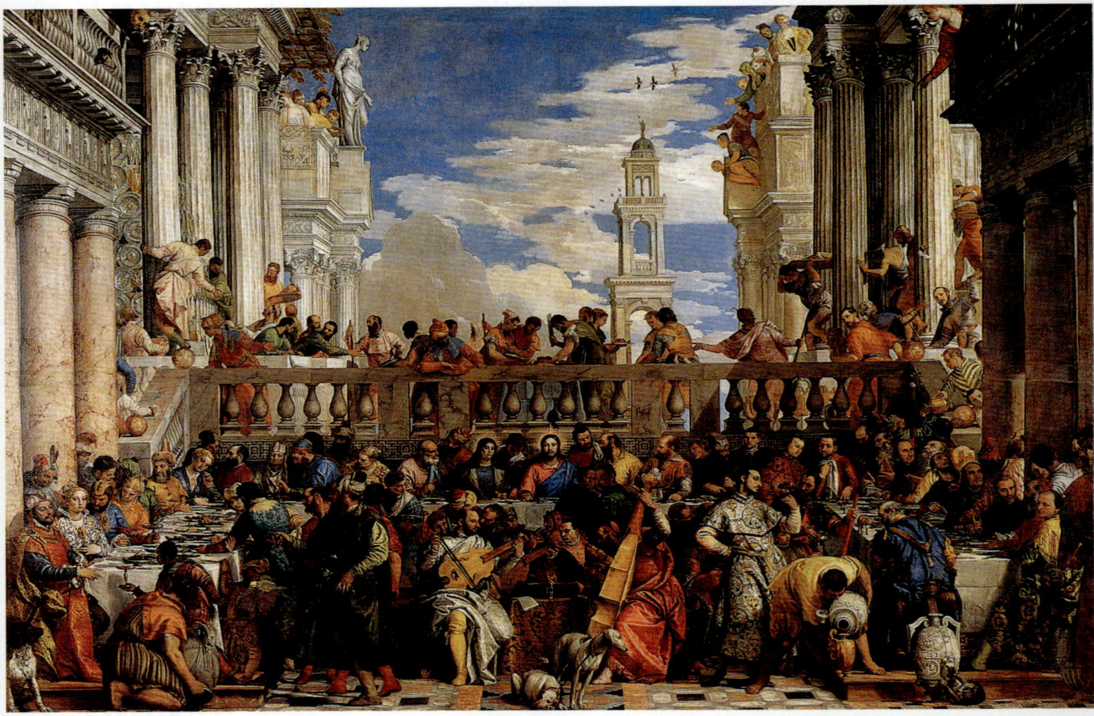

held the distinction of being the largest surviving work, and with a typical mixture of confidence and ambition, David planned a work of comparable, though slightly smaller, dimensions. The *Coronation* was therefore to be on a truly monumental scale – 6·8 × 9·8 m (22 × 30½ ft) – and to work on it David was given a new and more spacious studio in the deconsecrated church of Cluny in the Place Sorbonne (now demolished). He and all of the other artists had been expelled from their studios in the Louvre by Napoleon because the whole building was to be given over to the display of art and artefacts. In the studio David had models made of the cathedral interior and used dolls to help plan the figure groupings. A set designer with the Paris Opéra, Ignace-Eugène-Marie Degotti (b.1824), was also called in as an expert on architectural perspective (151). After almost a year of preparations, work on the huge canvas began on 21 December 1805 (152); David had as his assistant the faithful and reliable Georges Rouget (1784–1869), whom he called his 'right arm'. The painting was not finished until November 1807, but even then some changes had to be made in January of the following year.

150
Paolo Veronese, *The Wedding at Cana*, 1562–3.
Oil on canvas; 669 × 990 cm, $263\frac{3}{8} \times 389\frac{3}{4}$ in.
Musée du Louvre, Paris

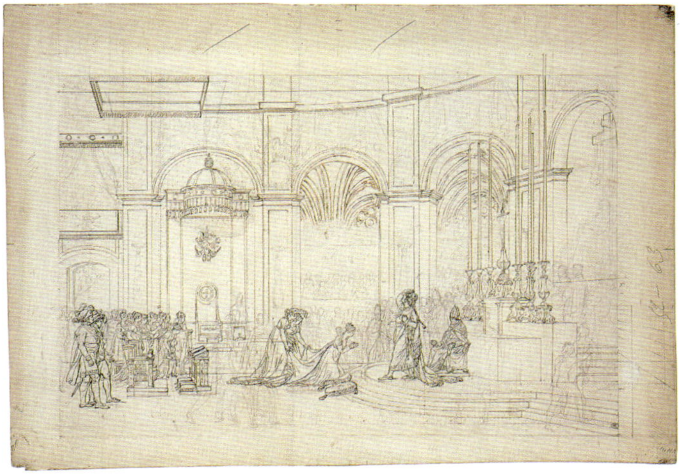

151
David and Degotti, Perspective study for the *Coronation*, 1805.
Black crayon and chalk; 34·5 × 48·5 cm, $13\frac{3}{8} \times 19$ in.
Musée du Louvre, Paris

While painting the scene David was faced with the problem of selecting the most significant moment of the ceremony to commemorate. At first, he planned to show Napoleon raising Josephine's crown above his own crowned head while pressing his ceremonial sword close to his heart (153). Although it is often said that this drawing and others show Napoleon crowning himself, it is known that he did not put on two crowns (itself a difficult task), and the crown he holds is certainly that of Josephine. David wrote that, 'This grandiose gesture reminds the spectators of the universally acknowledged truth that whoever can conquer something will be able to defend it. The

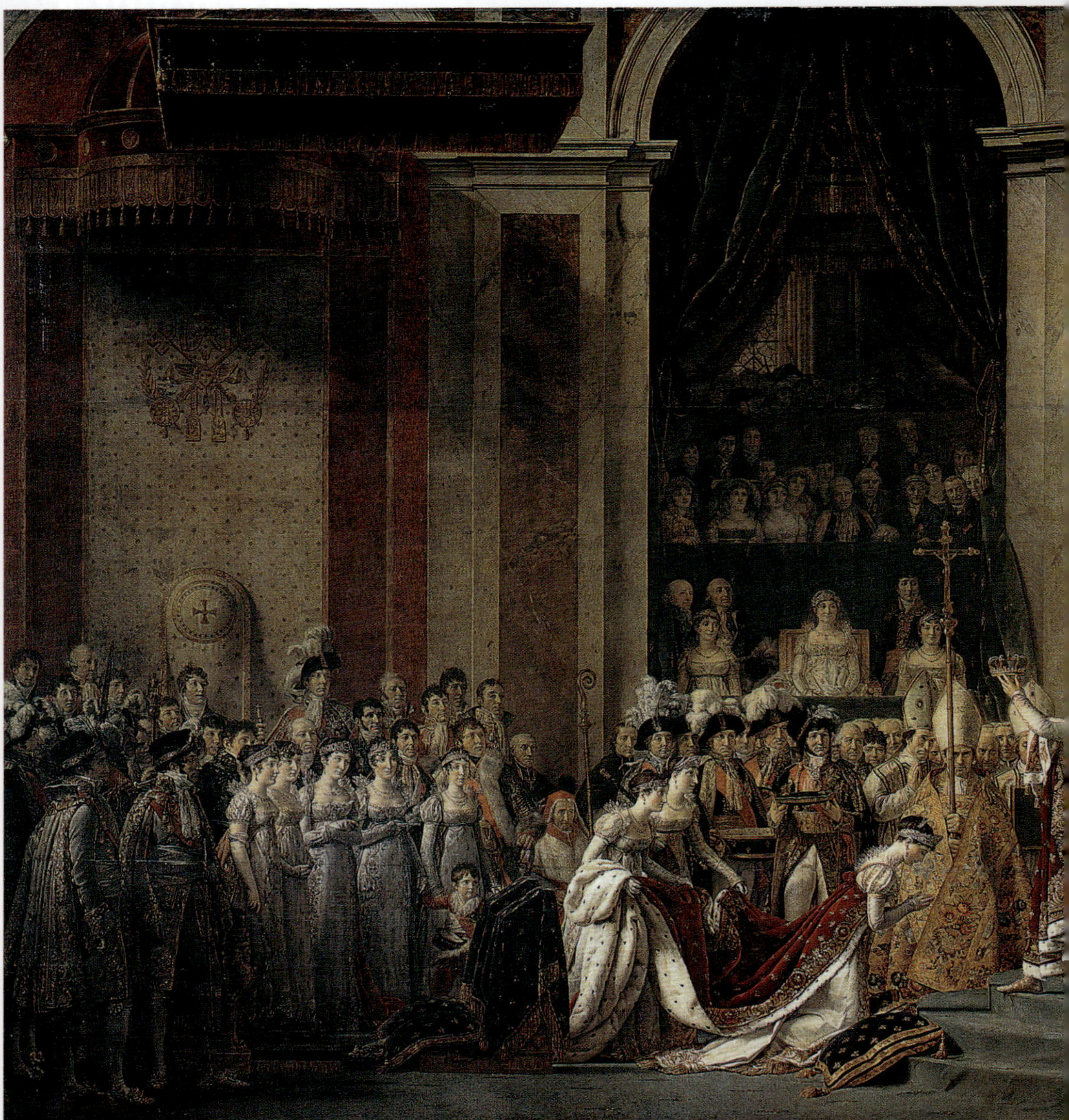

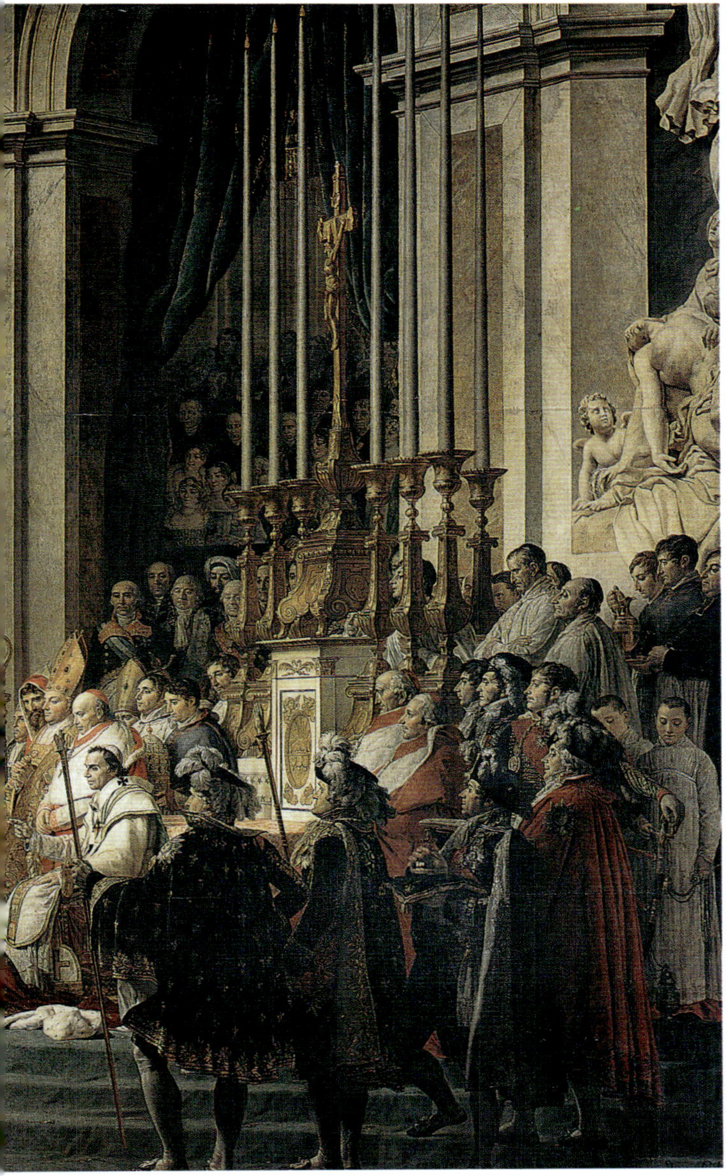

152
The Coronation of the Emperor and Empress, 1805–7.
Oil on canvas; 610 × 970 cm, $240^{1}/_{8} \times 381^{7}/_{8}$ in.
Musée du Louvre, Paris

empress is kneeling at the foot of the altar, her hands clasped, waiting for the crown her august husband is about to place on her head.' The emphasis on the sword may be an invention of David's to emphasize Napoleon's heroism and chivalry, as the programme of the coronation said that after the Pope gave him the sword, the emperor put it into its scabbard. But at quite a late stage in the development of the painting, certainly before May 1807, David was advised by his former student Gérard that this presentation lacked nobility and appeared faintly ridiculous. Such an arrangement would also have meant that both Josephine and the Pope were simply passive onlookers. David also planned to show the Pope watching the event with his hands on his knees (154), but Napoleon intervened and in his usual forthright manner exclaimed: 'I didn't have him come all that way to do nothing.' Therefore, in the final work, Napoleon is shown raising the crown in both hands before placing it on Josephine's head and the sword now appears on Napoleon's left side in the opening of his mantle (see 158). The Pope gives a blessing with his mitre at his feet and with his magnificent papal tiara, a gift from Napoleon, placed on the altar behind him. Napoleon was almost certainly consulted about these changes, but he could not have kept track of the picture's progress because he was away from Paris for most of 1807.

Working on such a large scale with such a huge cast to manipulate, David resorted to Renaissance working practices to plan and organize the *Coronation*. As well as drawings of Notre Dame, studies for groups and individuals (156) and details of uniforms and regalia, he also made full-scale cartoons of some figures. Two of these survive, the only examples of this practice in the whole of David's work. Both show Napoleon – one nude holding the crown; the other has him raising the crown in the position that he adopts in the final painting. These cartoons both demonstrate David's hesitation over the best pose to give to Napoleon, and also testify to his exhaustive working process. The cartoon of Napoleon crowning Josephine (157) is squared for transfer onto the final canvas which would

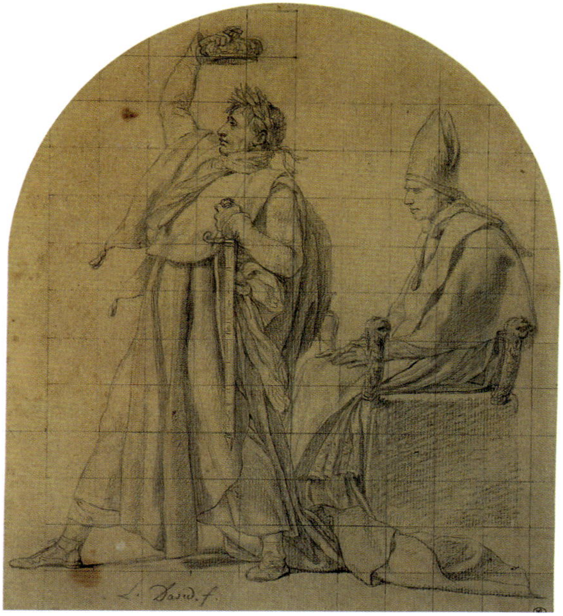

153
Napoleon Holding Josephine's Crown,
1805.
Black crayon;
29·3 × 25·3 cm,
$11\frac{1}{2}$ × 10 in.
Musée du Louvre, Paris

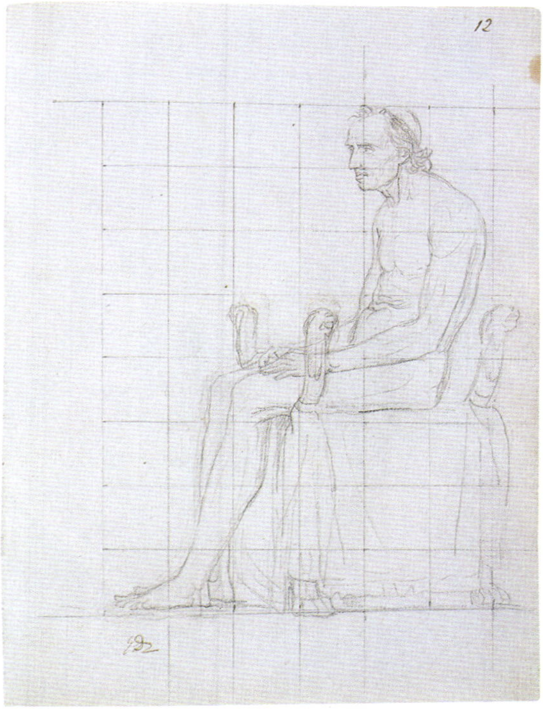

154
Nude study of Pope Pius VII,
1805.
Black crayon over graphite;
23·7 × 17·9 cm,
$9\frac{3}{8}$ × 7 in.
Fogg Art Museum, Harvard University Art Museums, Cambridge, Massachusetts

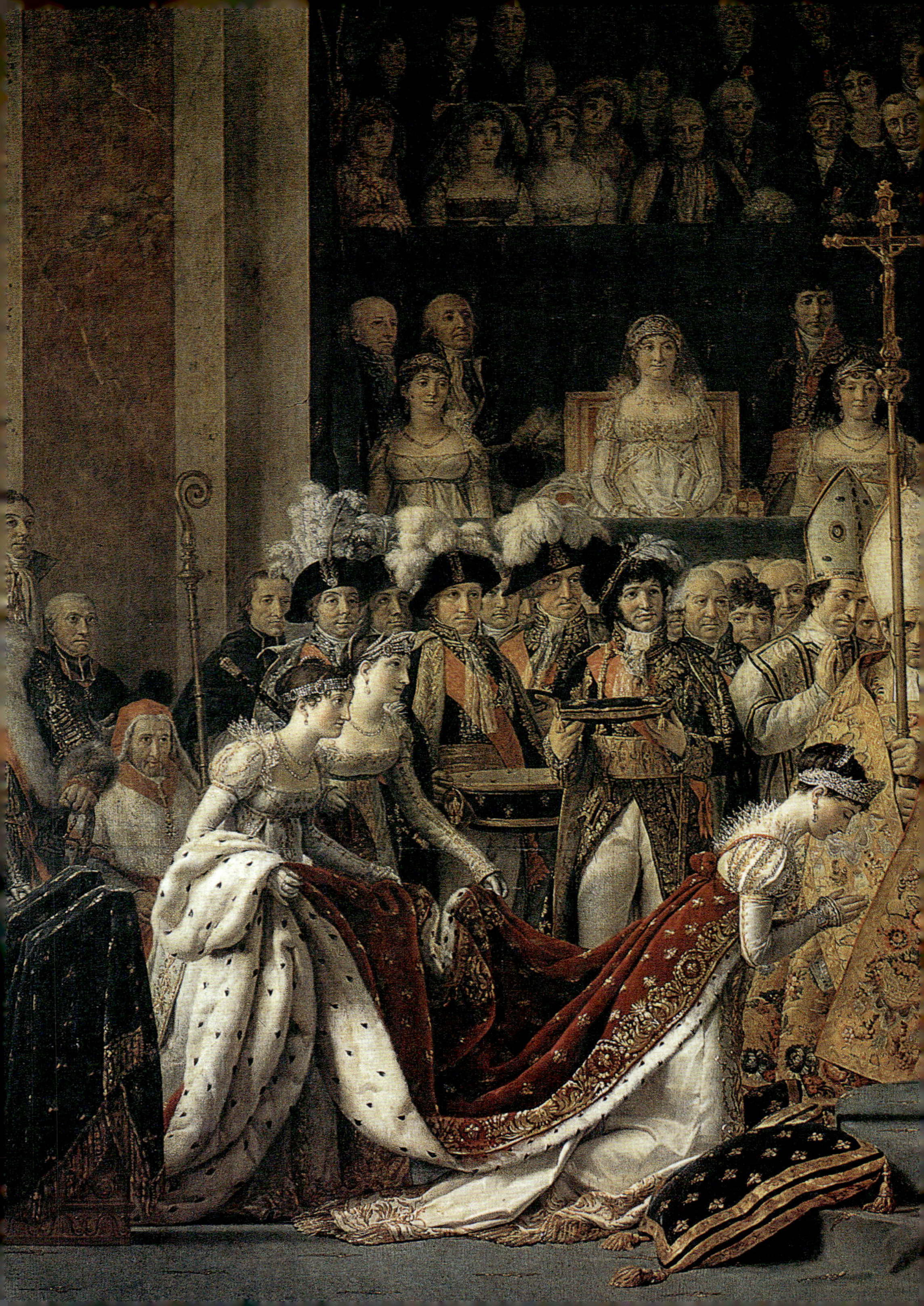

have been done by tracing the contours of the figure with a metal stylus. There would presumably have been other cartoons which David would have used to locate precisely the figures on the final work. However, they do not survive owing to their large scale and their strictly practical purpose and usage. David probably used cartoons for groups and for figures, especially Napoleon, who were too busy to pose.

In David's re-creation of the event the spectator is given a privileged close-up view and almost becomes part of the picture's space. David manipulated his large cast of characters with great finesse and for reasons of clarity and diplomacy he took

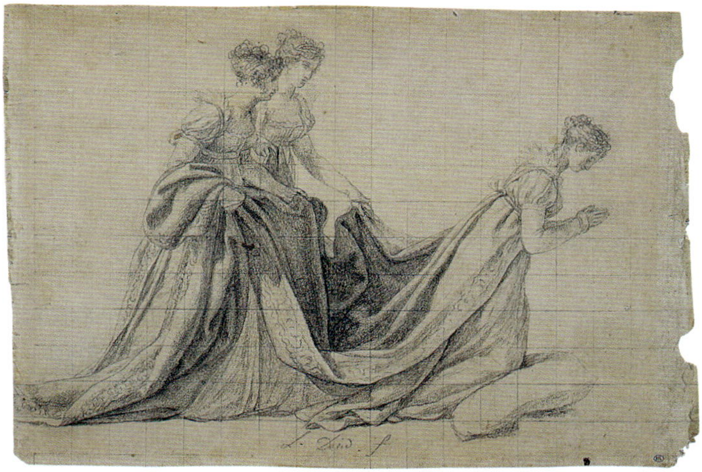

155
The Coronation
(detail of 152)

156
The Empress Josephine Kneeling with Madame de la Rochefoucauld and Madame de la Valette,
1806.
Black crayon and graphite;
27·4 × 39·1 cm,
$10^{3}/_{4} \times 15^{3}/_{8}$ in.
Musée du Louvre, Paris

some liberties with both the architectural setting and the personnel. Space is compressed and one tier of the side gallery is omitted. Napoleon's mother, Maria Letizia Bonaparte, known as Madame Mère, was not actually present at the ceremony, but she is the main figure in the central box, directly above Josephine (155). She and her son were not on particularly good terms, and she also disliked Josephine, and therefore decided to stay at home in Rome. Standing next to the Pope is Cardinal Caprara who was also absent because of illness. The *Coronation* is a spectacular portrait gallery of the new imperial court and there are nearly seventy recognizable likenesses.

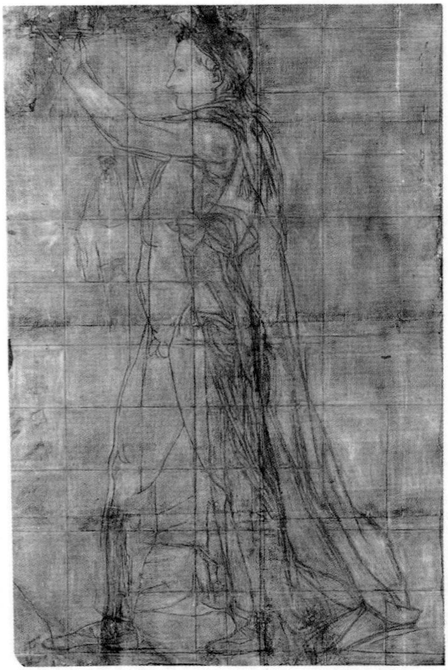

157
Cartoon for *The Coronation*, 1806. Red and black crayon. Musée des Beaux-Arts, Lille

158
The Coronation (detail of 152)

With his usual attention to detail, David asked the dignitaries to come to pose in the Cluny studio so that their heads might be painted directly onto the canvas, and to send him the clothes and uniforms that they had worn on the day. At the left are two of Napoleon's brothers, Joseph and Louis, both of whom were given kingdoms in 1806 by their brother – Joseph became King of Naples and Louis became King of Holland. Next to them are their sisters Caroline Murat, Pauline Borghese and Elisa Bacchiochi, with Louis's wife Hortense holding the hand of little Prince Charles, and Julie, wife of Joseph (159). In the gallery above Madame Mère we find not only the aged Vien (now a senator), but also David (with sketchbook and chalk; see 155) and his family. Josephine's long and heavy train is held by Madame Emilie-Louise de la Valette, Mistress of the Robes, and by Madame Chastulé de la Rochefoucauld, her principal lady-in-waiting, who though recorded as being small and misshapen, appears graceful and well proportioned. David also rejuvenated Josephine, who at forty-one was beginning to

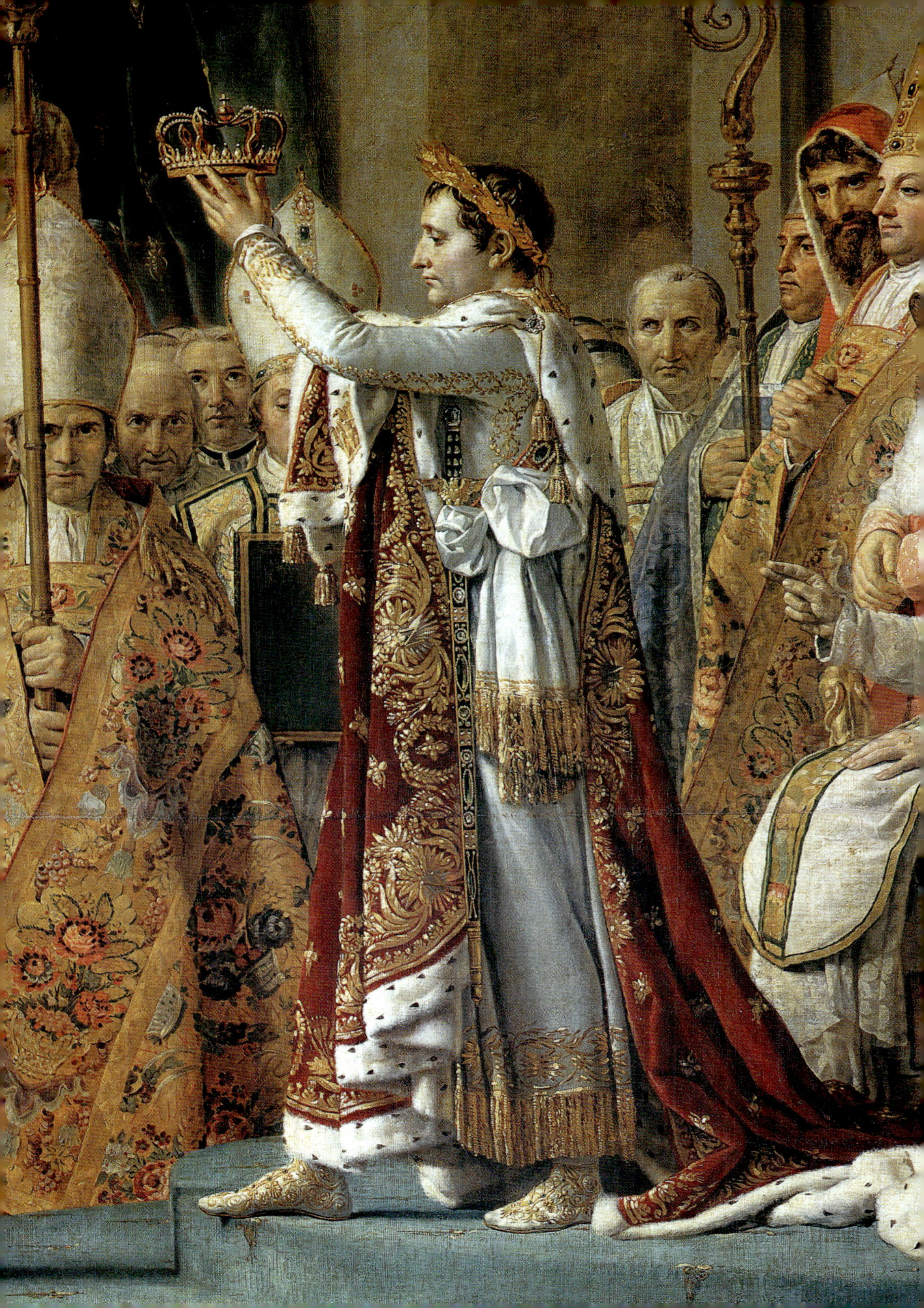

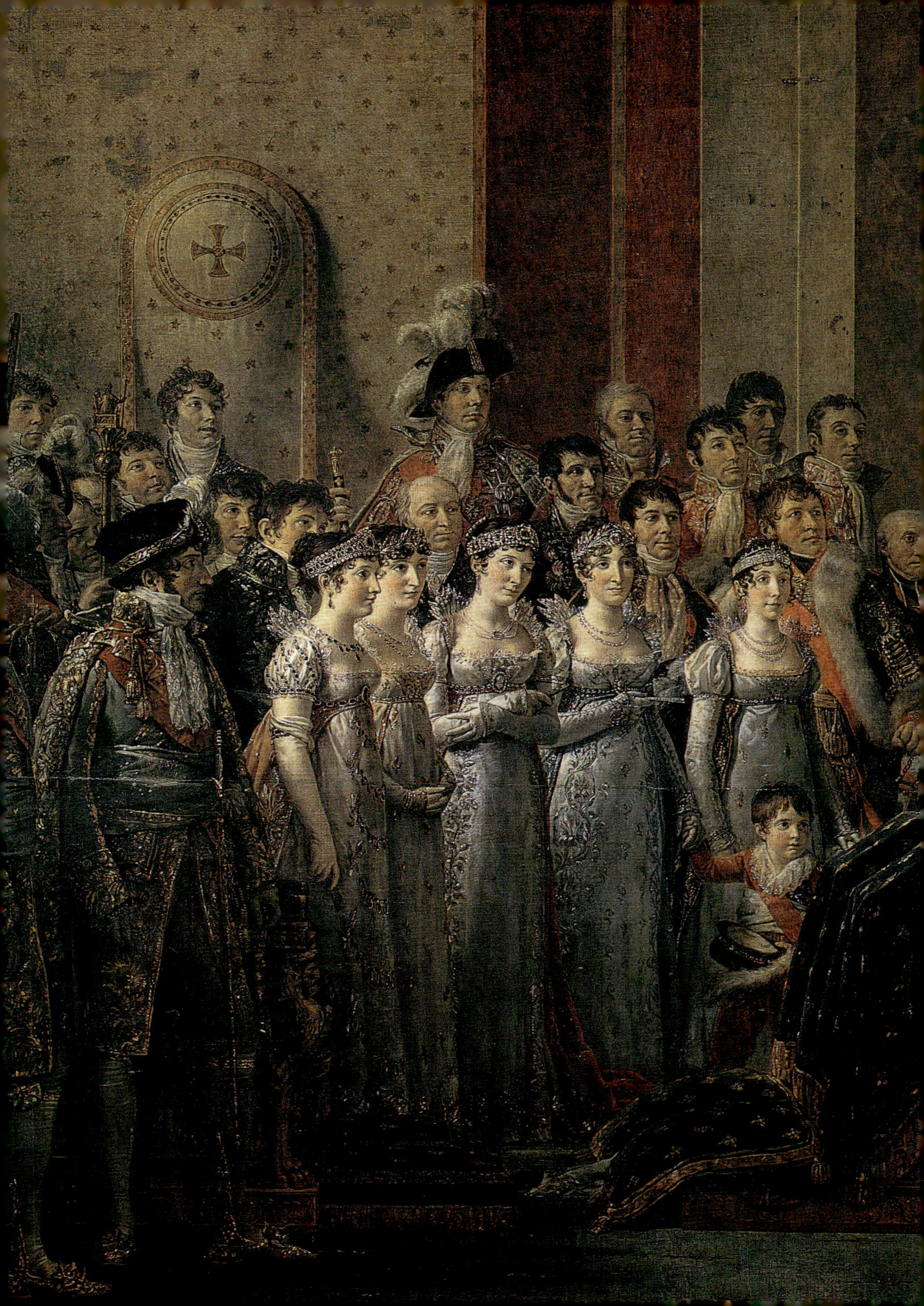

show her age; her features have the radiant bloom of her former beauty. In profile, Napoleon has a noble and severe quality and resembles the heads found on ancient coins and medals. At the extreme right are a semicircle of male courtiers, including Napoleon's former fellow consuls, Charles François Lebrun, now the arch-treasurer (with his back to the viewer) and the archchancellor Jean Jacques Régis de Cambacérès, both seen holding items of ceremonial regalia – the sceptre and the Hand of Justice. Next to them are Marshal Louis Alexandre Berthier, Grand Huntsman, who holds the orb on a velvet cushion and Charles Maurice de Talleyrand, the Grand Chamberlain (160).

By contrast Charlemagne's regalia is banished to the left of the painting. The crown, placed between Joseph and Louis Bonaparte, is almost swallowed up by the surrounding details, and above and behind them Marshal Lefebvre holds the sword and Marshal Pérignon the sceptre. As stated above, they had only played a marginal part in the proceedings, and by the time David came to paint the scene a change in political ideology meant that they were even less relevant. From 1806 the associations between Napoleon and Charlemagne were suppressed, since public opinion was increasingly critical of the territorial ambitions of Napoleon, which mirrored those of Charlemagne, and which continuously embroiled France in war. To be emperor also meant the denial of the ideals of the French Revolution and so Napoleon rejected Charlemagne in favour of a return to ancient Roman imagery which maintained revolutionary connections. Ingres's painting of *Napoleon on the Imperial Throne* of 1806 was condemned precisely because the artist had miscalculated the change in the political climate and emphasized the Carolingian associations.

159
The Coronation
(detail of 152)

For all its undoubted pomp, the *Coronation* also had an element of a family celebration about it and, true to his Corsican upbringing, Napoleon was determined to be surrounded by his clan at the moment of supreme glory. During the ceremony he whispered to his brother Joseph:

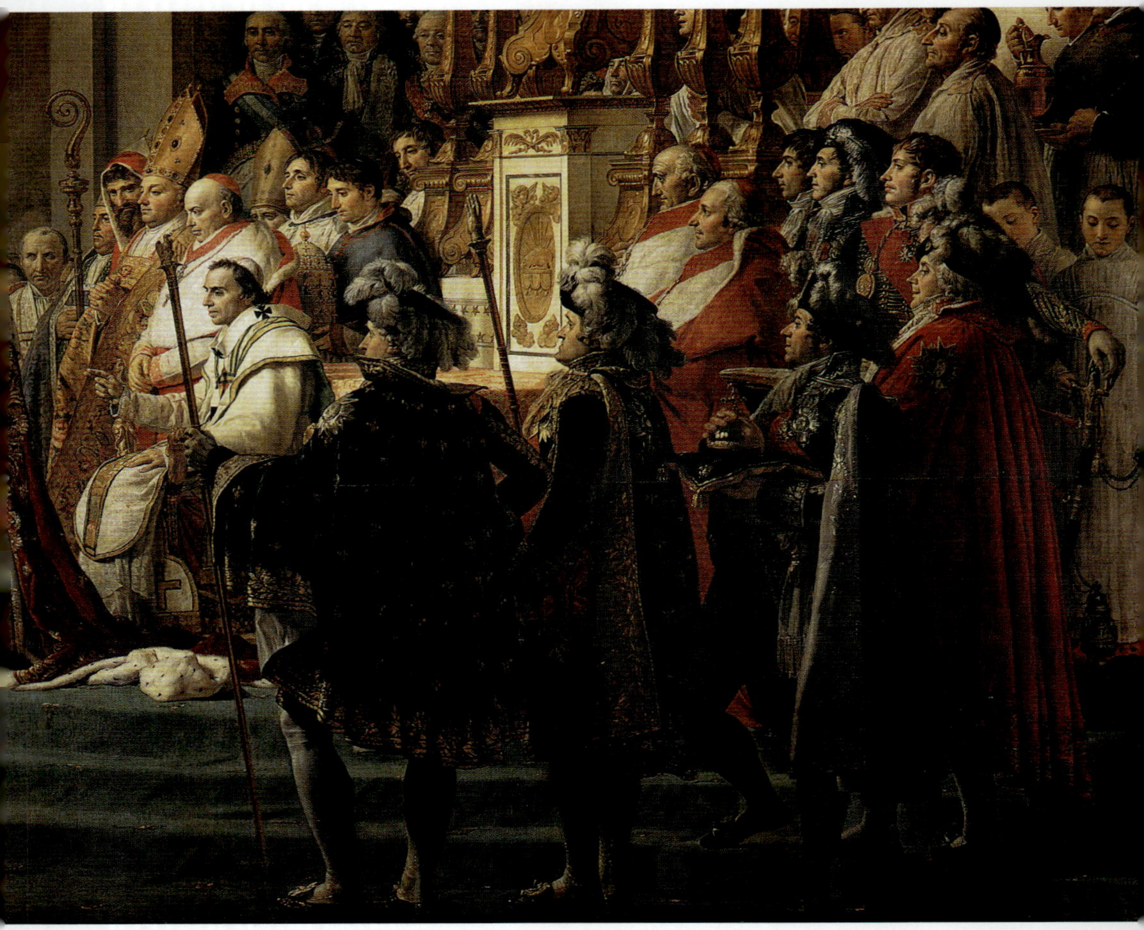

'If only our father could see us.' But even though a moment of great seriousness and solemnity is focused on, David introduced a lighter note: far from witnessing the momentous event, at the extreme right two choirboys are more intrigued by the magnificent sword held by Napoleon's stepson, Prince Eugène de Beauharnais (160).

Trying to keep so many important people happy with their assigned poses and positions in the *Coronation* proved to be a very difficult task for David. Minor points of protocol and priority were raised and the vanity of some courtiers severely tried David's patience. The Moslem Turkish ambassador, Mohamed-Sayd Halet Effendi, though present, refused to be shown in a church as it was contrary to the Koran and had to be persuaded to allow his inclusion; Cardinal Caprara, though ill on the day, requested to be shown wearing his ceremonial wig, which David flatly refused to do. More seriously, Louis Bonaparte, now King of Holland, was not satisfied with his and his brother Joseph's position at the left. To make the painting clear and uncluttered David had placed them there, whereas in fact they had been involved in the ceremony and had stood at the side of the altar. Louis wrote to David about this and the artist replied that if the king insisted, changes would naturally be made. He added, however, 'As you know, everything is calculated in a painting and changing a figure can lead to an incalculable number of adjustments that will completely disrupt an entire part of a painting and often the entire work.' David's tact meant that Louis grasped the problem and neither he nor his brother was re-positioned closer to Napoleon. The one minor change that did occur was that each figure was reworked so that both brothers stood apart and the profile of Joseph did not obscure Louis.

160
The Coronation
(detail of 152)

In order to commemorate the pageant and splendour of the coronation, something different from the purified and sculptural style of the *Sabines* was required and so David turned for inspiration to a previous artist-courtier who had painted grand state occasions – Peter Paul Rubens. In particular David looked at *The Coronation of Marie de' Medici* (161), which formed part of a cycle of twenty-one paintings produced between 1622 and 1625 to dramatize and aggrandize the rather mundane life of Marie, widow of Henry IV of France. David also looked to the example of the Old Master whom he sought to emulate, the great Venetian artist Veronese, who turned modest biblical events into large-scale pictures of feasts and celebrations (see 150). With its great number of portraits, concentration on colour and the sumptuous richness of materials, it is obvious that the *Coronation* is far removed from David's previous

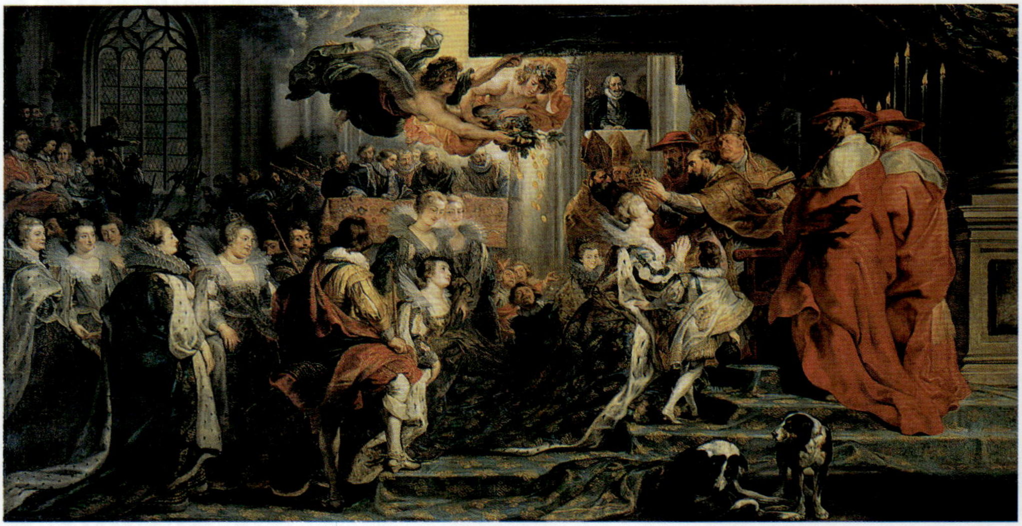

Neoclassicism and is further proof of his ability to change and develop his art. Perhaps it is better to speak of a newly created Empire style and certainly no other image captures so perfectly the glitter and opulence of Napoleon's imperial court.

Napoleon first saw the *Coronation* in David's studio on 4 January 1808 and spent a whole hour looking at it (162). He then said: 'This is not a painting; one can walk around in this picture; life is everywhere ... Good, very good, David. You have understood my thoughts, you have made me a French knight. I am grateful to you for recording for posterity the proof of the affection I wished to give to the woman who shares with me the burden of office.' The emperor then removed his hat, saying: 'David I compliment you', to which his First Painter replied: 'Sire, I receive your compliment on behalf of all artists, and am happy to be the one to whom you deign to offer it.' Nevertheless some minor changes, particularly the introduction of the papal blessing, were ordered. Josephine was also particularly keen on the painting, especially because of her youthful and sympathetic portrayal, although some courtiers said that she had been made to appear ridiculously young. When this was pointed out to David he very astutely replied: 'Then go and tell her so', a suggestion that was not taken up. The *Coronation* was publicly exhibited first at the Musée Napoleon in the Louvre in February and March 1808 and then at the Salon which opened on 14 October. As with the *Sabines*, David increased the sense of illusion by placing a large mirror opposite the work. Napoleon rewarded David for his service by promoting him to the rank of Officer of the Legion of Honour at the Salon on 22 October, an event that Gros planned to commemorate (163). David became a member of the imperial court, and was also granted a coat of arms (164) and a hereditary title. It is little wonder that he announced, 'I will slide into history in the shadow of my hero.'

161
Peter Paul Rubens, *The Coronation of Marie de' Medici*, 1622–5. Oil on canvas; 394 × 727 cm, $155\frac{1}{8} \times 286\frac{1}{4}$ in. Musée du Louvre, Paris

While Pope Pius VII remained in Paris David also painted his portrait (165) and thereby joined an illustrious band of past artists – Raphael, Titian (*c*.1485/90–1576) and Diego Velázquez (1599–1660) – as the painter of a pontiff. David broke with protocol by sitting down while he worked, as previously tradition had dictated that the humble artist should kneel to paint the Pope. David, though, did appreciate the honour bestowed upon him and apparently put on fine clothes and wore a sword as he worked. He responded warmly to the venerable old pontiff and was both delighted and moved by the benediction that he received from the hand of Pius. 'This dear old man, what a venerable face! How simple he is ... and what a fine head! ... This is a real Pope, a real priest ... He is as poor as

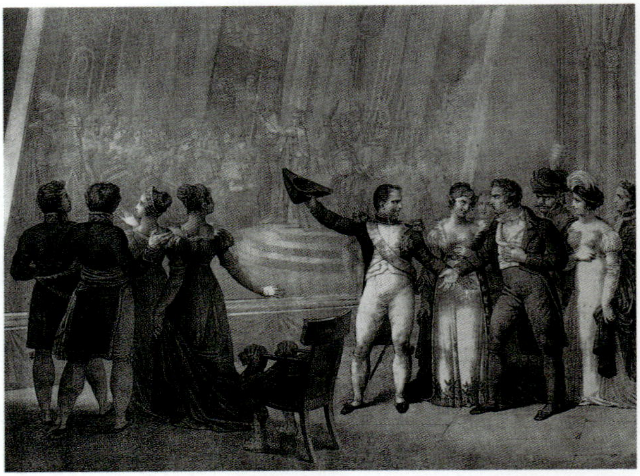

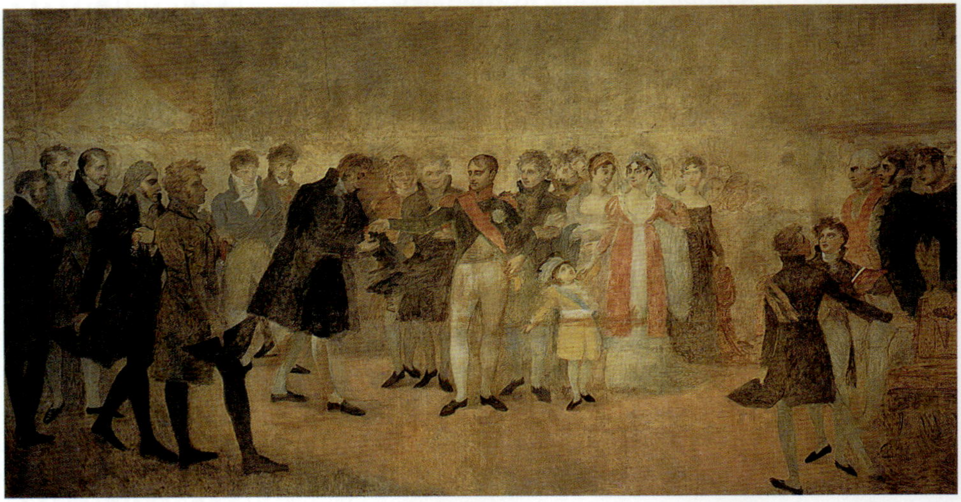

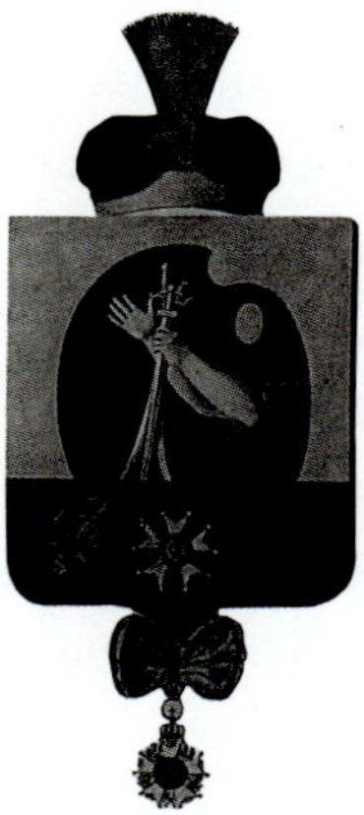

St Peter; the gold embroidery on his cape is artificial! He really lives according to the Gospel ... I must admit that I have long envied the artists who had lived before me for the opportunities that I thought I would never have. I shall have painted an Emperor and then a Pope.' David hesitated as he was about to start his attempt to capture the likeness and character of the Pope, saying: 'A true artist always trembles before struggling with nature', but the completed portrait is a very successful investigation, almost interrogation, of his sitter.

162
Charles-Etienne Motte,
The Visit of Napoleon and Josephine to David's Studio on 4 January 1808.
Engraving after Norblin; 34 × 40·7 cm, 13⅜ × 16 in

163
Antoine-Jean Gros,
Napoleon Visiting the 1808 Salon,
1808.
Oil on canvas; 350 × 640 cm, 137⅜ × 252 in.
Musée National du Château de Versailles

164
David's coat of arms, painted by himself, 1808.
Private collection

Despite the success of the *Coronation*, David's work for Napoleon did not always please. In 1805 he had to paint Napoleon in the robes of the coronation, a picture destined for the Appeals Court in Genoa – a painting which is now lost, although a small oil sketch remains (166). As usual, Napoleon refused to pose and the end result was rather feeble, probably because David had handed the work over to his student Georges Devillers. Napoleon disliked the work intensely and said: 'The portrait is so bad, so filled with defects that I do not accept it and do not wish it to be sent to any town, especially in Italy where it would give a very bad idea of our school.' Thanks to this disappointing piece of work David lost the chance to become Napoleon's favoured portraitist and much work was given instead to Gérard and Robert Lefèvre (1755–1830). David tried to cover up the embarrassment of the refusal at the expense of a rival artist, Jean-Baptiste Regnault. Regnault had also had a picture of Napoleon rejected and David quipped: 'Well Regnault, it appears the Emperor is not satisfied with our portraits. As likely as not, too, because I did not paint mine, as it is rumoured, and because you did paint yours.'

While their father was enjoying the privileges of the imperial court, David's sons and daughters were all affected by the Napoleonic experience. The eldest son, Charles-Louis-Jules, was a Greek scholar who became a government official under the Empire, and Eugène, after briefly studying with his father, went off to be an army officer. He fought at Austerlitz where the carnage appalled him, and after the Battle of Leipzig in 1813 news reached Paris that he had been killed. However, although he was left for dead, he managed to escape through enemy lines and arrived home after many adventures. At first, neither his father nor his mother recognized the pathetic figure, but were then overcome with joy and emotion. For his bravery Eugène was admitted into the Legion of Honour. Both of David's daughters were married to officers in the Napoleonic army. Emilie's

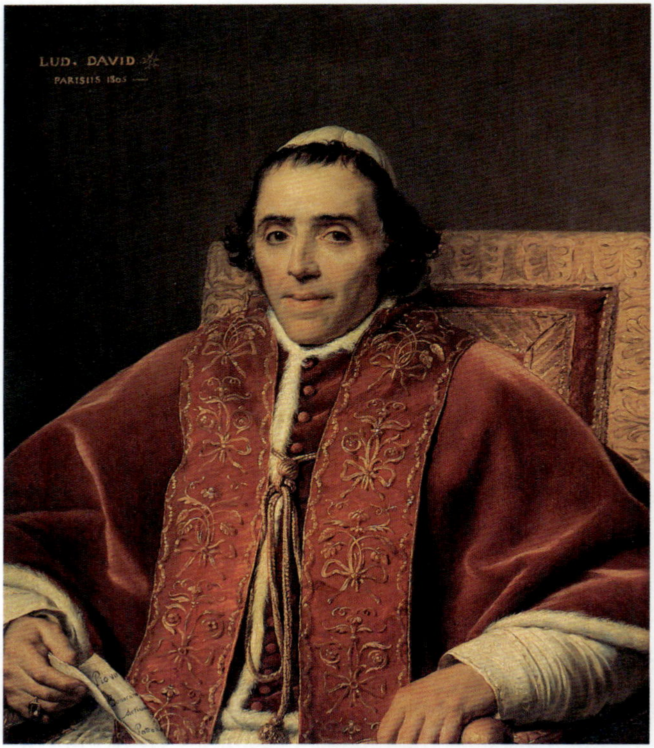

165
Portrait of Pope Pius VII, 1805.
Oil on panel; 86 × 71cm, $33\frac{7}{8}$ × 28in.
Musée du Louvre, Paris

166
Napoleon in Imperial Costume (sketch), 1805.
Oil on panel; 58 × 49cm, $22\frac{7}{8} \times 19\frac{1}{4}$in.
Musée des Beaux-Arts, Lille

husband was General (later Baron) Claude-Marie Meunier, of the 9th Light Infantry regiment, and Pauline married General Jean-Baptiste Jeanin who later also became a baron.

Almost as soon as the *Coronation* was finished, David began work on his second huge Napoleonic painting, *The Distribution of the Eagle Standards* (167), which he completed in November 1810. Napoleon had actually requested that David postpone work on another of the three remaining commemorative works, *The Arrival at the Hôtel de Ville*, which was then being prepared (168), because the military subject was his favourite and he preferred a painting that demonstrated the loyalty of his army to one that showed the allegiance of his people. The event had taken place three days after the coronation, on 5 December 1804, when, in an obvious imitation of the standards of the imperial Roman legions, Napoleon presented the

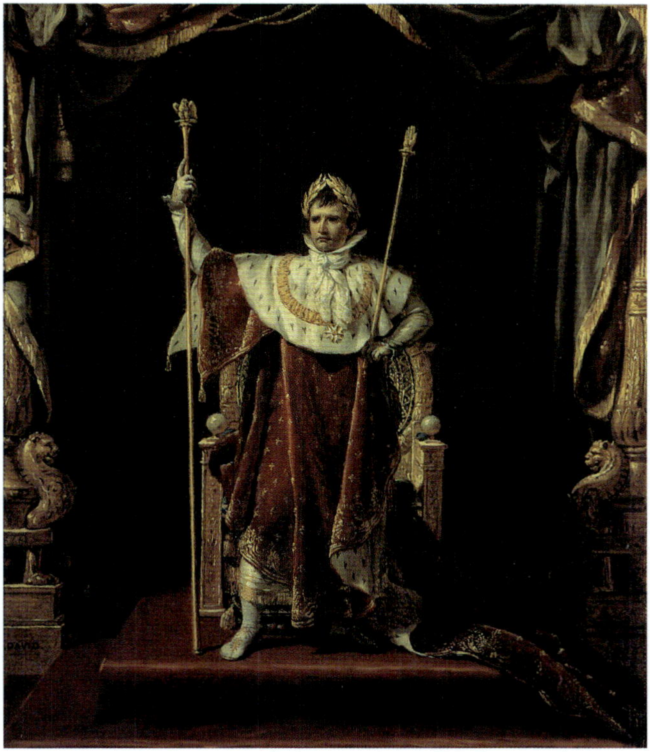

167 Overleaf
The Distribution of the Eagle Standards, 1810.
Oil on canvas; 610 × 970 cm, $240\frac{1}{8} \times 381\frac{7}{8}$ in.
Musée National du Château de Versailles

army regiments and the National Guard of the 108 departments of France with their own Eagle standards (169). 'Soldiers,' the emperor proclaimed, 'here are your flags! These Eagles will always be your rallying point; they will be wherever your Emperor deems them necessary to defend his throne and his people. You will swear to defend them with your life and to uphold them constantly by your courage on the road to victory. Do you swear?' In unison the army colonels raised the

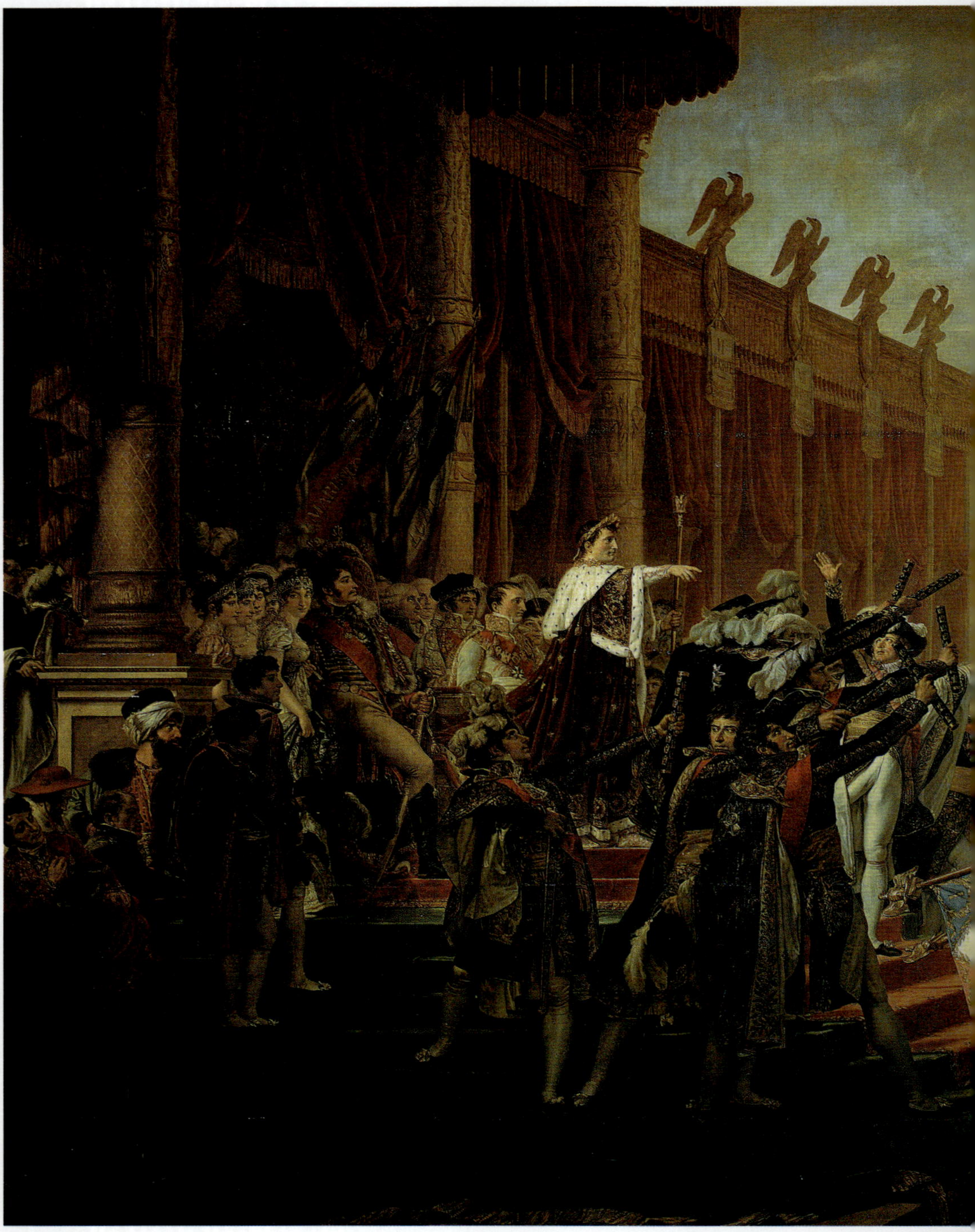

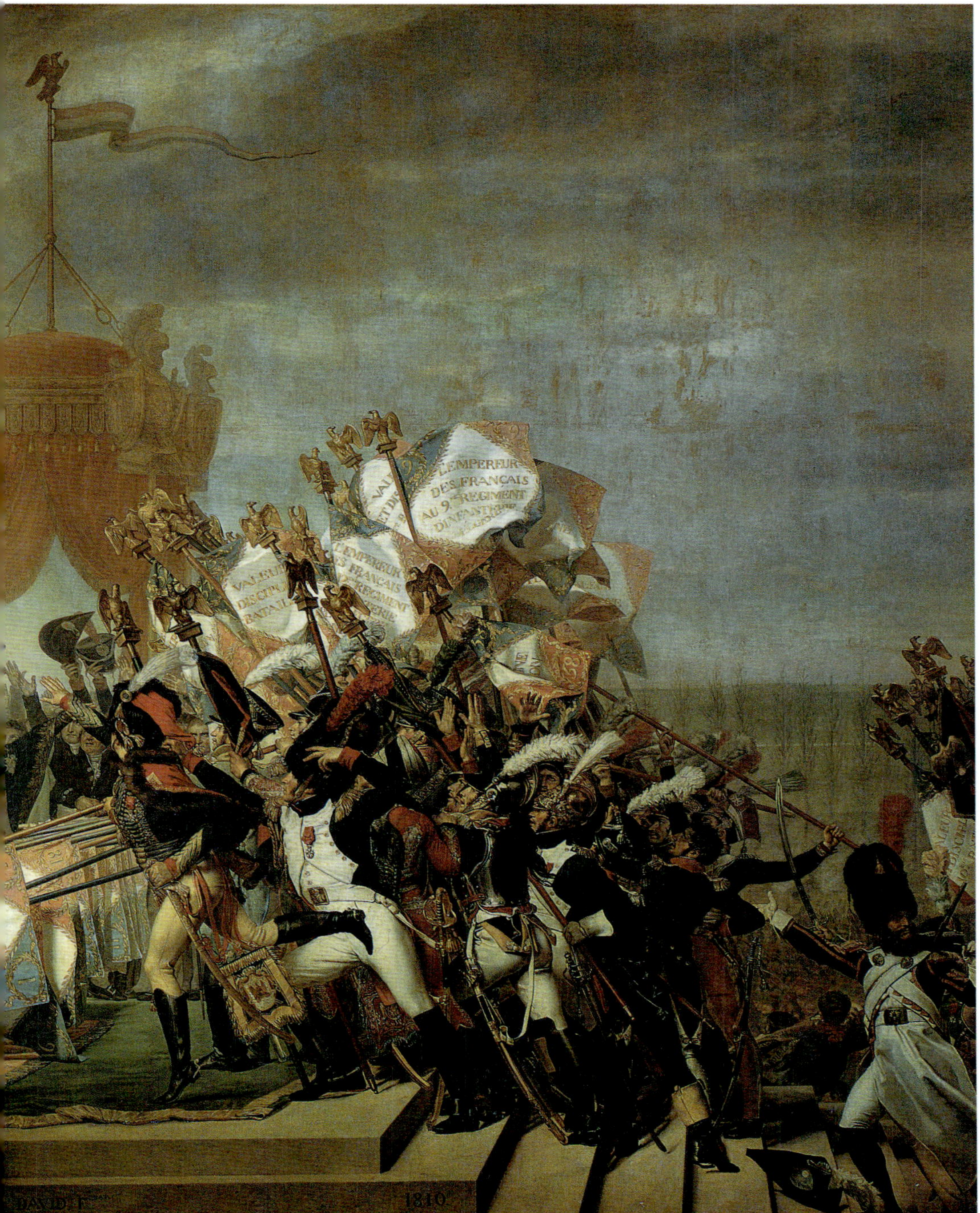
L'EMPEREUR
DES FRANCAIS
1810

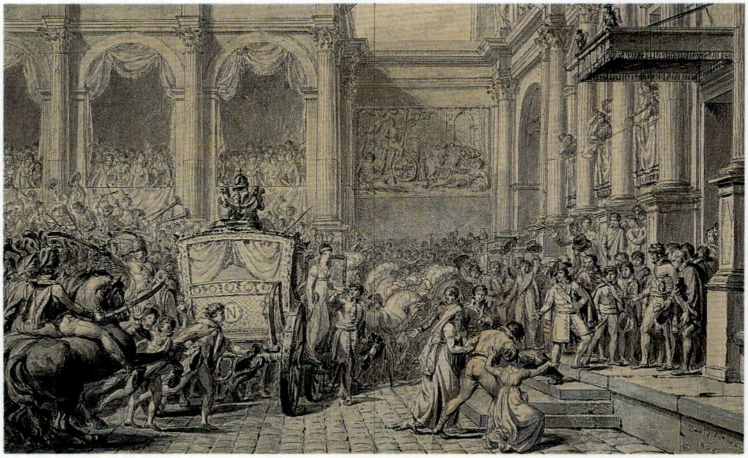

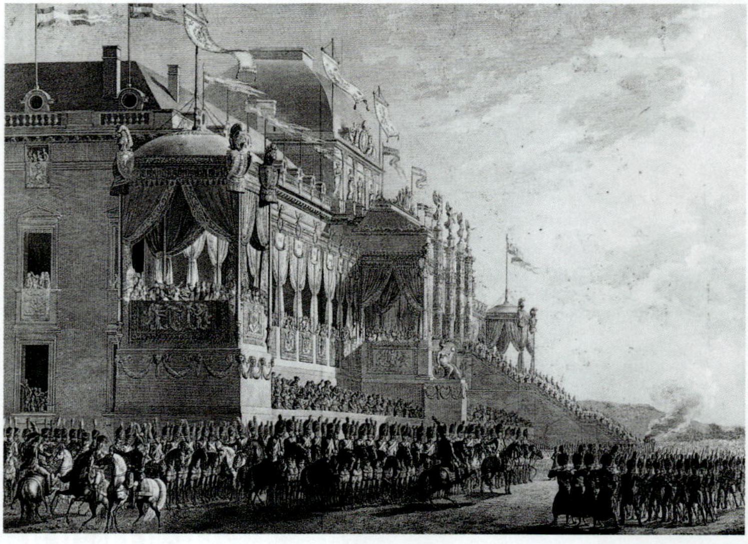

standards towards the emperor, and the marshals of France lifted up their batons and a chorus of 'We swear' rang out. The superstitious Napoleon attached great importance to banners and flags, seeing the capture of enemy colours as proof of complete victory and the loss of French standards as deeply humiliating and a disgrace to the regiment concerned. When first considering the painting in 1806, David was full of enthusiasm and wrote: 'Never was an oath better kept. What different stances, what a variety of expressions. There never was a finer subject for a painting.' But circumstances were to dilute and alter his vision. The initial composition had a crowd of soldiers rushing towards the static and diminutive emperor with a winged allegorical figure of Victory hovering at the right (170). The bluntly pragmatic Napoleon could not see the point of allegory and told David to remove it, a decision with which the painter did not agree, because without the figure of Victory, the marshals and courtiers look up into an empty sky. Josephine was also to be seated behind her husband, but her failure to produce the heir that Napoleon so wanted had led to their divorce in 1809; the emperor had then married the portly and plain Marie Louise of Austria on 2 April 1810. As both former wife and former empress, Josephine could no longer be present in the official image and so David simply removed her from the group at the left. But in doing so a compositional void was created next to Napoleon which was filled very awkwardly by extending the right leg of Eugène de Beauharnais into the space formerly occupied by Josephine. Such changes affected the painting's impact and meaning and it received only a muted response from the critics.

168
The Arrival at the Hôtel de Ville, 1805.
Pen, brown and black ink with white highlights and traces of graphite; 26·2 × 40·8 cm, $10^3/_8$ × 16 in. Musée du Louvre, Paris

169
Malbeste, *The Distribution of the Eagle Standards,* 1807.
Engraving after Jean-Baptiste Isabey and Charles Percier, from Percier and Fontaine, *Déscriptions des cérémonies et des fêtes ...,* Paris, 1807

Although *The Distribution of the Eagle Standards* demonstrated fervent patriotism and devotion, there is also a less appealing side to the imagery. Just as the Napoleonic Empire created a model to inspire twentieth-century dictators, David's paintings for the emperor provided artistic examples for their commemoration. Indeed, it later needed only a small leap of the imagination to turn such ideas into fascist and totalitarian art (171), and we are also reminded of the stage-managed propaganda of Hitler's Nuremberg rallies held between 1933 and 1938 (172).

With *The Distribution of the Eagle Standards*, David's official work for Napoleon ended. Over the past six years there had been constant haggling over prices and some very tense dealings with Baron Vivant Denon (Napoleon's Director-General of Museums) and with the officials of the imperial household. Delays in payment during the execution of the *Eagle Standards* prompted David to undertake a private commission for the

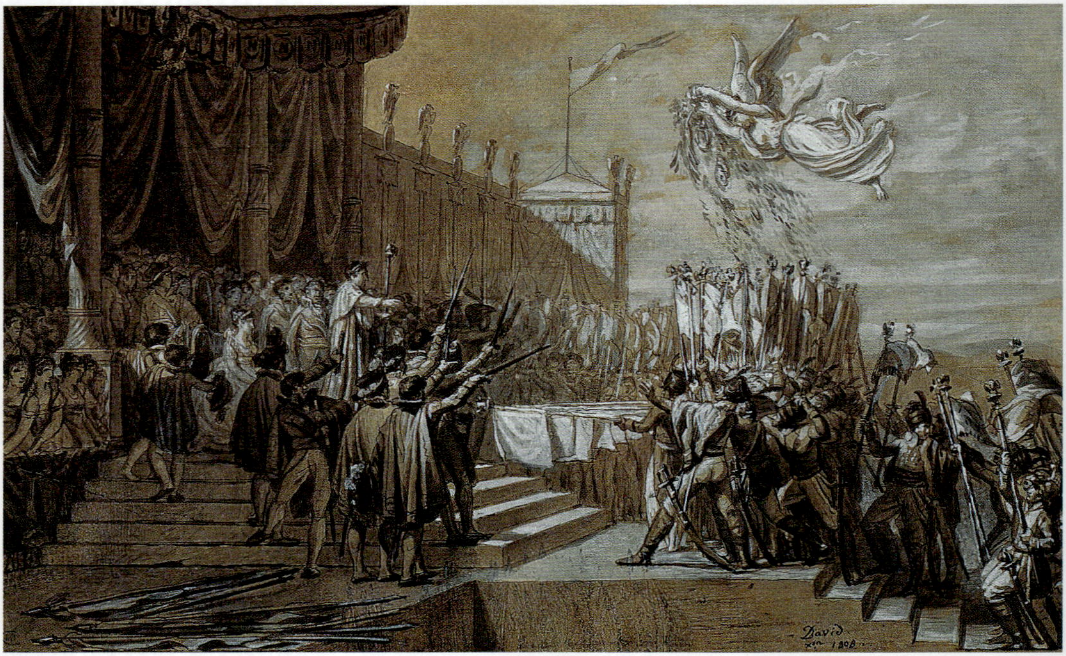

wealthy Russian diplomat and art collector Prince Nicolas Yusupov, who lived in Paris from 1808 to 1811. The painting *Sappho and Phaon* (173) was commissioned in July 1808 and completed in November of the following year. Sappho was a poetess on the Greek island of Lesbos and her affection for the young women of the cult of Aphrodite was the origin of the word 'lesbian'. However, she fell in love with the beautiful youth Phaon, the protégé of Venus, and when he only briefly reciprocated her love, she leapt to her death from the rocks at

Leucadia. Though this theme of legendary or mythological lovers was similar to that of *The Loves of Paris and Helen* of 1788 (see 74), in this painting the couple are not totally self-absorbed and instead look out at the viewer, Phaon staring intensely and Sappho intoxicated with delight at her lover's touch. Indeed, so transported is she that she still believes herself to be playing the lyre that is now held by Cupid. The poem she was in the midst of reciting had been dedicated to Phaon and the scroll on her lap bears his name and the verses: 'He appears to me as god's equal.' For this picture about the power of physical love and its effect on the individual, David gave his lovers an almost portrait-like degree of characterization, placing them very close to the edge of the picture plane and near to the spectator. To add to the almost unreal sense

170
Study for *The Distribution of the Eagle Standards*, 1808.
Pen, black ink, grey wash and white highlights; 18·1 × 29 cm, $7\frac{1}{8} \times 11\frac{1}{2}$ in. Musée du Louvre, Paris

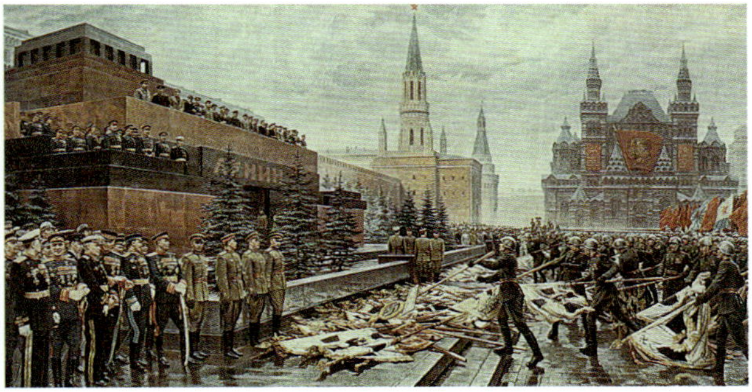

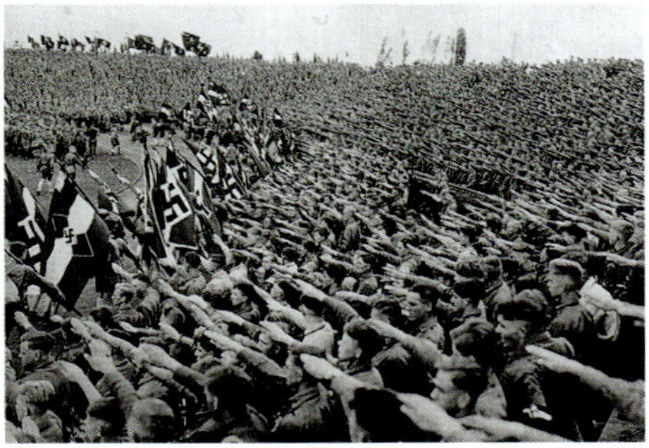

171
Mikhail Khmelko, *The Triumph of the Fatherland*, 1949.
Oil on canvas; 291 × 560 cm, $114\frac{5}{8} \times 220\frac{5}{8}$ in. Tretyakov Gallery, Moscow

172
Nazi Party rally, 1933

of mythology come to life he also bathed the scene in harsh daylight and used bright colours and hard contours. He would return to such subject matter and technical means later when once again forced to invent his own themes.

Though exacting a handsome payment of 12,000 francs for *Sappho and Phaon*, David's main concern was the outstanding payment for the Napoleonic works. As a courtier David's tactics were undiplomatic and clumsy, winning few friends and making him appear greedy and money grabbing. Not until February 1810 were the financial arrangements for the *Coronation*, the *Eagle Standards* and David's salary as Painter to the Emperor fixed and even then his price of 100,000 francs

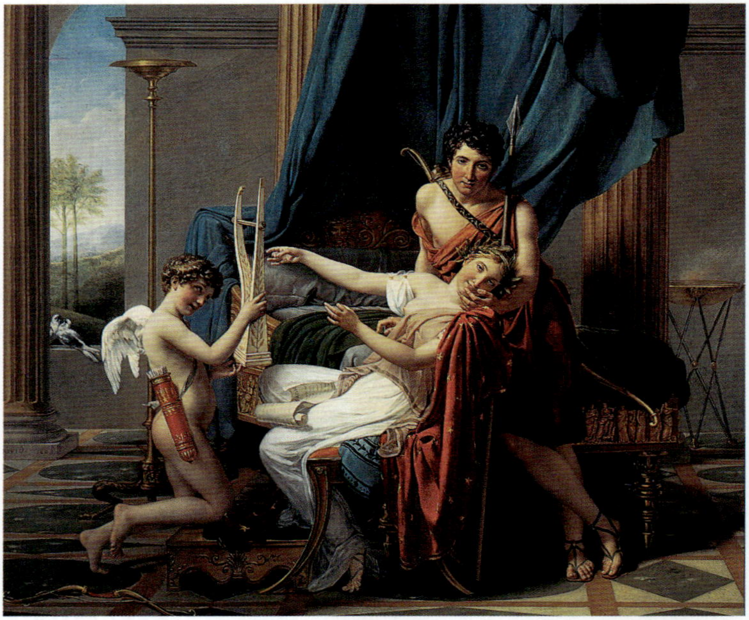

for the *Coronation* was rejected – he received only 65,000 francs. By this time the fees he demanded seemed exorbitant, and in effect he priced himself out of work, many commissions being given to cheaper artists who had formerly been his pupils, such as Gros, Girodet and Gérard. For the first time in over twenty years David began to face serious artistic competition and he also encountered opposition from government officials and from the Institute, the learned body that had replaced the Academy in 1795. In 1810 it was decided to award decennial prizes in the categories of best history painting and best national subject and all works produced over the past decade were eligible. Napoleon doubtless thought that his reign and that of his heirs would have both the creativity and the longevity to sustain a competition that only took place once every ten years, although subsequent events were to determine that the 1810 competition was both the first and the last occasion on which the prizes were judged. That *The Coronation of the Emperor and Empress* should be declared the best national subject of the decade was a foregone conclusion – how could it be otherwise? But the prize that David really coveted was that

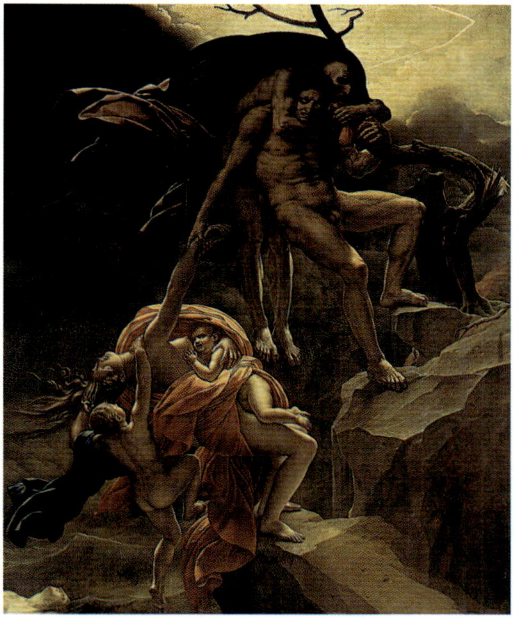

173
Sappho and Phaon,
1809.
Oil on canvas;
225 × 262 cm,
88⅝ × 103⅛ in.
Hermitage Museum,
St Petersburg

174
Anne-Louis Girodet,
Scene of a Deluge,
1806.
Oil on canvas;
441 × 341 cm,
173⅝ × 134¼ in.
Musée du Louvre, Paris

for history painting, and to his disbelief and huge disappointment the *Scene of a Deluge* (174) by his former pupil Girodet was placed ahead of *The Intervention of the Sabine Women*. The artistic world was consequently split into pro- and anti-David factions with pamphlets and articles both praising and criticizing the respective works. The result also displeased Napoleon and actually the cash prizes that were promised never materialized. Nevertheless, there was a suggestion that David's work was becoming outdated and that the public preferred the delicious thrill and dramatic lighting of Girodet's muscular figures to the smooth sculptural forms and posed gestures of the *Sabines*.

In Napoleonic Paris David and his wife were hardly a splendid or striking couple. The English novelist Fanny Burney called Madame David (175) 'a woman of no sort of elegance ... and if she ever possessed any beauty, it had deserted her at an early period', but in compensation she was clever, shrewd and penetrating, yet prone to sarcasm. David's features continued to be twisted by the growth of his tumour; the Scottish novelist

Sir Walter Scott said that the painter's face was the most hideous he had ever seen. We should remember, though, that this was a time when people were judged more on their abilities and achievements than on their appearance, and that people were not readily dismissed simply because they were plain or ugly – as is often the case today. Having been required to leave their lodgings in the Louvre, the couple moved to a

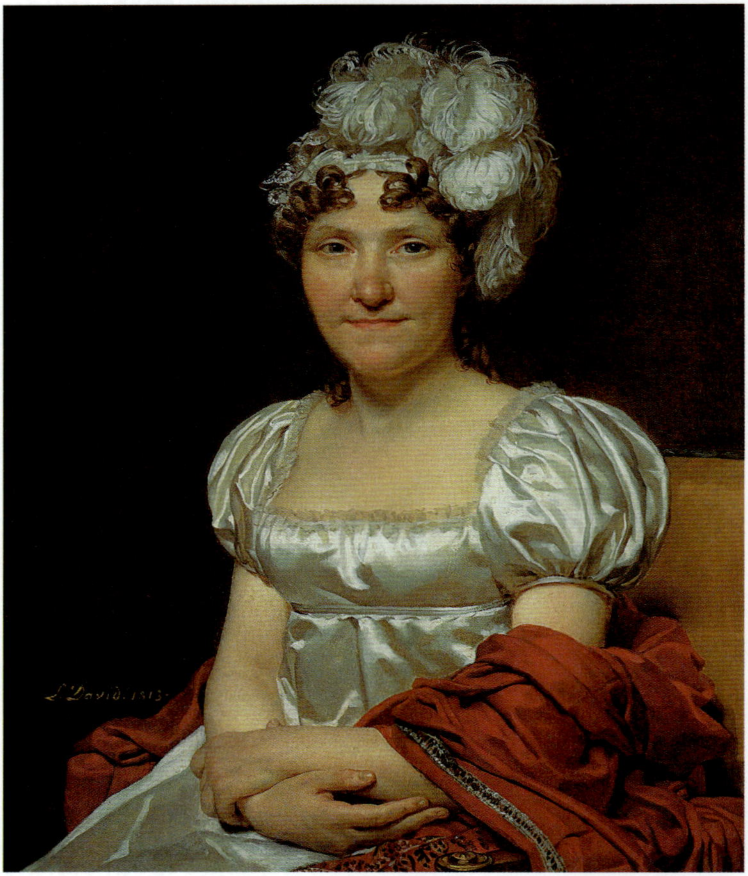

175
Portrait of Marguerite-Charlotte David,
1813.
Oil on canvas;
72 × 63 cm,
$28^{3}/_{8} \times 24^{3}/_{4}$ in.
National Gallery of Art, Washington, DC

176
J J Champin lithograph after Régnier,
David's house, 13 rue d'Enfer, from *Habitations des personnages célèbres en France,*
1834

spacious house at 13 rue de l'Enfer (176) and enjoyed a comfortable lifestyle with five servants, stabling for four horses and a carriage and two gigs.

David did paint Napoleon once more, in 1812, but this commission came from a most unexpected source. Britain and France had been at war since 1803 but such was the emperor's fame that a Scottish aristocrat, Alexander Douglas, later Duke of Hamilton, paid David the enormous sum of 1,000 guineas (18,650 francs) for a full-length portrait (see 140). This was not Napoleon the athletic and heroic warrior (his waistline had increased at approximately the same rate as his hairline had decreased), but Napoleon the statesman and lawgiver who, as the burnt-down candle and the clock with a time of 4·13 am show, works far into the night for the benefit of his subjects. A scroll of paper in the bureau bears the word 'Code', which refers to the new Civil Code, actually in operation since 1804 but which was renamed the 'Code Napoleon' in 1807 in an

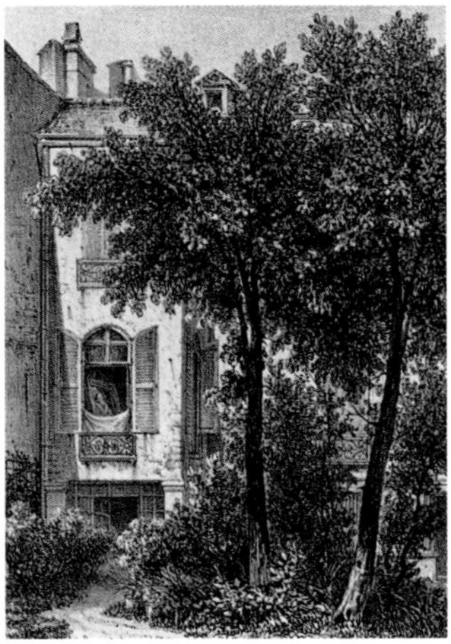

obvious propaganda move to promote him as a legislator. In the portrait the emperor has evidently just stopped work and, as the sword on the chair indicates, now prepares to review the troops wearing the uniform of a colonel of the Foot Grenadier Guards. David perhaps also intended the portrait to make a political point to the British by showing their hated enemy as approachable, modest, magnanimous and a figure worthy of peace negotiations. Although he did not pay for it, Napoleon liked the picture and said: 'You have found me out, dear David; at night I work for my subjects' happiness, and by day I work for their glory.'

David tried in vain to drum up support for more official work and with time on his hands he returned to the project for *Leonidas at Thermopylae* which he had begun as far back as 1798 as a companion piece to the *Sabines*. The subject concerned Leonidas, King of Sparta, who in 480 BC held the pass at Thermopylae against the invading Persian army of Xerxes. Vastly outnumbered, Leonidas and his 300 hand-picked volunteers were killed, but only after their heroic defence had ensured the safe retreat of the Greek fleet. This episode gave birth to the legend that Spartans always fought to the death; David wanted the painting to be a hymn to patriotism and sought to capture the deep intensity of devotion and self-sacrifice inspired by the love of one's country. He said that:

I want to endow this scene with something more serious, more reflective, more religious. I want to paint a general and his soldiers preparing for a battle like veritable Spartans, knowing full well that they will not be spared; some absolutely calm, others weaving wreaths of flowers in preparation for the banquet they will attend in Pluto's domain. I want neither movement nor passionate expression, except on the faces surrounding the man who inscribes on the rock: *Passer-by, tell Sparta that her sons died for her.*

However, the final painting (177) is not nearly as static or restrained as David's description would suggest. As the sentinel trumpeters sound the call to arms, on the right two soldiers rush to gather their weapons that are hanging from the branches of an oak tree. Leonidas sits on a rock facing out at the viewer, contemplating his and his soldiers' fate. Seated at his right is Agis, his wife's brother, who looks to his commander for orders. To emphasize the fervent patriotism of the Spartans, David once again includes an oath, and behind Leonidas three young soldiers lift up wreaths above two altars dedicated to Hercules and Aphrodite. Hercules was invoked for strength and courage but also because Leonidas and all kings of Sparta were supposed to be descended from him. Aphrodite, although usually associated with love, was honoured as a goddess of war among the Spartans, though David probably also meant to refer to the bonds of love forged between comrades. Though fierce and disciplined warriors, the Spartans were deeply religious and always made sacrifices before battle. The priest Megistias read the message of Leonidas' death in the face of the sacrificial she-goat and thus instigated the combination of action and meditation that forms the subject of the picture. Though not a soldier, Megistias remained and died at Thermopylae, and he can be seen in the background on the right, bearded and pointing up to heaven, rather as Socrates had been portrayed nearly thirty years before (see 66). Like many of the warriors, he wears a garland, as was the custom of the Spartans before battle, but David also included these to suggest the forthcoming and inevitable meeting with Pluto in the Underworld. With this fate in mind, a lyre, the instrument capable of soothing Pluto, also hangs on the tree. Neither youth nor infirmity were a barrier to taking part in this heroic rearguard action. On either side of Leonidas are two very young warriors, hardly more than boys, one of whom ties his sandal, while the other bids a last farewell to his aged father. Leonidas had tried to send the two young men away from the battle under the pretext of carrying a message, but they had refused to go. It is perhaps this undelivered scroll that is partially visible at Leonidas' feet; it reads in Greek, 'Leonidas, son of Anaxandrides, King to the Gerousia [Spartan Council of Elders]. Greetings.' The staunch resolution to fight is perhaps most evident at the left where the blind soldier Eurytas, who had also been sent away, returns led by his slave, carefully negotiating a step with his sandalled foot (178). David had used the device of the determined invalid before – Eurytas makes his entrance at a similar point to the infirm Maupetit de la Mayenne being carried into *The Oath of the Tennis Court* (see 86). The final sacrifices having been made, all these men are ready to die for the glory of Sparta and in the background the baggage train departs with the possessions they will no longer need in this world. At the top left the soldier climbs the

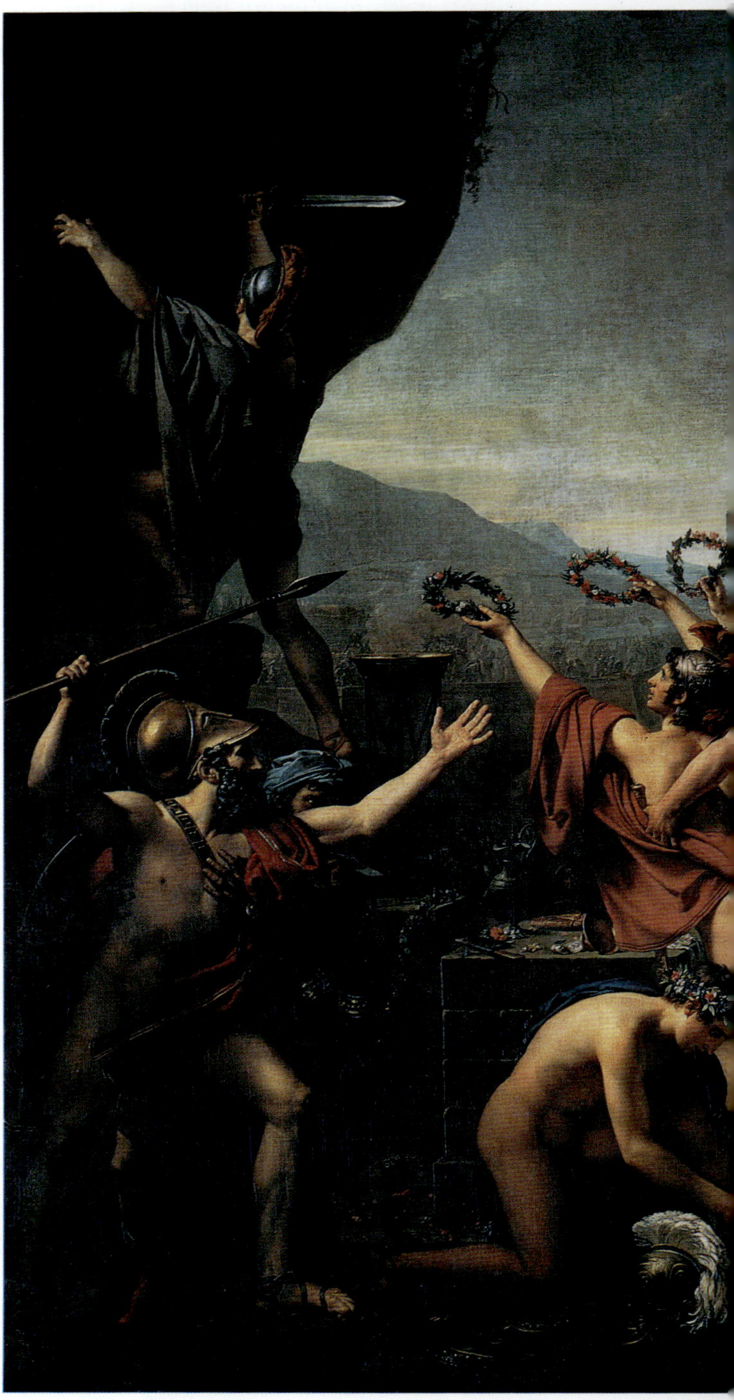

177
Leonidas at Thermopylae,
1814.
Oil on canvas;
395 × 531cm,
$155^{1}{}_{2}$ × 209in.
Musée du
Louvre, Paris

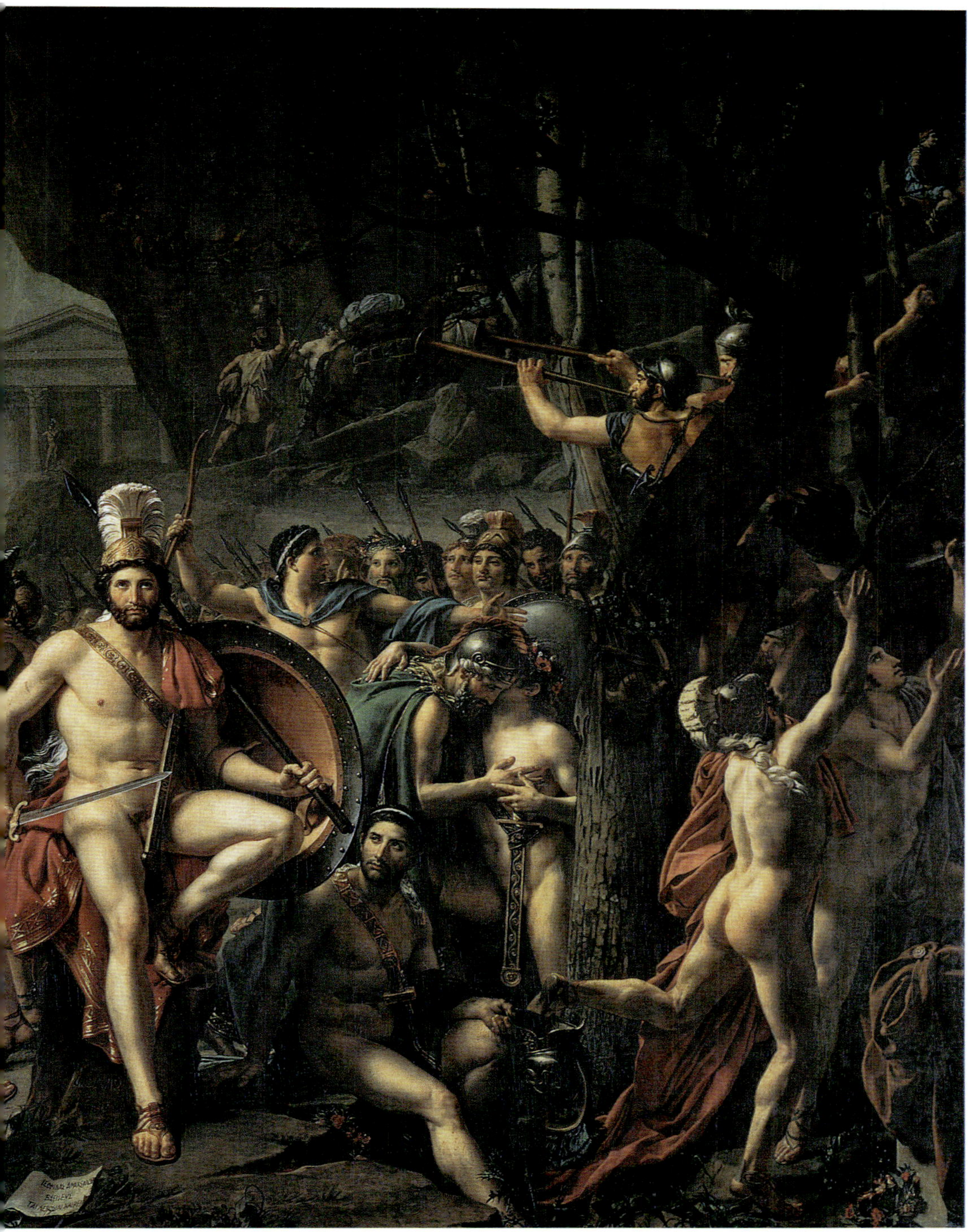

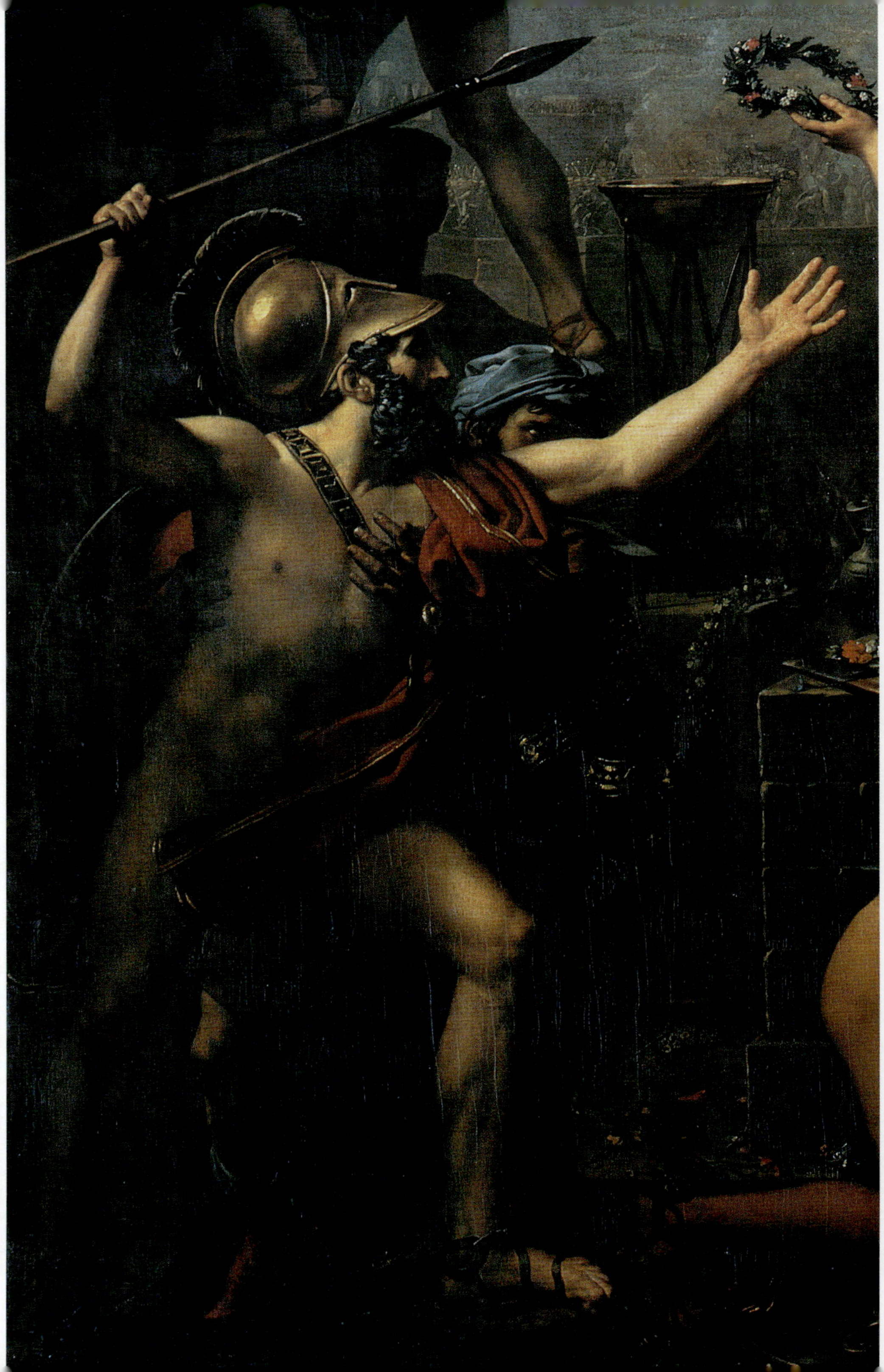

rock to inscribe the poignant message with the pommel of his sword. Initially, David wanted it to be in French but was persuaded by his pupil Paul-Emile Destouches (1794–1874) that it would be more accurate to have it written in Greek. Typically, when Napoleon saw the work in progress, he told David not to waste his time painting the defeated. Leonidas, though a hero, was a loser and Bonaparte had no time for the vanquished. The painting was eventually finished in 1814 and by then the subject of defeat had become a bitter reality both to Napoleon and to the whole of France.

In 1812 Napoleon mounted a campaign against Russia which proved to be an unmitigated disaster. He was so obsessed with conquering the country that he overreached himself and his resources. Although France and Russia were allies, the alliance was becoming increasingly strained as a result of the continental system: a form of economic warfare, instigated by Napoleon, that sought to close all continental ports to British commerce. However, Russian trade slumped, and in December 1810, Tsar Alexander I began admitting neutral ships into Russian ports in order to alleviate the economic situation. This action infuriated Napoleon, and he resolved to teach the Tsar that it was useless to defy French imperial power. A force of 600,000 troops, the 'Grand Army', was raised for this campaign, but only around 20,000 men returned. None of the objectives was achieved and the French were out-thought and out-fought by the Russians who, although beaten at Borodino in September, then refused to fight conventional battles and instead burnt and destroyed as they fell back. The tattered remnants of the less than 'Grand' army limped back on the infamous retreat from Moscow (179), where the soldiers had to endure a catalogue of misery – cold, hunger and fierce attacks from marauding Cossacks. Characteristically, to save face, the Napoleonic propaganda machine tried to turn this terrible ordeal into the heroic struggle of his brave soldiers against the unrelenting savagery of a Russian winter, but in reality it was less the weather than a lack of food and supplies

178
Leonidas at Thermopylae (detail of 177)

combined with Napoleon's tactical blunders that condemned the French to their Russian fate. It was the beginning of the end for the Napoleonic dream; in the following year Austria joined Russia and Prussia in the war against France and these allies inflicted a crushing defeat on Napoleon at Leipzig. France could no longer defend herself and the enemy armies poured across the borders. A series of last-ditch battles were fought but Paris capitulated on 30 March 1814 and Napoleon was forced to abdicate on 11 April. On the night of 12–13 April he attempted suicide with the poison that he had carried with him since the Russian campaign, but after prolonged vomiting, he recovered. A final and moving farewell to his faithful Imperial Guard took place in the courtyard of the Château of Fontainebleau on 20 April and he was then exiled to the British-held island of Elba, just off the west coast of Italy. Although he was allowed visitors, Napoleon was separated from the Empress Marie Louise and their three-year-old son François-Charles-Joseph, the King of Rome, who were sent to Vienna. He was never to see them again.

179
The Retreat from Moscow, 1812. Coloured etching; 21·6 × 17·5cm, 8½ × 6⅞in

David exhibited *Leonidas at Thermopylae* with the *Sabines* in his studio at the former Cluny church in November and December 1814, and also produced a short explanatory pamphlet. For him to exhibit *Leonidas* six months after the defeat of France and the fall of Napoleon struck some as evidence of the picture's subject having been a bad omen, while others felt that the calm and poised resignation of these ancient warriors had nothing in common with the desperate struggles endured by present-day soldiers. For the first time David's work appeared positively out of step with contemporary events, and this notion was enforced by the exhibition at the Salon in November 1814 of two paintings by a brilliant young artist, Théodore Géricault (1791–1824): *An Officer of Chasseurs Commanding a Charge* (180) and *The Wounded Cuirassier* (181). These pictures dramatically captured the highs and the lows of the Napoleonic period. The first, actually painted in 1812 when victory still appeared possible, celebrates the excitement and frenzy of battle, while the second is a painting about defeat. No longer mounted, the cavalryman (called a cuirassier because of the metal breastplate he wears) stumbles down a bank looking apprehensively behind, while his horse snorts with wide-eyed fear. The only evidence of an injury is a slight reddening around the temple, ear and neck; the implication is that this is more of a mental than a physical wound and that this single figure stands for the whole French nation. Unlike David's *Leonidas*, both of Géricault's figures were anonymous – no great heroes or generals – but regular soldiers.

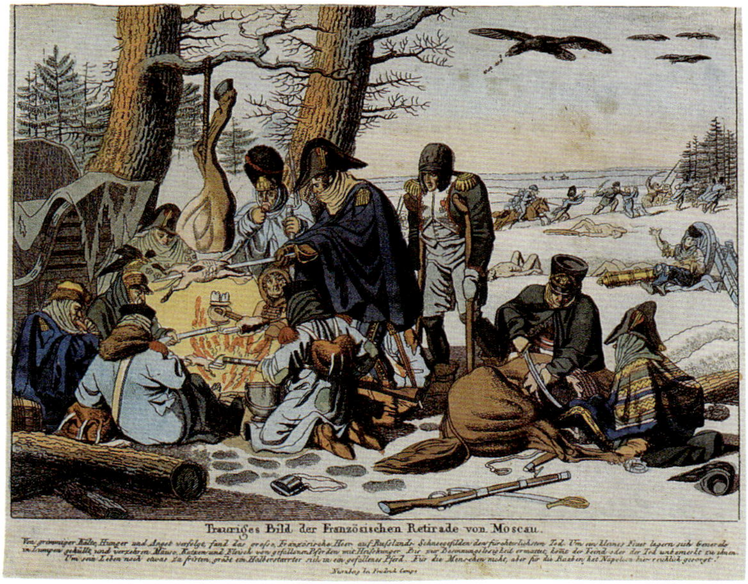

Géricault's colour scheme and freer way of painting also set his work apart from the smoothly sculptural and even surfaces of David's works; the older man, when viewing Géricault's work, is supposed to have said: 'Where does that come from? I do not recognize the touch.' Taken together, David's *Leonidas* and Géricault's *Wounded Cuirassier* both show images of defeat, but each uses a completely different visual language that emphasizes the growing gulf between the emotional limitations of Neoclassicism and the energetic and dramatic responses of the emerging younger generation of Romantic artists.

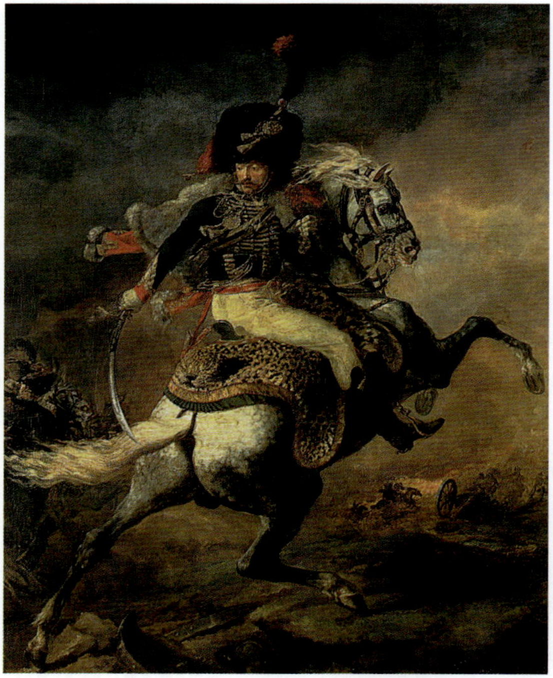

180
Théodore Géricault,
An Officer of Chasseurs Commanding a Charge,
1812.
Oil on canvas; 349 × 266 cm, $137^3/_8$ × $104^3/_4$ in.
Musée du Louvre, Paris

181
Théodore Géricault,
The Wounded Cuirassier,
1814.
Oil on canvas; 358 × 294 cm, 141 × $115^3/_4$ in.
Musée du Louvre, Paris

For many people the French Revolution and the triumphs and defeats of the Napoleonic era had brought into question (and sometimes destroyed) the age-old certainties of Church, monarchy and social stability. The values derived from the past that had governed Enlightenment thought – reason, logic, order and human perfectibility – were unable to explain the horror and misery of recent events. Such changes were best explained in terms of organic and dynamic processes rather than by mechanistic and rational conceptions. Many artists came to consider that expression replaced imitation as the goal of art, and the term 'Romanticism' began to be used in an attempt to define the new currents and directions that were developing in reaction to the inability of Neoclassicism to capture the enormous changes in society and the individual suffering that had occurred. A whole range of responses emerged throughout Europe, and the term 'Romanticism' covers a wide diversity of artists; these differences ensure that there is no such thing as a single 'Romantic' style. Indeed the poet and critic Charles

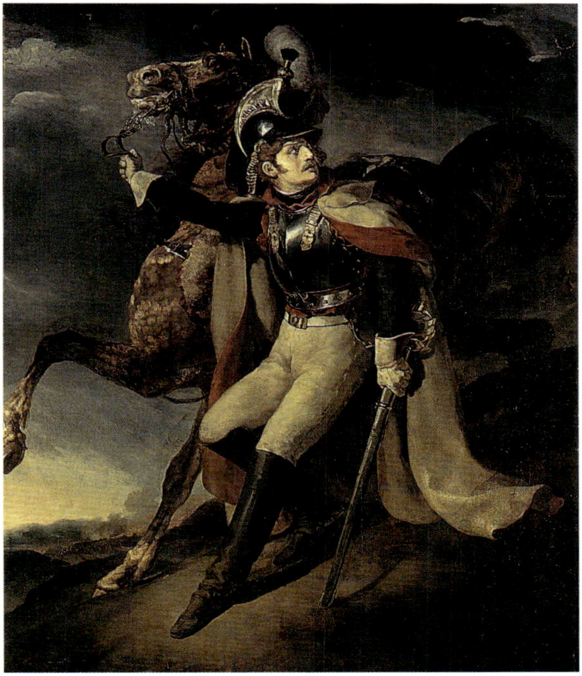

Baudelaire (1821–67) wrote that, 'Romanticism is precisely situated neither in choice of subjects nor in exact truth, but in a way of feeling.' What linked the Romantics was their desire that art should be judged by its emotional authenticity and spontaneity, and by the refusal to recognize any 'formula' or 'norm'. The artist's own sensibility was to be his guide, and so traditional methods of training were looked on with suspicion and academies that emphasized uniformity were considered as obstacles to the development of natural talent.

With Napoleon's abdication, the Allies occupied Paris and Cossacks bivouacked along the Champs Elysées (182). David had to billet two Russian officers in his house, but fortunately they spoke excellent French and were pleased to share the house of Europe's greatest painter. The Bourbon dynasty returned with Louis XVIII on the throne, the brother of Louis XVI. The presence of the former emperor's First Painter was not welcome at official artistic events and so David retreated from public life and worked very little.

Napoleon was only to endure a brief exile on Elba. Nursing a grievance against the Bourbon monarchy and heartened by news of public disaffection with the new regime, he escaped after ten months and returned to France, landing at Golfe Juan on 1 March 1815. This was the start of the 'Hundred Days' when, by the force of his own personality and with just a thousand soldiers, he won the French nation back and attracted great popular support. Louis XVIII and his court were forced into a swift exit from Paris to the safety of Ghent in Belgium and Napoleon reoccupied the Tuileries Palace and proclaimed himself emperor once more. David rushed to pay his respects and was warmly greeted, reinstated as First Painter and made

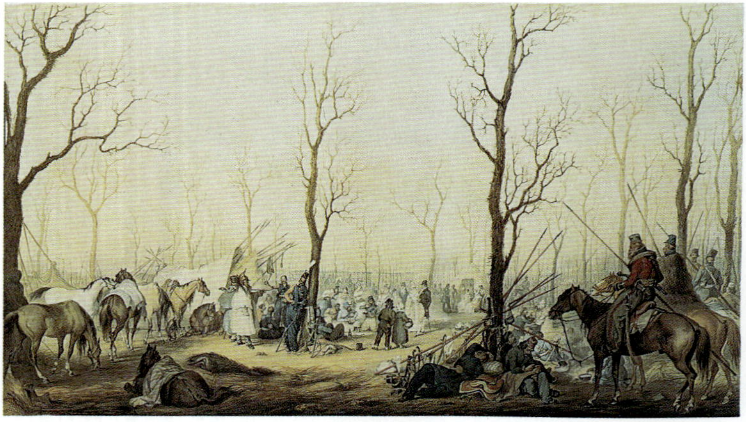

a Commandant of the Legion of Honour. His sons and sons-in-law were either restored to or promoted from their previous ranks in the army or government. Napoleon also visited David's studio where he revised his earlier critical opinion of the *Leonidas*, saying: 'Continue David, to illustrate France. I hope that copies of the picture will soon be hung in military academies: they will remind cadets of the virtues of their calling.' One month later David signed the *Addendum to the Constitution to the Empire* – a concession to liberal democracy by Napoleon which categorically refused to recognize the right of the Bourbons to rule France. In putting his name to this document David irrevocably aligned his own future with that of the returned emperor. Because his re-formed army was outnumbered and ill-equipped, Napoleon staked all on a quick victory over the Allies, and he very nearly succeeded – the decisive Battle of Waterloo on 18 June was, in the words of the victorious Allied commander, the Duke of Wellington, 'the nearest run thing you ever saw in your life'. Napoleon abdicated for the second time and was sent to the rocky south Atlantic island of St Helena, 1,600 km (1,000 miles) off the African coast, where he died in 1821.

David's last dealings with the Napoleonic court were, typically, financial. The day after the Battle of Waterloo he put in a claim for outstanding payments as First Painter, which he received a week later. In Paris, David, the anti-royalist who had voted for the death of Louis XVI and who was also a Napoleonic courtier and supporter of the 'Hundred Days', would have been in some danger from the firmly restored Bourbons. The *Coronation*, *Eagle Standards*, *Sabines* and *Leonidas* as well as his portrait of Napoleon were rolled up and sent away to the west coast of France for safe keeping. David then decided to leave France for a while and applied for passports to England and Switzerland. In these documents he was described as '1·71 m tall, greying hair, brown eyebrows, grey eyes, large nose, large mouth, rounded chin and high forehead.' In July and August 1815 David went with his servant Geoffroy to Besançon in eastern France and thence over the border into Switzerland, visiting Neuchâtel, Lausanne, Geneva and the Chamonix valley. Although he made a few landscape drawings (183), they seem to have been done simply to pass the time.

182
Alexandre Ivanovitch Sauerweid, *Cossacks Bivouacking Along the Champs Elysées, 31 March 1814*, 1814. Watercolour; 56·5 × 96·5 cm, 22¼ × 38 in. Musée Carnavalet, Paris

In Paris Louis XVIII's new government took action against former revolutionaries and Napoleon's supporters. On 12 January 1816 a law was passed whereby all regicides who had signed the *Addendum* and accepted work and offices from Napoleon were to be banished and had to leave France within a month. They were also to lose all the goods, titles and pensions that the former emperor had granted them.

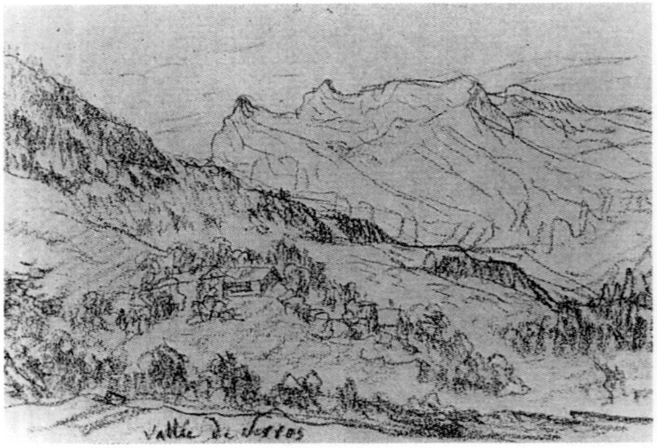

183
The Valley of Servoz,
1815.
Private collection

But although this law covered David exactly, his high reputation meant that the minister of police, Count Decazes, informed him that he might be exempted from it and stay. However, the return of the Bourbon monarchy held no attraction for David and so with great dignity he announced that he would obey the law and go into exile. If David had ever been accused of opportunism before, this was certainly not the case in 1816. He thought of returning to Rome, but this was forbidden by the authorities and instead he made preparations to go to Brussels in the newly created kingdom of the Netherlands, which then comprised both Holland and Belgium. Brussels had the advantages of being only 274 km (170 miles) from Paris, French speaking and the home of some of David's former students. On the eve of his departure David invited his favourite pupil (and later biographer) Etienne-Jean Delécluze to dinner. It was a sad affair with only David, his wife and Delécluze present. David served the food himself and talked only of trivial things, without making a single mention of the circumstances that were forcing him to leave, the coming journey, or of his uncertain future abroad. At the end of his time in Paris David was taking consolation in an act of silent virtue worthy of the ancient heroes he had been painting for the past thirty-five years. The following day, he and his wife took the coach to Brussels, and France's greatest living painter left the city of his birth, never to return.

Declining Years? Exile in Brussels

6

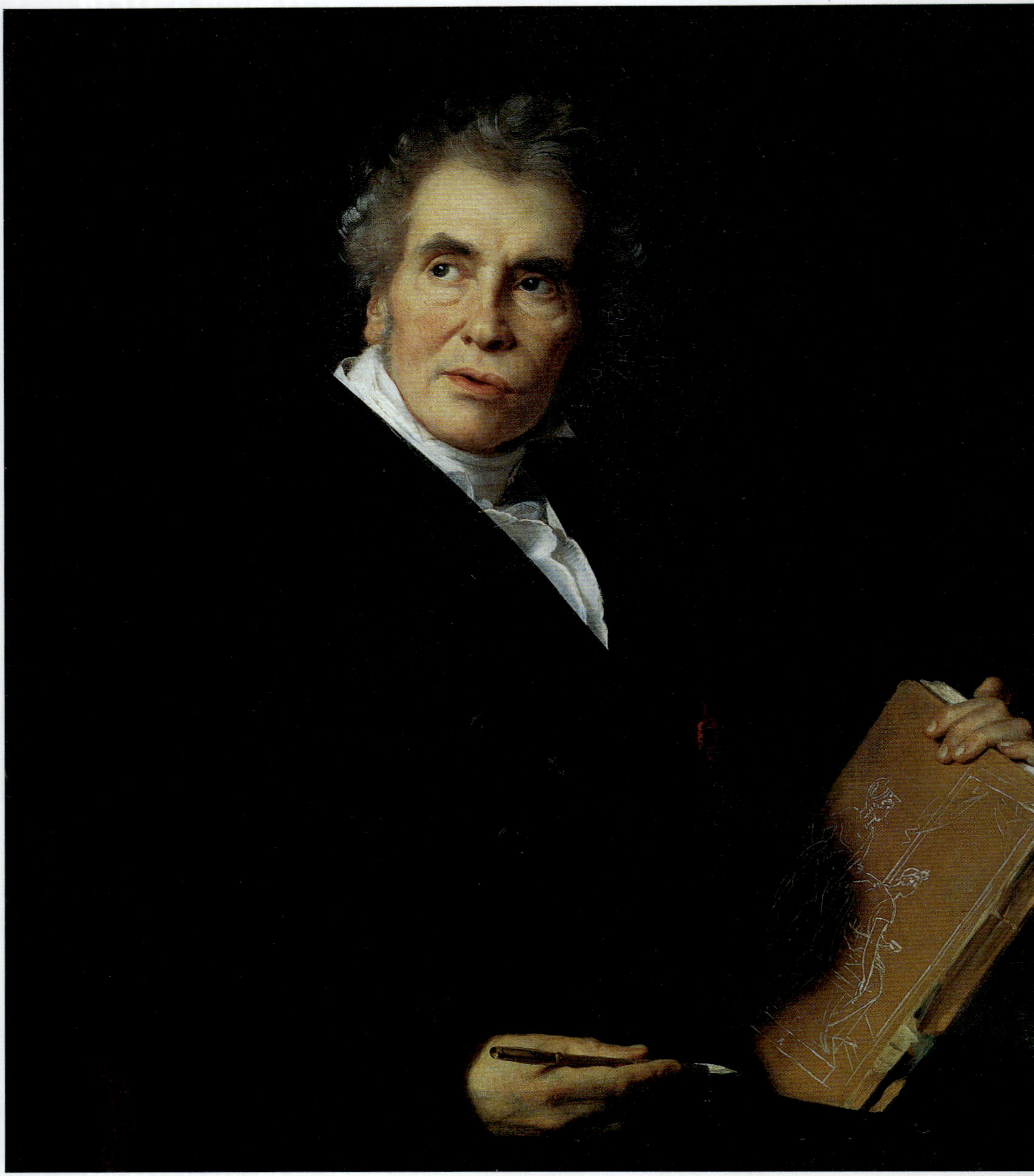

A 67-year-old man, uprooted and exiled to a foreign country, could be expected to have some problems in picking up the threads of a career, but nothing of this sort happened to David. In Brussels he approached his art with a renewed enthusiasm and energy, though at times he felt a weakening of his physical strength. Soon after his arrival on 27 January 1816 he found a large studio in the former bishop's palace, and his Belgian ex-students, Joseph-Denis Odevaere (1775–1830) and François-Joseph Navez (1787–1869), helped him settle into the artistic life of the city. For leisure, David continued his interest in the theatre, which he attended almost every night and where a special seat was reserved for him. He and Madame David also promenaded regularly in the city's public park. David tried to make the best of the situation, and praised Brussels for its amenities, clean streets, helpful local administration and artistic freedom, though in moments of honest soul searching and self-reflection he had to concede that it was not, and never could be, Paris. He spent time with another former member of the Convention and regicide, Bertrand de Barère de Vieuzac, whom David had depicted in *The Oath of the Tennis Court* (see 86). Barère recounted that, when they were talking about France, 'I saw a wave of sadness pass over David's face; for some time he did not speak, but sought a secluded seat whereon to rest with me. His melancholy and abstracted air pained me, and I tried to interest him by talking of his fame as an artist. "Are you not in Brussels," I said to him, "the object of the admiration of all her citizens, of all literary men, and all those artists who are mainly your own pupils? Do you not enjoy the consideration and benevolence of a liberal king, who is the kindly patron of Belgian hospitality in our favour? What more can you want? What can be the reason for your sadness?"'

184
Jérôme-Martin Langlois,
Portrait of David,
1824.
Oil on canvas;
88 × 74·5 cm,
$34\frac{5}{8} \times 29\frac{3}{8}$ in.
Musée du Louvre, Paris

David only broke the silence with these words: '*Amor patriae*' (Love of one's own country). Inevitably, there were also traces of bitterness and anger – David wrote that: 'I have never ceased to be persecuted, tormented in my work by all of the most odious means, and if heaven had not favoured me with a certain resolution I would have succumbed.'

Brussels was a haven for French political exiles, people who, like David, had been determined revolutionaries and/or loyal followers of Napoleon. Not surprisingly, he sought out their company and they in turn often asked him to paint their portraits. David started in 1816 with *General Etienne-Maurice Gérard* (185), a serious and formal full-length portrait of one of Napoleon's commanders. The general appears stiff and almost overwhelmed by his dress uniform and large bicorn hat. He has the air of a man of action ill at ease with the inactivity of exile, though he was later to return to France and became minister of war, a marshal of France and a senator. At this time David received a tempting and lucrative offer from Frederick William III, King of Prussia, to go to Berlin and become the minister of fine arts and director of the Academy. In his new position David would be paid more than his salary under Napoleon and some pressure was put on him to accept. The king's brother, Prince Mansfeld, visited David's studio, where he saw the Gérard portrait and was so impressed that he offered to drive David all the way to Berlin in his own coach. However, David did not want to move again so soon, and refused the offer with the excuses that he was settled and that his wife was in ill health. David also wrote to the governor of Brussels, the Comte Mercy d'Argenteau, telling him of his decision to stay and serve the king of the Netherlands, William I. He probably did this in the hope that William I would in turn offer him a similar position to the one he had just turned down in Prussia. Unfortunately, the key positions in the art world were already occupied by David's former pupils, and besides, to have given David high office would have given offence to the king of France, and such a diplomatic insult was to be avoided.

In his first years in Brussels David was under police surveillance and the Duke of Wellington, now commanding the allied army of occupation, also took an interest in what the painter was doing. A number of old stories are related about contacts between Wellington and David but, although they may have met, there is no conclusive evidence that they ever did. All these anecdotes are calculated to show how David's inflexible patriotism and sense of honour forbade him to have any dealings with the English duke who had defeated Napoleon. In

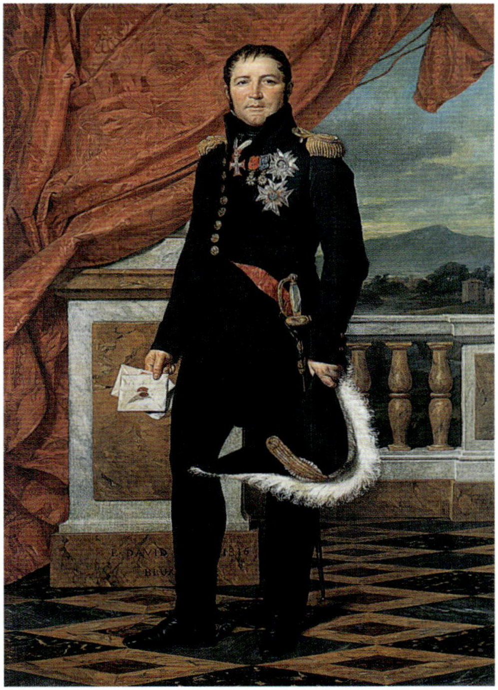

185
Portrait of General Etienne-Maurice Gérard,
1816.
Oil on canvas;
197 × 136 cm,
$77\frac{1}{2} \times 53\frac{1}{2}$ in.
Metropolitan Museum of Art, New York

1818, with the Countess de Hatzfeld, wife of the Prussian ambassador, acting as intermediary, Wellington informed David that he wished to have his portrait painted. This request was unceremoniously dismissed, with the artist saying: 'I have not almost reached the age of seventy just to dirty my palette. I would rather cut off my own hand than paint an Englishman ... I do not paint the enemies of my country.' A further embellishment to the story places Wellington and David together and adds that when asked to paint the portrait David stated that he only painted historical works. At this, Wellington pointed to one of the replicas of *Bonaparte Crossing the St Bernard Pass* (see 144) hanging on the studio wall. 'As I said, Milord,' responded David, 'I only paint historical works', neatly diminishing Wellington's achievements in comparison to Napoleon's.

Also in 1816, David painted the tender portrait of the *Comtesse Vilain XIIII and her Daughter* (186), which was bought by the National Gallery in London in 1994 for £3·75 million ($5·75 million). The 36-year-old comtesse had formerly been lady-in-waiting to the empress Marie Louise and had held Napoleon's son, the king of Rome, at his christening in 1811. Her husband, Philippe Vilain XIIII, had been the mayor of Ghent and had been raised to the nobility by Napoleon in 1811. (The numerals XIIII after the family name were a reminder of a seventeenth-century ancestor who had presented the keys of Ghent to Louis XIV.) In the picture David gives a very frank yet affectionate portrayal of mother and daughter, although the comtesse complained about being forced to pose for hours on end. In May 1816 she wrote that '[David] made me wait and dress from eleven until three, only to paint my hair. I suggested that to make me dress was a caprice on his part but he insisted that it was necessary for the general effect.' However, she was forced to concede that such hardships were worthwhile and that the end result was not only faithful and lifelike but also a beautiful piece of work. Like many of his Brussels portraits, the sitters are closely framed, bringing them near to the spectator. Perhaps this is due to David's failing eyesight – he had been obliged to wear glasses for detailed work for the last twenty years. In the following year David painted the portrait of one of the prominent political figures of the Revolution and the Empire – Emmanuel-Joseph Sieyès (187). Sieyès had been a radical clergyman and was the author of the pamphlet *What is the Third Estate?* (see 71) which had been so influential in the events of 1789. He had been present at the Oath of the Tennis Court (David had planned to include him in the never-completed commemorative painting;

186
Portrait of the Comtesse Vilain XIIII and her Daughter, 1816.
Oil on canvas; 95 × 76 cm, $37\frac{3}{8} \times 29\frac{7}{8}$ in.
National Gallery, London

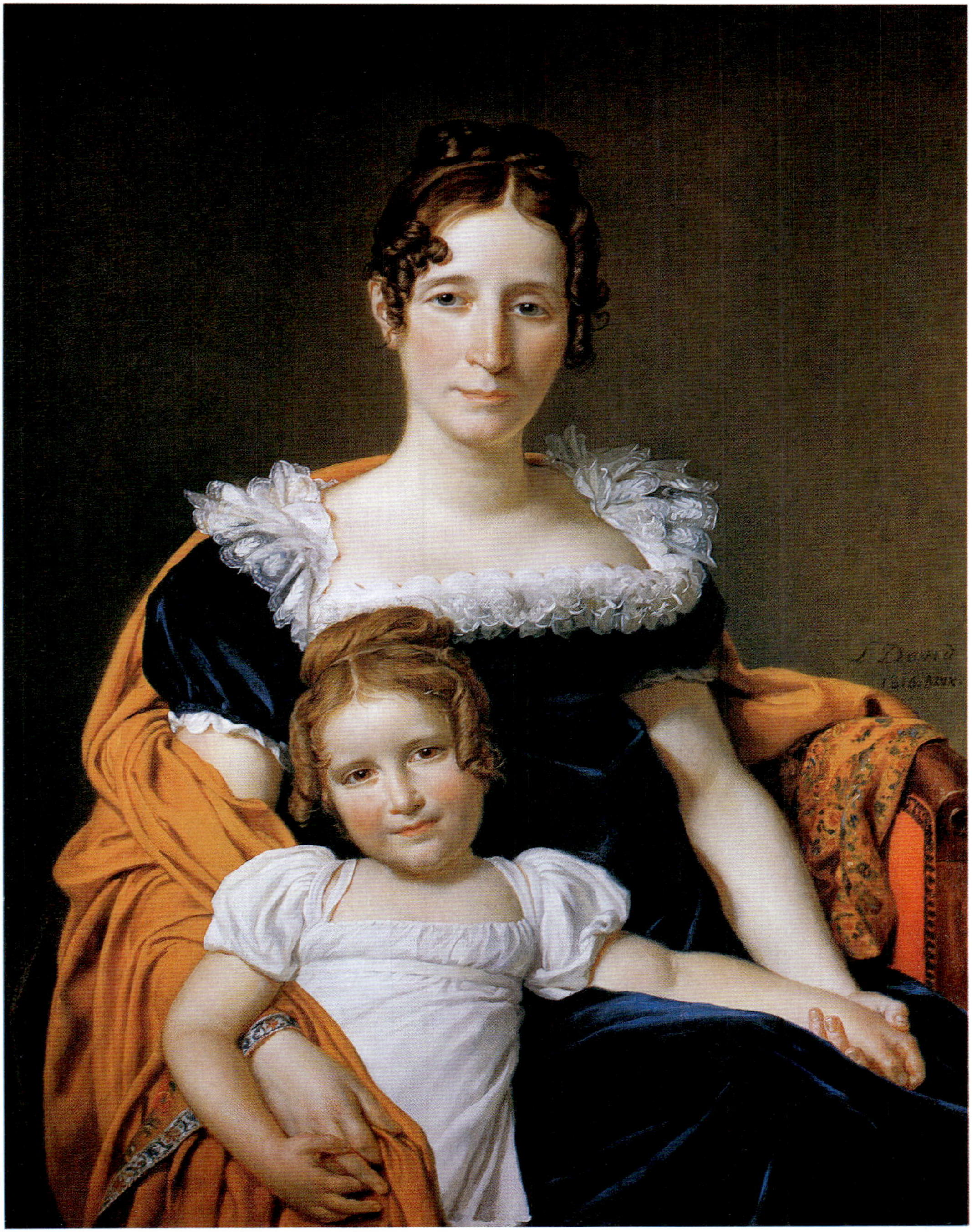

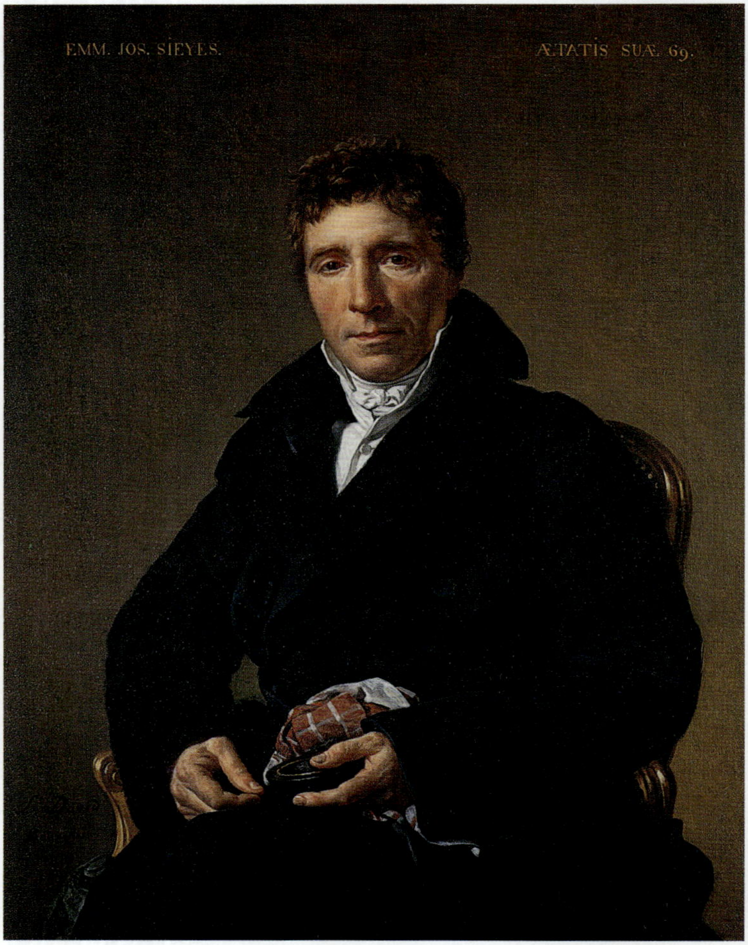
EMM. JOS. SIEYES.
ÆTATIS SUÆ 69.

see 90), voted for the death of Louis XVI and helped Napoleon to seize power in the Brumaire coup of 1799. As the Latin inscription at the top of the painting tells us – AETATIS SUAE 69 – in 1817 he was David's exact contemporary, but he appears much younger. Dorothy Johnson, in her book *Jacques-Louis David; Art in Metamorphosis*, asserts that this was a conscious decision and that David, with a sense of posterity, decided to paint Sieyès in his prime. This seems somewhat unlikely, given that David's sitters are often painted with flatteringly youthful features – both Josephine (see 155) and David himself in his prison *Self-Portrait* (see 122) are much rejuvenated. Like the Vilain XIIII portrait (186) there is a direct contact between sitter and viewer and from Sieyès's pose and facial expression we get strong ideas about this man's determination and obstinacy – characteristics with which David readily identified. In fact, it had been Sieyès who had advised David not to accept the king of Prussia's offer and retain his freedom and independence.

187
Portrait of Emmanuel-Joseph Sieyès, 1817.
Oil on canvas; 97·8 × 74 cm, 38½ × 29⅛ in.
Fogg Art Museum, Harvard University Art Museums, Cambridge, Massachusetts

In contrast to the confident informality of the Sieyès portrait, the painting of the daughters of Napoleon's brother Joseph, Charlotte and Zénaïde Bonaparte, of 1821 (188), seems tense and contrived. Although royal princesses, these sisters appear stiff and nervous, and this sense is increased by the hard enamel-like finish of the paint. Neither are they stunning beauties – in fact they both seem rather plain. Yet David succeeds in showing that they were temperamentally different by the way that he posed and dressed each of them. While Charlotte wears a modest high-collared and long-sleeved dress, timidly lowers her head and clutches her sister, Zénaïde stares out in an almost aggressive way, and her confident and outgoing nature is emphasized by her low-cut dress and bare arms. What David tried to do in his Brussels portraits was to suit his painting style to the personalities of his sitters, an approach that accounts for the different formats and techniques he used. His advancing years also meant that his pupils assisted him more than before, and at times we can see more than one hand at work on a single portrait.

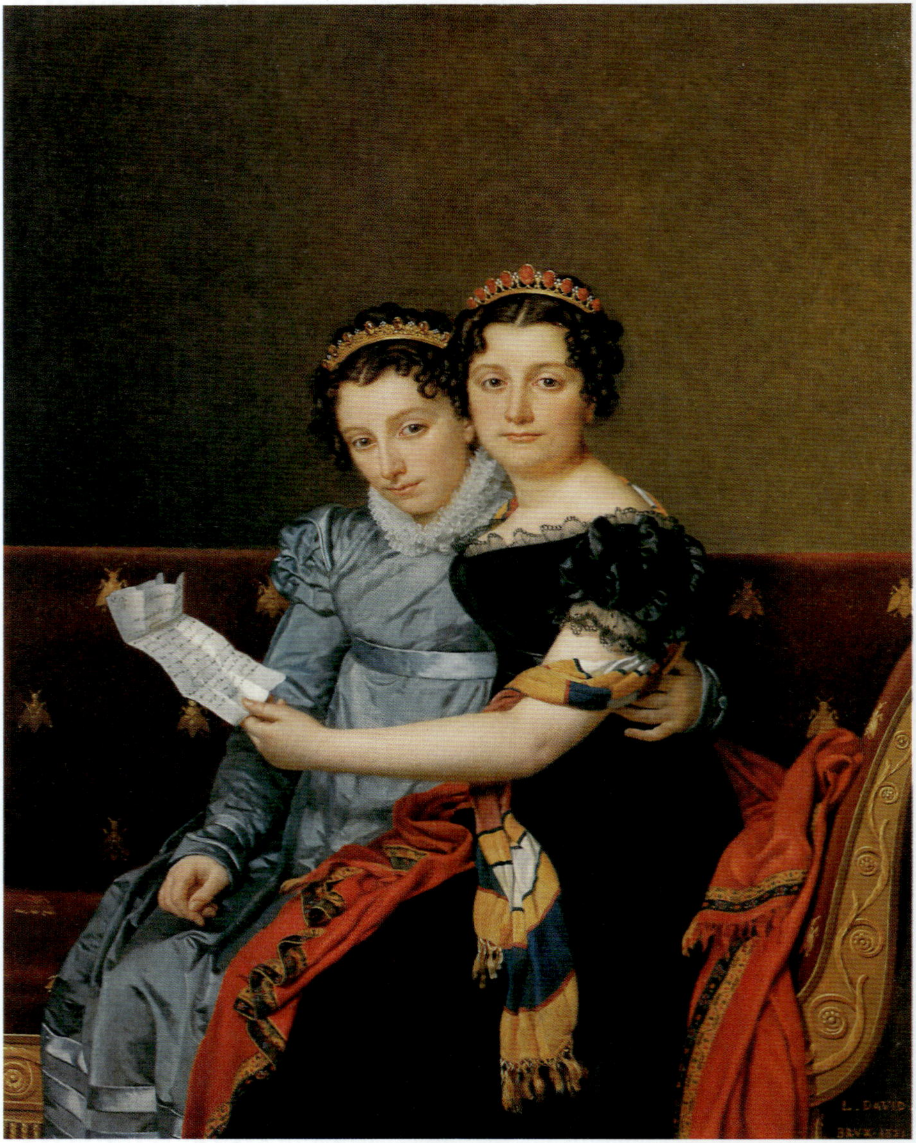
L. DAVID

The question of a return to France frequently came up, but although he was undoubtedly very homesick David refused to make the first move and approach representatives of the restored Bourbon monarchy. He wrote to his son Jules on 1 January 1819: 'My colleagues are all returning to France. I would certainly do the same if I were weak enough to ask in writing to be recalled. You know your father and his pride. I could not do such a thing. I did what I did knowingly, not out of passion; time will reveal the truth. In this country I have the esteem of those who respect rectitude and probity.' As early as 1816 David's pupils in Paris had organized a petition to the king requesting his return, and Gros (who had taken over David's teaching studio) kept up a detailed and regular correspondence with his former master. At times these letters are painful to read because David and Gros, though closely attached, never really understood one another, and their lack of candour led to misunderstandings and irritation. Gros knew that if David made the first move the king would pardon him and allow him to come back to Paris. Indeed, when the Count d'Artois, David's patron for *The Loves of Paris and Helen* (see 74), became King Charles X in 1824, this seemed an ideal and opportune time. Gros organized a petition which only needed David's signature, but David stubbornly refused and angrily rebuked Gros: 'Never speak to me again of things I ought to do to get back. I do not have to do anything; what I ought to have done for my country I have already done. I founded a brilliant school; I painted classic pictures that the whole of Europe came to study. I have fulfilled my part of the bargain; let the government now do the same.' In truth, David would probably have welcomed an invitation to return to France – for the supreme pleasure of embarrassing the government by refusing it. In his letters to Gros, David urged his former pupil to return to painting heroic antique subjects – themes for which Gros had little interest or aptitude – and give up the much less noble depiction of the boots and uniforms of modern events. Gros's sense of loyalty meant that he took such advice seriously even

188
Portrait of Charlotte and Zénaïde Bonaparte, 1821. Oil on canvas; 129·5 × 100 cm, 51 × 39⅜ in. J Paul Getty Museum, Los Angeles

though it was not in his best interests. For Gros the transition from the excitement and glamour of Napoleonic works to commemorating the mundane and uninspiring Bourbon regime was hard to take, but even so he was showered with honours by Louis XVIII and made a baron, thus making a tense situation with David worse. In 1835, long after David's death, the pressures on Gros proved unbearable. Trapped in an unhappy marriage, ridiculed by critics and convinced that he had lost his ability, he drowned himself in shallow water in a tributary of the Seine at Meudon, just south of Paris.

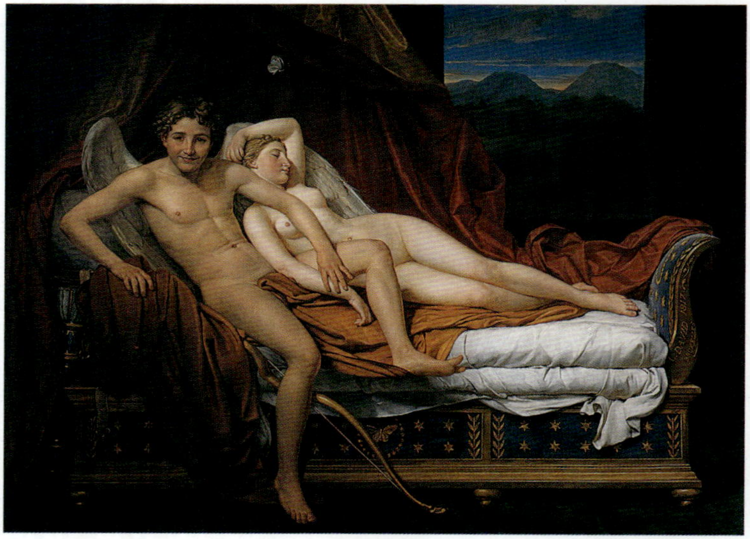

As well as setting up a sizeable portrait practice, David continued to produce paintings from ancient history and mythology. These works from the last nine years of his life are somewhat puzzling and unexpected, though hints about their direction had been made in the *Sappho and Phaon* of 1809 (see 173). It has been suggested by some that David's art went into a sad decline in this period and that the late paintings betray a dramatic loss of artistic powers. This is too harsh a judgement. It is true that David's history paintings executed in Brussels do look very different to the muscular figures of the *Horatii* (see 62), the unity and sculptural forms of the *Sabines* (see 131), or the crowded Napoleonic panoramas (see 152 and 167), but the differences come from a conscious change of emphasis and direction by the artist and should not just be seen as an old man's confused ramblings. David has an identifiable late style and the Brussels pictures need to be considered with the same degree of thought as any of his previous works.

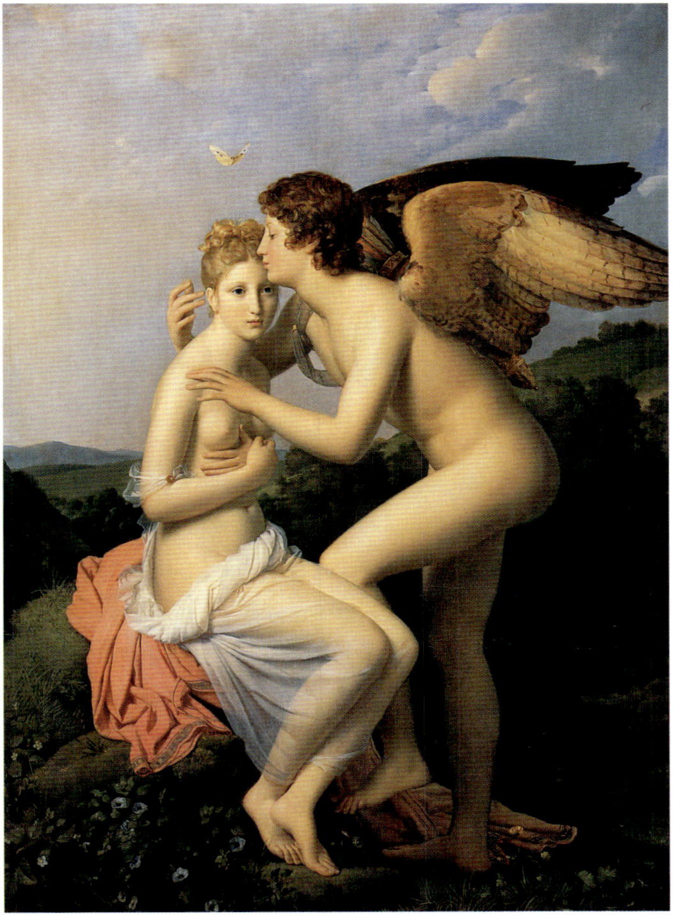

189
Cupid and Psyche,
1817.
Oil on canvas;
184·2 × 241·6 cm,
52⅝ × 95⅛ in.
Cleveland Museum of Art

190
François Gérard,
Cupid and Psyche,
1798.
Oil on canvas;
186 × 132 cm,
73¼ × 52 in.
Musée du Louvre, Paris

David's first history painting in exile was an extremely original and disturbing interpretation of the late antique myth of Cupid and Psyche (189). It was painted for the wealthy Italian patron and connoisseur Count Giovanni Battista Sommariva and, although planned in Paris, it was only finished in Brussels in 1817. In Paris, David persuaded James Gallatin, the seventeen-year-old son of the United States envoy, to pose nude for the figure of Cupid. In his diary, itself a fascinating document of the adventures of a fashionable man about town, Gallatin recorded: 'I don't think my father will approve of the picture Monsieur David is painting: it is Cupid and Psyche. I have not seen the model but would like to. She must be very pretty, only seventeen.' Gallatin added wistfully, 'We are not to pose together.'

As related by the Roman writer Lucius Apuleius in *The Golden Ass* (late second century AD), Cupid, the god of love, fell in love with the beautiful Psyche and brought her to his palace, where he visited her every night without ever letting her see his face. But curiosity got the better of her, and one night Psyche looked at Cupid while he was asleep. Unfortunately a drop of hot oil fell from her lamp and awakened him, whereupon he abandoned her and the palace disappeared. From then on Psyche was condemned to wander the earth and perform impossible tasks in the vain hope of winning her lover back. Many other artists, such as David's ex-pupil Gérard (190), saw the lovers as innocent, tender and poetic, but David deliberately drew attention to the sexual aspect of the relationship. Normally Cupid was shown as a beautiful young man, but David depicted him as a grinning adolescent who seems proud of his recent conquest. A great contrast is set up between Cupid's coarse ruddy features and awkward angular limbs, and the pale, smooth and languid beauty of the sleeping Psyche. Above their heads is a butterfly which symbolizes the soul, although the whole encounter seems more physical than spiritual. Unusually for David, the colours are bright and intense; in Brussels he looked at the colours used by Flemish Renaissance artists such as Jan van Eyck (*c*.1395–1441). *Cupid and Psyche* is meant to disconcert the viewer. Mythological painting depends for its effects on the creation of an ideal fantasy world distanced from everyday reality, but when we get the combination of the real and the ideal, as with the figures of Cupid and Psyche, the result is unexpected, unsettling and discordant. Certainly the people who saw the work in 1817 found it hard to appreciate.

191
The Farewell of Telemachus and Eucharis, 1818.
Oil on canvas; 87·2 × 103 cm, $34\frac{3}{8} \times 40\frac{1}{2}$ in.
J Paul Getty Museum, Los Angeles

In the following year, as an imaginary companion piece to *Cupid and Psyche*, David painted *The Farewell of Telemachus and Eucharis* (191), a story of true lovers forced to part. Telemachus, son of Penelope and Odysseus, and Eucharis, one of the nymphs of the goddess Calypso, had an intense physical passion for one another but still remained pure and chaste because this physical love expressed a higher, spiritual love. Telemachus stares out at us with an expression of regret and sadness at his departure, while Eucharis throws her arms around her lover's neck, making the most of their last moments together. In contrast to

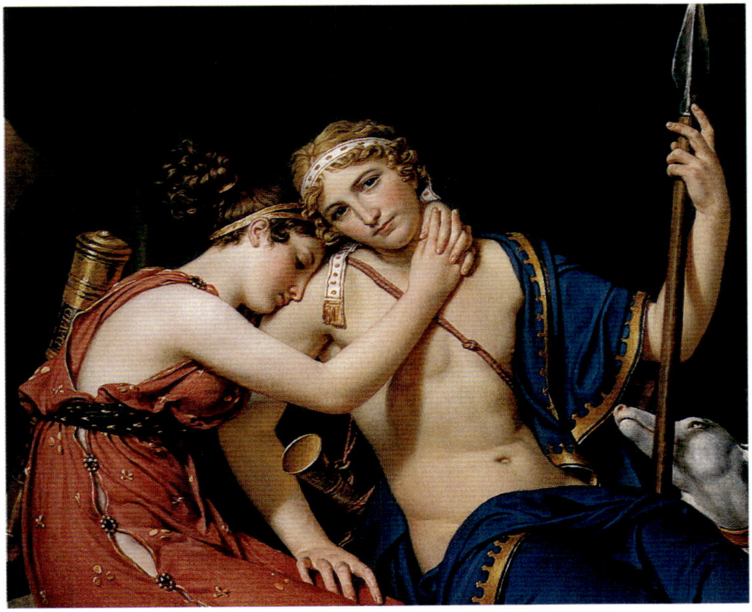

the lust and desire of *Cupid and Psyche*, *Telemachus and Eucharis* has as its theme love, fidelity and painful separation.

In his last history paintings David showed moments of psychological drama just before an important and decisive action was taken, and this tendency reached its climax in *The Anger of Achilles at the Sacrifice of Iphigenia* of 1819 (192). Iphigenia was the daughter of King Agamemnon, commander of the Greek forces in the Trojan War, and it was decreed that she must be sacrificed to the goddess Diana to ensure the victory

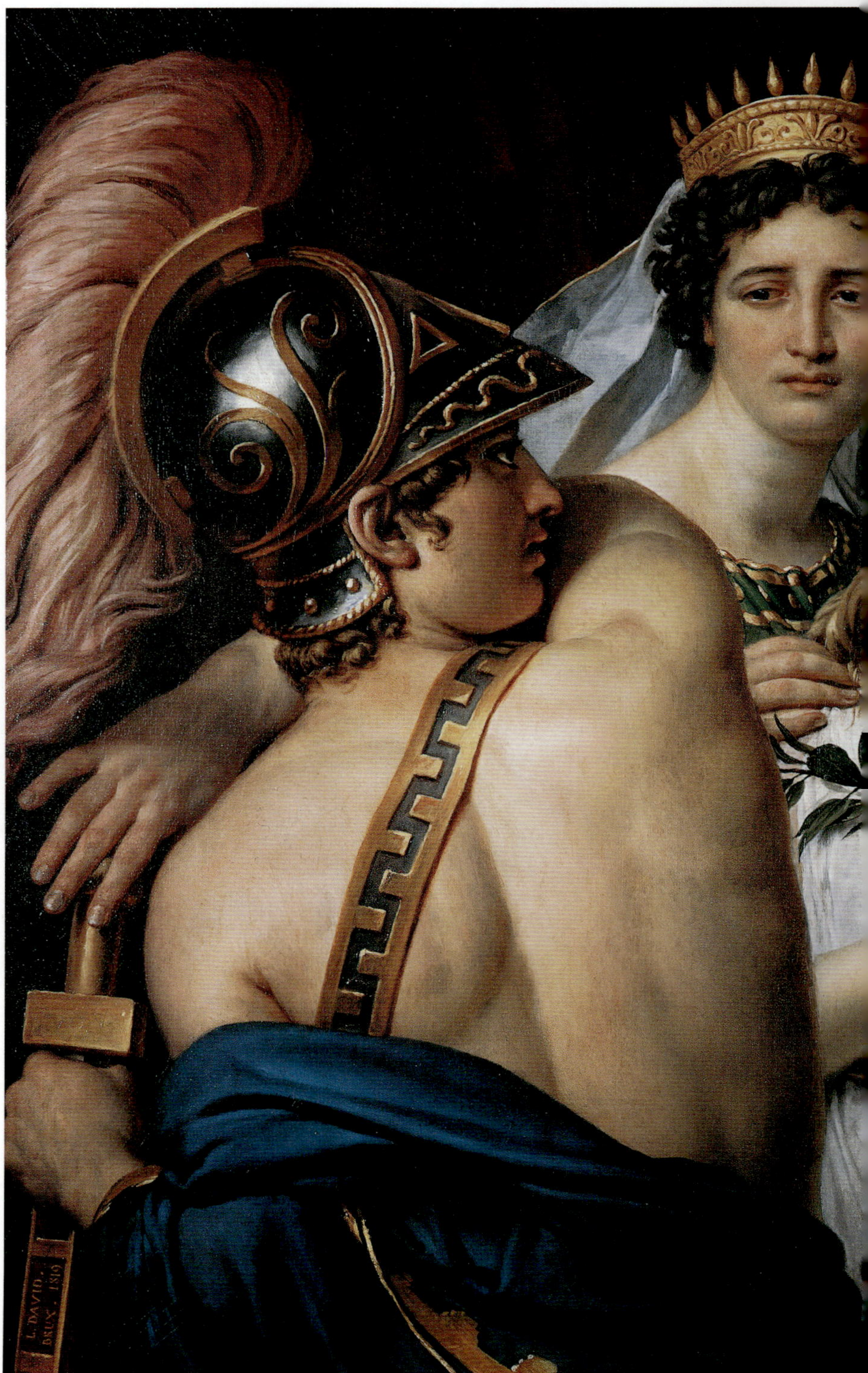

192
The Anger of Achilles at the Sacrifice of Iphigenia, 1819.
Oil on canvas; 105 × 145cm, $41^3/_8$ × 57in.
Kimbell Art Museum, Fort Worth

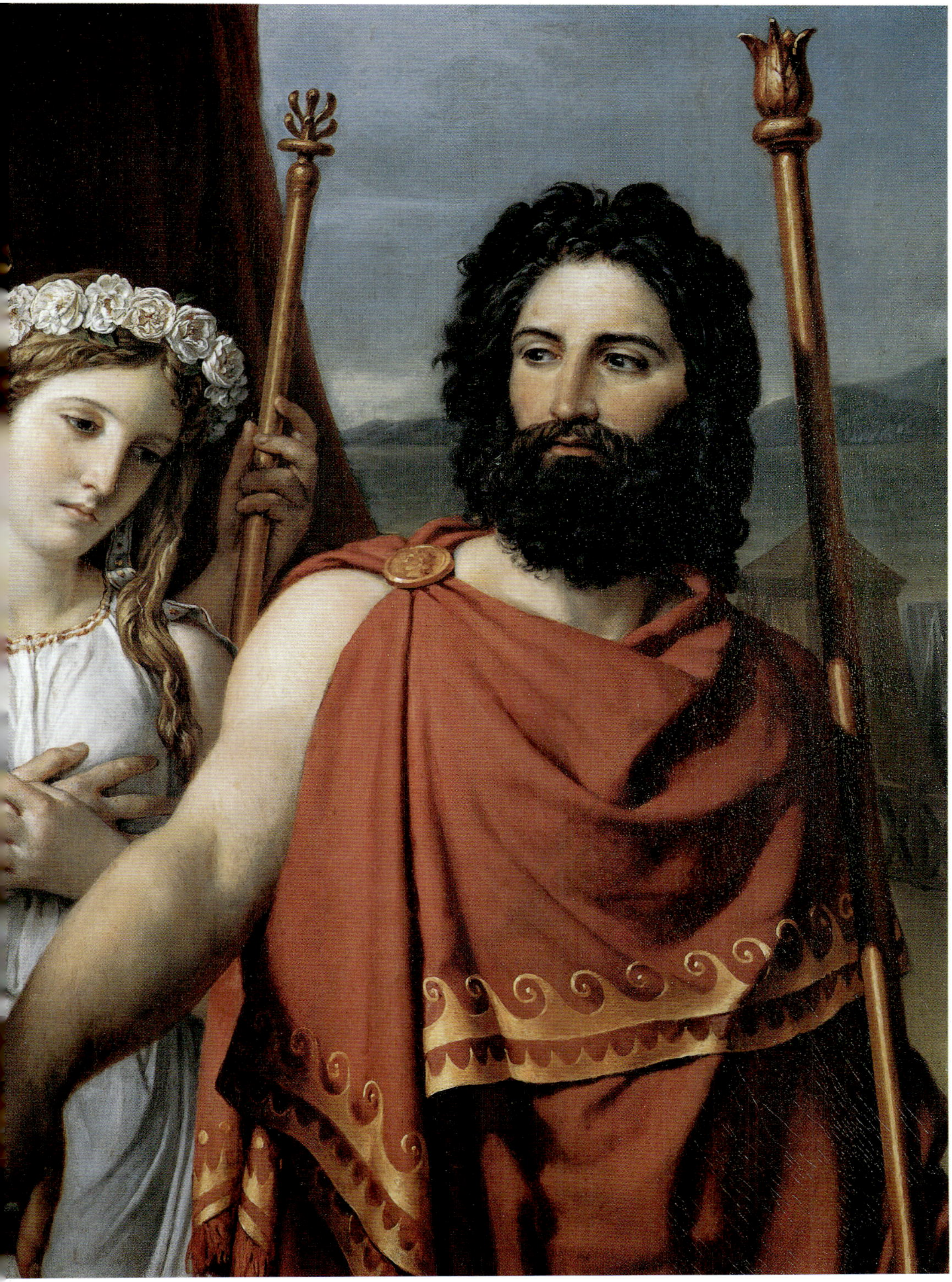

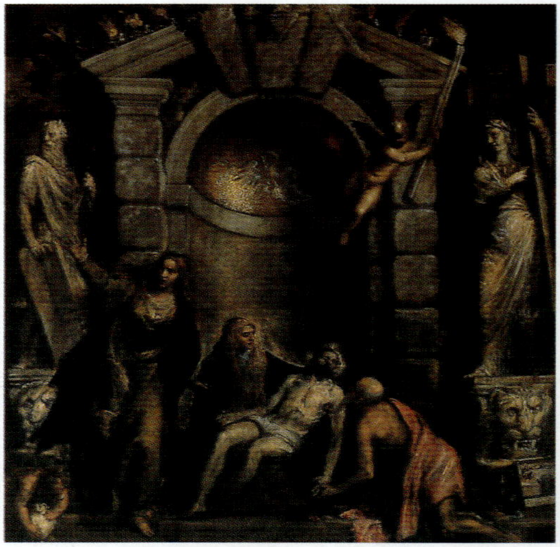

193
Titian,
Pietà,
1573–6.
Oil on canvas;
353 × 348 cm,
139⅛ × 137⅛ in.
Galleria dell'Accademia,
Venice

of the Greeks. As she was about to be killed, the warrior Achilles attempted to save her but was turned back by the masterful gaze of Agamemnon. David tried very hard to characterize the differing emotions and responses of the four figures to the event. The headstrong Achilles has an antique profile while the authoritative Agamemnon is bearded and middle aged. In the background is Queen Clytemnestra, wife of Agamemnon and mother of Iphigenia, close to tears as she gently rests her hand on her daughter's shoulder. Iphigenia appears delicate and fragile, dressed in white and wearing a garland of roses, she bows her head in wistful melancholy and resignation. By showing Agamemnon controlling Achilles by the sheer force of his will, David was perhaps recalling the pseudo-scientific theories of animal magnetism of Friedrich Anton Mesmer (see Chapter 2), who said that certain powerful individuals could control others with an invisible fluid that came from their fingertips and eyes. The tension of the scene is increased by the way that David forces these half-length figures into a uncomfortably narrow space, so narrow that Achilles' back is flattened and compressed. David was clearly pleased with this new type of work and wrote of *The Anger of Achilles*: 'Never have I done better works ... in the simple and energetic taste of Ancient Greece.' He exhibited *Cupid and*

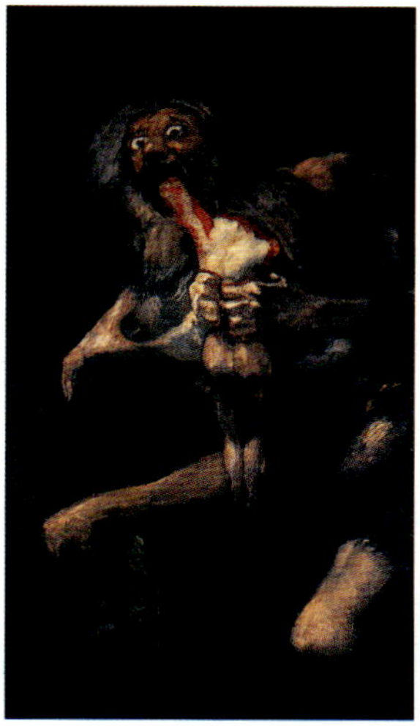

194 Francisco Goya, *Saturn,* c.1821–3. Oil on canvas (transferred from plaster); 146 × 83 cm, $57\frac{1}{2} \times 32\frac{5}{8}$ in. Museo del Prado, Madrid

Psyche, The Farewell of Telemachus and Eucharis and *The Anger of Achilles* in Brussels, Ghent and Mons for an admission fee before they were sent off to their owners – the receipts from the shows were then given to religious and civic charities.

Many artists when they reach old age become anxious about how posterity and future generations will judge them. Some are eager to make sure that their best works are in major collections, others try to buy back their old works with which to surround themselves (David's pupil Ingres was later to do this). Another common characteristic of elderly artists – painters, writers and composers – is a profound sense of independence or isolation and a loss of the desire to communicate. The artist wants to be taken on his or her own terms with few concessions to anyone else, and so the results are often highly personal. In painting, we can think of Titian's highly expressive and technically breathtaking works (193), and also of Francisco Goya (1746–1828), two years older than David, who, in 1819, removed himself to La Quinta del Sordo (The House of the Deaf Man) outside Madrid and produced powerful and aggressive virtuoso works on the absurd nature of humanity for his own private consumption and with little regard for the public's gaze (194). Though we can see that David's work at this time became more personal, he never cut himself off from the artistic life around him. To remind the French public of their greatest living painter's continued creativity, he was determined that his works be shown in Paris whenever possible, although to many critics he seemed totally out of touch with what was going on. Yet, interestingly, one of the most gifted young artists of the day, Géricault, went with his fellow artist Horace Vernet (1789–1863) to see David in Brussels in November 1820. Shortly afterwards David wrote: 'Two skilful painters,

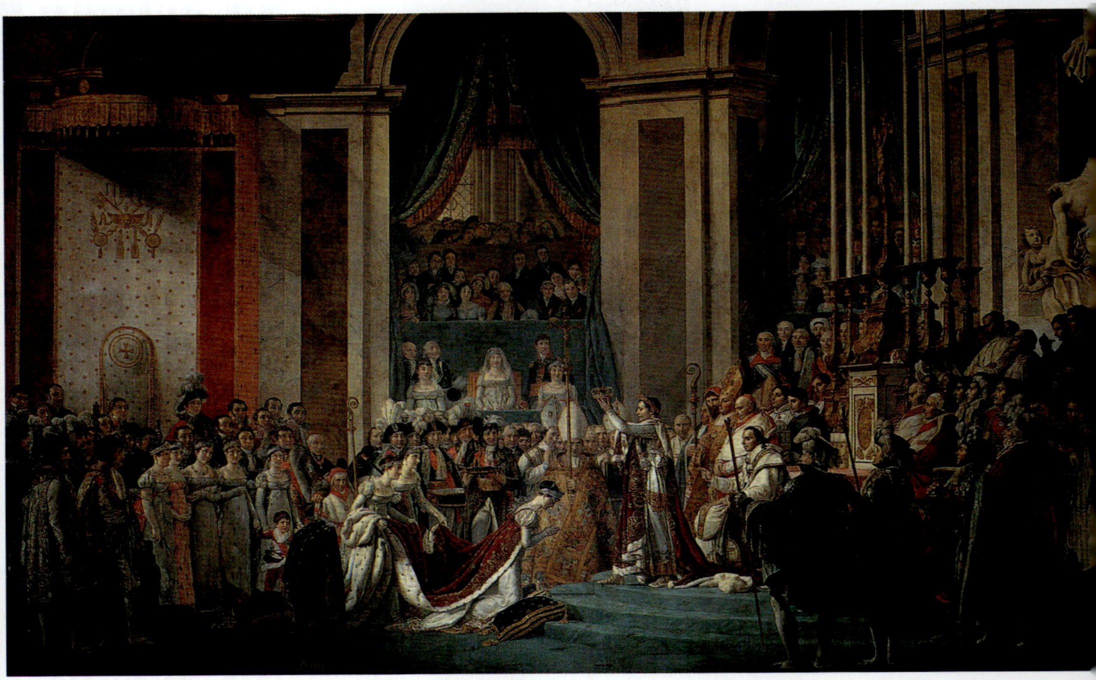

Messieurs H Vernet and Géricault ... have overjoyed me with their presence. They came to Brussels in order to see me and embrace me. We drank to the health of my students who have never grown cold in their filial attachment to me.'

As for posterity, David's place in the pantheon of French art was already assured by paintings such as the *Horatii* (see 62) and the *Brutus* (see 77), which were in the Luxembourg Museum in Paris, and although he sold other works to the government in France this was to maximize his income rather than expressly to ensure that they entered a state collection. Early in 1820 the *Sabines* (see 131) and *Leonidas at Thermopylae* (see 177) were placed in the Luxembourg after having been bought by the government for a total price of 100,000 francs. As part of this deal David also handed over *The Coronation of the Emperor and Empress* (see 152) and *The Distribution of the Eagle Standards* (see 167), which he had held on to at the fall of Napoleon and put into store in Paris when he left for Brussels. No money changed hands for these works because he had already been paid for them, albeit by a different regime. However, the Napoleonic paintings were not put on public display – their obvious political content meant that they were placed in the storerooms of the Louvre. Although he was enjoying a high standard of living in Brussels, David sought to increase his income still further by negotiating contracts for his paintings to be engraved. For artists of the eighteenth and nineteenth centuries, selling the engraving rights of their successful and popular paintings was a highly important venture which meant that they were paid twice for a work – once by the picture's buyer and then by the engraver. In many cases they made more money from the engravings than from the original painting. Given David's shrewd business sense it is no surprise that he eagerly pursued such sources of revenue; he was even supposed to have made a suggestion about the engraving of *Leonidas* on his deathbed.

195
Replica of *The Coronation of the Emperor and Empress*, 1822.
Oil on canvas; 610 × 970 cm, 240⅛ × 381⅞ in.
Musée National du Château de Versailles

David's health was poor in 1820 and it was even rumoured that he would never paint again, but he recovered somewhat and, after painting *Charlotte and Zénaïde Bonaparte* (see 188) in 1821, he supervised the completion of an almost full-sized replica of *The Coronation of the Emperor and Empress* (195). This had been begun back in 1808, probably at the instigation of some American entrepreneurs who planned to put the painting on tour and charge an admission fee to see it, but the plan foundered and was abandoned. With Napoleon's death in 1821, public interest in the former emperor was revived and a new group of businessmen approached David to finish the project. About two-thirds of the painting was already complete and David asked his assistant Georges Rouget, who had worked on the original, to bring the canvas to Brussels from Paris and then stay to help. David was given a large room in the town hall as a studio and work probably began in the autumn of 1821. Although David had an extremely good visual memory and was often able to redraw the faces and features of people he had not seen for a decade and a half, in some cases he had to substitute local dignitaries and friends for Napoleonic courtiers. Hairstyles and clothes were also updated, as were the figures – David's wife and daughter in the central box were aged to show the passing of the years – though in his self-portrait next to them the painter himself has aged little. Also in the central box, behind the long dead Vien, he placed one of his former pupils, Odevaere, who was then a successful court painter to King William I of the Netherlands. Odevaere had painted David's portrait in 1820 (196) and it was said that David returned the favour by including him in the replica. In the same painting we therefore see people from two different eras twenty years apart, a combination that disrupts the overall effect and which people at the time remarked upon. Because David was still weak through ill-health, almost all of the remaining work was done by Rouget and this, combined with a lack of fine detail, makes the replica appear dry and lacking the immediacy and splendour of the original. David was surely deluding himself when he said that he preferred it to the original, and his former pupil François-Joseph Navez said that it was feeble and 'completely bad'. When the painting was shown in London in 1822, *The Times* found in it 'nothing deserving of particular praise' and called it 'an imitation of a waxwork', and the review in the *Literary Gazette and Journal of Belles Lettres* was even more scathing: 'Never, in a Coronation scene, did we see such vile countenances, such dingy colouring', and added that many of the individual portraits were reminiscent of pub signs. Before being sent off to London and then a tour of America, David had hoped to show the painting to the Brussels public and once again raise money for charity, but the government denied his request, fearing that the painting would be a rallying point for radicals and Bonapartists and thereby cause an unwelcome diplomatic incident with the Bourbon regime in France.

With the illness of 1820, David began to sense the end of his life and was determined to paint one last grand statement. In 1821 he began work on *Mars Disarmed by Venus and the Three Graces* (197). He said of it: 'It is the last of the paintings I want to

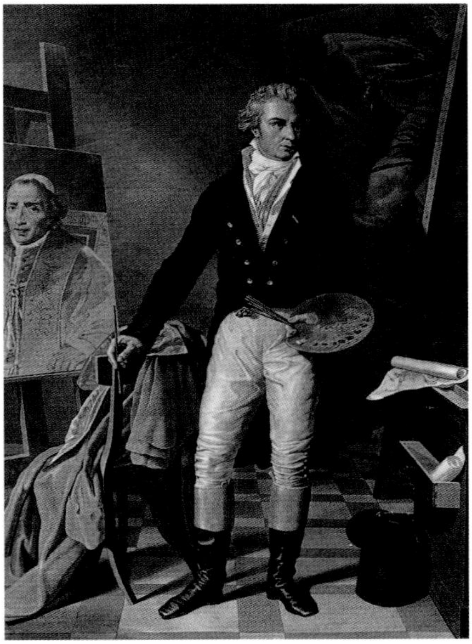

196
Jean-Pierre-Marie Jazet,
David from Life,
1820.
Engraving after Joseph-Denis Odevaere;
76 × 56 cm,
30 × 22 in

do, but I want to surpass myself in it. I will inscribe it with the date of my seventy-fifth year, and after that I never want to touch a brush again.' Completed in 1824, the work is bold, surprising and puzzling, and many people then and now have wondered exactly what he meant by this strange scene played out against an ornate marble pavilion in the sky. Is it is the manifesto of someone re-examining the meaning of classical mythology and tradition to arrive at a parody of conventional mythological painting? Or is the picture a genuine, but misguided and

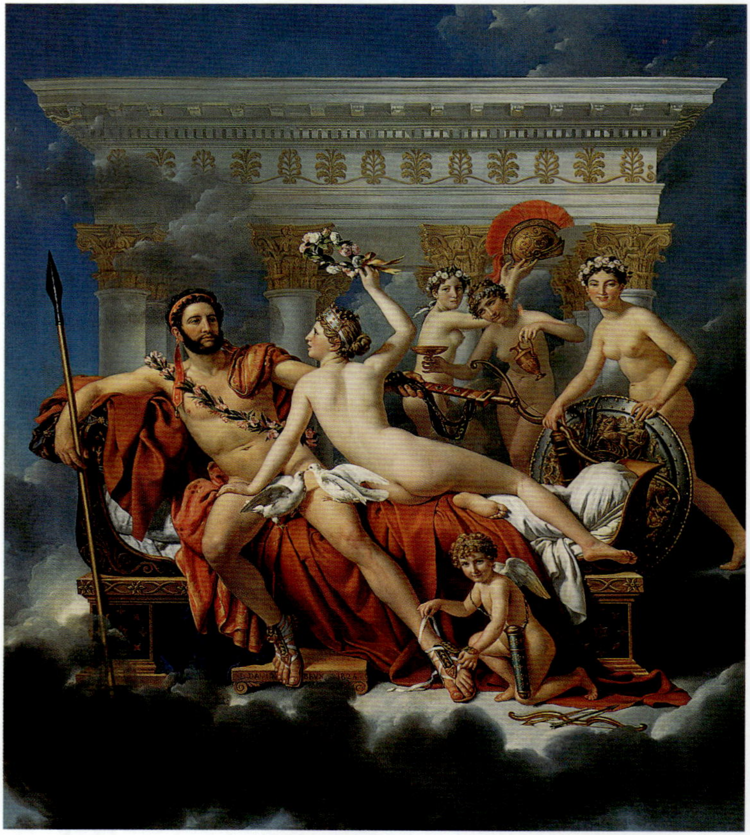

197–198
Mars Disarmed by Venus and the Three Graces, 1824.
Oil on canvas; 308 × 262 cm, 121¼ × 103⅛ in.
Musées Royaux des Beaux-Arts, Brussels
Right
Detail

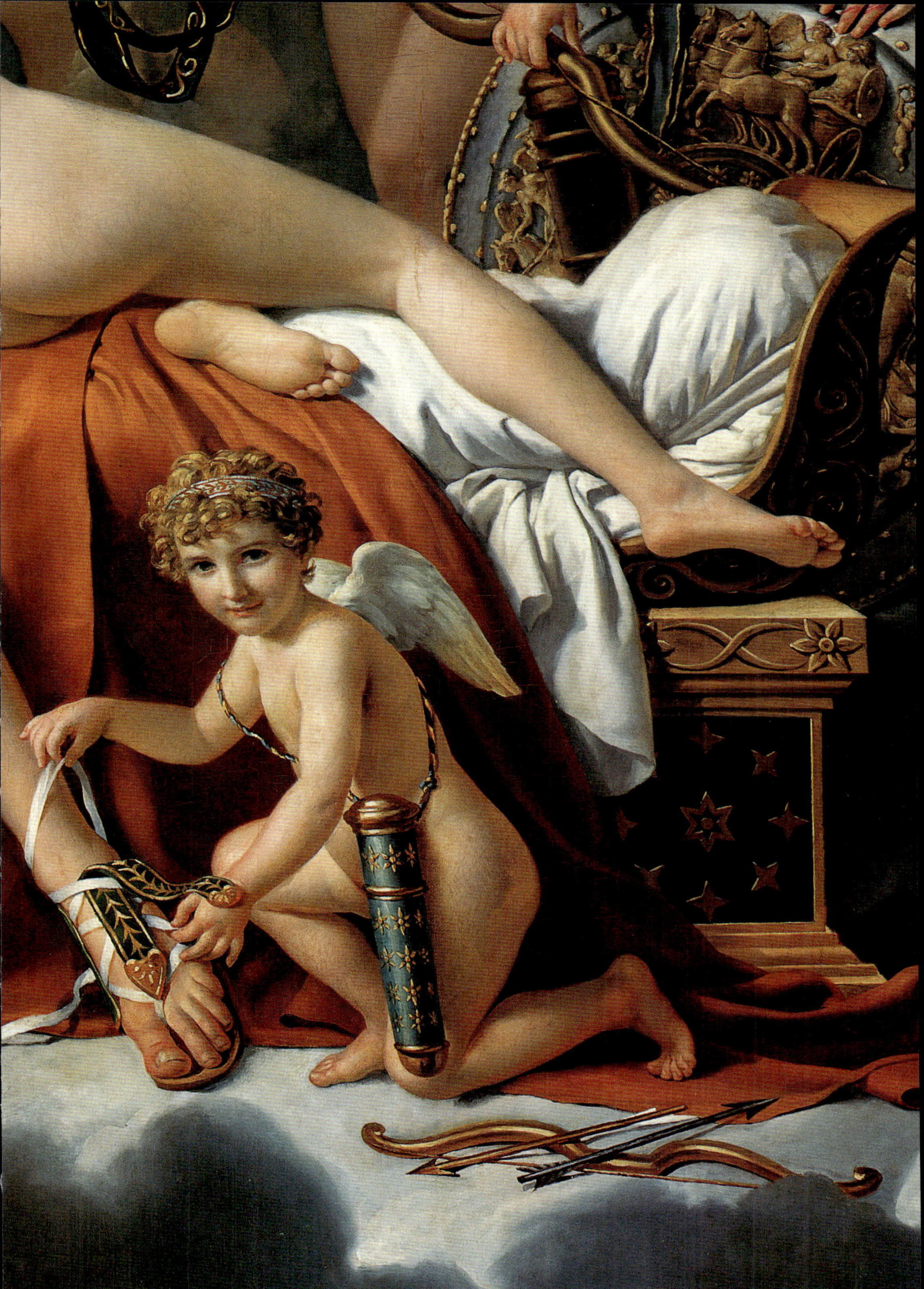

anachronistic revisiting of the themes that David had painted fifty years before (see 13)? Both explanations have been offered and it remains a point of contention between scholars.

Mars, the god of war, is succumbing to the charms of Venus, but the outcome is still in doubt. Venus hesitates to place the crown of roses on his head – an emblem of submission to the pleasures of the flesh – and Cupid, who unties Mars' sandal, has put down his bow with the golden arrow of desire and the leaden arrow of repulsion side-by-side and not yet fired (198). A psychoanalytic reading of the subject might conclude that in handing his sword, a symbol of masculine power, to one of the Graces, Mars, and by extension David, recognizes his

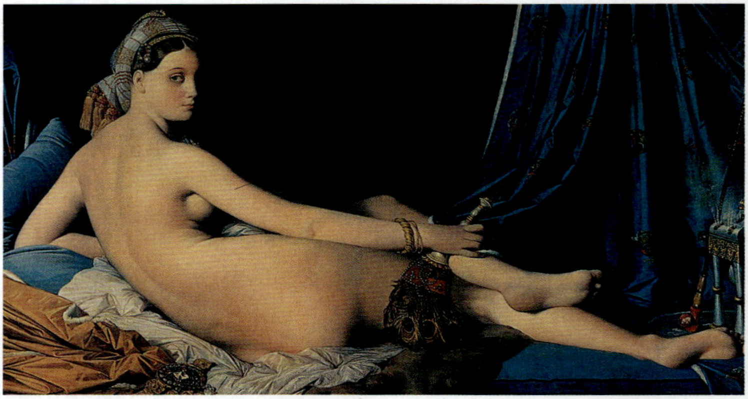

enfeeblement and withdraws from the competitive arena of war/art. Mars is shown nude and David delicately placed one of a pair of rather scruffy cooing doves to conceal his genitals for the sake of propriety. The pale Venus is an extremely delicate and sinuous form and much thinner than this voluptuous goddess is usually depicted. The slow and sensual curve of the back and arms is reminiscent of *La Grande Odalisque* of 1814 (199) by Ingres, David's student at the turn of the century – perhaps the master was now taking inspiration from the pupil. David had great trouble in finding a beautiful and unblemished pair of feet as a model for those of Venus and although many ladies of Brussels high society presented themselves, finally he found the solution in a young working girl who had only ever worn clogs. To model Venus herself, he hired the principal dancer of the Théâtre de la Monnaie in Brussels, Marie Lesueur, who had danced the title role in Marius Petipa's ballet *The Birth of Venus and Love* in June 1821. Behind the divine couple on the antique couch are the Three Graces who perform aimless tasks. One offers a cup of wine to Mars who has no free hand to take it, another rolls his shield as if it were a child's hoop and we can only wonder where the Grace on the left thinks she is putting Mars' helmet. Traditionally, the Graces were the beautiful handmaidens of Venus, but these are patently 'graceless Graces' and their gestures and expressions border on the absurd and comical.

199 Jean-Auguste-Dominique Ingres, *La Grande Odalisque,* 1814. Oil on canvas; 91 × 162 cm, 35⅞ × 63¾ in. Musée du Louvre, Paris

For the Graces David had used the unidealized forms of the corps de ballet of the Monnaie and an uncomfortable juxtaposition of the real and the ideal is achieved. Was David incapable of painting 'graceful Graces' or was it a deliberate choice? In the past the credibility of David's works had rested on his careful selection of models and his capacity to establish a convincing gestural interplay between his figures. In *Mars and Venus* different criteria are used and, contrary to the upbeat tone of David's letters, one suspects a misplaced confidence in novelty. The overall effect is certainly perplexing and unnerving and it is also painted in a highly coloured hard-edged style that perhaps suggests considerable contributions from his Belgian assistants.

To show off his 'final adieu' to painting, David instructed his son Eugène to rent three rooms in Paris in a corner apartment at 115 rue de Richelieu. The first room contained some of his past paintings, including *Andromache Mourning Hector* (see 43) and the *Hector* (see 35) and *Patroclus* (see 36) *académies,* while the second room was set aside for *Mars and Venus*. The walls were covered with green drapery and opposite the painting hung a large mirror which completely reflected the painted image. Standing between the two, an extraordinary sensation

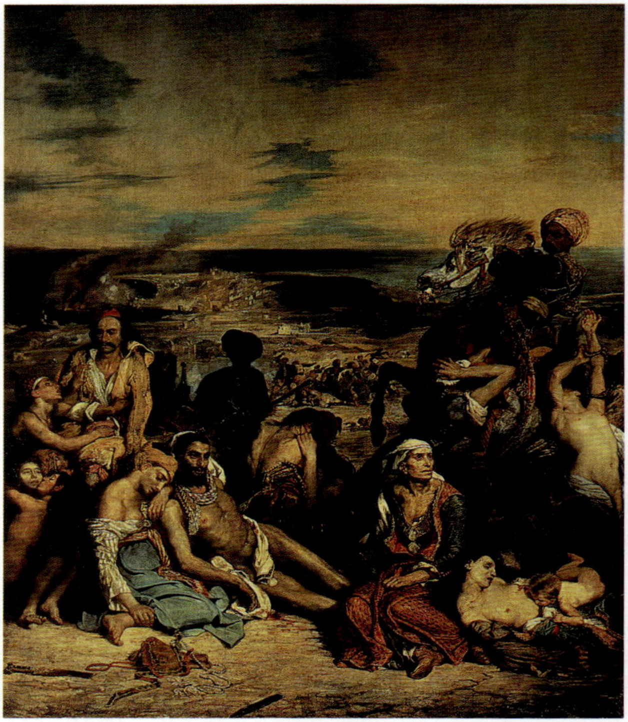

200
Eugène Delacroix,
Scenes from the Massacres at Chios,
1824.
Oil on canvas;
419 × 354 cm,
165 × 139½ in.
Musée du Louvre, Paris

201
John Constable,
The Haywain,
1821.
Oil on canvas;
130·2 × 185·4 cm,
51⅜ × 73 in.
National Gallery, London

was gained as the spectator was caught between art and illusion. As with the *Sabines* (see 131) a quarter of a century before, David once again sought to promote the act of viewing as an active and participatory experience. The final room was furnished with chairs and meant as a place for discussion and recovery from the effects of the spectacle. Most viewers did not know what to make of this huge picture, though high praise was given to David's brilliant and vibrant colour and the subtle treatment of Venus' flesh. The exhibition lasted from May 1824 to March 1825 with a two-franc entry fee. Attendances were little more than modest, and in the eight and a half months of the exhibition only 9,358 tickets were sold – two-thirds of them in the first three months – and by the end only about six people a day were entering. The profit amounted to about 15,000 francs compared to the figure of about 75,000 francs for the *Sabines* exhibition. For all his attempts at breaking new ground, no one bought the picture, and much more interest was created by the appearance

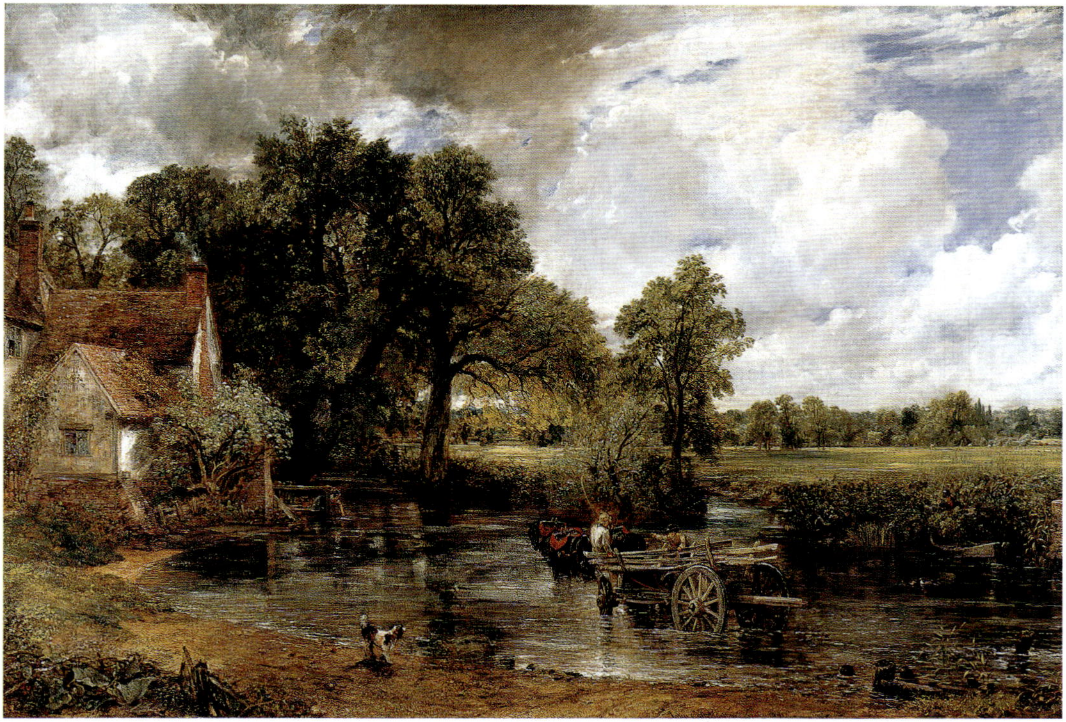

at the 1824 Paris Salon of two works representing different facets of Romanticism – the topical but anti-climactic recreation of the sufferings of the Greek War of Independence, *Scenes from the Massacres at Chios* (200) by Eugène Delacroix (1798–1863), and *The Haywain* (201) by John Constable (1776–1837), a naturalistic rendition of an English summer's noon.

David had been assisted on *Mars and Venus* by a pupil, Michel Ghislain Stapleaux (1799–1881) – another, Isidore Dupavillon (1790–1856), had been sacked for poor work – but even so the effort of creating this huge work weakened an already fragile old man. Work had also been interrupted after David was knocked down by a horse-drawn cab returning from the theatre early in 1824. In 1825 David was gravely ill with heart disease and, to make matters worse, his wife was also unwell and had returned to Paris for treatment. David briefly felt strong enough to have his portrait painted for the last time by his loyal pupil Jérôme-Martin Langlois (see 184). He seems alert and vital, which was probably not the case, and is also shown at work on a drawing for *Apelles and Campaspe* (202), a painting begun in Paris but which was never finished. In the autumn of 1825 David wrote very touchingly: 'I feel my imagination to be as vivid and as fresh as it was in the first part of my youth, I compose with the same facility all of the subjects that come into my mind; but when I pick up my pencils to sketch them onto the canvas, my hand refuses.' He then became confined to bed, dictated his will on 21 November and became calm, courageous and resigned as the end approached, finally dying in the arms of his son Eugène on the morning of 29

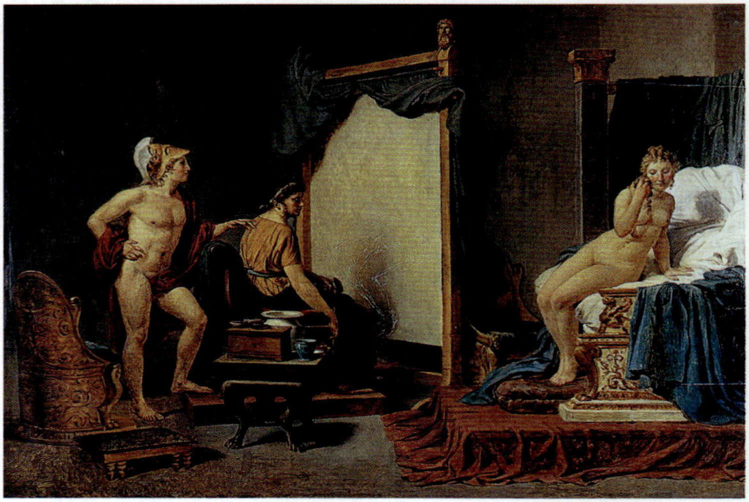

December. His friends and colleagues realized that a truly great artist had been lost and barely was the body cold before a death mask and plaster cast of his right hand were made, as well as a drawing of his face. The postmortem showed a grossly enlarged heart which was removed, placed in a silver urn and given to his family. Then, in a curious parallel with the arrangements for Marat over thirty years before, the body was embalmed and the public admitted to see the famous man for the last time. An impressive funeral was organized by the government and the cortège included a hearse drawn by six black horses, a military band playing sombre music, art students carrying banners with the names of David's most famous paintings, friends and fellow artists holding flaming torches, and David's valet in mourning dress carrying his uniform of the Institute of France and the decorations of the Legion of Honour. When news of his death reached Paris his ex-pupils rushed to the Luxembourg Museum and placed laurel crowns above his pictures. This display of devotion so upset the authorities that the gallery was briefly closed to prevent any further outbursts. In his will David left annual pensions to both his servants, and his family then began to assemble his works together in Paris for auction. David had managed to keep many of his own works, and the sale of his studio contents included *Bara, Le Pelletier de Saint-Fargeau, Andromache Mourning Hector, Mars Disarmed by Venus and the Three Graces*, the drawing for *The Oath of the Tennis Court*, one version of *Bonaparte Crossing the St Bernard Pass* and the unfinished portraits of Madame Pastoret and Madame Récamier. Although David had also retained the *Marat*, it was still considered too controversial and, although included in the catalogue, it was not offered for sale. However, few works were sold and prices did not match the family's inflated expectations. From some quarters at least, the charge of greed was once again levelled.

202
Apelles and Campaspe (unfinished), begun *c*.1813. Oil on panel; 96 × 136 cm, 37¾ × 53½ in. Musée des Beaux-Arts, Lille

David had not been buried immediately because it was hoped that his remains would be allowed to return to France, but in a show of petty vindictiveness the government refused. It was not until 11 October that David's body was laid to rest in a specially constructed tomb and memorial in the cemetery of Saint-Josse-ten-Noode. This cemetery was later closed and in 1882 the monument and David's remains were transferred to the cemetery of Evere outside Brussels; recently an anonymous benefactor paid for the lease of the plot to be renewed until the year 2021. Madame David, who was in Paris when her husband died, did not long survive him and died on 9 May 1826. She was buried in Père Lachaise cemetery, and, without alerting either the government or the press, Eugène David placed his father's heart next to her.

But the story does not end there. In 1989, when the French government was in the midst of celebrating the two-hundredth anniversary of the Revolution, plans were made to bring David's remains back to Paris and place them with great ceremony with the heart in a specially prepared vault in Père Lachaise. All the arrangements were made and hundreds of invitations were sent out to honoured guests by the French minister of culture at the time, Jack Lang. Then, at the eleventh hour, a Brussels city councillor went to court to object to this 'political body snatching', David's remains were deemed 'a historic monument' and permission for their removal was withdrawn. Over 160 years after his death, and from beyond the grave, David was still causing controversy.

Gross David with the Swoln Cheek   David's Afterlife

7

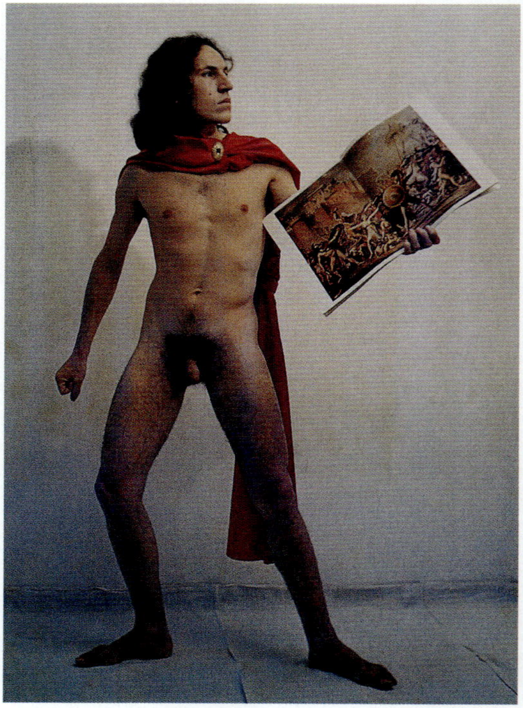

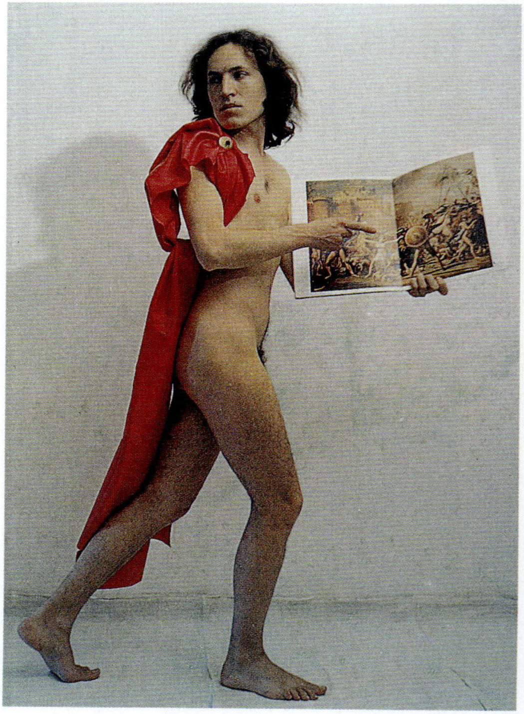

At the time of his death David was considered by modern French critics to be an anachronism; a remnant of a way of life and a type of painting that had long since passed. Yet, thanks to his vast number of pupils, the influence of David was felt for another half century. Many of the painters honoured by the restored Bourbons had been his pupils, and both Gérard and Gros enjoyed even more official honours than they had under Napoleon, both being created barons. His former pupil Ingres became the most important artist of the Academy and the figurehead of the Classical School to counter the attacks of the Romantics (204). Ingres saw himself as the defender of timeless and universal values, and maintained that the great tradition of art had remained unbroken from classical times until the present day. These values were most cogently expressed in his 1827 painting *The Apotheosis of Homer*, where Homer is celebrated as the source for all European culture, and is paid homage to by the major artistic figures of ancient and modern civilization. The Romantics, led, as far as the public were concerned, by Delacroix, considered that each new generation must find its own particular form of artistic expression, and that subjects from the modern world and from literature were emotionally superior to those from ancient history. However, Delacroix was an admirer of David's paintings, and always distinguished between the invention and originality of his work and the servile copying of his style by some of his weaker pupils.

203
Luigi Ontani,
After David (The Rape of the Sabines),
1972

In some quarters, to have been a student of David carried with it a certain status, and all over France academies and art schools were administered by his former students. In scanning both Parisian and provincial newspapers one would almost certainly find an advertisement from 'a former pupil of Monsieur David's' willing to give tuition in painting and drawing at a reasonable

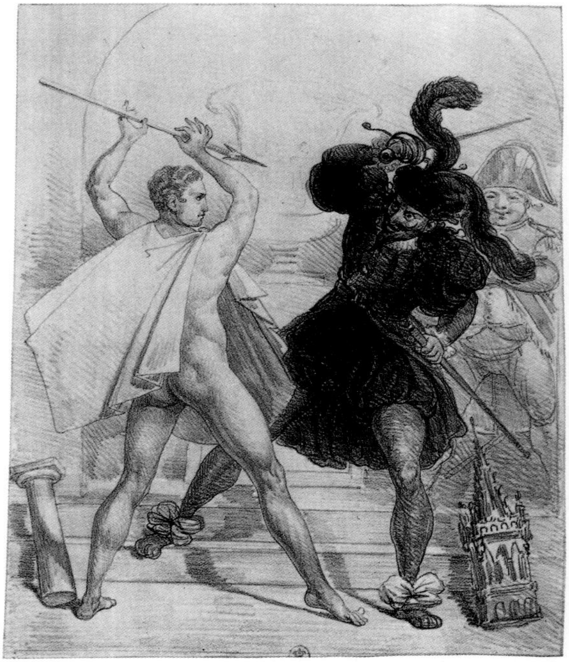

cost. To keep alive the cherished memory of their beloved master, David's former pupils also held a dinner annually from 1836 to 1845; it was an opportunity to meet old comrades and reminisce as well as to drink a toast to their late lamented teacher.

Almost inevitably, as well as producing tributes and appreciations, David's death was also accompanied by some hostile accounts of his work and on the part he had played in the development of French art. What had been a whispering campaign of opposition to his methods in the previous decade was now openly and vociferously stated. It was said that David had had a pernicious and prejudicial effect on art because of his concentration on drawing and on static scenes, which led to a sterile uniformity and a conservative orthodoxy. The blame for the moribund state of history painting was laid squarely at the feet of David, and it is ironic that his stylistic innovations, which had begun as a radical and vibrant art form, were reduced to a rigid formula when practised by less gifted artists. Of course, to shift the burden of guilt onto David alone is too harsh – he certainly never intended art to become a matter of rules and stock poses, and always wanted his pupils to find the method of artistic expression that best suited them. Yet, if he was innocent of this charge, he had no such defence when accused of encouraging students to concentrate on the intellectual aspects of art with a consequential neglect of technical matters. Delacroix in particular was scathing both about David's lack of sound technique and of the cold appearance of his paintings.

204
The Salon of 1827. Will they Enter, Won't they Enter? The Great Battle between the Romantic and the Classic at the Door to the Museum, 1827. Lithograph; 34 × 23·8 cm, $13\frac{3}{8} \times 9\frac{3}{8}$ in

To David the manual craft and tricks of the trade of painting had always been objects of scorn and contempt, and he endured rather than enjoyed the physical act of holding a brush and applying oil paint. Even though he is said to have claimed, when bored by a man insistent on discussing processes, 'I knew all that before I knew anything at all', this was patently not the case. His insistence on artistic intellect and invention meant that he had little time for the craft of painting and paid scant attention to many technical details such as the preparation of canvas and the selection of good quality materials. In doing so he was, of course, ignoring a valuable source of accumulated artistic wisdom and this resulted both in shortcomings in his own technique and in the training of a whole generation of painters who had lost the skills of their socially inferior, though technically advanced, artistic forbears. In effect, this was the final rupture between the artist and the craftsman that had slowly been in progress ever since the Academy was founded in Paris in 1648.

Not only was David's artistic reputation put under the most severe scrutiny, his life and work was also subjected to much harsh criticism. British artists and writers were especially hard on him and could not (or would not) disentangle David the artist from David the politician who had voted for the death of Louis XVI. The Scottish essayist and historian Thomas Carlyle referred to 'Gross David with the swoln cheek', and Constable, after visiting an exhibition of David's pictures in London in 1835, was especially extreme in his views. He wrote: 'I have seen David's pictures, they are indeed loathsome ... David seems to have formed his mind from three sources, the scaffold, the hospital and a brothel.' William Makepeace Thackeray, author of *Vanity Fair* (1848), said that David 'died about a year after his bodily demise in 1825', adding, 'was there ever anything so absurd as this passion for the nude, which was followed by all the painters of the Davidian epoch?', and finally likened Romulus in the *Sabines* (see 131) to 'the exact action of a telegraph'. The critic and writer John Ruskin thought David a painter of limited ability, and although he saw in *The Oath of the Horatii*, 'handsome and well-made men; their countenances courageous, determined and noble', he felt that a more distinguished artist would have attempted greater characterization of the brothers. As a supporter of the Pre-Raphaelite Brotherhood, it is not surprising that Ruskin condemned David for merely depicting the 'outward verities of passing events', and praised artists who invented poetic stories on a par with literature – especially John Everett Millais (1829–96) and William Holman Hunt (1827–1910). It should be noted though that there is one link between an artist in the Pre-Raphaelite circle and David. Ford Madox Brown (1821–93) had briefly been a student of Albert Gregorius (1774–1853) in Bruges, and then Pieter van Hanselaere (1786–1862) in Ghent, both of whom had studied with David.

In France too there was much mudslinging of a personal nature and this inevitably affected later opinions of David and his art. The episode where David was either unable or unwilling to help the unfortunate Madame Chalgrin during the Revolution (see Chapter 3) was much embellished to cast David in an even less favourable light. His refusal to act now seems to have stemmed from sheer spitefulness after the vulnerable woman had rejected his amorous advances! In an attempt to set the record straight, David's former pupil Etienne-Jean Delécluze wrote his long biography, *Louis David, son école et son temps*, in 1855, and stated that: 'The object of these souvenirs is to restore David's proper genius and the principles which this great artist passed onto his pupils.' This book concentrated on David's work and relationship with pupils, and avoided asking any awkward questions about his involvement with the Revolution. Then, in 1880, David's grandson Jules produced his monumental work, *Le Peintre Louis David*, which contained reprints of many letters and documents, and still forms the basis for any serious study on David.

But although debts to David were still being incurred by many of the history paintings on the walls of the official Salon, there were new forces and artistic currents at work that made his example even less relevant. With the advent of the Impressionists and their small-scale, highly coloured landscapes, which were painted outdoors in a single sitting, it is hard to conceive of an art form more divorced from the principles and practice of David. Although it took some little time for the public to be converted to the charms of Claude Monet (1840–1926), Pierre-Auguste Renoir (1841–1919), Edgar Degas (1834–1917), Alfred Sisley (1839–99) and Camille Pissarro (1830–1903), once it was accomplished the Impressionists became the most popular and accessible of artists, their scenes of nature touching a chord of nostalgic recognition in their audience as well as providing a soothing balm for the eyes, two characteristics that are distinctly absent in David's work. In the later nineteenth century and at the start of the twentieth century the course of Post-Impressionism, Fauvism, Cubism and abstraction created an artistic atmosphere not so much hostile as redundant of the need to consider David, although the writer and critic Guillaume Apollinaire did write an appreciative review of the 1913 *David and his Pupils* exhibition that was held at the Petit Palais in Paris. Colour became the dominant mode of expression in art, and if any nineteenth-century predecessor were sought it was Delacroix. For those artists exploring the subtlety and sobriety of pure form and line, such as Paul Cézanne (1839–1906) and Piet Mondrian (1872–1944), David had little relevance since Poussin's lucid and geometrical landscapes provided a more valuable guide from the past.

To some recent artists and critics, David's work, in particular *The Intervention of the Sabine Women* (see 131), appear concerned with brutal masculine values that have no place in a civilized modern society. In 1972 the Italian artist Luigi Ontani (b.1943) cast himself as one of the nude grooms from *The Sabine Women* while holding a reproduction of the whole work in his hand (203). Entitled *After David (The Rape of the Sabines)*, this photograph of a performance by Ontani was meant to be a critique of past culture by updating artistic quotations. Then, in Britain in December 1996, the *Guardian* newspaper carried an article condemning David's painting for its 'vile' and 'despicable' depiction of 'the terrified, soon-to-be brutally slaughtered female figures.' Both cases mistake the reconciliation of the women's intervention for the earlier scene of rape, and illustrate how present-day unfamiliarity with ancient history means that half-remembered stories can be used to confirm current beliefs and attitudes.

205
The Coronation of the Emperor and Empress being moved for the David exhibition, September 1989, Musée du Louvre, Paris

For an artist with such a degree of political involvement, it is little wonder that David has attracted a huge amount of interest from critics and historians, and it often seems that he has been used as a starting point from which to demonstrate personal opinions and arguments. He has been praised and reviled by both the right and left, and seen as both a true revolutionary artist and, according to the French Marxist historian Daniel Guérin, a cynical bourgeois betrayer of the proletariat. In many ways these discussions and interpretations are a small-scale version of the much larger debate that continues to this day concerning the causes, nature and effects of the French Revolution.

It was not until after World War II that David's public rehabilitation began to take place. An exhibition to celebrate the two-hundredth anniversary of his birth was mounted at the Musée de l'Orangerie in Paris and at the Château de Versailles in 1948. Placed against the backdrop of a France requiring massive reconstruction and having to come to terms

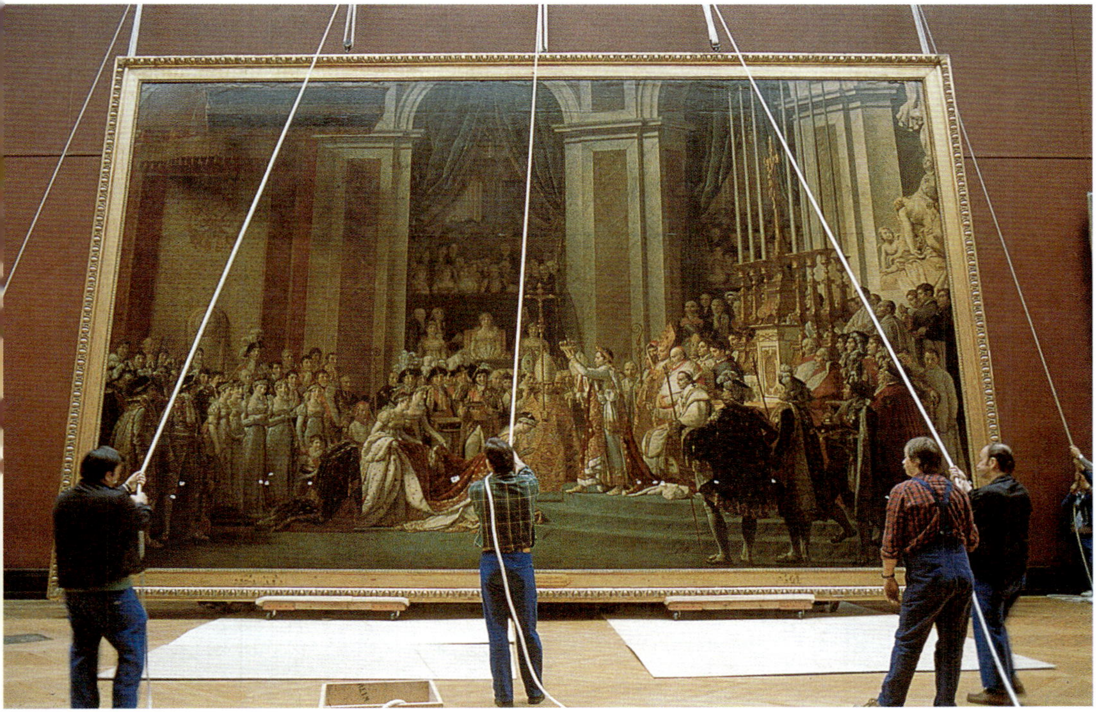

with past collaboration with the Nazis, David provided a symbol of national pride and identity. Characterized as a quintessentially French artist with a passion for painting the truth, David was seen as part of an unbroken chain of French art that stretched from the Renaissance to the time of Cézanne. The catalogue introduction solemnly concluded, 'he remains one of the giants of French painting'. Since then, books and studies on David have blossomed, reaching their peak at the 1989–90 exhibition at the Louvre (205) and at Versailles, which also included a five-day academic conference. Present-day scholarly debate on David's art has matched and even surpassed the controversies that his paintings provoked at the time of their exhibition, with the ingenious theories of some researchers being dismissed as far-fetched and over-inventive by their more traditionalist colleagues.

Yet no amount of tightly constructed argument can replace or diminish the thrill and excitement of directly experiencing David's major creations. To view in close proximity the *Horatii, Sabines, Coronation* and *Leonidas* in the Louvre leaves one marvelling at the breadth of invention and clarity of thought and purpose. Better still, make the pilgrimage to Brussels and stand in silent awe before the sublime *Marat*. In a time of sound bites, thirty-second news clips and ever decreasing attention spans here is a painting that requires our gaze and richly repays the demands it makes. David's art has the ability to speak across the centuries to us, and at a time when calls for a return to order come from every shade of the political spectrum, it still has much to offer the modern viewer.

Glossary | Brief Biographies | Key Dates | Map |
Further Reading | Index | Acknowledgements

Glossary

Academy (Royal Academy of Painting and Sculpture) The Royal Academy of Painting and Sculpture was founded in 1648 to increase the status of artists by demonstrating that they were cultivated men of intellect rather than manual craftsmen. Great emphasis was placed on teaching and a high standard of draughtsmanship resulted. The Academy also had an outpost in Rome where winners of the **Prix de Rome** would go to study. Although an Academician himself, David agitated against the privileges of senior members and the uniform teaching methods, and succeeded in having the institution abolished in 1793. In 1795 the Academy was replaced by the **Institute**.

Barbus (Bearded Ones) Also known as the *Penseurs* (Thinkers), *Méditateurs* (Meditators) or *Primitifs* (Primitives). A breakaway sect in David's studio led by Pierre-Maurice Quay (*c*.1779–1802/3), that wanted art to return to the primitive purity of ancient Greek vase-painting and the simplicity of the early Italian Renaissance. They wore outlandish clothing, practised vegetarianism and had plans for a utopian society. David ejected them from his studio when they criticized his work and the group dispersed after Quay's death in 1802/3.

Baroque The most important artistic style in Europe from the late sixteenth to the early eighteenth century, the Baroque originated in Rome. Embracing painting, sculpture and architecture, it was an art of movement, virtuosity, drama and spectator involvement, and flourished mainly in Catholic countries as an expression of the Counter Reformation. Leading exponents of the Baroque included Gianlorenzo Bernini (1598–1680), **Caravaggio**, Francesco Borromini (1599–1667) and Peter Paul Rubens (1577–1640).

Committee of General Security One of the two major committees established in 1793 at a time of peril for the new French Republic. Though less powerful than the **Committee of Public Safety**, it was responsible for the police and internal security. David was one of its members.

Committee of Public Safety A 'war cabinet' operating from 6 April 1793 to 26 October 1795 consisting of twelve **Convention** members – known as the 'twelve who ruled'. Their main tasks were to mobilize the economy and organize the war effort, though **Robespierre** maintained the ideology of the **Reign of Terror**. Members were often dispatched to the provinces to supervise activity and implement policies.

Consulate Established by **Napoleon** after the Brumaire coup of 1799, the consulate consisted of Napoleon as First Consul and Jean Jacques Cambacérès and Charles François Lebrun as his subordinates. In 1802 Napoleon was made Consul for life and this dictatorial position was strengthened when he was crowned emperor in May 1804.

Convention The republican Convention replaced the Legislative Assembly in September 1792. It consisted of the left-wing **Mountain**, the independent Plain, and the moderate **Girondins**. The Girondins were arrested in June 1793 and the Mountain, led by **Robespierre**, were themselves overthrown in July 1794. The **Directory** replaced the Convention in October 1795.

Direction des Bâtiments du Roi (Direction of the King's Buildings) The equivalent of a ministry of fine arts. From 1774 until the Revolution, the **Comte d'Angiviller** was director of this branch of the royal administration. As well as commissioning works of art, the officials supervised the upkeep and maintenance of royal buildings and gardens, oversaw the **Academy** and sometimes acted as censors.

Directory Following the fall of **Robespierre**, in August 1795 five directors were appointed to wield executive power. They instituted some monetary reforms in an attempt to revive trade and agriculture but their inefficiency, corruption and increasing repression led to discontent. On 9–10 December 1799 **Napoleon** overthrew the Directory with the coup of 18–19 Brumaire and established the **Consulate**.

Girondins Moderate and idealistic **Convention** deputies, numbering about 180, so called because many of them came from the Gironde region in south-west France. Led by Jacques Pierre Brissot de Warville and Jean Marie Roland de la Platière, they tried to counter the radicalism of the Paris-centred **Mountain**. Their deputies were expelled from the Convention in June 1793 and the prominent members executed.

Institute The learned body that replaced all former Academies of Arts and Science in 1795. The painting section was limited to six members – compared to about ninety full and associate members at the old

Academy. David was a founder member and the Institute acted only as a forum for deliberation and had no teaching responsibilities.

Jacobin Club A political pressure group so called because they met in the former monastery of the Dominican friars of St James (Jacobus in Latin). Moderate at first, they became increasingly revolutionary. David was a member from September 1790. The club was abolished in November 1795.

Mountain The name given to the radical **Jacobin** deputies of the **Convention** because they occupied the top benches of the steepsided former royal riding hall of the Tuileries Palace where the Convention met. Standing in opposition to the moderate **Girondins** and numbering 250–300 deputies, they were led by **Robespierre** and had David as a member.

National Assembly The representatives of the Third Estate, meeting at the Estates General at Versailles in May 1789, termed themselves the National Assembly on 17 June when discussions with the other two Estates were deadlocked. On 20 June they met in the Tennis Court and swore an oath not to disperse until a new constitution was adopted. This National Assembly was replaced by the elected Legislative Assembly in October 1791.

Neoclassicism The dominant movement in European art and architecture from the late eighteenth to the early nineteenth century, Neoclassicism was both a reaction to the playful **Rococo** and an expression of Enlightenment morality. Ancient Roman and Greek ideals of nobility and heroism were transmitted in pure yet grand paintings and sculptures. David was the the most important Neoclassical painter and Antonio Canova (1757–1822) the major sculptor.

Prix de Rome (or Grand Prix) The premier student prize for history painting at the **Academy** in Paris. The best students were selected and given two and a half months to produce a picture on a given subject, executed in individual studios. The winners spent between three and five years of further study at the French Academy in Rome. The subject of intense competition and bitter rivalry, the prize was won by many of the major painters of the eighteenth and early nineteenth centuries, including David, **Girodet**, **Ingres**, **Regnault** and **Vincent**.

Reign of Terror The ruthless purging of all elements hostile to the Revolution, the Reign of Terror lasted for about ten months from September 1793 to July 1794 and was directed by the **Committee of Public Safety**. Not all victims were sent to the guillotine, some were shot or drowned and many died in filthy and overcrowded prisons. About 30–40,000 perished, the majority of whom were not nobles but ordinary people.

Revolutionary Calendar In 1793 a new republican calendar was introduced with the intention of removing all ecclesiastical associations. The republican year ran from 22 September to 21 September, with Year I dating back to the declaration of the Republic on 22 September 1792. The year was divided up into twelve equal months of thirty days, the five remaining days were festivals. Each month had three periods of ten days called 'Decades'. The months of the year were renamed with meteorological and agricultural associations and began with Vendémiaire (vintage) and continued through Brumaire (mist), Frimaire (frost), Nivôse (snow), Pluviôse (rain), Ventôse (wind), Germinal (seed), Floréal (blossom), Prairial (meadow), Messidor (harvest), Thermidor (heat) and Fructidor (fruit). The calendar lasted until 1803 when the Gregorian calendar was re-introduced.

Rococo A style of art, architecture and interior design that appeared mainly in France *c.*1700–*c.*1780. Characterized by grace, lightness and frivolity, it was a sensual art that was swept away by the austerity and seriousness of **Neoclassicism**. Leading Rococo artists included Jean-Antoine Watteau (1684–1721), **Boucher** and **Fragonard**.

Romanticism Following the massive upheavals of the French Revolution and the Napoleonic era, artists all over Europe began to treat subjects in a more personal way, and valued instinct, intuition and emotion over the cool, universal order of **Neoclassicism**. The irrational, the horrific and the force and mystery of nature were also explored. The Romantics also laid great emphasis on colour rather than line. The term is truly international and covers such diverse artists as **Géricault**, Eugène Delacroix (1798–1863), John Constable (1776–1837), J M W Turner (1775–1851) and Francisco Goya (1746–1828).

Comte d'Angiviller (Charles-Claude de Flahaut de la Billaderie) (1730–1809) A former soldier, d'Angiviller was appointed head of the **Direction des Bâtiments du Roi** at Louis XVI's accession. He promoted the cause of history painting and diverted funds from other projects to maintain official commissions. Though the protector of **Peyron**, he recognized David's talent and commissioned both royal and private works from him. D'Angiviller went into exile at the Revolution and died in Germany.

Joseph Bara (1779–93) A boy soldier with the revolutionary army of General Desmarres d'Estimauville, Bara was killed during a skirmish for refusing to hand over two horses to royalist soldiers. **Robespierre** used this incident to turn Bara into an emblem for republican youth, killed for refusing to say 'Long live the King' and dying with 'Long live the Republic' on his lips instead. David started a commemorative painting of the martyr, but it was never completed.

Pompeo Batoni (1708–87) A major figure in the Roman art world, Batoni painted religious and historical subjects before specializing in portraits, particularly of Englishmen on the Grand Tour. He admired David and urged him to establish himself in Rome where his talent would be truly appreciated. At his death he bequeathed David his palette and brushes.

Josephine de Beauharnais, née Tascher de la Pagerie (1763–1814) Attractive and charming, though extravagant and shallow, Josephine was first married to the Vicomte de Beauharnais, who was executed during the Revolution. In March 1796 she married the dashing young general **Napoleon Bonaparte** in a civil ceremony (they were remarried in church in 1804). With Napoleon absent in Italy and the Middle East, she spent lavishly on the house of Malmaison and its decorations. Though crowned empress by Napoleon in 1804, she was unable to provide him with an heir and so he divorced her in December 1809. But he remained very fond of her and made generous financial arrangements on her behalf.

François Boucher (1707–70) The leading **Rococo** artist, Boucher was the most productive and successful artist of his day. After training with François Lemoyne (1688–1737), Boucher won the **Prix de Rome** in 1720 and spent 1727–31 in Italy. Becoming a full Academician in 1734 he was made First Painter to the king in 1765. His later works were decorative and sensual, depicting an idyllic pastoral world and amorous scenes from mythology. Distantly related to David, he refused to take him as a pupil, though he probably exercised some influence over his early style.

André Chénier (1762–94) Born of Greek–French parentage, Chénier was a poet and political writer. An outspoken critic of privilege and champion of democracy and artistic freedom, he probably met David through the **Trudaine** brothers and helped in the artist's political education. Initially enthusiastic for the Revolution, he and David fell out in 1793 when Chénier remained moderate and David became a committed activist. Chénier perished during the **Reign of Terror**, but much of his poetry, including the *Iambes* and *Odes*, was published posthumously.

Charlotte Corday (1768–93) The well-educated daughter of a Norman nobleman, Corday at first welcomed the Revolution but was then shocked at its bloody course, and sided with the moderate **Girondins**. She decided to assassinate **Jean-Paul Marat** to save France from violent extremism. Reaching Paris, she stabbed Marat while he was in the bath and, her virtuous deed done, did not try to escape. She remained calm and composed during her trial and went to the guillotine four days after the murder.

Georges Jacques Danton (1759–94) Trained as a lawyer, Danton entered politics at the Revolution and his energy and determination attracted much support. Elected minister of justice in 1792, he became a leading political figure and member of the **Committee of Public Safety**. However, doubts were raised about his honesty and integrity and he was removed. Fearing that he might emerge as an opponent, the committee had him arrested, tried and sent to the guillotine on 6 April 1794.

Etienne-Jean Delécluze (1781–1863) An artist, writer and critic, Delécluze became David's pupil in 1797 and spent 3–4 years in his studio. Though active as a history painter, little of his work survives. In 1822 he became an art critic for the conservative *Journal des débats* and later wrote about literature and music. His great book on David – *Louis David, son école et son temps* – was published in 1857 and combined warm reminiscences with a solid and sober account, free from political controversy.

Jean-Germain Drouais (1763–88) Coming from a dynasty of portrait painters, Drouais was David's favourite pupil and the two were very close. Exceptionally gifted, he also enjoyed great independence thanks to a large inheritance. After winning the 1784 **Prix de Rome**, Drouais went to Rome with David. Drouais became sullen and rebellious when David returned to France, but his *Marius at Minturnae* (1786) was the first flowering of the Davidian school. Expected even to surpass David, Drouais tragically died of smallpox and his name became associated with youthful talent prematurely extinguished.

François-Xavier Fabre (1766–1837) A history and portrait painter, Fabre became David's pupil in 1783. He developed quickly and was entrusted with the replica of *Belisarius* and won the 1787 **Prix de Rome**. He stayed in Rome until 1793, but fled to Florence because of the anti-French backlash following the execution of **Louis XVI**. He stayed in Florence for over twenty years, mostly painting portraits and entering high society. On his return to France he set up a museum in Montpellier that bears his name.

Jean-Honoré Fragonard (1732–1806) One of the foremost practitioners of the **Rococo**, Fragonard studied under Jean-Siméon Chardin (1699–1779) and **Boucher**, won the 1752 **Prix de Rome** and spent 1756–61 in Italy. At first a history painter, he abandoned it from lack of patronage and financial security and instead devoted himself to paintings of erotic frivolity and gallantry, which were highly successful. However, such subjects became outdated with the advent of **Neoclassicism**, and he fell from favour. Though admired and supported by David in hard times, he died in poverty.

Théodore Géricault (1791–1824) Though a pupil of Carle Vernet (1758–1836) and Pierre-Narcisse Guérin (1774–1833), Géricault was mostly self-taught. One of the new generation of artists dedicated to the depiction of modern life and capturing extremes of emotion, he was a leading figure in the birth of **Romanticism**. He spent ten months in Rome, 1816–17, before returning to Paris to paint *The Raft of the Medusa* (1819), a topical and controversial picture. His self-confessed ambition was 'to shine, to illuminate, to astonish the world', but he died young following a riding accident.

Anne-Louis Girodet (1767–1824) Artist and poet and one of David's most talented pupils. Disqualified from the **Prix de Rome** in 1787 for cheating, Girodet won the competition in 1789. Though starting as a faithful follower of David, Girodet then tried his hardest to produce original and imaginative works free from his master's influence. The results were novel, yet often bizarre. David was outraged when Girodet's *Scene of a Deluge* was placed ahead of his *Intervention of the Sabine Women* in **Napoleon**'s Decennial Prize of 1810. Girodet had an erratic lifestyle, alternating between being a dandy and a secretive recluse.

Jean-Baptiste Greuze (1725–1805) Greuze made his name as a painter of morally uplifting narrative genre scenes such as *The Village Betrothal* (1761), which was praised by Diderot for rendering the simple virtues of a rustic family. Such scenes later influenced David, particularly the closely observed gestures and facial expressions. When Greuze tried to become a history painter, the result was a fiasco and his *Septimius Severus Reproaching Caracalla* of 1769 was harshly criticized by the **Academy**. Thereafter Greuze refused to exhibit at the Salon and came to specialize in heads of tearful young girls.

Antoine-Jean Gros (1771–1835) Gros was one of David's best pupils and remained on good terms with his master. He commemorated a number of **Napoleon**'s noble and heroic deeds in such paintings as *The Plague House at Jaffa* (1804) and *The Battle of Eylau* (1808). When David was exiled to Brussels, Gros worked for his return and kept up a faithful correspondence. Though created a baron in 1824 by the restored monarchy, Gros's work was unpopular and severely criticized. This, coupled with an unhappy marriage, led him to drown himself in a tributary of the Seine.

Phillippe-Auguste Hennequin (1763–1833) A history painter trained in Lyon and then in Paris, Hennequin was for about two years a favoured pupil of David's, before being expelled from the studio in 1782. He spent five years in Rome and during the Revolution was an active **Jacobin** and only just avoided execution. He produced political allegories such as *The Remorse of Orestes* (1800) as well as Napoleonic battle scenes. At **Napoleon**'s defeat he went into exile in Belgium, becoming the director of the Tournai **Academy**. His valuable *Memoirs* were published a century after his death.

Jean-Auguste-Dominique Ingres (1780–1867) Arriving in Paris in 1797, Ingres entered David's studio and won the **Prix de Rome** in 1801. Political instability prevented a Roman trip until 1806, but once in Italy he stayed until 1824. Returning to France, he became the champion of orthodox classicism in the battles against **Romanticism**, with his preference for line over colour and his insistence on accurate borrowings from source material. Though David's pupil, he and his master failed to comprehend fully each other's art.

Antoine-Laurent Lavoisier (1743–94) French chemist and the founder of modern chemistry. From an aristocratic background, he became rich as a tax farmer and from his wealth he built a large laboratory in which he discovered the composition of air and experimented on combustion. A political liberal, he frequented the circle of the **Trudaine** brothers, where he met David. As a tax farmer and Commissioner for Gunpowder, Lavoisier came under suspicion during the Revolution and was executed during the **Reign of Terror**.

Louis Michel Le Pelletier de Saint-Fargeau (1760–94) An aristocrat turned revolutionary and member of the **Convention**, to many Le Pelletier was a turncoat and an opportunist. Having voted for the death of the king, Le Pelletier was assassinated on the eve of the king's execution while eating dinner in a restaurant. Given a splendid state funeral, Le Pelletier was celebrated as a republican martyr and commemorated in a painting by David. This work has not survived as Le Pelletier's daughter grew up to be an ardent royalist, bought the picture and had it burnt.

Louis XVI (1754–93) King of France 1774–93, Louis was a well-intentioned but weak and misguided ruler who failed to enact the reforms necessary to prevent power being seized from him. Though hard working, he found state business onerous, preferring hunting and scientific engineering. During the Revolution he was unwilling to work within the constitution and his attempted flight with the royal family to Brussels, which was halted at Varennes, meant that he was considered a traitor. In December 1792 he was put on trial, found guilty and sent to the guillotine on 21 January 1793.

Jean-Paul Marat (1743–93) A journalist and radical politician, Marat initially practised as a physician in England and then in France, where he craved admission into the Academy of Science, but was consistently rebuffed. At the Revolution he founded the newspaper *L'Ami du peuple* (*The Friend of the People*) and wrote virulent denunciations and inflammatory prose. Eventually elected a deputy at the **Convention**, Marat helped to instigate the **Reign of Terror**. Already gravely ill, Marat was stabbed in his bath by **Charlotte Corday** on 13 July 1793. He quickly became a revolutionary martyr and is the subject of David's most forceful painting.

Marie Antoinette (1755–93) Daughter of the Habsburg empress Maria Theresa, Marie became the wife of the future king **Louis XVI** at the age of fifteen. As queen, from 1774, she was spendthrift and headstrong, and her extravagances generated much malicious gossip. As her unpopularity grew, she was accused of adultery and lesbianism and for many was the epitome of decadent self-indulgence. The target of popular hatred during the Revolution, she was tried and found guilty of treason and conspiracy in 1793. She met her end at the guillotine with great composure on 16 October 1793.

Napoleon Bonaparte (1769–1821) Son of a Corsican noble and a soldier by profession, Napoleon gained rapid promotion in the aftermath of the Revolution, and as General of the Army of Italy gained a series of brilliant victories. He broke off his Middle Eastern campaign to stage the Brumaire coup of 1799, whereby he became First Consul. Enjoying huge popular support, Napoleon became increasingly repressive and dictatorial, and was made emperor in 1804. Continuing warfare brought defeat, abdication and exile to Elba in 1814. He escaped and mounted the 'Hundred Days' campaign that ended at Waterloo in June 1815. He was finally exiled to St Helena where he died of stomach cancer.

Pierre Peyron (1744–1814) A history painter and pupil of Louis Lagrenée (1724–1805), Peyron beat David in the 1773 **Prix de Rome**. Considered the best talent of his generation and supported by **d'Angiviller**, Peyron spent seven years (1775–82) at the French **Academy** in Rome. While Peyron was in Rome, David's career in Paris blossomed and at the Salons of 1785 and 1787 David totally eclipsed his rival and thereafter condemned Peyron to a minor role in French painting. At his funeral David paid tribute to Peyron by saying: 'He opened my eyes.'

Jean-Baptiste Pierre (1714–89) Artist and administrator who trained under Charles-Joseph Natoire (1700–77), won the **Prix de Rome** in 1734 and was admitted to the **Academy** in 1742. Becoming the king's First Painter and director of the Academy in 1770, he virtually gave up painting and then exercised a considerable influence on art during the reign of **Louis XVI**. Pierre's arrogant and autocratic manner and his condescension towards socially inferior fellow artists made him unpopular and feared. He and David had an extreme dislike of one another.

Count Stanislas Potocki (1755–1821) Polish nobleman, collector and connoisseur, Potocki's scholarship and love of antiquity led to him being called 'The Polish **Winckelmann**'. He made the Grand Tour in 1779–80 and met David in Rome, where he commissioned his equestrian portrait (1781). Potocki greatly appreciated David's art and wrote very favourably about it in a critique of the 1787 Salon. Back in Poland, Potocki pursued a political career and held a number of offices; as minister of education he helped found Warsaw University.

Jean-Baptiste Regnault (1754–1829) Regnault was a history painter and one of David's chief rivals. A precocious draughtsman, his early life was adventurous – he was a cabin boy for five years before returning to Paris to study art. He won the **Prix de Rome** in 1775 and was admitted to the **Academy** in 1783. Later a member of the **Institute**, Regnault was also responsible for the training of many students. His elegant and refined mythological paintings contrasted with the austere masculinity of much of David's work.

Maximilien Robespierre (1758–94) A dominant figure in the **Convention** and the **Jacobin Club**, Robespierre also helped to instigate the violent cleansing of the **Reign of Terror**. A lawyer and supporter of the ideals of the Enlightenment, Robespierre was a founder member of the **National Assembly**, becoming its president in 1790. Nicknamed 'The Incorruptible' because of his high sense of moral duty and refusal to compromise with royalty, his dynamic personality attracted many followers, including David. But the tide turned against him and he was overthrown on 9 Thermidor, Year II (27 July 1794) and went to the guillotine the following day.

Georges Rouget (1783–1869) A history painter, for ten years Rouget was David's principal assistant on works such as *The Coronation of the Emperor and Empress*, *The Distribution of the Eagle Standards* and *Leonidas at Thermopylae*. An excellent draughtsman and technician, Rouget was referred to as 'my right arm' by David, but his almost filial devotion to his master meant that his own career suffered and he had trouble in establishing an independent artistic personality. When David called him to Brussels in 1822 to work on the replica of the *Coronation*, Rouget went without hesitation.

Abbé Emmanuel-Joseph Sieyès (1748–1836) A radical clergyman and author of the influential pamphlet *What is the Third Estate?*, Sieyès took part in the Oath of the Tennis Court and was a deputy at the **Convention**. He helped **Napoleon** stage the Brumaire coup in 1799 but then retired from politics. At the Restoration he went to Brussels and had his portrait painted by David. He returned to France after the 1830 Revolution.

Charles-Louis Trudaine de Montigny (1765–94) and **Charles-Michel Trudaine de la Sablière** (1766–94) Sons of a wealthy financier, the two brothers held important gatherings of the liberal and intellectual élite at their grand town house in the Place Royale, Paris. Both David and **André Chénier** attended and the 'Trudaine Society' helped to shape David's opinions. The younger brother, Charles-Michel, an enthusiastic Greek scholar, commissioned *The Death of Socrates* (1787) from David. Though no great royalists, they were both executed during the **Reign of Terror**.

John Trumbull (1756–1843) American artist, diplomat and patriot. Largely self-taught, Trumbull was the first college graduate in America to become a professional artist. In the War of Independence he served as George Washington's aide-de-camp and on resuming painting he specialized in battle scenes from the war. In 1817 he was commissioned by the United States government to paint four scenes from the Revolutionary War for the Rotunda of the US Capitol. The most famous of these is *The Declaration of Independence*. He met David on several occasions and called him 'my warm and efficient friend'.

Joseph-Marie Vien (1716–1806) A history painter, Vien was one of the first French artists to take a serious interest in antiquity; many of his students went on to become major artists of their day. Vien enjoyed much official recognition and was director of the French **Academy** in Rome and First Painter to the king. David was one of his pupils, and although disagreeing about the Revolution, he and Vien remained on close terms. Under **Napoleon** he was made a senator and a count and was awarded the Legion of Honour. On Vien's death David proclaimed: 'Our father has ceased to live.'

Elisabeth-Louise Vigée-Lebrun (1755–1842) The foremost woman artist in pre-revolutionary France, Vigée-Lebrun specialized in sympathetic portraits, particularly of aristocratic female sitters. A socialite, courtier and favourite of **Marie Antoinette**, she married the picture dealer Jean-Baptiste Lebrun in 1776 and became an Academician in 1783. During the Revolution she lived in exile in Florence, Rome and St Petersburg, before returning to France in 1802. Though initially friendly with David, they fell out at the Revolution, although they maintained a mutual professional admiration. In her old age she composed her interesting *Memoirs*.

François-André Vincent (1746–1816) A pupil of **Vien**'s, Vincent was one of David's chief rivals in Paris. After winning the 1768 **Prix de Rome**, he was in Italy from 1771 to 1775. He became an Academician in 1777 and thereafter regularly exhibited at the Paris Salon. At the Revolution he was a royalist, causing further tensions with David. A founding member of the **Institute**, in his later years Vincent painted less because of ill health, but still received official recognition. Like David, he operated a large teaching studio.

Johann Joachim Winckelmann (1717–68) German archaeologist, antiquarian and art theorist. The most important eighteenth-century advocate of a return to antique-inspired art, his writings were highly influential in the birth of **Neoclassicism**. He established his reputation with *Thoughts on the Imitation of Greek Works in Painting and Sculpture* (1755) and later wrote *The History of Ancient Art* (1764). Winkelmann placed ancient Greek sculpture above everything else, although his experience of it was mostly through Roman copies. Travelling back to Rome from Vienna, he was murdered by a petty thief.

Key Dates

Numbers in square brackets refer to illustrations

The Life and Art of Jacques-Louis David

1748 Jacques-Louis David born in Paris, 30 August

1757 David's father, Louis-Maurice, dies following a pistol duel

1758–64 Attends boarding school and the Collège des Quatre Nations in Paris

1765 Enters the studio of Joseph-Marie Vien

1766 Enrols as a student at the Royal Academy of Painting and Sculpture

1770 Competes in the Prix de Rome for the first time. Eliminated before the final stages

1771 Comes second in the Prix de Rome with *The Combat of Mars and Minerva* [13]. Joseph-Benoît Suvée wins first prize

1772 Victim of conspiracy that denies him the Prix de Rome for *Apollo and Diana Attacking Niobe and her Children* [16]. Half-hearted suicide attempt

1773 Defeated in the Prix de Rome by Pierre Peyron. Competition painting is *The Death of Seneca* [19]. Wins Academy prize for Expressive Head with *Sorrow* [20]

A Context of Events

1748 Discovery of ruins of Pompeii. Britain: Samuel Richardson, *Clarissa*

1751 First volume of the *Encyclopédie* published [4]

1755 Britain: Samuel Johnson, *Dictionary of the English Language*

1756–63 Seven Years' War between Britain, Prussia and Hanover on one side and France, Austria, Russia, Saxony, Sweden and Spain on the other

1757 Britain: Edmund Burke, *A Philosophical Inquiry into the Origin of Our Ideas of the Sublime and Beautiful*

1760 Britain: Accession of George III

1762 Jean-Jacques Rousseau, *The Social Contract*

1763 Treaty of Paris ends Seven Years' War and confirms Britain as the major world power

1764 Johann Joachim Winckelmann, *The History of Ancient Art*

1765 François Boucher becomes director of the Academy and painter to King Louis XV

1766 Execution of the Baron de Tollendal

1767 Jean François Marmontel, *Belisarius*

1768 Britain: Foundation of the Royal Academy of Arts in London. Sir Joshua Reynolds elected first president

1770 Captain James Cook charts the east coast of Australia and claims it for Britain

1773 America: The Boston Tea Party. Britain: Sir Joshua Reynolds, *Three Ladies Adorning a Term of Hymen*

	The Life and Art of Jacques-Louis David	A Context of Events
1774	Finally wins Prix de Rome with *Antiochus and Stratonice* [22]. Living with his godfather Sedaine in the Louvre	**1774** Death of Louis XV and accession of Louis XVI
1775	Travels to Rome with Vien to take up his place at the French Academy in the city	**1775** America: Start of War of Independence against the British (to 1783)
1776–7	Pursues his studies of the antique and Old Masters in Rome	**1776** USA: Declaration of Independence **1777** Britain: Richard Brinsley Sheridan, *School for Scandal*
1778	Exhibits *The Funeral of Patroclus* [33] at the French Academy in Rome	**1778** Deaths of Voltaire and Rousseau. Houdon, *Bust of Benjamin Franklin*
1779	Visits Naples with the sculptor Suzanne	
1780	Completes and exhibits first independent commission, *St Roch* [39]. Begins work on Potocki portrait [41]. Returns to Paris in the autumn and takes studio in the Hôtel de Ville	
1781	Made an Associate member (*agrée*) of the Academy and exhibits about a dozen works at the Salon. *Belisarius Receiving Alms* [45] is a spectacular success. Visits Flanders	**1781** Immanuel Kant, *Critique of Pure Reason*. Britain: Henry Fuseli, *The Nightmare*
1782	16 May: Marries Marguerite-Charlotte Pécoul	
1783	15 February: Birth of son, Charles-Louis-Jules. Made a full Academician (*reçu*) for *Andromache Mourning Hector* [43]	**1783** Under the Treaty of Paris, Britain recognizes the independence of America. Britain: Copley, *The Death of Major Peirson*
1784	27 April: Birth of second son, Eugène. September 17: Accompanied by his wife and Drouais, leaves for Rome to work on a royal commission, *The Oath of the Horatii* [62]	**1784** Pierre Augustin Caron de Beaumarchais, *The Marriage of Figaro*. 31 July: Death of Diderot
1785	The *Horatii* shown to great acclaim in Rome and Paris	**1785** USA: Thomas Jefferson, The State Capitol, Richmond, Virginia
1786	Working on *The Death of Socrates* [66] for Charles-Michel Trudaine. 26 October: Birth of twin daughters, Emilie and Pauline	**1786** Jean-Germain Drouais, *Marius at Minturnae* [65]. Britain: Robert Burns, *Poems, Chiefly in the Scottish Dialect*
1787	Exhibits *The Death of Socrates* at the Salon. Supported by the Marquis de Bièvre in his (unsuccessful) attempt to become director of the French Academy in Rome. Mixing with liberal intellectuals and court society	**1787** Italy: Antonio Canova, Tomb of Clement XIV for Church of Santi Apostoli in Rome. Britain: William Beckford, *Vathek*
1788	Paints portrait of Lavoisier and his wife [82]	**1788** Death of Drouais in Rome
1789	Exhibits *The Lictors Returning to Brutus the Bodies of his Sons* [77] and *The Loves of Paris and Helen* [74] at the Salon. Lavoisier portrait suppressed. Joins dissidents pressing for reform in the Academy	**1789** Sieyès, *What is the Third Estate?* [71]. 20 June: Oath of the Tennis Court sworn at Versailles. 14 July: Storming of the Bastille. July–August: The 'Great Fear'. 26 August: *Declaration of the Rights of Man and Citizen*. George Washington becomes the first president of the United States
1790	Continues to agitate against the Academy. Visits Nantes for commission that never materializes. *Oath of Tennis Court* project begun [86–90]. 14 July: Contributes to Festival of Federation. Joins the Jacobin Club	**1790** Suppression of most religious orders. Revival of Voltaire's play *Brutus* (written in 1730). Britain: Edmund Burke, *Reflections on the Revolution in France*

	The Life and Art of Jacques-Louis David	A Context of Events
1791	Exhibits finished drawing of *The Oath of the Tennis Court* at the Salon [86]. 11 July: collaborates in the Procession for the Transfer of Voltaire's Ashes to the Pantheon. *Tennis Court* project abandoned	**1791** 20–25 June: Flight of Louis XVI to Varennes. Alexandre Lenoir opens the Museum of French Monuments to preserve medieval architecture and sculpture from revolutionary vandalism. André Chénier, 'The Tennis Court'. Britain: Thomas Paine, *The Rights of Man* (completed 1792). Austria: Death of Mozart
1792	Executes drawings of Louis XVI and the dauphin [95]. Organizes festival for the Swiss soldiers of Châteauvieux. July: Appointed an Associate Professor at the Academy. September: Elected deputy for Paris at the National Convention. Sits with the Mountain faction. December: Elected to the Committee of Public Instruction	**1792** France at war with Austria and Prussia. 21 September: Abolition of the monarchy. Rouget de Lisle, *La Marseillaise*
1793	17 January: Votes for the death of Louis XVI. Exhibits memorial painting of Le Pelletier de Saint-Fargeau at the Salon. April: Resigns from the Academy. June–July: Made president of the Jacobin Club. Begins work on *Marat Breathing his Last* [110]. 8 August: Makes speech at the Convention demanding the suppression of the academies. His motion is adopted and all academies are closed. 10 August: Organizes the Festival of Unity and Indivisibility. 14 September: Becomes member of the Committee of General Security. 7–8 October: Assists at the interrogation of the dauphin. 16 October: Sketches Marie Antoinette on the way to the guillotine [116]. *Marat* and *Le Pelletier* paintings exhibited at Louvre. 30 December: Organizes the Festival of the Capture of Toulon	**1793** France declares war on Britain, Spain and Holland. Conscription introduced. 10 August: Louvre opened as a public museum. June: Reign of Terror begins. July: Death of Jean-Paul Marat. October: Revolutionary calendar introduced
1794	January: Serves one month as president of the National Convention. 18 March: Divorced from his wife. 8 June: Organizes the Festival of the Supreme Being. 27 July: Absent, claiming illness, at the arrest of Robespierre at National Convention. 2 August–28 December: Imprisoned first at the Hôtel des Fermes Générales then in the Luxembourg Palace. Paints *Self-Portrait* [122]. Released from prison. Paints the Sériziat family [127, 128]	**1794** 26 July: André Chénier sent to the guillotine. 28 July: Execution of Robespierre and his followers. Britain: William Blake, *Songs of Experience*
1795	28 May: Re-arrested and imprisoned at the Collège des Quatre Nations until released due to ill-health on 3 August. Paroled and receives a final amnesty on 26 October. Paints portraits of Jacobus Blauw [129] and Gaspar Mayer [130]. 20 November: Becomes a member of the Institute	**1795** France signs peace treaties with Prussia, Holland and Spain
1796	12 November: Re-marries his former wife	
1797	Works on *The Intervention of the Sabine Women* [131]. Meets Napoleon and is granted a single portrait sitting [142]	**1797** Treaty of Campo Formio confirms peace between France and Austria
1798	Declines to accompany Napoleon to Egypt. Contemplates resumption of the *Oath of the Tennis Court* project, but then finally abandons it	**1798** Napoleon victorious at the Battle of the Pyramids. Britain: Samuel Taylor Coleridge, *The Rime of the Ancient Mariner*

	The Life and Art of Jacques-Louis David	A Context of Events
1799	21 December: Opening of the *Sabine Women* exhibition. Entrance fee of 1 franc 80 centimes	**1799** 9–10 November: Napoleon stages the coup of 18–19 Brumaire and becomes First Consul. War declared on Austria
1800	Offered, but refuses post of Painter to the Government. Begins *Portrait of Juliette Récamier* [146]	**1800** 14 June: Napoleon defeats the Austrians in the Battle of Marengo
1801	*Bonaparte Crossing the St Bernard Pass* [144] completed. 30 October: Purchases country property of Marcoussis at Ozouer-le-Voulgis [139]	**1801** Peace of Lunéville with Austria. Napoleon agrees Concordat with Pope Pius VII for the return of Catholicism to France
1802	Paints *Portrait of Cooper Penrose* [148]. Working on *Leonidas at Thermopylae* [177]	**1802** Napoleon made Consul for life. Peace of Amiens ends war with Britain
1803	18 December: Named Knight of the Legion of Honour	**1803** Renewal of war with Britain
1804	16 July: Receives Legion of Honour. 2 December: Appointed First Painter to the emperor, commissioned to paint *The Coronation of the Emperor and Empress* [152]	**1804** Antoine-Jean Gros, *The Plague House at Jaffa*. 4 December: Coronation of Napoleon as emperor
1805	Preparatory work for the *Coronation* [151–7]. Paints Nelson at the Battle of Trafalgar (21 October) and *Portrait of Pope Pius VII* [165]	**1805** War against Austria and Russia brought to an end with the French victory at the Battle of Austerlitz (2 December)
1806	Assisted by Rouget, working on *The Coronation* in a new studio in the deconsecrated Cluny church. Three other Napoleonic works commissioned – *The Distribution of the Eagle Standards* [167], *The Enthronement* and *The Arrival at the Hôtel de Ville* [168]. July: Napoleon refuses to accept the *Portrait in Coronation Robes*	**1806** Prussia enters war against France but is defeated in the battles of Jena and Auerstadt (14 October). Anne-Louis Girodet, *Scene of a Deluge* [174]. Jean-Auguste-Dominique Ingres, *Napoleon on the Imperial Throne*
1807	October/November: Completion of *The Coronation of the Emperor and Empress*	**1807** 8 February: Napoleon defeats Russians and Prussians at Battle of Eylau. Peace made with Treaties of Tilsit (8 July). France invades Spain and Portugal
1808	4 January: Napoleon sees the *Coronation* in his studio. 10 September: Granted a hereditary title and a coat of arms [164]. The *Coronation* is shown at the Salon. 22 October: Promoted to Officer of the Legion of Honour	**1808** Gros, *Napoleon at the Battle of Eylau*. Beethoven, *Fifth Symphony*. 6 June: Joseph Bonaparte installed as King of Spain
1809	Working on *The Distribution of the Eagle Standards*. Paints *Sappho and Phaon* [173] for Prince Yusupov	**1809** Wellington begins his peninsular campaign against the French. December: Napoleon divorces Josephine
1810	Disappointed that the *Sabines* fails to win the Decennial Prize for History Painting, although the *Coronation* is deemed best National Subject of the decade. 5 November: Exhibition of the *Eagle Standards* at Salon	**1810** 2 April: Marriage of Napoleon and Marie Louise of Austria
1811	Resumption of work on *Leonidas at Thermopylae*	**1811** Birth of a son to Napoleon. Britain: George III declared insane, his son, the Prince of Wales, declared Regent
1812	Paints *Napoleon in his Study* [140] for Alexander Douglas	**1812** Napoleon invades Russia but is forced to retreat after disastrous defeats. Théodore Géricault, *An Officer of Chasseurs Commanding a Charge* [180]

	The Life and Art of Jacques-Louis David	A Context of Events
1813	Continuation of *Leonidas at Thermopylae* with assistance of Rouget	**1813** Coalition of allies (Britain, Russia, Prussia, Austria and Sweden) against Napoleon. Napoleon defeated at the Battle of Leipzig (16–19 October)
1814	Completes *Leonidas at Thermopylae* which is shown in his studio rather than at the Salon	**1814** 31 March: Allies enter Paris. 11 April: Abdication of Napoleon and first restoration of Louis XVIII. Géricault, *The Wounded Cuirassier* [181]. Ingres, *La Grande Odalisque* [199]
1815	6 April: Visited by Napoleon for the last time and made a Commandant of the Legion of Honour. May: Signs *Addendum to the Constitution of the Empire*. July–August: Travels to eastern France and Switzerland with his servant Geoffroy	**1815** 20 March: Napoleon returns from Elba and mounts 'Hundred Days' campaign. 18 June: Napoleon defeated by Wellington at Waterloo. 22 June: Napoleon abdicates. July: Second restoration of Louis XVIII. August: Napoleon banished to St Helena
1816	Complies with law banishing all regicides. He and his wife go into exile in Brussels, arriving on 27 January. Paints portraits of *General Gérard* [185] and *Comtesse Vilain XIIII and her Daughter* [186]. May–June: Refuses offer to become Prussian minister of arts and director of the Academy	**1816** Italy: Rossini, *The Barber of Seville*. Britain: Jane Austen, *Emma*
1817	Paints *Portrait of Emmanuel-Joseph Sieyès* [187] and *Cupid and Psyche* [189]	
1818	Paints *The Farewell of Telemachus and Eucharis* [191]	**1818** Britain: Byron, *Don Juan*. Mary Wollstonecraft Shelley, *Frankenstein*
1819	Paints *The Anger of Achilles at the Sacrifice of Iphigenia* [192]. The *Sabines* and *Leonidas* are sold to the French government	**1819** Géricault, *The Raft of the Medusa*. Britain: John Keats, *Ode to a Nightingale*
1820	Visited by Géricault and Vernet. In poor health	**1820** Britain: Death of George III and accession of George IV. Spain: Francisco Goya begins his 'Black Paintings' [194]
1821	Paints *Portrait of Charlotte and Zénaïde Bonaparte* [188]. Visited by Gros	**1821** 5 May: Death of Napoleon on St Helena. Britain: John Constable, *The Haywain* [201]
1822	Completion of replica of the *Coronation* [195]. Majority of work done by Rouget	**1822** Eugène Delacroix, *The Barque of Dante*
1823	Begins work on *Mars Disarmed by Venus and the Three Graces* [197, 198]	
1824	February: Knocked down by a carriage returning from the theatre. Completes *Mars* painting. Shown first in Brussels and then as the centrepiece of a large exhibition in Paris. Entrance fee is 2 francs	**1824** Death of Louis XVIII and accession of Charles X (the former Count d'Artois). Delacroix, *Scenes from the Massacres at Chios* [200]. Constable's *Haywain* shown at the Salon
1825	Gravely ill with heart disease. Refuses to consider negotiations for a return to France. 21 November: Writes his will. Dies at 10 am on 29 December	**1825** Britain: Opening of the world's first effective railway from Stockton to Darlington
1826	January: State funeral in Brussels. French government refuses family request that he be buried in Paris. 9 May: Death of Madame David. 11 October: His remains are placed in a specially constructed memorial at the Saint-Josse-ten-Noode cemetery, Brussels	**1826** Britain: Death of John Flaxman

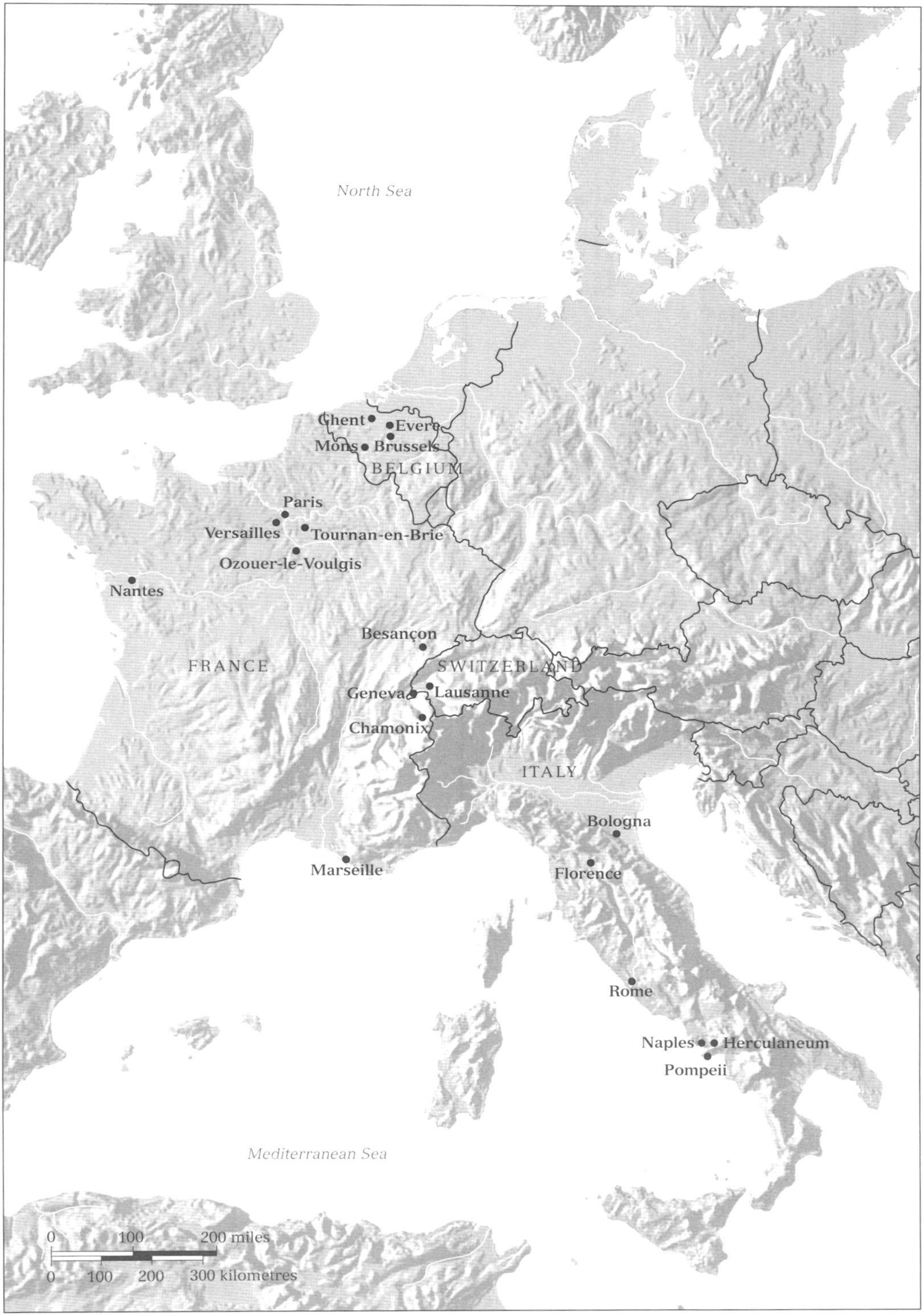
North Sea
Ghent
Evere
Mons
Brussels
BELGIUM
Paris
Versailles
Tournan-en-Brie
Ozouer-le-Voulgis
Nantes
Besançon
FRANCE
SWITZERLAND
Geneva
Lausanne
Chamonix
ITALY
Bologna
Marseille
Florence
Rome
Naples
Herculaneum
Pompeii
Mediterranean Sea
0
100
200 miles
0
100
200
300 kilometres

Further Reading

Some works covering the whole of David's career are listed only in the General section. Specialized sources on particular topics appear under the relevant chapter. Exhibition catalogues should also be consulted for entries on individual paintings.

General

The Age of Neo-Classicism (exh. cat., Royal Academy and Victoria & Albert Museum, London, 1972)

Anon, *Notice sur la vie et les ouvrages de M. J L David* (Brussels, 1824) [written with information provided by David to accompany the exhibition of his works in Paris]

Philippe Bordes, *Le Serment du Jeu de Paume de Jacques-Louis David. Le peintre, son milieu et son temps de 1789 a 1792* (Paris, 1983)

Anita Brookner, *Jacques-Louis David* (London, 1980)

Publicola Chaussard, *Le Pausanias Français. Etat des arts du dessin en France a l'ouverture du XIX siècle* (Paris, 1806)

P A Coupin, *Essai sur J-L David, peintre d'histoire, ancien membre de l'Institut, officier de la Légion d'honneur* (Paris, 1827)

Matthew Craske, *Art in Europe 1700–1830* (Oxford, 1997)

Thomas E Crow, *Painters and Public Life in Eighteenth-Century Paris* (New Haven and London, 1985, repr. 1987)

David (exh. cat., Musée du Louvre and Château de Versailles, Paris, 1989–90)

David contre David (The texts of 44 papers presented by an international panel of scholars at the David colloquium in the Louvre Auditorium, 6–10 December 1989), 2 vols (Paris, 1993)

Jules Louis David, *Le Peintre Louis David 1748-1825, I Souvenirs et documents inédits; II Suite d'eaux fortes d'après des oeuvres gravées par J L Jules David, son petit-fils*, 2 vols (Paris, 1880–2)

Etienne-Jules Delécluze, *Louis David, son école et son temps. Souvenirs* (Paris, 1855, reissued with introduction and notes by J P Mouilleseaux, Paris, 1983)

David Dowd, *Pageant Master of the Republic. Jacques-Louis David and the French Revolution* (Lincoln, Nebraska, 1948)

Louis Hautecoeur, *Louis David* (Paris, 1954)

Hugh Honour, *Neo-classicism* (Harmondsworth, 1977, repr. 1996)

Donna Hunter, *Second Nature: Portraits by J-L David (1769–1792)* (PhD dissertation, Harvard University, 1988)

David Irwin, *Neoclassicism* (London, 1997)

Dorothy Johnson, *Jacques-Louis David: Art in Metamorphosis* (Princeton, 1993)

Alexandre Lenoir, 'David. Souvenirs historiques', *Journal de l'Institut historique*, 3 (1835), pp.1–13

Miette de Villars, *Mémoires de David, peintre et député à la Convention* (Paris, 1850)

William Olander, *Pour transmettre à la posterité. French Painting and Revolution 1774–1795* (Ann Arbor, 1984)

Warren Roberts, *Jacques-Louis David, Revolutionary Artist: Art, Politics and the French Revolution* (Chapel Hill and London, 1989)

Robert Rosenblum, 'Reconstructing David', *Art in America* (May 1990), pp.188–97 and p.257

Marie-Catherine Sahut and Régis Michel, *David l'art et le politique* (Paris, 1988)

Antoine Schnapper, *David* (New York, 1982)

Arlette Sérullaz, *Inventaire Général des Dessins. École Française. Dessins de Jacques-Louis David, 1748–1825* (Paris, 1991)

A Th [probably Antoine Thibaudeau], *Vie de David, Premier Peintre de Napoléon* (Brussels and Paris, 1826)

Tradition and Revolution in French Art 1700–1880 (exh. cat., National Gallery, London, 1993)

Daniel and Georges Wildenstein, *Documents complementaires au catalogue de l'oeuvre de Louis David* (Paris, 1973)

Chapter 1

Sylvain Bédard, *Une académie peinte de Jacques-Louis David. Le Saint Jérôme de Québec. Etude stylistique et historique du tableau* (MA dissertation University of Montreal, 1991)

C B A Behrens, *The Ancien Régime* (London, 1967, repr. 1989)

Jacques de Caso, 'Jacques-Louis David and the style *all'antica*', *Burlington Magazine* (October 1972), pp.686–90

David a Roma (exh. cat., French Academy in Rome, 1981–2), pp.29–113

Thomas Gaehtgens, 'David et son maître Vien', in *David contre David*, op. cit., vol. 1, pp.19–34

T W Gaehtgens and J Lugand, *Joseph-Marie Vien, Peintre du Roi (1716–1809)* (Paris, 1988)

Seymour Howard, *Sacrifice of the Hero: The Roman Years. A Classical Frieze by Jacques-Louis David* (Sacramento, 1975)

Barthélemy Jobert, 'The "Travaux d'encouragement": an aspect of official arts policy in France under Louis XVI', *Oxford Art Journal*, 10:1 (1987), pp.3–14

Simon Lee, *Jacques-Louis David and the Prix de Rome* (PhD dissertation, University of Reading, 1984)

Pierre Rosenberg, 'Fragonard et David', in *David contre David*, op. cit., vol. 1, pp.5–16

Robert Rosenblum, 'David's Funeral of Patroclus', *Burlington Magazine* (September 1977), pp.567–76

Arlette Sérullaz, 'La Jeunesse', in *David*, op. cit., pp.37–41

—, 'Le séjour à Rome', in *David*, op. cit., pp.59–64

Chapter 2

Colin Bailey, 'Les clients de David avant la Révolution', in *David contre David*, op. cit., vol. 1, pp.141–64

Albert Boime, 'Marmontel's *Bélisaire* and the Pre-Revolutionary Progressivism of David', *Art History*, 3 (March 1980), pp.81–101

—, 'Les Themes du Serment: David et la franc-maconnerie', in *David contre David*, op. cit., vol. 1, pp.259–91

Philippe Bordes, 'Dessins perdus de David, dont un pour la Mort de Socrate, lithographiés de Debret', *Bulletin de la Societé de l'Histoire de l'Art Français* (1979), pp.179–84

—, 'Jacques-Louis David's anglophilia on the eve of the French Revolution', *Burlington Magazine* (August 1992), pp.482–90

Thomas Crow, *Painters and Public Life in Eighteenth-Century Paris*, op. cit., chapters 6 and 7

—, *Emulation: Making Artists for Revolutionary France* (New Haven and London, 1995), pp.5–102

Leopold Ettlinger, 'Jacques-Louis David and Roman Virtue', *Journal of the Royal Society of Arts* (1967), pp.105–23

Michael Fried, *Absorption and Theatricality. Painting and Beholder in the Age of Diderot* (Berkeley and London, 1980, repr. Chicago, 1988), pp.145–60

Felicité de Genlis, *Memoirs of the Countess de Genlis, illustrative of the history of the eighteenth and nineteenth centuries* (London, 1825)

Francis Hamilton Hazlehurst, 'The artistic evolution of David's *Oath*', *Art Bulletin* (March 1960), pp.60–3

Philippe Auguste Hennequin (ed. Jenny Hennequin), *Un peintre sous la révolution et le premier Empire* (Paris, 1933)

Simon Lee, 'Jean-Germain Drouais and the 1784 Prix de Rome', *Burlington Magazine* (May 1988), pp.361–65

Alexandre Péron, 'Examen fait par M. Alexandre Péron, du tableau du Serment des Horaces, peint par David; suivi d'un notice historique sur ce tableau', *Annales de la Société libre des Beaux-Arts*, 9 (1839–40), pp.231–91

Pierre Rosenberg and Udolpho Van de Sandt, *Pierre Peyron 1744–1814* (Neuilly, 1983)

Robert Rosenblum, 'A Source for David's *Horatii*', *Burlington Magazine* (May 1970), pp.269–73

Antoine Schnapper, 'De Bélisaire à Brutus', in *David*, op. cit., pp.113–23

Jean Silvestre de Sacy, *Le Comte d'Angiviller, dernier Directeur Général des Bâtiments du Roi* (Paris, 1953)

Donald Wisner, 'Jacques-Louis David and André Chénier: *The Death of Socrates, The Tennis Court Oath* and the quest for artistic liberty', *Proceedings of The Consortium on Revolutionary Europe, 1750–1850* (Athens, Georgia, 1986)

Chapter 3

David Bindman, *The Shadow of the Guillotine* (exh. cat., British Museum, London, 1989)

T C W Blanning, *The French Revolution; Aristocrat versus Bourgeois?* (Basingstoke, 1987)

Albert Boime, 'Jacques-Louis David, Scatological Discourse in the French Revolution and the Art of Caricature', in *French Caricature and the French Revolution 1789–1799* (exh. cat., Grunwald Center for the Graphic Arts, Los Angeles, 1989), pp.67–82

Philippe Bordes, 'Jacques-Louis David's "Serment du Jeu de Paume", Propaganda without a cause?', *Oxford Art Journal* (October 1980), pp.19–25

—, *Le Serment du Jeu de Paume de Jacques-Louis David. Le peintre, son milieu et son temps de 1789 à 1792* (Paris, 1983)

—, 'L'Art et le Politique', in Régis Michel and Philippe Bordes (eds), *Aux Armes et Aux Arts! Les Arts de la Révolution 1789–1799* (Paris, 1988)

Timothy J Clark, 'Painting in the Year Two', *Representations*, 47 (Summer 1994), pp.13–63

Claude Cosneau, 'Un grand projet de J-L David (1789–1790). L'Art et la Révolution à Nantes', *Revue du Louvre*, 38:4 (1983), pp.255–63

Thomas Crow, *Emulation: Making Artists for Revolutionary France*, op.cit., pp.117–88

David Dowd, *Pageant Master of the Republic. Jacques-Louis David and the French Revolution*, op. cit.

—, 'Les Vernet et les chevaux: un manuscrit inédit de David trouvé dans les registres du Comité du Sûreté Générale', *Bulletin de la Société de l'Histoire de l'Art Français* (1953), pp.64–9

Ian Germani, *Jean-Paul Marat: Hero and Anti-hero of the French Revolution* (Lewiston, NY and Lampeter, PA, 1992)

Stefan Germer and Hubertus Kohle, 'From the theatrical to the aesthetic hero: on the privatization of the idea of virtue in David's *Brutus* and *Sabines*', *Art History*, 9:2 (June 1986), pp.168–84

Tom Gretton, 'Representing the Revolution', *History Today*, 39 (May 1989), pp.39–44

Robert Herbert, *David, Brutus and the French Revolution: an essay in art and politics* (London, 1972)

Klaus Herding, 'Utopie concrète à l'échelle mondiale: L'Art de la Révolution', in *La Révolution Française et l'Europe* (exh. cat., Grand Palais, Paris, 1989), pp.21–50

Lynn Hunt, *Politics, Culture and Class in the French Revolution* (Berkeley and London, 1984, repr. London, 1986)

Donna Hunter, *Second Nature: Portraits by J-L David (1769–1792)*, op. cit., pp.323–52

Wolfgang Kemp, 'The Theater of the Revolution: A new interpretation of Jacques-Louis David's *Tennis Court Oath*', in N Bryson, M A Holly and K Moxey (eds), *Visual Culture. Images and Interpretations* (Hannover, ND and London, 1994)

Yvonne Korshak, '*Paris and Helen* by Jacques-Louis David: Choice and Judgement on the Eve of the French Revolution', *Art Bulletin*, 69 (March 1987), pp.102–16

Yvonne Korshak and Francis Dowley, 'Discussion. An Exchange on Jacques-Louis David's *Paris and Helen*', *Art Bulletin*, 70 (September 1988), pp.504–20

Simon Lee, 'Artists and the Guillotine', *Apollo* (July 1989), pp.14–18

Virginia Lee, 'Jacques-Louis David: The Versailles Sketchbook', *Burlington Magazine* (April and June 1969), pp.197–208 and pp.360–9

Régis Michel, 'L'Art des Salons', in Régis Michel and Philippe Bordes (eds), *Aux Armes et Aux Arts! Les Arts de la Révolution 1789–1799*, op. cit.

Jean-Rémy Mantion, 'David en toutes lettres', in *David contre David*, op. cit., vol. 2, pp.805–25

La Mort de Bara. De L'évènement au mythe. Autour du tableau de Jacques-Louis David (exh. cat., Musée Calvet, Avignon, 1989), contributions by M-P Foissy-Aufrère, J-C Martin, R Michel, E Pommier and M Vovelle

William Olander, *Pour transmettre à la posterité. French Painting and Revolution 1774–1795*, op. cit., chapters 4 and 5

A Ottani Cavina, 'Louis Gauffier and the question of J-L David's *Vue presumé du jardin du Luxembourg*', *Burlington Magazine* (January 1992), pp.27–33

Mona Ozouf, *Festivals and the French Revolution*, trans. by Alan Sheridan (Cambridge, MA and London, 1988, repr. 1991)

Harold Parker, *The Cult of Antiquity and the French Revolutionaries* (Chicago, 1937)

Alex Potts, 'Beautiful Bodies and Dying Heroes: Images of Ideal Manhood in the French Revolution', *History Workshop Journal* (Autumn 1990), pp.2–21

Thomas Puttfarken, 'David's Brutus and Theories of Pictorial Unity in France', *Art History* (September 1981), pp.290–304

Simon Schama, *Citizens: A Chronicle of the French Revolution* (London, 1989)

—, 'David et les enfants de la patrie', in *David contre David*, op. cit., vol. 2, pp.741–57

Antoine Schnapper, 'La Révolution', in *David*, op. cit., pp.207–29

1789: French Art during the Revolution (exh. cat., Colnaghi USA Ltd, New York, 1989)

Robert Simon, 'David's martyr portrait of Le Pelletier de Saint-Fargeau and the conundrums of revolutionary representation', *Art History* (December 1991), pp.459–87

Joseph Sloane, 'David, Robespierre and "The Death of Bara"', *Gazette des Beaux-Arts* (September 1969), pp.143–60

John Trumbell (ed. T Sizer), *The Autobiography of Colonel John Trumbell, Patriot Artist, 1756–1843* (New Haven and London, 1953)

Chapter 4

Anon, *Le tableau des Sabines exposé publiquement au palais national des sciences et des arts, salle de la ci devant Academie d'architecture par le citoyen David*, (Paris, 1799), probably written by David

Stephanie Carroll, 'Reciprocal Representations: David and the Theater', *Art in America* (May 1990), pp.198–206 and pp.259–61

Stefan Germer and Hubertus Kohle, 'From the theatrical to the aesthetic hero: on the privatization of the idea of virtue in David's *Brutus* and *Sabines*', op. cit.

Ewa Lajer-Burcharth, 'David's *Sabine Women*: Body, Gender and Republican Culture under the Directory', *Art History* (September 1991), pp.397–430

John Leighton, *Jacques-Louis David; Portrait of Jacobus Blauw* (London, 1987)

Alexandre Lenoir, *Concours pour les prix décennaux. Peinture. Examen du tableau des Sabines et de l'ecole de M. David* (Paris, 1810)

George Levitine, *The Dawn of Bohemianism. The Barbu Rebellion and Primitivism in Neoclassical France* (University Park, PA and London, 1978)

Robert Rosenblum, 'Essai de synthése: *Les Sabines*', in *David contre David*, op. cit., vol. 1, pp.461–70

James Henry Rubin, 'Painting and Politics II: Jacques-Louis David's Patriotism, or the Conspiracy of Gracchus Babeuf and the legacy of Topino Lebrun', *Art Bulletin* (December 1976), pp.547–68

Antoine Schnapper, 'Les Sabines', in *David*, op. cit., pp.323–38

Michael Wilson, 'A new acquisition for the National Gallery: David's portrait of Jacobus Blauw', *Burlington Magazine* (November 1984), pp.694–8

Chapter 5

Anon., *Explication du tableau des Thermopyles par M. David* (Paris, 1814), written with the help of David

Anon., *Account of the celebrated picture of the Coronation of Napoleon, by M. David, First Painter to the Emperor* (London, 1821)

Albert Boime, *Art in an Age of Bonapartism, 1800–1815* (Chicago and London, 1990, repr. 1993), pp.3–95

Philippe Bordes and Alain Pougetoux, 'Portraits de Napoléon en habit du Sacre', *Gazette des Beaux-Arts* (July–August 1983), pp.21–34

Ferdinand Boyer, 'Napoléon et l'attribution des Grands prix décennaux', *Bulletin de la Société de l'Histoire de l'Art Français* (1947), pp.66–72

T C Bruun Neergard, *Sur la situation des Beaux-Arts en France, ou lettres d'un Danois à son ami* (Paris, 1801)

Fanny Burney (ed.J Hemlow), *The Journals and Letters of Fanny Burney (Madame d'Arblay)*, vol. 6 (Oxford, 1975)

José Cabanis, *Le Sacre de Napoléon* (Paris, 1970)

Martin Kemp, 'J-L David and the prelude to a moral victory in Sparta', *Art Bulletin*, 51:2 (June 1969), pp.178–83

Joachim Le Breton, *Rapports à l'Empereur sur le progrès des sciences, des lettres et des arts depuis 1789. V Beaux-Arts* (Paris 1808, repr. 1989 with preface by D Woronoff and annotated by Udolpho Van de Sandt)

Pierre Leliévre, *Vivant Denon, directeur des Beaux Arts de Napoleon. Essai sur la politique artistique du Premier Empire* (Angers 1942, repr. Paris, 1995)

Philip Mansel, *The Eagle in Splendour. Napoleon I and his Court* (London, 1987)

Fréderic Masson, *Napoleon and his Coronation* (London and Leipzig, 1911)

Agnes Mongan, *David to Corot: French Drawings in the Fogg Art Museum* (Cambridge, MA and London, 1996), pp.57–112

Napoléon (exh. cat., Grand Palais, Paris, 1969)

Charles Percier and Pierre Fontaine, *Recueil de decorations exécutés dans l'eglise de Notre-Dame* de *Paris* et *au Champ de Mars, d'après les dessins et sous la conduite de C Percier et P F L Fontaine* (Paris, 1807)

Christopher Prendergast, *Napoleon and History Painting: Antoine-Jean Gros's La bataille d'Eylau* (Oxford, 1997)

Antoine Schnapper, 'David et Napoléon', in *David*, op. cit., pp.359–78

Jean Tulard, *Procès-verbal de la cérémonie du Sacre et du couronnement de Napoléon* (Paris, 1993)

Chapter 6

Bertrand Barère de Vieuzac (ed. Henri Carnot and Pierre-Jean David d'Angers), *Memoirs of Bertrand Barère* (London, 1896)

Catalogue des Tableaux de Galerie et de Chevalet, Dessins, Etudes, Livres de Croquis de M. Louis David, Peintre d'histoire (Paris, 1826) [the catalogue of the sale of the contents of David's studios]

David Dowd, 'Louis David et le gouvernment des Pays-Bas. Documents inédits sur le second "Sacre de Napoléon"', *Bulletin de la Societé de l'histore de l'art Français* (1955), pp.153–9

James Gallatin (ed. Count Gallatin), *The Diary of James Gallatin* (New York and London, 1916)

Dorothy Johnson, *Jacques Louis David; Art in Metamorphosis*, op. cit., pp.221–72

Jean-Claude Lebensztejn, 'Histoires Belges', in *David contre David*, op. cit., vol. 2, pp.1011–23

Antoine Schnapper, 'L'exil', in *David*, op. cit., pp.513–22

Chapter 7

Donna Hunter, '*David contre David*. Réflexions sur un colloque', *Revue de L'Art*, 91 (1991), pp.68–70

Lisa Jardine, 'It may be art, but is it violence?', *The Guardian* (2 December 1996), p.5

Neil McWilliam, 'Life and Afterlife: Jacques-Louis David, nineteenth-century criticism and the construction of the biographical subject', in Michael Orwicz (ed.), *Art Criticism and its Institutions in Nineteenth-Century France* (Manchester and New York, 1994), pp.43–62

Simon Schama, 'Book Reviews: Art as History', *Journal of Modern History* (December 1981), pp.683–91

Index

Numbers in **bold** refer to illustrations

Acknowledgements

Any present-day student of David must be indebted to the work of Antoine Schnapper, Philippe Bordes and Thomas Crow who have reshaped our view of the artist in the last two decades. Alex Potts was generous both with his time and his advice and Alan Windsor encouraged this project from the start. I am also extremely grateful to Sylvain Bédard and Donna Hunter for very kindly loaning me copies of their doctoral dissertations. Research has been greatly facilitated by the holdings on French art of the eighteenth and nineteenth centuries in the Department of History of Art, University of Oxford and in the library of the Ashmolean Museum. Travel to France has been assisted by a grant from the Research Board at the University of Reading. I must also thank many of my students whose questions in front of David's works in the Louvre forced me to sort out my own ideas about the artist.

Simon Chaffin-Johnson of the University of Reading photographic unit has been unfailingly helpful and acceded to strange requests without demur. At Phaidon Press, Pat Barylski, Cleia Smith, Juliet Duff and Giulia Hetherington have been exceptionally helpful, diligent and good humoured despite my irritating changes of mind. They must take part of the credit for this book. The rigours of writing have been offset by spiritual sustenance from Preston North End and Old Salesians football clubs. Numerous other debts have been incurred during the course of writing but most especially to Bernadette Devlin for her constant inspiration and support.

S L

For my parents, Reginald and Lilian, with love and affection

Photographic Credits

AKG, London: 40, 71, 99, 172, photo Erich Lessing 10, 41, 54; Albright-Knox Art Gallery, Buffalo, NY: 8; The Art Institute of Chicago: Clyde M Carr Fund and Major Acquisitions Endowment (1967.228) 94, Helen Regenstein Collection (1943.153) 126; Artothek, Peissenberg: 92; Bibliothèque Nationale de France, Paris: 18, 72, 118, 162, 176, 196, 204; Bildarchiv Preussischer Kulturbesitz, Berlin: 179; Bridgeman Art Library, London: 5, 34, 58, 83, 97, 101, 173, 177, 178, 180, 200; British Library, London: 138; British Museum, London: 30, 135; Photographie Bulloz, Paris: 6, 11, 12, 16, 23, 103, 113, 120, 149, 169; Jean-Loup Charmet, Paris: 119; Christie's Images, London: 21; Cleveland Museum of Art: 1998 Leonard C Hanna Jr Fund (1962.37) 189; Courtauld Institute of Art, Witt Library, University of London: 183; Crocker Art Museum, Sacramento, CA: E B Crocker Collection 38; École Nationale Supérieure des Beaux-Arts, Paris: 15, 20, 22; École Polytechnique, Palaiseau: photo J B Debreux 46; Edimedia, Paris: 98; ET Archive, London: 74, 106; Fogg Art Museum, Harvard University Art Museums: Bequest of Grenville L Winthrop 154, 187; Fotomas Index: 4, 134; Galerie Cailleux, Paris: Private collection 84; Galleria dell' Accademia, Venice: photo Oswaldo Böhm 193; J Paul Getty Museum, Los Angeles: 105, 188, 191; Photographie Giraudon, Paris: 39; Kimbell Art Museum, Fort Worth, Texas: 192; David King Collection, London: 171; Lord Zetland, Aske, Richmond, North Yorkshire: 29; Metropolitan Museum of Art, New York: Harris Brisbane Dick Fund (1948) 27, Catherine Lorillard Wolfe Collection, Wolfe Fund (1931) 66, 67, Purchase Mr & Mrs Charles Wrightsman, Gift in honour of Everett Fahy (1977) 82, Purchase Rogers and Fletcher Funds, Bequest of Mary Wetmore Shively in memory of her husband, Henry L Shively, MD (1965) 185; Mountain High Maps, © 1995 Digital Wisdom Inc: p.341; Musée des Augustins, Toulouse: 49; Musée des Beaux-Arts, Dijon: 104; Musée des Beaux-Arts, Rouen: photo Didier Tragin/Catherine Laucien 17; Musée des Beaux-Arts et d'Archéologie, Besançon: photo C Choffet 89; Musée Calvet, Avignon: 114; Musée Fabre, Montpellier: photo Frédéric Jaulmes 35, 50, 53; Musée Thomas Henry, Cherbourg: photo Martine Seyre 36; Musée de l'Hotel de Ville, Amboise: 51; Musée Lambinet, Versailles: photo F Doury 107; Musée du Louvre, Paris: 205; Musée Municipal Frédéric Blandin, Nevers: 57; Musée de Peinture et de Sculpture de Grenoble: 37; Musée de Poitiers: photo C Vignaud 137; Musées Royaux des Beaux-Arts de Belgique, Brussels: photo Cussac 110, 197, 198, photo Speltdoorn 112; Museo del Prado, Madrid: 194; National Gallery, London: 129, 186, 201; National Gallery of Art, Washington, DC: Samuel H Kress Collection 140, 175; National Gallery of Ireland, Dublin: 33; Nationalmuseum, Stockholm: 76; Photothèque des Musées de la Ville de Paris: photo Andreani 102, 111, 117, Ladet 70, 147, 182, Lifermann 1, Pierrain 19, Svartz 121, Toumazet 100; Pierpont Morgan Library, New York: Collection of Eugene Victor Tham 75; The Putnam Foundation, Timken Museum of Art, San Diego: 148; RMN, Paris: 2, 9, 13, 14, 24, 31, 32, 55, 59, 73, 85, 86, 87, 88, 90, 91, 95, 96, 108, 116, 122, 124, 130, 141, 142, 144, 146, 150, 151, 152, 153, 155, 157, 159, 160, 163, 165, 170, 184, 199, photo Jean Arnaudet 131, 132, 133, 145, 158, Michèle Bellot 125, 156, J G Berizzi 136, 168, P Bernard 166, Gerard Blot 25, 44, 62, 63, 77, 88, 91, 127, 128, 181, 190, Francis Dubuisson 202, C Jean/H Lewan 161, Hervé Lewandowski 45, 48, R G Ojeda 43, 60, 64, 65, 174, Peter Willi 167, 195; Scala, Florence: frontispiece, 26, 28, 42, 79, 80, 93, 115; Courtesy Gian Enzo Sperone, New York: 203; Statens Museum fur Kunst, Copenhagen: photo Hans Petersen 69; Studio Edition, Mâcon: Philippe Lafarges 52; Tate Gallery, London: 3; Wildenstein and Co, Inc, New York: Private collection 7; Yale Center for British Art, Paul Mellon Collection, New Haven, Connecticut: 56

Phaidon Press Limited
Regent's Wharf
All Saints Street
London N1 9PA

First published 1999

ISBN 0 7148 3804 7

A CIP catalogue record for this book is available from the British Library.

Text typeset in Versailles

Printed in Singapore

Cover illustration Detail from *Bonaparte Crossing the St Bernard Pass*, 1800 (see p.232)